Largesse

Jean Starobinski

Largesse

Translated by Jane Marie Todd

The University of Chicago Press
Chicago and London

Jean Starobinski is professor emeritus at the University of Geneva and is author of several books, including *Jean-Jacques Rousseau: Transparency and Obstruction.*

Jane Marie Todd is the translator of major French works, among them, Georges Didi-Huberman's *Fra Angelico: Dissemblance and Figuration,* also published by the University of Chicago Press.

The University of Chicago Press, Chicago 60637
The University of Chicago Press, Ltd., London

Printed in the United States of America
06 05 04 03 02 01 00 99 98 97 5 4 3 2 1

ISBN (cloth): 0-226-77135-0
ISBN (paper): 0-226-77136-9

Originally published as *Largesse,* © Editions de la Réunion des musées nationaux, 1994. © Jean Starobinksi, 1994. The French edition of this book was published in conjunction with an exhibition conceived and organized by the Department of Graphic Arts at the Louvre. The exhibition dates were 20 January to 18 April 1994.

Library of Congress Cataloging-in-Publication Data

Starobinski, Jean.
[Largesse. English]
Largesse / Jean Starobinski ; translated by Jane Marie Todd.
p. cm. — (Parti pris)
Exhibition was presented at the Louvre by the Dept. of Graphic Arts, Jan. 20–Apr. 18, 1994.
Includes bibliographical references.
ISBN 0-226-77135-0. — ISBN 0-226-77136-9 (pbk.)
1. Generosity in art—Exhibitions. 2. Art, European—Exhibitions. 3. Generosity. I. Musée du Louvre. II. Title. III. Series: Parti pris (Réunion des musées nationaux (France))
N8217.G43S713 1997
704.9'491799—dc20 96-34058
CIP

This book is printed on acid-free paper.

Contents

Parti Pris, To What End?

A first series of exhibits at the Louvre, entitled *Parti pris,* concludes with Jean Starobinski, exegete of the gift, under the expansive title *Largesse. Parti pris* is a common enough expression, but it speaks volumes. It points out the partisan—in the best sense of the term—nature of any reading. It forcefully reminds us that a reader is never neutral, that is, dead; never impartial, that is, utopian, or no place. A reader's being is always situated somewhere; a reader's speech is always contingent; every gloss is also a projection. Jean Starobinski knows this better than anyone. Like all the great readers of this fin de siècle, he has constantly questioned the status of the interpreter and the grounds of discourse—what we commonly call the critical relation. Hence the rule that governs these exhibits: the guest curator (the author, that is, to give him the courtesy he deserves), has complete freedom in choosing the material for his subject from among the Louvre's collections and from works lent by other museums. Thus, it is the discourse that produces the works of art and not the reverse. But it produces them in a different way each time: as thesis in Jacques Derrida, whose *Memoirs of the Blind* argued for the blindness of the draftsman; as dramaturgy in Peter Greenaway, whose *Flying Out of This World* imitated the fall of Icarus on the ogee moulding of the museum; and as literature in Jean Starobinski, whose *Largesse* is a novel of sorts about an evil spell, that is, a maleficent gift.

The idea of the gift has been a constant preoccupation of this century and its philosophy. It obviously remains relevant during this time of crisis, which is marked, for better or for worse, by the return of good intentions, of so-called humanitarian feelings. But Starobinski's meditation is more ambitious: it is a vast overview of the figures of the gift, from the ancient *sparsio*—the shower of gold by Roman emperors—to the modern giving of alms encouraged by the Christian conscience. And it all begins with Rousseau. Why should this be surprising? Like Derrida and Paul de Man, Starobinski is one of the most expert exegetes of the solitary dreamer. The episode of the patricians throwing gingerbread to young peasants, which Rousseau evokes in his ninth reverie as the corruptive model of familiar forms of largesse, serves as an eloquent epigraph to that long saga. Through it, we see immediately that the gift is drama: the peasants quarrel over cake crumbs under their masters' eyes. Power, contempt, domination, and destruction all contribute toward the giver's pleasure, including the pleasure of looking. Rousseau tries to redeem the scene with a more peaceful distribution of apples (true symbols), but it is no use. There is no escape. The moral to this profound fable is dark: the gift is ruinous because of the inequality it entails. Such corrosive ambiguity lends a strikingly sinister aspect to the astonishing adventure that follows. This story of the gift is a kind of double-entry bookkeeping: it has a light side and a dark side. Each of its stages is burdened or cursed with the fundamental duality at work in the act of giving, where good has become inseparable from evil. First and foremost, the gift was the newly anointed prince's act of throwing coins to a greedy crowd of people, who slaughtered one another at his feet. Next came pagan Fortune, which governed the world as sovereign mistress, blind and fickle. Then Christian humanism, through its reading of the Bible, forged the ideal creature for its merciful designs, the creature fit to receive its good works or good conscience: the poor man.

And finally, the Enlightenment invented charity, where the sentimental itch of philanthropy spread in dubious profusion. But the worst was yet to come: with Baudelaire, giving became a spectacle. Huysmans was the great witness to this perverse aestheticism, which uses the gift only as an instrument of evil: Des Esseintes, consuming the *vile snack* belonging to the offspring of the plebeian class, is the rich man who pretends to be poor by stealing the poor man's bread—or his soul. Jean Starobinski concludes with more cheerful postulates on the poetic gift, but this masterful account is, in fact, poignantly pessimistic. In it, the gift never frees itself from its primitive curse, never stops being Pandora's box or Eve's apple. There is only one antidote to this deleterious role: the contract, which is a relation of power, but a relation nonetheless. With the contract, we return to Rousseau—for another meditation perhaps. . .

But what is the purpose of *Parti pris*? As this trilogy of dissimilar exhibits—bearing such different signatures—comes to an end, the question deserves to be articulated. But there is no answer to it, because it is badly phrased: the impact of such a series cannot be measured in the prosaic terms of direct utility. *Parti pris* serves no purpose. Or rather, it serves only the tenacious, but not tenuous, imperative for the pluralist destiny of a public space, in this case the museum. The objective of those who pioneered this genre was simply to enrich the reading of a museum's collections beyond the limits recognized by historical discourse. Hence they turned to skilled practitioners in every discipline who were moved by the concern to look anew at works of art, to look with critical, reflexive eyes. The practice of this genre here and there goes back a long time. It has had uneven success. The novelty in this case, if there is one, has to do with the place where it is practiced: the Louvre. The goal was to introduce into the museum readings that came from the outside. You may judge the pertinence of the undertaking as you like, based on the evidence—that is, on the three panels of this triptych. The audience is all the more to be praised since these readings are sometimes difficult, which proves that there is always a public for language games. Let the historians meditate on what that augurs for the future.

But the limits of such a reception can be guessed. Are not such exercises in the margin in fact marginal? Are they not merely the modernist showcase, the critical alibi, the luxury insurance of a giant museum with many projects under way? That question is even more undecidable, because, today, the course of ideas meanders far too much through the collective consciousness. It is reckless to use language to describe the patience of the concept, the force of precedent, the influence of the model, the logic of imitation. Or of rejection. That latent osmosis can be translated only through metaphors of orality or even alchemy. The discourse on art, after all, is only one idiom among others: it evolves in the same way, by uncertain paths, and its secret causes have nothing rational about them. And then one day, the words change and the vulgate is enriched—and our eyes along with it. Although the profit realized is clandestine, its claim is constant. In these subtle matters, one is compelled to produce not a result but only a means: a way of making all languages—from the most learned philology to the boldest exegesis—coexist in a single space, which, because it is public, belongs to no one. Hence, a democratic community begins to form around works of art, a community endowed with free speech and a plural gaze.

Françoise Viatte
Régis Michel

Preliminaries

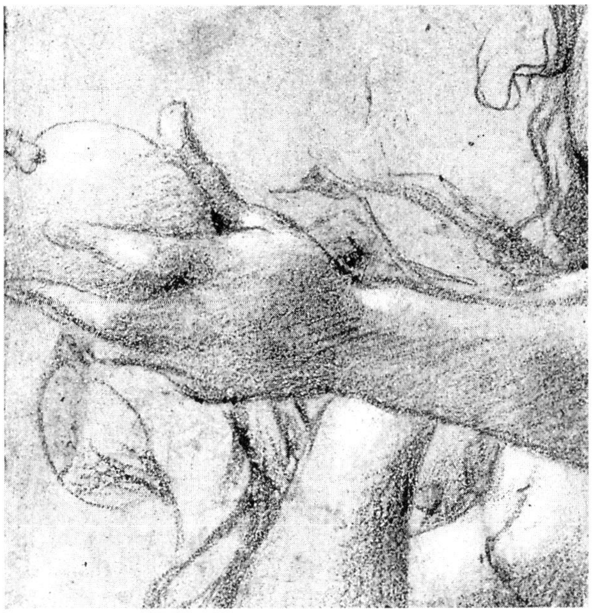

The exquisite flavor surprised her mouth. Her arm is drawing away; the hand that picked the fruit is already presenting it. Her fingers are still closed on the apple, but will soon open. Correggio's *Eve,* one of the most beautiful drawings ever executed, figures this gesture. The miracle of the drawing is that the object extended is not distinct from the smile, the naked flesh, the hand presenting the gift. The fruit and the person belong together to such a degree that they form a single gift. Delight brightens the face of Woman, who has tasted the apple and offers to share it. She is without shame: she still does not know that in giving, she is giving herself. In its imminence, the gesture thus drawn, with its gentle innuendo, is an immediate conquest. Accepting entails endless desire.

This is one of the strong images of the gift, but not the only one. In the pages that follow, I shall examine texts and images that stage the act of giving—of making a gift—in a number of its many different senses. I shall inventory, distinguish, and oppose.[1] There are infinite variations on this gesture: for example, we will need to distinguish between symmetrical exchange and asymmetrical exchange. Gifts can circulate on the basis of equality, but also on the basis of disparity, in which case they involve rich and poor, sovereign dispenser and humble beneficiary. Things can be given, but so can signs, words, missions, and duties. Gifts do not always pass from one hand to another. . . . In truth, giving and receiving (in which a substance offered becomes mine) form the very fabric of every life, beginning with the first mouthful of food. Giving and receiving are
48 first behaviors, which belong to a language of the body prior to speech: the maternal breast in contact with the child's lips. Simultaneously, as the human being is constructed, the acts of appropriating and giving, of monopolizing and dispensing, are made manifest through different intermediaries, through more complex paths—from the mother's lips to the child's ear—and through a changing series of more or less codified symbolic
46 elements. The gift of speech cannot be separated from the gift of the first nourishment.[2] That is a universal, anthropological fact, the point from which everything else diversifies.

1. I shall limit and circumscribe as well. The semantic field I explore is that of a few gestures—let me insist on that point—and not of the French verb *donner,* "to give," which is much broader. What gift is bestowed when someone *donne les coups* [deals blows] or *donne la charge* [leads the charge], when one gives voice to something, when someone *donne dans le panneau* [falls into a trap], or *donne prise* [lays himself open]? . . . The extension of the uses of the verb *donner* is certainly not a matter of indifference. The verb *rendre,* "to render," would also require our attention. What do we mean when we speak of a "given"? Whence does it come, and from whom? Every *given* seems to be offered, but it is in fact an "object" that must first be *projected* before we can *take* it into consideration. On this point, the philosopher would have a great deal to consider. Keep in mind that, in the past, the French used *donner* or similar terms to express deception: *la bailler belle, en donner à garder,* or quite simply *en donner* [to fool] (in seventeenth-century French), *se donner pour* [to pass oneself off for], *en jeter* [to charm], etc. In remaining close to both the material and the substantial content of the gift, I have found it difficult to include a consideration of *pardon* or forgiveness, which is, however, closely linked to the gift etymologically: *perdonare, vergeben, forgive,* etc.

2. We are no doubt stretching the meaning of the word "gift" to its very limit when we use it to designate the conditions without which there would be no physical or mental life: giving the breast, giving a verbal response to the newborn's cry. The gift is thus ubiquitous and fundamental, excluding pathological exceptions. The fact that a "world" and "one's own body" are given to consciousness has been a matter for philosophical reflection beginning with modern phenomenology. The inquiries of Jean-Luc Marion "intend to place giving at the center of reduction, hence at the center of phenomenology." *Réduction et donation: Recherches sur Husserl, Heidegger et la phénoménologie* (Paris: PUF, 1989). This discussion has been reopened in a recent work by Jacques Derrida devoted entirely to the study of the gift: *Donner le temps* (Paris: Galilée, 1991). [*Given Time,* trans. Peggy Kamuf (Chicago: University of Chicago Press, 1992).]

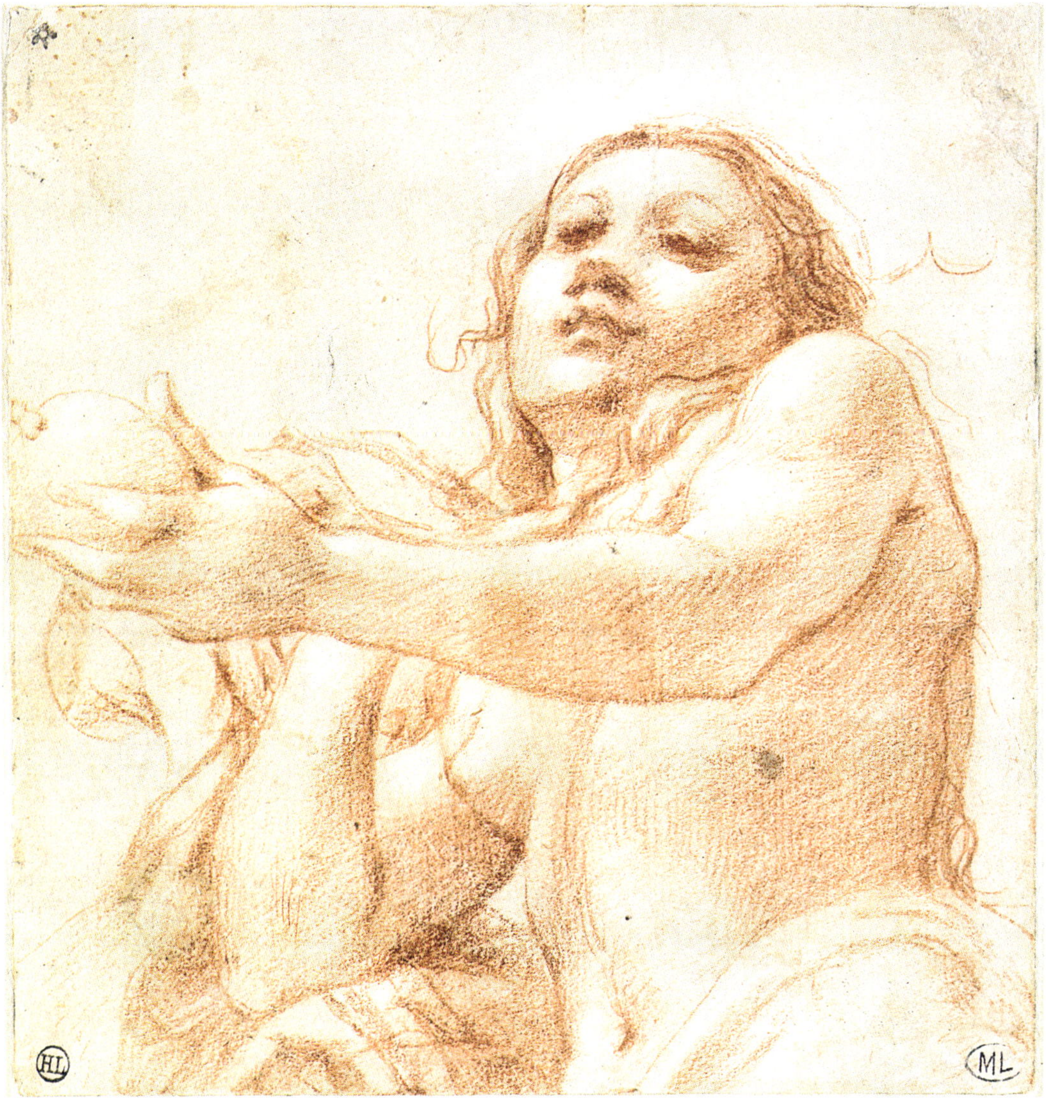

1. Correggio, *Eve Offering the Apple,* Louvre Museum.

Would it be too much to maintain that the entire course of history manifests itself as a process that fashions and reworks the forms of exchange, finding applications for them in particular behaviors, customs, shared practices, linguistic structures, institutions, dogmas, in the rules of civility, ties of gratitude and reciprocity, and so on? Such diverse aspects have rarely been the object of a comprehensive look, and the pages that follow do not claim to constitute the synoptic history of the gift that has been missing so far. Anthropologists, philosophers, theologians, and social historians have directed their attention to the gift. In light of Marcel Mauss's famous *Essai sur le don* [Essay on the gift], it is certainly appropriate to include giving in a history and psychology of expenditure: to be understood, the phenomenon must be inscribed within the context of the general circulation of goods within a particular culture.[3] But the economistic perspective would be inadequate if it were not accompanied by a consideration of the status of beliefs and feelings implied at every moment by the gift. Not only are feelings manifested in different ways during different eras, they are also encouraged or repressed to different degrees. They are modified according to the values attributed to them; they take on different nuances and have different names. Extravagance, largesse, and charity have been the object of changing assessments. Largesse has sometimes been obligatory, sometimes suspect. Treasures have sometimes been sacrificed on gaming tables, at other times for the salvation of the soul, but in each case, it was because this was the requisite behavior. There are social rules that fix the invariable distance between giver and receiver, others that oversee the possible reversal of roles. . . . The best evidence of these rules lies in mythic narratives and poems, in the pages of a few great texts of history or fiction, and, often, in the images that reflect them.

The object given always has a history. The piece of fruit given by Eve is the handiwork of the tree. The gift she makes to Adam is the result of the wily discourse of the serpent, who is "more subtil than any beast of the field" (Genesis 3:1).[4] Nothing given—whether it be a natural object or the product of art—is without cost. That is, it has always been improved or perfected, through the grace of nature or the work of man: water drawn from the well, a flower, an ear of corn, a young goat, a coin, a poem. . . . Certain crafted gifts are themselves receptacles for other gifts: a vase, a goblet, a book.

Between human individuals, the gesture of giving transmits something that has blossomed or borne fruit. The desirable object must first have been gathered, must have grown and ripened; the valuable object must have been imagined and produced before the act of giving can dispose of it and allow it to pass into another's hands. Nonetheless, I will not make the claim that my theme figures the very operation of the artist. In the work of art, the gift is something like the power, of obscure origin, that precedes and supports labor, or something like the future of the work of art. Labor itself, which adds to the world, is the surging up of a force that leaves its mark, then takes off again, moves away, reasserts itself, and propagates with all the more vigor. Yes, the artist's creation—

3. This was George Bataille's undertaking in *La part maudite: Essai d'économie générale,* vol. 1: *La consumation* (Paris: Minuit, 1949). [*The Accursed Share,* vol. 1: *Consumption,* trans. Robert Hurley (New York: Zone Books, 1988–91).] The second volume announced by Bataille never appeared.

4. [Biblical passages are taken from the King James Version.—*Trans.*]

a surplus of visibility—comes from an "internal" gift. If the creation receives the artist's approval, it may, in a last gesture, be offered, handed over to the reader or beholder. But in the interval, the artist gives up nothing: in the torment and joy of labor, he holds on to his work, hides it jealously, keeps it secreted away, anxious only to make what can be given increase, ready to destroy whatever does not give of itself as the artist had hoped and which, as a result, cannot be surrendered to the public. For every gift granted, how many have remained incomplete or have been rejected.

Consider the drawing or painting hand. It is not like Eve's hand: it is not a giving hand. In his labor, the artist holds his instrument in the firmest and yet most delicate manner possible as it sets down lines and colors, takes possession of the space and the material. The draftsman's questioning gaze is divided in two; it moves from one thing to another. His eyes leave the model (if there is one) for the paper, then abandon the paper for the model. His hand hazards a stroke in the hope of capturing a shifting resemblance. He wants effective control over the resemblance, but he knows he will never master it fully. At some point—not too soon and not too late—the stroke hazarded must be retained. (Even in the drip painting, the hand does not project the paint haphazardly.) The gaze questions the gesture; the hand makes it, but as if it were continuing to question the object. Hence the artist at work persists, worrying about what *that* will produce, ready to persevere, ready to abandon the game. And while he *gives himself* to his work, while he *gives form* to his work of art, he puts off the decision to accept or reject the result. The destination remains open. Will he finally consent to his work, will he *give* his assent? He may make it a gift to the public, or to a friend, who for the moment assumes the role of the beholder par excellence. The possibility of this final gift illuminates all of his earlier labor.

I have thus opted to shed light on some of the most significant forms of the gesture of giving, as it appears in a few great historical, literary, philosophical, and religious texts of European culture. Art is also implicated since, whatever its material, its means, its motives, or its pretexts, it almost always seeks to fulfill an expectation. Furthermore, it often takes as its theme the very representation of the act of giving, its glorious or satirical staging. In more than one case, drawings will be not the subject of my argument, but an extension of it. If I do not always comment on these drawings, it is because I am asking them to come to the aid of my reflection. I shall be dealing with eloquent works of art (sometimes too eloquent). They are works of beauty, but they are also demonstrations. They illuminate the texts I cite; they set thought or reverie back in motion. They are so good at offering themselves as examples that they allow me to avoid excessive developments.

The present work owes its definitive form to the exhibit organized by the Department of Graphic Arts at the Louvre Museum, held between 20 January and 18 April 1994. The complementarity of the text and the illustrations in this book was made possible through the skill and inexhaustible attention of Françoise Viatte and Régis Michel. I am also indebted to Catherine Goguel and Madeleine Pinault Sørensen for their valuable information. The realization of this project owes a great deal to Geneviève Picon's encouragement. I am grateful for her friendship.

I also wish to thank all those whose conversations and letters have contributed toward enriching my list of examples and my bibliography: Bronislaw Baczko, Jacques Berchtold, Yves Bonnefoy, Jacqueline Cerquiglini-Toulet, Lydia Fleur, Lucie Galactéros de Boissier, Alain Grosrichard, John E. Jackson, Hans Robert Jauss, David Lowenthal, Richard Macksey, Walter Magass, Simon Markish, Hellmut Pappe, Gérard de Puymège, Aline Rousselle, Karlheinz Stierle, Jean-Pierre Vernant, and Paul Zumthor.[5]

I wish to express my warmest gratitude to Bernard Ducret and André Vifian, administrators for the Villa Laret in Sils-Maria. During the summer of 1993, they provided the residency that allowed me to complete the final draft of this book. This villa, a generous gift from Olga Spitzer to the Université de Genève, was the most propitious place for writing this book.

5. The present volume is an expanded and completely recast version of several earlier studies: "Sur Rousseau et Baudelaire: Le dédommagement et l'irréparable," in *Le lieu et la formule: Hommage à Marc Eigeldinger* (Neuchâtel: La Baconnière, 1979), 47–59; "Rousseau, Baudelaire, Huysmans (les pains d'épice, le gâteau et l'immonde tartine)," in *Baudelaire, Mallarmé, Valéry: New Essays in Honour of Lloyd Austin* (Cambridge: Cambridge University Press, 1982), 128–41; "Don fastueux et don pervers," presented at the Conférence Marc Bloch, 13 June 1985, published in *Annales ESC* 1 (January–February 1986): 7–16. The work of the seminar on French literature beginning in 1965 and of the meetings of the study group on the eighteenth century of the Faculté des Lettres at the Université de Genève allowed me to test the historical research, of which this book represents the final version. For the present publication, I had to omit or abbreviate certain stylistic analyses.

CHAPTER ONE

The Ostentatious Gift

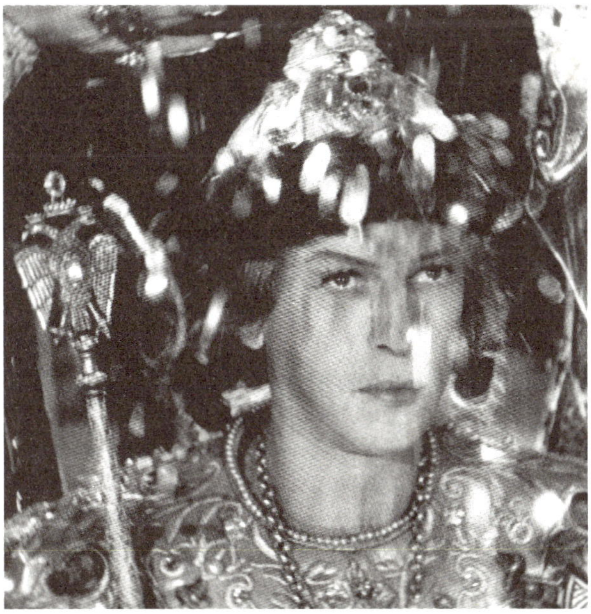

A Fete in a Garden

A passage from the ninth reverie in Rousseau's *Rêveries d'un promeneur solitaire* [Reveries of a solitary walker] continues to demand my attention.[6] It is one of the passages in Rousseau that most reveals or exposes the age in which he lived, one of the decisive moments in the history of ideas and sentiments. The writer evokes the memory of a fete, given in honor of the master of the house, on the property of Mme d'Epinay, his protector. On the grounds-turned-fairground, a young man of society decides to scatter gingerbread to the wind: "herds" of young peasants brutally fight over it. "Everyone"—that is, everyone in the "good company"—imitates the young man's gesture. Rousseau himself joins in "out of bashfulness." But soon, "bored with emptying [his] purse to see people get crushed," he distances himself and, in another corner of the fair, sees "five or six Savoyards around a little girl who still had about a dozen sorry-looking apples on her tray, which she would very much have liked to be rid of." He buys the fruit and distributes it to the children who were coveting it. "I then was witness to one of the sweetest spectacles that can flatter a man's heart, that of seeing joy and the innocence of youth spreading around me. For when the spectators saw it, they too shared it, and I, who shared that joy at so little expense, had the additional joy of feeling it was my doing."

Why does Rousseau tell this story? To supply proof that he does not hate children, despite the vicious gossip; to prove to himself that he possesses inner resources, happy memories that can heal the wounds that evildoers continue to inflict upon him. In the series of peaceful images in the ninth reverie, the scenes of distributing treats to children give rise to three reminiscences in succession. And when the memory of an encounter with an old invalid finally emerges, a small largesse (hindered this time by "shame") is once more at stake. As in many other passages, Rousseau leads us to discern, almost unbeknownst to him, a problematic of extreme importance. Concerned with defending himself personally, he hits the mark when he dramatizes the opposition between two manners of giving: on the one hand, a prodigality linked to violence and disorder; on the other, an equitable and orderly distribution. The first reveals and aggravates social ills and the distance between rich and poor; the second is frugal, and produces the reign of goodness "at . . . little expense." Rousseau acknowledges that he participated in evil works at the beginning, but only to let us know immediately that he tired of them, that he went over to the other side, that, on his own initiative, he established a little paradise in which he was the central figure. He had felt impoverished among the rich, who took pleasure in seeing "all those peasants rush forward, fight, and knock one another down." He felt almost like a god among the children whose joy he elicited. In associating pleasure with goodness, he felt the joy of being the cause of it.

Although he distributed a few apples, Rousseau does not claim he carried out an act of charity. It was, he tells us, only a better amusement. On the fairground, he improvised a different spectacle: not the scuffle, but shared contentment. In his text, Rousseau insists on the sensation produced, that is, on the aesthetic aspect of the scene, both for

6. See "Texts on the Gift," no. 1, at the end of this volume. [Unless otherwise noted, quoted passages throughout this book are my own translation.—*Trans.*]

himself and for those who witnessed it: "When I reflected back on the sort of pleasure [*volupté*] I had experienced I found that it consisted less in a feeling of beneficence than in the enjoyment of seeing contented faces. That aspect has a charm for me which[,] even though it penetrates my heart[,] seems to be solely a matter of sensation. If I did not see the satisfaction I caused[,] even if I were sure of it[,] my pleasure [*jouissance*] would be cut in half."[7] And, he assures us, he could easily enjoy such a spectacle in a disinterested manner, without having contributed to it. But in this instance, in this distribution of apples, he occupies multiple roles: he is the creator of the event, the giver, and also the final addressee. He is the stage director and the spectator of the happy "denouement" of this children's "comedy" that had long remained in abeyance. It is as if Rousseau were appropriating not only the general euphoria, but also the fruit he gave away. In his own past, this same fruit had cruelly failed to satisfy his desire. We may suppose that the pleasure of the little Savoyards compensates for a desire belonging to Rousseau's childhood and that the frustration of this desire had left traces in Jean-Jacques's memory.

Do we have proof of this? As often happens in art and literature, one detail, one similarity in the choice of vocabulary, can serve as an index. Let us reread a sentence from the scene in *Rêveries:* "For them, this tray was the garden of Hesperides, and the little girl was the *dragon* guarding it" (my emphasis). The mythological commonplace ironically solemnizes the forbidden treat. But it is no mere ornament, and its content is not immaterial. Note that the same comparison accompanies another story of apples in the first book of the *Confessions* and reinforces a similarity in theme: the impoverished child's covetousness for a fruit beyond his reach. Rousseau recounts his years of apprenticeship as an engraver under a bad master: "All . . . that I saw became for my heart an object to covet, solely because I was deprived of everything." A painful incident, relived from a distance, becomes the object of a comic narration:[8]

> One memory of an apple-hunt that cost me dear still makes me shudder and laugh at the same time. These apples were at the bottom of a cupboard which was lit from the kitchen through a high lattice. One day when I was alone in the house I climbed on the kneading trough to peer into this *garden of the Hesperides* at those precious fruits I could not touch.

Armed with a spit on the "kneading trough" *(may),* Jean-Jacques is unable to reach his goal, but he persists: "Next day, when the opportunity offered, I made a fresh attempt. I climbed on my perch, fastened the two spits together, straightened them, and was just going to probe.[. . .]But unfortunately the *dragon* was not asleep; the larder door suddenly opened; my master came out, folded his arms, looked at me, and said 'Bravo!' . . . The pen falls from my hand."[9] The writer interrupts his narrative. He was depicting himself, spit in hand, trapped by the master; but now, he claims, it is the pen he has dropped (though its fall is indicated only through the use of ellipses). Rousseau

7. The manuscript of the ninth reverie is a draft. Rousseau is not strict about punctuation. The signs conforming to modern usage are given here in brackets.

8. Note that Rousseau likes to evaluate the *cost* of every happiness. In La Chevrette, the pleasure of distributing the apples is acquired "at so little expense."

9. Jean-Jacques Rousseau, *Confessions,* English translation by J. M. Cohen (Middlesex and New York: Penguin Classics, 1953), 42; emphasis mine. [Translation is slightly modified; nonbracketed ellipses are Rousseau's own.—*Trans.*]

can speak with good cheer of the unlucky spit only because he has perfectly mastered the nib dipped in ink that has replaced it. Our gaze shifts from the adolescent hero to the adult author who is speaking to us about him. In the space between one pointed tip and another, we can measure all the distance that now separates the illustrious writer from the mistreated apprentice. The story of that humiliation is the occasion for a triumph of writing: the revenge is complete. What satisfaction is then to be had when, in a new text, the fashionable writer recalls that he distributed, on the grounds of a great Parisian financier, the fruit that the sorry apprentice from Geneva had not managed to steal. Here, by the power of writing, he vanquishes a single dragon twice over. He is twice master of the fruit in the forbidden garden. But the very ancient desire for an apple is not abolished for all that. The story is without end.

Is there a beginning? The theft of the apples was already a substitute for a previous, unsatisfied desire. The petty larcenies not only compensated for ill treatment and prohibitions, but also symbolized or replaced other objects, whose lack was only vaguely felt: "I have never been concerned with my belly except when my heart has been disengaged."[10] We can thus trace the chain of frustrations and compensations back a long time. In the rhetoric used to exonerate himself, Rousseau excuses his guilty desire because the coveted object is only the substitute for another, which he had the full right to possess, but which an unjust destiny refused him or only let him glimpse obscurely.[11] It is up to us (or you) as readers to make conjectures about what the primitive frustration, the disappeared person or voice, the refused breast—or the wrong he groundlessly imagined he suffered—might have been.

The Antecedents of a Gesture

At the fete of La Chevrette, the young man who throws the gingerbread is repeating an immemorial gesture. It is a gesture he had seen many times, upon leaving church during great feasts, or at weddings and baptisms.[12] He may have seen the crowds at public

10. Ibid., 43.

11. Some of the other apples to be found in Rousseau include those he gathers by climbing trees during his autumn stay of 1765 on the Ile de Saint-Pierre (*Confessions,* book 12, and the fifth reverie in *Rêveries*). Other fruits distributed by Rousseau: the cherries he throws from the top of the tree into the blouse of the two charming girls (*Confessions,* book 4, episode of the "cherry idyll"). In all this, of course, we discern the symbolic affinity between the apple and the breast. This is a legitimate interpretation, but it is only *partial.* In all idyllic and bucolic literature, apples and other small gifts require that kisses be received or given in exchange. See Meyer Schapiro, "The Apples of Cézanne: An Essay on the Meaning of Still-Life," chap. 1 of *Modern Art: Nineteenth and Twentieth Centuries* (New York: George Braziller, 1978); see also Marguerite-A. Sechehaye, *La réalisation symbolique* (Bern: Hans Huber, 1947): in a case of schizophrenia, the author, a psychoanalyst, used apples given to her patient to symbolize the maternal breast the latter had been deprived of. This belated compensation was effective. In mythology, Paris marks his choice between three goddesses with the gift of a golden apple. The chosen one, Venus, thanks him with the catastrophic return gift of Helen, the most beautiful of women. See Karl Reinhardt, "Das Paris-Urteil," in *Tradition und Geist* (Gottingen: Vandenhoeck & Ruprecht, 1960); and Hubert Damisch, *Le jugement de Pâris* (Paris: Flammarion, 1992).

12. Confetti is a form of *missilia* that still survives today. Arnold Van Gennep has made numerous documents available regarding the throwing of Jordan almonds, treats, and coins at baptisms *(natalitia)* and weddings; see *Manuel de folklore français,* tome 1 (in 2 vols.) (Paris, 1946), esp. 2:469–72, 488–92, 530–39. Van Gennep asserts the universality of the ritual and is skeptical regarding the search for sources. It is clear that the gesture described by Rousseau at the fete of La Chevrette persisted into the nineteenth century. In *Les mémoires d'un âne,* a baptism is the occasion for the traditional throwing of almonds and pennies; poor children fight "like animals." And the wise mama, sadistic enough not to miss a bit of the scene, adopts, like Rousseau, the moral principle of an equitable distribution: "Children become like dogs fighting over a bone. If ever I become a godmother in this region, I will give out almonds and will have the money we spend in pennies, which are for the most part lost, taken to the poor." Comtesse de Ségur, *Les mémoires d'un âne* (Paris: Bibliothèque Rose, 1860), chap. 18: "Un baptême," 199–203. See "Texts on the Gift," no. 6, below.

festivities rushing to collect the gifts announced by the ritual cry, "Largesse." It is in this manner that the idealized sower scatters seed,[13] that the heavens pour down fertilizing rain. There is magic in this gesture. In making it, its agents take on the role of sovereign dispensation. In dispersing wealth, they call down upon them the blessings of the gods and a new influx of wealth. They attribute to themselves the mastery of overabundance, which will engender a new abundance; what was produced by the land will be returned to the land so that new crops can grow. "And they throw all sorts of seeds at the people, as if to appease the land with its own fruit."[14] Those who give in that manner, "divine kings," assure themselves of their own superiority, even as they repeat the ritual gesture required for safeguarding general prosperity. If such kings are to be considered a source of happiness, wealth has to pass through their hands.

Behind the episode of the largesse of the gingerbread narrated by Rousseau, we can make out an entire historical context. And etymology points the way. *Largesse* stems from *largitio,* whose meaning is shored up by the material sense of the adjective *largus,* defined by the lexicographers as "abundant; that which surges forth in abundance (especially of springs, rivers)," and thus, as "that which gives in abundance; generous; expansive (in the moral sense)."[15] Once we have a better sense of this welling up of spring or river, we can use our imaginations to extend it to various mythical gifts of the earth and sky. Images flow from every direction, evoking miracles that satisfy hunger and thirst:
nourishing manna that falls from the sky or a rock that, when struck, allows water to 41
flow from it. The images also evoke a generative power: the master of gods metamorphosized into a shower of gold so that he can possess a mortal woman, Danaë. From that 2
gold (divine seed), Perseus is born. That hero decapitates the dangerous Medusa, she of the petrifying gaze; but from the blood of Medusa Pegasus comes forth, and from beneath the hoof of the winged horse the generous spring of Hippocrene surges up. Hippocrene is the spring that flows for the Muses and for poets.[16]

In Latin, *largitio* took on a very broad meaning. The word designates the liberalities

13. "Il marche dans la plaine immense, / Va, vient, lance la graine au loin, / Rouvre sa main, et recommence" (He walks on the immense plain, / Goes, comes, throws the seed into the distance, / Opens his hand, begins again). We find these lines in a poem by Victor Hugo, who celebrates "le geste auguste du semeur" (the august gesture of the sower) ("Saison des semailles: Le soir," in *Les chansons des rues et des bois,* 2.1.3). Jules Renard's parody in *La lanterne sourde* (in *Oeuvres* [Paris: Gallimard, "Bibliothèque de la Pléiade," 1970], 1:628), deserves to be cited at length. The city dweller Eloi asks country dweller Jaquot:

> "Jaquot, here's a good opportunity: Make the august gesture of the sower for me."
>
> "I beg your pardon?"
>
> "I want to see the famous gesture of the sower that our great painters have so often painted and our great poets have so often described. Well, go ahead! Don't you get it? I'm asking you to show me how you sow what you sow."
>
> "There," said Jaquot.
>
> "No, my poor friend," cried Eloi, "that's not right! Don't be so timid. You look like you're feeding chickens. Have no fear. I wish you no harm. Imagine you're alone and let's start all over. First, you're facing the wrong way, toward the dark woods. Turn toward the light. Stand out against the horizon. Then, slowly dip your hand into your apron, pull it out full of wheat, throw the fertilizing grains this way and that, and let your free gesture seem to travel over immense nature, like a bird set free. Careful now, one! two! . . . Now, Jaquot, why do you look so bewildered?"

14. This is the ancient gloss of Persius's *Satire* 5, line 177. Cited by P. Fabia in the article entitled "Missilia," in Saglio-Pottier, *Dictionnaire des antiquités classiques* (Paris, 1904), 1934–38.

15. A. Ernout and A. Meillet, *Dictionnaire étymologique de la langue latine: Histoire des mots* (Paris: Klincksieck, 1939).

16. The river imagery of *largitio* in no way excludes a metaphorical reference to the rays of the sun. In *La part maudite,* Georges Bataille privileges solar exuberance and "consumption" in his references to Mexican myths and sacrifices. But on other occasions, he also uses the river image: the "overall movement of energy" on the surface of the globe "cannot accumulate without limit" in the productive forces of economic activity. "In the end, *like a river into the sea,* it must escape and be lost to us" (27–28; emphasis added).

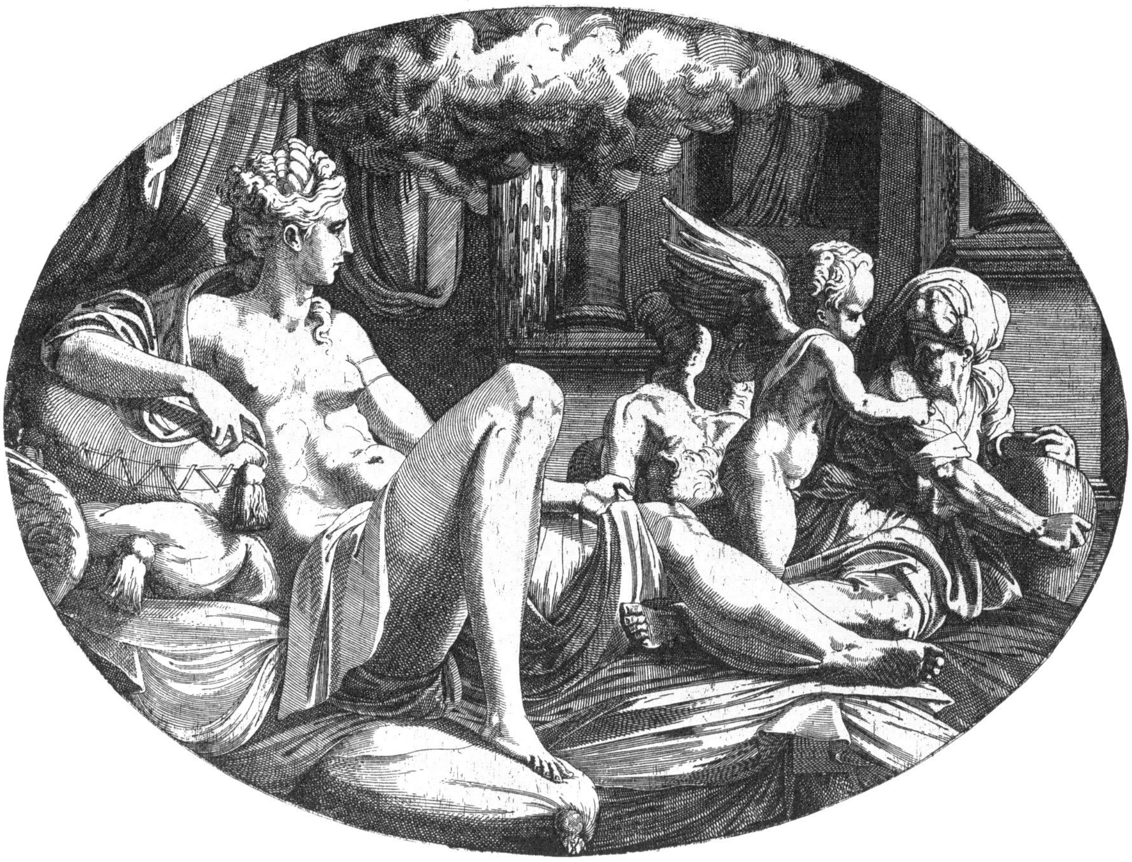

2. Master L. D., *Danaë,* Bibliothèque Nationale.

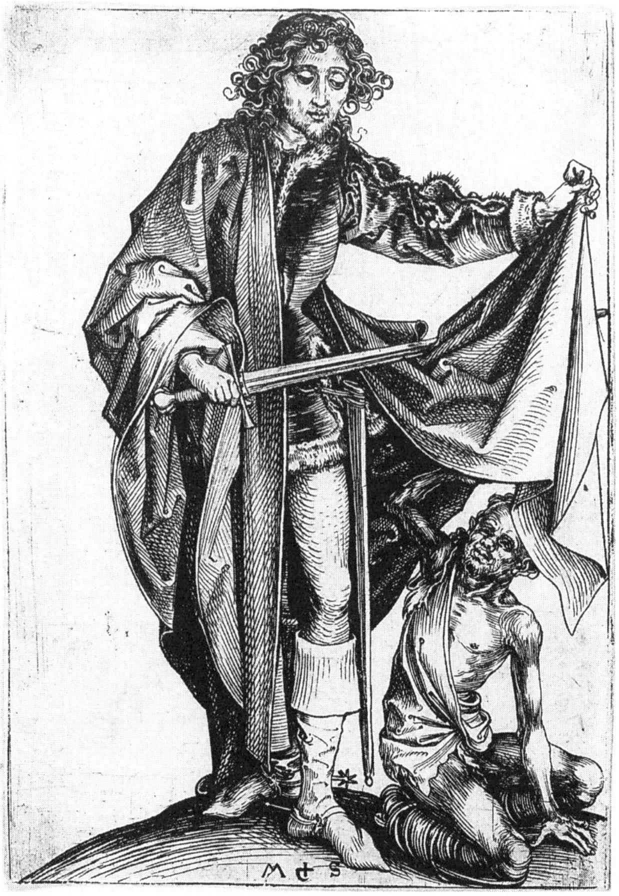

3. Martin Schongauer, *Saint Martin,* Louvre Museum, Edmond de Rothschild Collection.

of the prince and of important personages in a province or city: these might be public meals, lands, individual bonuses in cash or kind, or games—in short, anything that an aedile, consul, emperor, or benefactor (*évergète*) could offer.[17] Those who had resolved that their *authority* would be respected had to manifest in various ways their faculty for augmenting and increasing the prosperity around them. True authority was the act of an *auctor,* the origin of our word *author.*

Latin has another term with more restricted meanings: *sparsio,* to designate what is scattered or dropped, an act that most resembles sowing.[18] During circus games, when the people were gathered together, the dispenser of the feast performed a *sparsio* in person or had it done by someone else.[19] It consisted of throwing the most various sorts of gifts to the crowd. The objects thus dispersed were called *missilia.*[20]

That gesture was obviously connected to "divine kingship," to use Frazer's terminology. The practice has been documented in the ancient Middle East and in Mediterranean cultures. The wealthy man in Athens was obliged to provide for the *liturgies:* he took responsibility for equipping the choir *(chorégie),* for providing a public meal *(hestiaisis),* and so on.[21] The rich, however, did not show any excessive zeal in fulfilling these costly obligations. Less expensive variants existed. During the time of Aristophanes, poets solicited the favor of the theater public in Athens by throwing out sweets—*tragèmata, trogalia:* these consisted of "figs, nuts, and grilled barley corns," similar to the treats thrown out to bring good luck to newlyweds.[22] The good company's diversions at M. d'Epinay's fete continued a practice that was many centuries old.

Emperors and Kings

In a poem from Statius's *Silvae* that describes the saturnalia and exalts the generosity of **14**
the emperor Domitian, the author first celebrates *largitio* and *sparsio.* The laudatory image is deft and alive, and skillfully takes up the old established formula:

> Scarce was the new dawn stirring, when already sweetmeats were raining from the lines, such was the dew the rising East wind was scattering; the famous fruit of Pontic nut-groves, or of Idume's fertile slopes, all that devout Damascus grows upon its boughs or thirsty Canunus ripens, falls in a generous profusion. Biscuits and melting pastries, Amerian fruit not over-ripe, must-cakes, and bursting dates from invisible palms were showering down. Not with such torrents do stormy Hyades o'erwhelm the earth or Pleiades, dissolved in rain, as the hail that from a sunny sky lashed the people in the theatre of Rome. Let Jupiter send his tempests through the world and threaten the broad fields, while our own Jove sends us showers like these!
>
> But lo! another multitude, handsome and well-dressed, as numerous as that upon the benches,

17. In the eastern empire, the emperor was called the creator of wealth, *ploutopoios.* This practice was linked to clientelism. See Paul Veyne, *Le pain et le cirque: Sociologie historique d'un pluralisme politique* (Paris: Seuil, 1976); and, by the same author, the very incisive notes in the translation of Seneca, *Entretiens: Lettres à Lucilius,* ed. Paul Veyne (Paris: Laffont, "Bouquins," 1993). In the *donativa* given to soldiers or in the *congiaires* offered to beneficiaries of every category, the portions were divided up exactly. To each the same share: when Rousseau distributes the apples to the little Savoyards, he remains faithful to a model of largesse proposed by Roman antiquity.

18. "*Spargo . . .* to disperse *(n. semina);* to scatter; to strew." Ernout and Meillet, *Dictionnaire étymologique.*

19. By a *dispensator* selected beforehand for that duty, and rewarded with the munificence granted petitioners.

20. See Fabia, "Missilia"; and Louis Robert, "Sur un décret d'Acraiphia pour l'évergète Epaminondas," *Arkhaiologiké Ephemeris* (1969), 34–39.

21. See Aristotle, *Ethica Nicomachea* 4.1119–1125a.

22. Fabia, "Missilia," n. 14 above.

makes its way along all the rows. Some carry baskets of bread and white napkins and more luxurious fare; others serve languorous wine in abundant measure. . . . Come now, Antiquity, compare with ours the age of primeval Jove and the times of gold: less bounteously then did the vintage flow, not thus did the harvest anticipate the tardy year. One table serves every class alike, children, women, people, knights, and senators; freedom has loosed the bonds of awe. Nay even thyself—What god could have such leisure, or vouchsafe as much?—thou didst come and share our banquet. And now everyone, be he rich or poor, boasts himself the Emperor's guest.

Now as the shades of night draw on, what commotion attends the scattering [*sparsio*] of largess! Here enter maidens easily bought; here is recognized all that in theatres wins favour or applause for skill or beauty. Here a crowd of buxom Lydian girls are clapping hands, here tinkle the cymbals of Cadiz. . . . Amid the tumult dense clouds of birds swoop suddenly down through the air. . . . Too few [hands] are there to seize them all, exultantly they grasp their fill and ever clutch fresh plunder. Countless voices are raised to heaven, acclaiming the Emperor's festival; with loving enthusiasm they salute their Lord. This liberty alone did Caesar forbid them.[23]

More troubling episodes accompanied these images of abundance and the lifting of prohibitions:[24] gladiator fights between women or between dwarves, for example. Statius does not spare his amazement: these monstrosities are part of the surprises of the day.

When we look through the historians' texts, we see similar scenes unfolding, even before Domitian, attesting to the same pleasure on the prince's part, the same demands from spectators. Here is Gaius Caligula: "He also threw various sorts of gifts among the people to be scrambled for, and gave each man a basket of victuals."[25]

The prince exposes himself, exposes his life, through this gesture. The conspirators who put Caligula to death chose the very day of a *sparsio:*

In [Chaerea's] eyes any opportunity for action was good enough. Indeed he had frequent opportunities when he went up to the Capitol on occasions when Gaius offered sacrifice for his daughter's benefit. For . . . Gaius stood above the palace and scattered gold and silver money among the people. . . . [Gaius] turned to the spectacle and took his seat surrounded by the most prominent of his companions. . . . A considerable quantity of fruit was scattered among the spectators with a number of such birds as are prized by their possessors for their rarity; and Gaius watched with amusement as the spectators fought over them and snatched them from one another.[26]

Soon after, mortal blows from a sword struck down the tyrant. The aggressiveness

23. Statius, *Silvae* 1.6, English translation by J. H. Mozley (Cambridge and London: Harvard University Press and William Heinemann, 1961), 1:65–71. For a less flattering view of the emperor celebrated by Statius, see Suetonius, *Domitianus* 4. Following a similar fete on the occasion of the new year, Martial (8.78) rants about receiving heteroclite objects as New Year's presents, which a tiresome person had collected at a *sparsio* or acquired from someone who had resold them.

24. In Martial's Latin, *dare* is the absolute verb in the expression "to give oneself" in the erotic sense. Hence the play on words concerning a lewd and stingy old woman: "You want to give and not to give" *Vis dare nec dare vis* (7.75). Rabelais uses the expression *donner la secousse* [give the shake]. In *Gargantua and Pantagruel* (book 3, chap. 2), when Panurge praises prodigality, he expresses his admiration for the "wanton lasses" of Gaul because "they do acknowledge their being born into this world, not to be for themselves alone, but that in their proper persons their acquaintance may claim one share, and their friends another." In *The Urquhart-Le Motteux Translation of the Works of Francis Rabelais,* ed. Albert Jay Nock and Catherine Rose Wilson (New York: Harcourt Brace, 1931), 1:445. Valéry is more elegant when he evokes "the last gifts, the fingers that defend them" *(Cimetière marin).*

25. Suetonius, *Caligula* 8.2, in *The Lives of the Caesars,* ed. Joseph Gavorse (New York: Random House, "Modern Library," 1931), 177.

26. Flavius Josephus, *Jewish Antiquities* 19:70–71, 88, 93–94, English translation by Louis H. Feldman (Cambridge and London: Harvard University Press and William Heinemann, 1965), 249–59.

of the conspirators, who put an end to the monstrous misdeeds the prince had delighted in, corresponds to the aggressiveness that was mingled with Caligula's gifts.

Nero attends to his popularity in the same way:

> Every day all kinds of gifts were thrown to the people. These included a thousand birds of every kind each day, various kinds of food, tickets for grain, clothing, gold, silver, precious stones, pearls, paintings, slaves, beasts of burden, even trained wild animals, and finally, ships, blocks of houses, and farms.[27]

Jealous of the performers, Nero outbids them: he gives himself as spectacle, serves himself up for public consumption, provided the crowd applauds him. The habit took hold among the people, and even though emperors did not often hazard into the arena, they scattered the expected munificences at the theater and circus. Those of Elagabalus were extravagant.[28] The eastern religious rituals, the frenzied theatricality, and the mater-
nal figures associated with this peculiar adolescent attracted the attention of Antonin 4
Artaud, who, in retracing his history, left nothing out of the scenes of *sparsio.* In one of the strangest events from the ancient world (at least to our eyes), Artaud found the ele-
ments for a scene from the "theater of cruelty." The episode is without equal, except in 5
the rituals of ancient Mexico, which also fascinated Artaud:

> A strange rhythm imposes itself in Heliogabalus's cruelty; this initiate does everything with art and everything twice. I mean he does everything on two levels. Each of his gestures cuts both ways.
>
> Order, Disorder,
> Unity, Anarchy,
> Poetry, Dissonance,
> Rhythm, Discord,
> Greatness, Puerility,
> Generosity, Cruelty.
>
> From the heights of the newly erected towers of his temple to the god Pythia, he throws wheat and male members.
>
> He feeds a castrated people.
>
> Of course, there are no theorbos, no tubas, no orchestra of asors amid the castrations he imposes, but imposes each time as so many personal castrations, as if it were he, Elagabalus, who was being castrated. Sacks of sex organs are thrown from the top of the towers with the cruelest abundance, on the feast day of the god Pythia.
>
> I would not swear that an orchestra of asors, or of nebels with squeaking strings, with hard bellies, is not hidden somewhere in the dark recesses of the spiral towers, to mask the cries of the parasites being castrated; but to these cries of tortured men there corresponds, almost at the same time, the acclamations of a people in jubilation, with whom Heliogabalus shares the value of several wheat fields.
>
> Good, evil, sperm, rose wines, embalming oils, and the most expensive perfumes surround Heliogabalus's generosity with limitless irrigation.
>
> And the music emerging bypasses the ear and reaches the mind, without instruments and without orchestra. I mean that the pom pom pom, the maneuvers of inept orchestras, are nothing next to

27. Suetonius, *Nero* 11, in *The Lives of the Caesars,* 247.

28. "Elagabalus," *Scriptores historiae augustae,* ed. E. Hohl, 2 vols. (Leipzig: Teubner, 1927); Herodian, *History of the Empire from the Time of Marcus Aurelius* 5.3.3–8; and Dio Cassius, *Romaika,* 78–79.

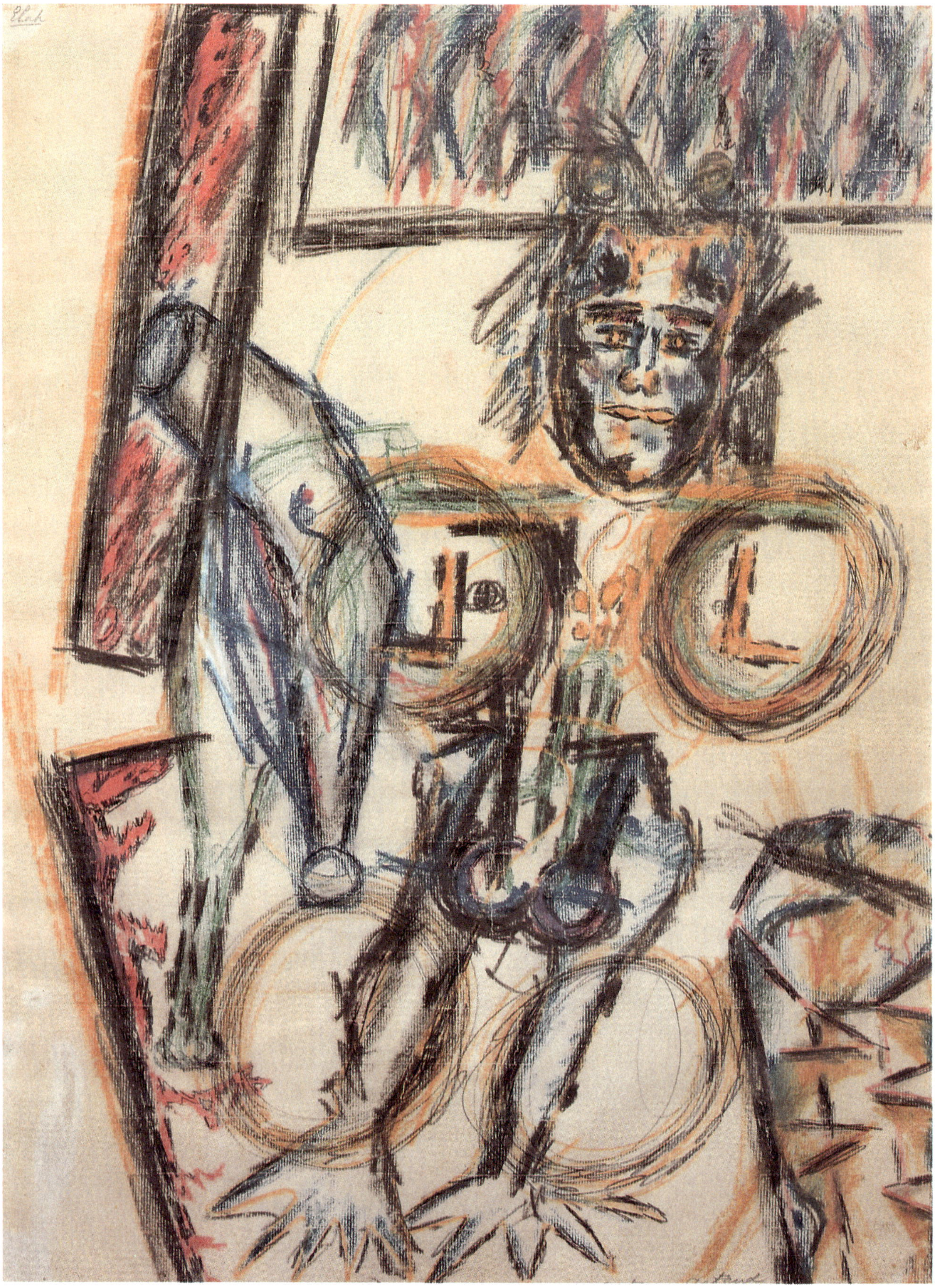

4. Antonin Artaud, *The Inca,* private collection. "It is a matter of rediscovering and resuscitating the vestiges of the ancient solar culture" (letter to Jean-Louis Barrault, Mexico City, 10 July 1936).

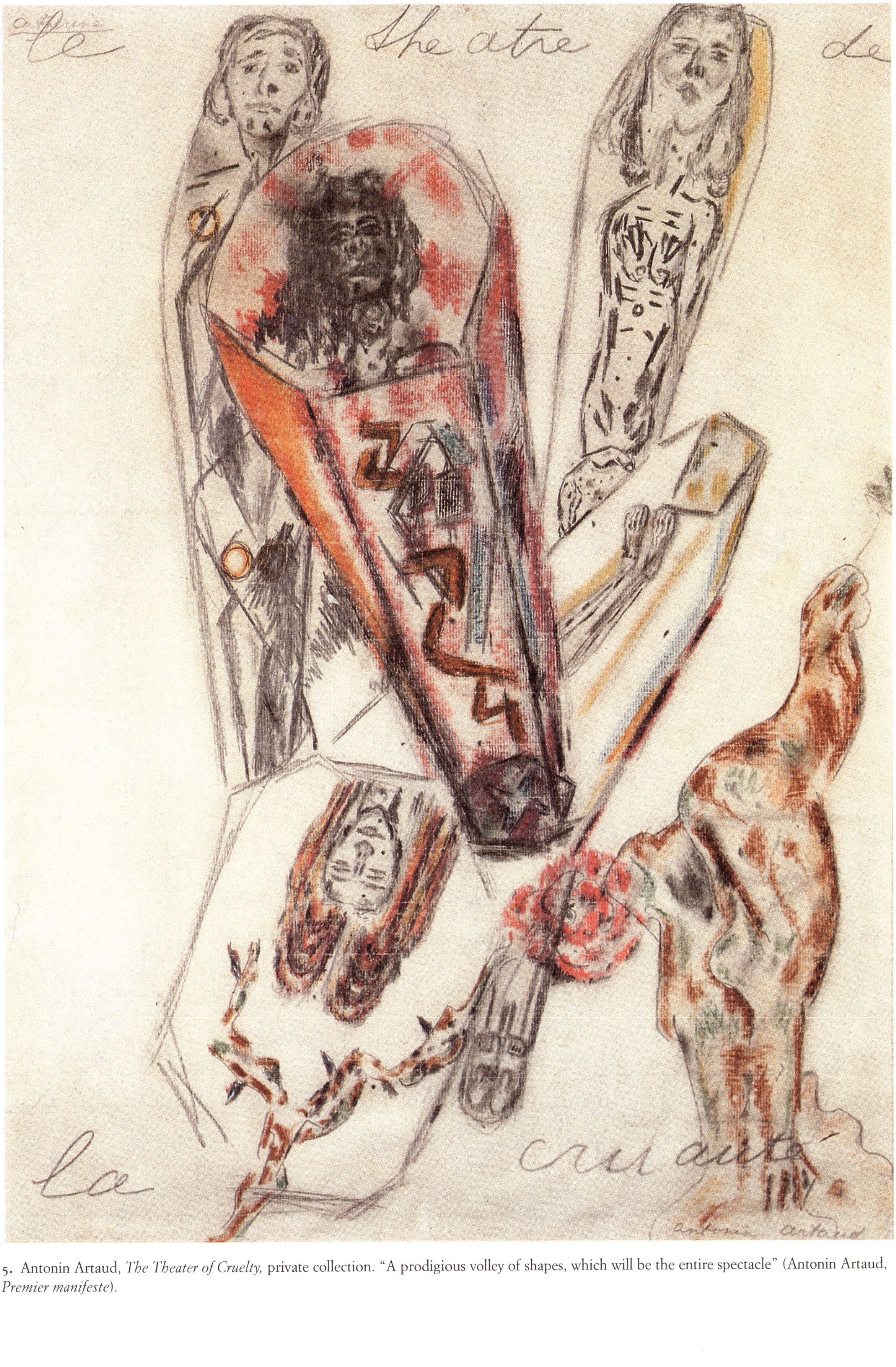

5. Antonin Artaud, *The Theater of Cruelty,* private collection. "A prodigious volley of shapes, which will be the entire spectacle" (Antonin Artaud, *Premier manifeste*).

> this ebb and flow, this tide that comes and goes with its strange dissonances, its generosity and its cruelty, its taste for disorder and its search for an order inapplicable to the Latin world.[29]

Artaud projects his own ambivalence onto Elagabalus and, in a spectacular escalation of violence, he elevates dismemberment, which illness has imposed upon him in the image of his own body, to the dignity of the triumphal *sparsio.* For the text refers both to an apotheosis of the phallic idol and to an orgy of castration. In an association by analogy that has nothing but scorn for the principle of noncontradiction, wheat, which is seed, and the sacks of sex organs, which are sperm (also seed, stemming from the same etymology, the verb *spargo*), are thrown simultaneously from the top of the tower. This delirious text, traversed by archaic images, belongs to the corpus of the "avant-garde" of our literary consciousness. The *sparsio* is not some curiosity for the erudite: it is an archetype for behavior that is easily found in the gestures of children, in dreams, in speech animated by drives.

Is it mere coincidence that Caligula, Nero, and Elagabalus—three "monsters" whose taste for dispatching *missilia* to the people has been related by historians—were all stigmatized for their incestuous attachments? For "modern" (and therefore anachronistic) psychology, there is a great temptation to establish a correlation between this type of ostentatious gift and the infantilism of desire.

During imperial processions, at the consuls' entrance or to mark a solemn entry into a city, gold and silver were regularly scattered among the crowd. The practice continued during the Byzantine Empire.[30] And while Christian emperors undertook to suppress obscenities and gladiator games, they did not in any way renounce the gesture of monetary *sparsio.* In Eusebius of Caesarea's *De vita Constantini* [Life of Emperor Constantine], the panegyrist sets forth the Christian concern with alms; but we also find the persistence of the image of the sun's profusion: "He was not satisfied with merely distributing money to the poor who were begging in the streets and in public squares, but also took care for their food and clothing. . . . And finally, he spread his beneficence to all his subjects with the same profusion that the sun spreads its light to all men. Never did anyone in need implore his help in vain nor leave his sight without receiving some favor."[31] Beginning at daybreak, "he gave largesse to his subjects, to imitate the liberality with which the Lord spreads his light."[32]

In his *History of the Franks,* Gregory of Tours made sure that the example of Clovis, the founder of the Frankish monarchy, would not be forgotten:

> Clovis received letters from the emperor Anastasius conferring the consulate, and in the church of the blessed Martin he was vested in the purple tunic, and in a mantle, and set the diadem upon his head. Then, mounting his horse, he showered with his own hand [*praesentibus populis manu propria*

29. Antonin Artaud, *Héliogabale ou l'anarchiste couronné,* in *Oeuvres complètes* (Paris: Gallimard, 1970), 7:102–5. In reading the work of Artaud, we might conclude that the emperor Elagabalus, assassinated in the latrines and thrown into the sewer, incarnates in a caricatural manner the Freudian homologies of the *gift:* child, money, feces.

30. See Roland Delmaire, *Largesses sacrées et* res privata: *L'*aerarium *impérial et son administration du IVe au VIe siècle* (Rome: École Française de Rome, 1989), esp. 532–93. This book studies primarily the resources that filled the public treasury or the emperor's personal coffers, and their administration. We find very complete information in Fergus Millar, *The Emperor in the Roman World* (London: Duckworth, 1977), 133–39, 368–75.

31. Eusebius de Caesarea, *De vita Constantini,* 1.43.

32. Ibid., 4.22.

> *spargens*] in the generosity of his heart pieces of gold and silver among the people all along the road between the gate of the atrium of the holy Martin's church. From that day he was hailed as consul or Augustus.[33]

The order of events narrated is very important. The passage refers to a twofold
gift: first, the title of consul, conferred by Emperor Anastasius; and second, the coins
distributed by King Clovis to the people. In the interval between the two gifts, the reli- 7
gious ceremony or consecration takes place. The articles of clothing and the crown are
the solemn signs of this consecration. The first gift—the title—should be considered a 12
legitimizing gift. It confers on its beneficiary superior rank, new power, additional au-
thority, which are immediately manifested by an overabundance, a show of wealth that
the people take possession of in the fistfuls of precious metal scattered among them. In
each of these stages, the gift in question is vertical: it descends from the distant emperor 6,9
to the king, from the supreme suzerain to the powerful vassal, and asserts in a benevolent
way a relation of preeminence. It requires submission. Note also that the confirmation
of the legitimizing gift takes place in Tours, in the basilica dedicated to a saint; one of
the illustrious works of Saint Martin, in fact, consisted in giving half his coat to a beggar. 3
Political legitimation is thus sanctified, and the *sparsio,* heir to a magical and pagan prac-
tice, is now nothing more than a supplemental public gesture. Precellence is attributed
to an entirely different form of gift, namely, to charity given the poor. We will need to
consider this again in some detail.

The public gesture of distributing goods to the people was part of the royal ceremony among the high clergy and nobility in Catholic Europe and in the Byzantine East.[34] In the twelfth century, Saint Bernard of Clairvaux's treatise *On Consideration* criticized the behavior of the Roman church and described the pagan customs that had survived Christianization:

> What shall I say of the practice of buying the cheers that ring out as you pass with the booty of the Church of Rome? The bread of the poor is thrown by the handful into streets inhabited by the rich. Silver coins shine in the mud; on every side, people make a rush for them. These coins are the prey, not of the poorest, but of the strongest and most alert. . . . Who do we see advancing in the middle of all that? You, the pastor of this people, shimmering in gold and bespeckled with the richest colors.[35]

33. Gregory of Tours, *History of the Franks* 2.28, English translation by O. M. Dalton (London: Oxford, Clarendon Press, 1927), 78.

34. See Otto Treitinger, *Die oströmische Reichsidee* (Darmstadt, 1969). In *Les rois thaumaturges* (rev. ed., preface by Jacques Le Goff [Paris, 1983], 96–114), Marc Bloch recalls the alms and distributions of money that accompanied the rite of touching scrofula. He links them to the ancient English custom of distributing "maundy money" on Maundy Thursday, when the king washes the feet of the poor. The English expression has survived independent of this ritual. In the *ordo* of the anointing ceremony for the kings of France in Rheims, the "tokens" thrown to the people appeared only with the anointing of Henri II in 1547. See Richard A. Jackson, *Vivat Rex—Histoire des sacres et couronnements en France, 1364–1825* (Strasbourg: Associations des Publications, 1984); and Jacques Le Goff, "Reims, ville du sacre," *Lieux de mémoire,* vol. 2: *La nation,* 98–184, ed. Pierre Nora (Paris: Gallimard, 1986).

35. Bernard of Clairvaux, *Oeuvres complètes,* trans. Charpentier, 8 vols. (Paris: Vivès, 1866), 2:193. The religious criticism of the wealth of the Church appealed not only to the Gospels but also to the legend of martyred saints. The Counter-Reformation often evoked Saint Lawrence distributing the goods of the Church of Rome to the poor, or presenting the poor to the pagan emperor, who had asked him to hand over his treasures. In the beginning of the seventeenth century, Giovanni Serodine painted at least two versions of *The Charity of Saint Lawrence.* See the catalog *Serodine: La pittura oltre Caravaggio,* exhibition in Locarno and Rome, 1987 (Milan: Electa, 1987).

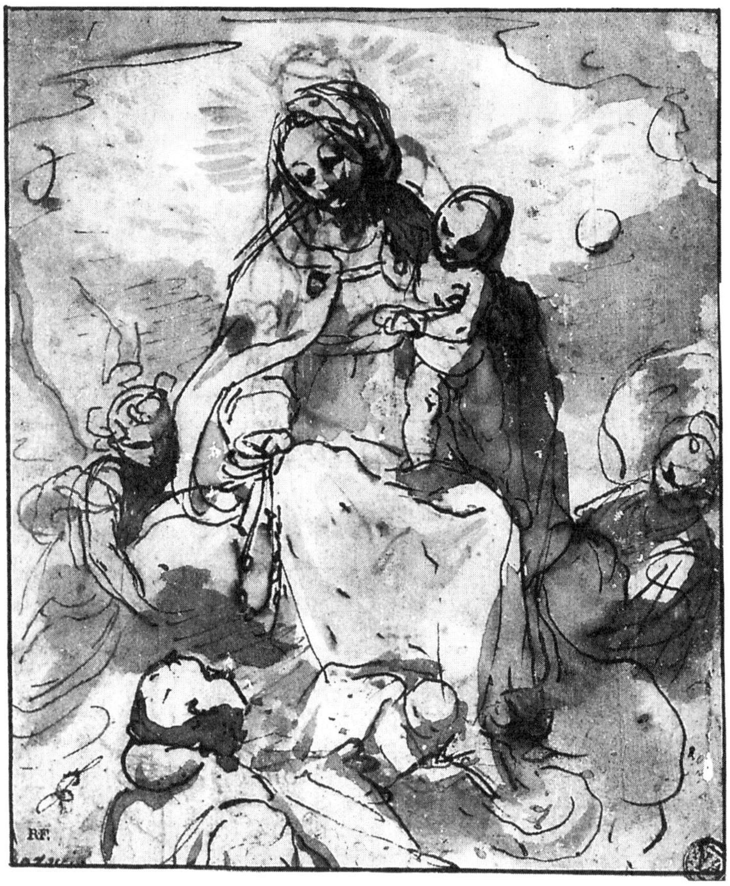

6. Federico Barocci, *The Madonna of the Rosary,* Louvre Museum. The vertical gift: the Madonna appears to Saint Dominic and gives him the first rosary.

7. Tommaso Vincidor, *The Wedding of Alexander and Roxane,* Louvre Museum. Copy after a lost drawing by Raphael. A vertical gift, a horizontal gesture: having conquered a prince of Sogdiana, Alexander falls in love with his daughter and makes her his wife.

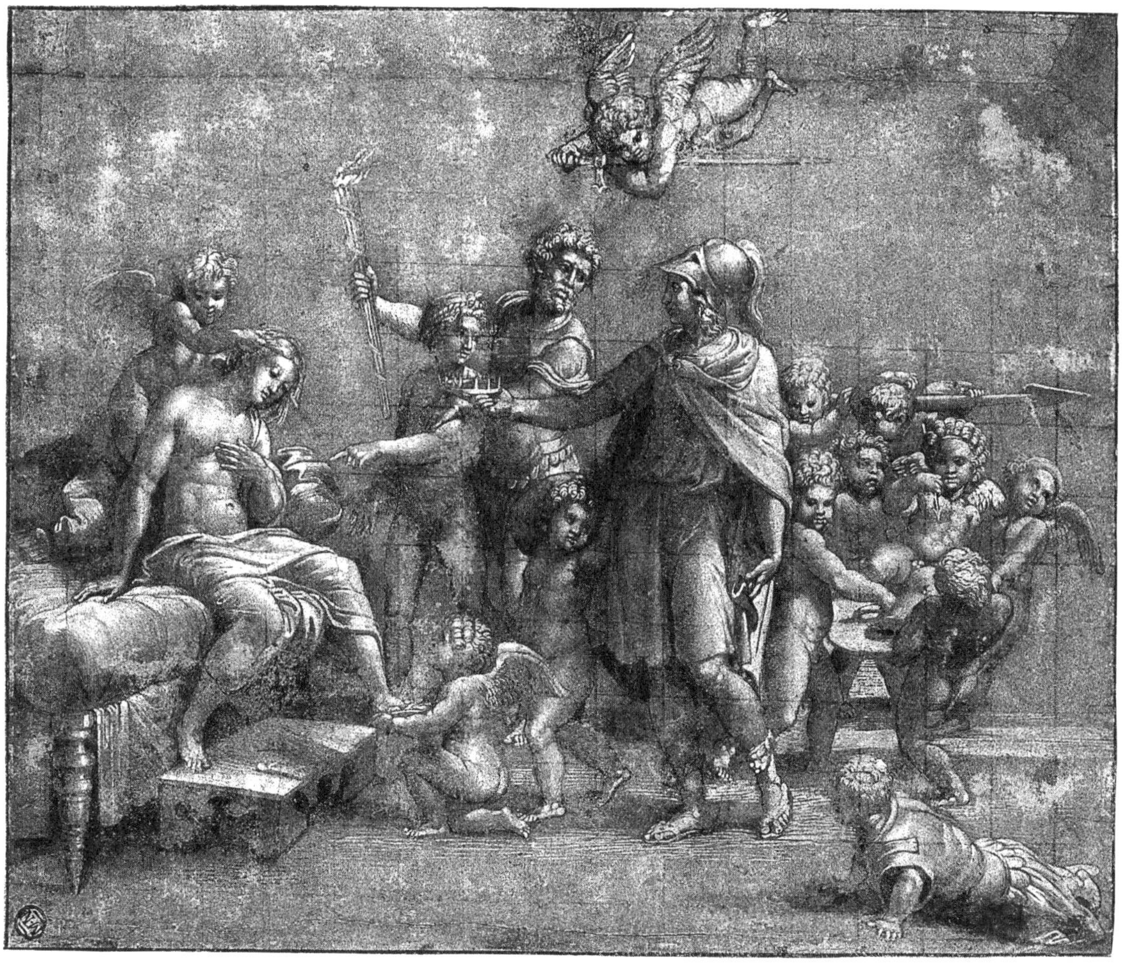

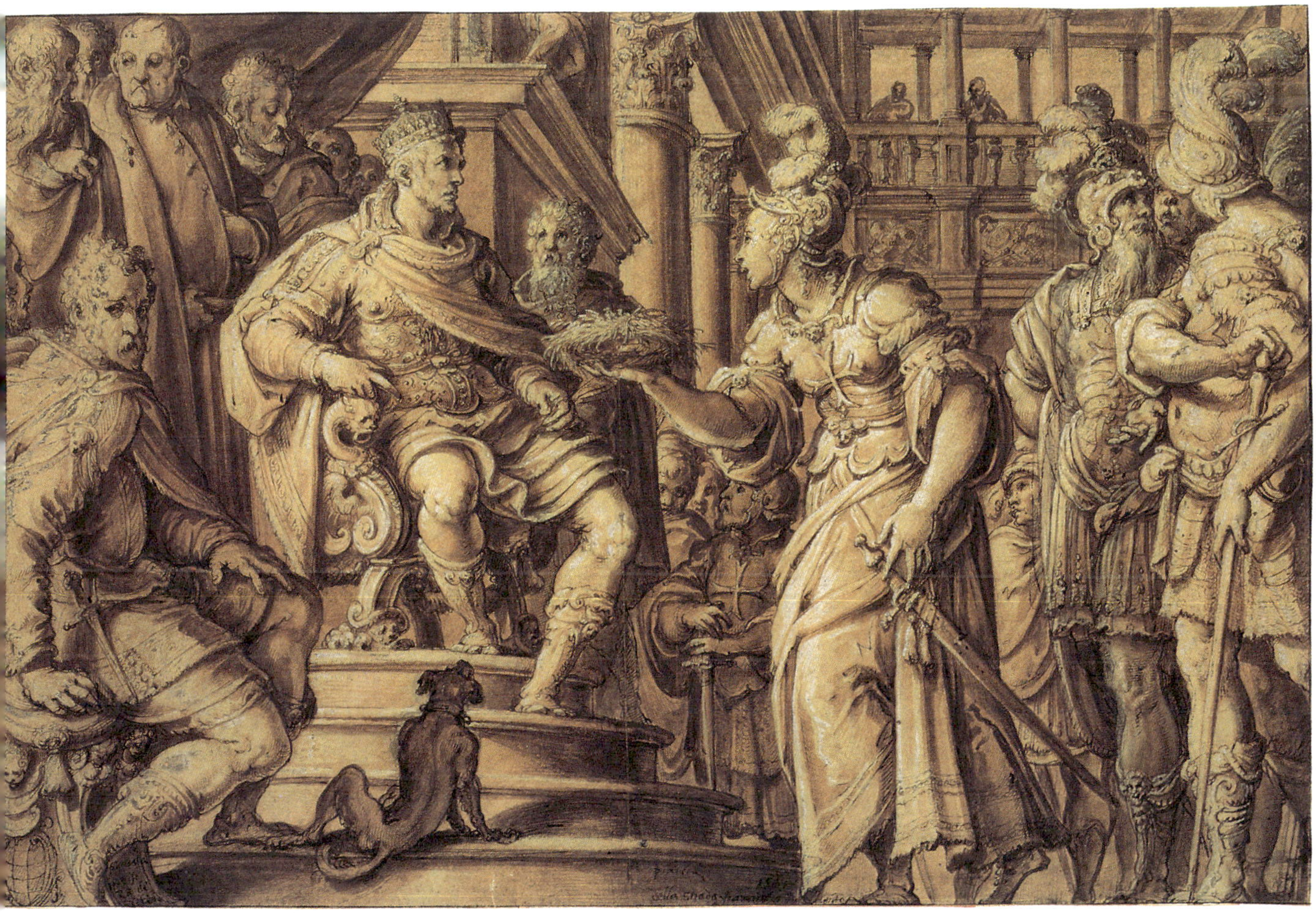

. Jan van der Straet (Stradanus), *Philip II Receiving the Tribute of Malta,* Louvre Museum.

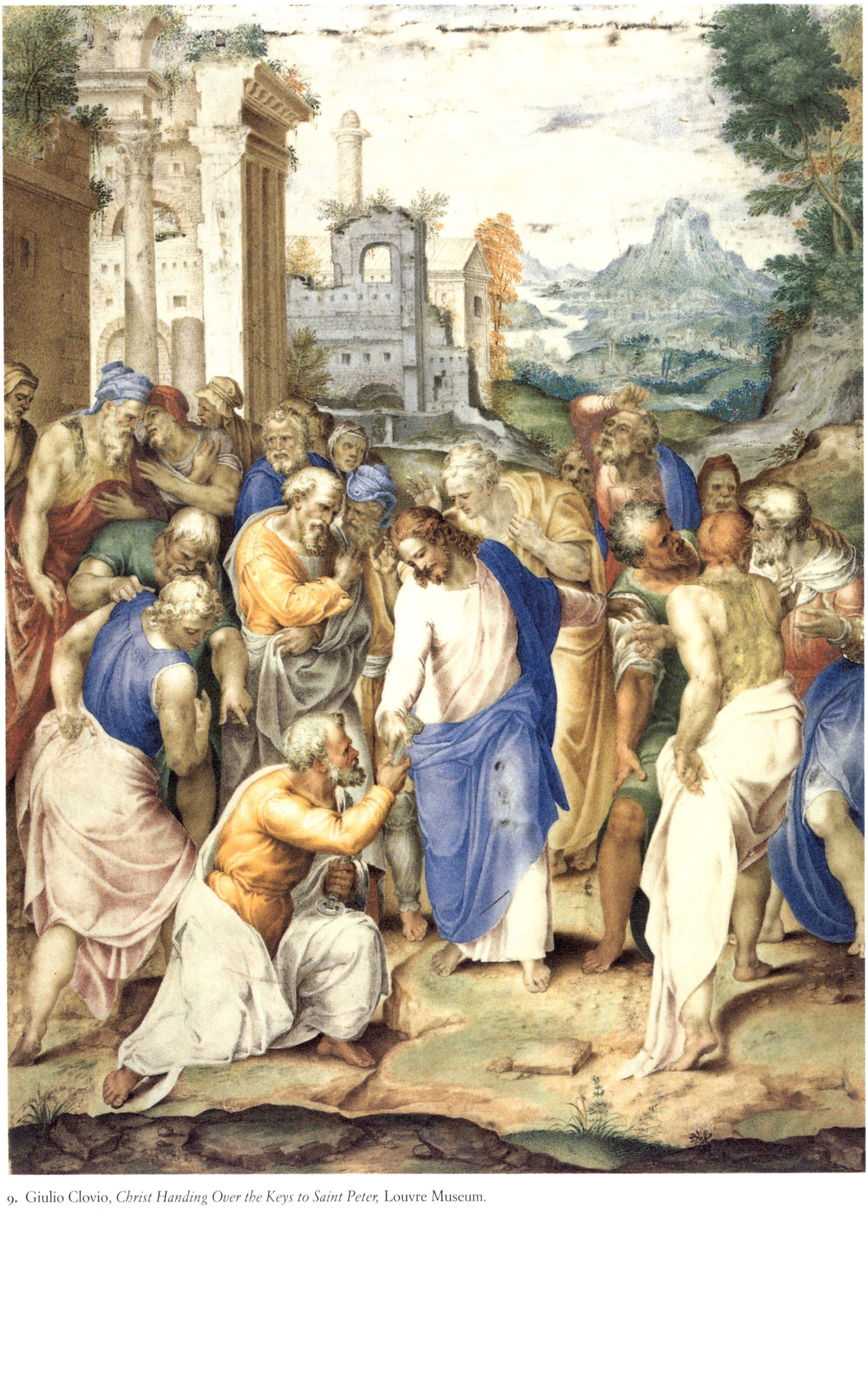

9. Giulio Clovio, *Christ Handing Over the Keys to Saint Peter,* Louvre Museum.

In the world of chivalry, spending is a noble gesture. The allegorical figure of Largesse exemplifies an entire pattern of behavior, closely associated with other personified virtues. Chrétien de Troyes proclaims in his *Cligès:* "Largece est dame et reïne, Qui totes vertus anlumine" (Largesse is lady and queen, who illuminates all virtues; ll. 193–94). And we read in *L'histoire de Guillaume le Maréchal:* "Gentilesce fu nurie en l'ostel Largece" (Nobleness was nourished in the hotel Largesse; ll. 5067–68).[36] At the beginning of *Le roman de la rose,* in the Garden of Mirth, Largesse dances the carol with other characters called Gladness, Beauty, Riches, Courtesy, and Youth. But there is also the risk of consuming all one's wealth in largesse; should Largesse be represented as two-faced, then, should her garb be half one way, half another? Instead, a new character, known as Foolish Largesse, is created, and allegory accepts her into its expanding repertoire. There is a place for her too in the space of *Le roman de la rose.* The lover must avoid wandering into her territory.

The figure of Largesse is well known throughout Europe. In Italian, she is "Larghezza," in Spanish "Largueza." In England during the Elizabethan Age it was believed that "bountie and largesse is befallyng for kinges" (John Udall).[37] Whenever it was a matter of manifesting power, Renaissance courts punctuated profane fetes with the paroxysm of throwing out largesse. The act of crying out names and titles goes hand in hand with that of making profuse gifts of minted coins: the verbal act is "jaculatory" speech, like the motto on coins made of precious metal. Consider this scene, which occurred on 10 June 1520, at the Field of the Cloth of Gold, during the banquet offered by King Henry VIII of England:

> At the third service the kings of arms and the heralds, having a large pot of very rich gold, cried out, "Largesse!" in the name of the king of England. "Largesse from his highness, the powerful, the excellent Prince Henry, King of England and Lord of Ireland by the grace of God: Largesse, largesse." So cried Montjoie. Then the officers at arms came into the great hall, and among them was the duke of Alençon and other princes and lords, who toasted the princes of England, and cried: "Largesse Britain, King of Arms." Then they went to the pavilion, where the feast and public banquet were being held, and there were a great number of people there, and again they cried "largesse." Afterward, they played various instruments, and there were dances, songs, and other amusements.[38]

36. Georges Duby notes: "The knight's duty is to keep nothing in his own hands. Everything that comes to him, he gives away. He draws his strength and most of his power—in any case, all his renown and the warm friendship surrounding him—from his generosity. The only praise Guillaume le Maréchal liked to hear about his father was that he had spread wealth abundantly, and the hero himself no doubt wanted to be admired first and foremost for his own munificence, for not knowing how to hold anything back, for his boundless spending, for everything he distributed to please those he loved.

"But it is this aspect of the underlying ethics of chivalry that runs up against reality. It had grown up during a time when gold coins rarely circulated, when gifts and countergifts were almost the only way wealth passed from one person to another, with the exception of inheritances. But during the very abrupt growth in the last quarter of the twelfth century, the invasion of money turned everything upside down." *Guillaume le Maréchal ou le meilleur chevalier du monde* (Paris: Fayard, 1984), 108–9. See also Marian P. Whitney, "Queen of Mediaeval Virtues: Largesse," in *Vassar Mediaeval Studies,* ed. Christabel Forsyth Fiske (New Haven: Yale University Press, 1923). In Bocaccio's *Decameron,* we find the story of the falcon, where a knight deprives himself of all his wealth for the lady he loves: he impoverishes himself to the point of having to sacrifice his last possession, an admirable falcon. He kills the precious bird to offer food to his lady.

37. I shall confine myself to recalling the use of "Larghezza" and its allegorization in Dante's *Il fiore,* which is derived from *Le roman de la rose* (in particular, in sonnets 71–75). The virtue of largesse is considered in chap. 27 of part 4 of Dante's *Convivio.* Shakespeare, who occasionally uses the term "largesse," is above all the poet of "bounty." Need we recall Cleopatra's eulogy of Antony? (*Antony and Cleopatra,* 5.2.76–100; see "Texts on the Gift," no. 14.) Or sonnet 4? (See "Texts on the Gift," no. 13.) The addressee of that poem is criticized for not procreating and thus for making improper use of his beauty: "Why dost thou abuse / The bounteous largess given thee to give?"

38. Théodore Godefroy, *Le cérémonial français,* 2 vols. (Paris: Cramoisy, 1649), 2:742.

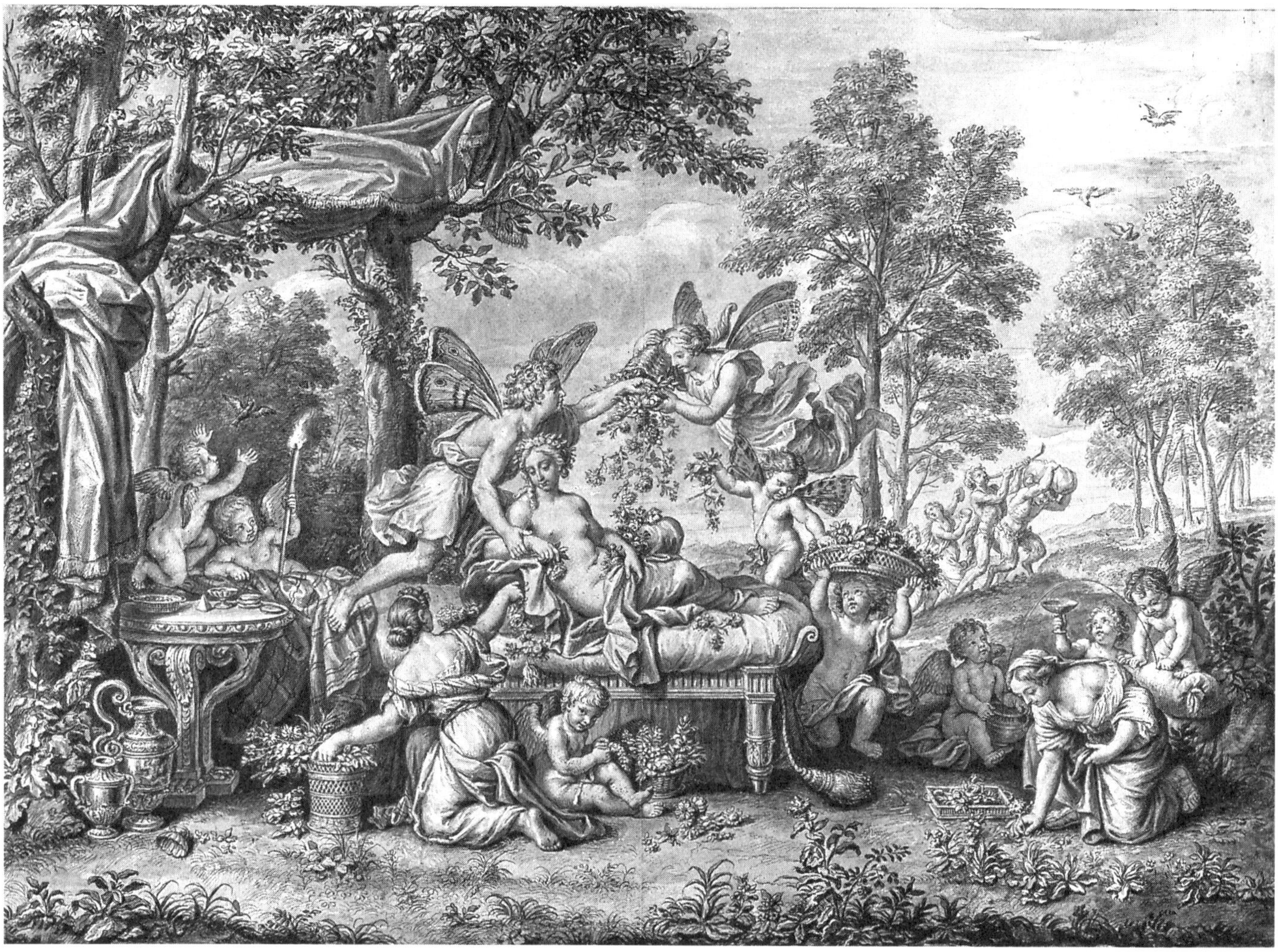

10. After Pierre Mignard, *Spring,* Louvre Museum.

In the age of humanism, the occasions for largesse repeat and deploy all the ancient emblems of profusion: horns of plenty, heavy garlands full of bunches of grapes and pomegranates, Cybele and Ceres (figures of nourishment), images of Spring scattering **10**
her flowers, of Summer and Autumn pouring forth their fruit, the personification of distant regions bringing their tributes, processions of Bacchus and Plutus, feasts of the gods. In Rabelais's *Gargantua and Pantagruel,* after the banquet at the home of the Queen of Lanterns and the copious enumeration of dances, the cry goes up, "Largesse from the queen!" The ceremonial is respected in the realm of pure fantasy.[39] Consider in particular the *contion* that Gargantua addresses to the vanquished enemies: he cites as an example the leniency of his father toward the Canary Island pirates he had conquered, who repaid him with a profusion of gifts in place of the tribute that was not imposed upon them.[40] Rabelais waxes euphoric about the relation of submission. The conquerors, who had conducted a just war, maintain that magnanimity toward the vanquished pirates is lucrative, since the pirates give a disproportionate largesse. These heteroclite riches thrown onto a boat are in fact a voluntary tribute, a return gift without measure. (The mythology of chivalry requires that surrender be presented as a generous gift. Stradanus suggests this when he represents the submission of the island of Malta: a vanquished power will **8**
not be humiliated if it can make the gesture of giving.) Of course, in Rabelais's text, the offerings enumerated at length are entirely imaginary: they are a cargo of words. In the literature of the sixteenth century, the profusion of words, the breathless enumeration, the *copia verborum,* are, for both the cleric and the poet, a way of playing a trick on the lords: the poet too has a treasure, something to give as largesse.

In Théodore Godefroy's *Cérémonial français,* which appeared during the Fronde (1649) and was the authoritative text during the absolute monarchy, the compiled documents present multiple accounts and programs regarding princely fetes accompanied by largesse. At the marriage of Elisabeth of France to the duke of Albe (21 June 1559), money was thrown both inside and outside Notre Dame:

> While the solemn mass was being said, the king's heralds at arms, one standing on the stage in front of the great portal of Notre Dame, the other on the wooden ramp in the nave, threw a great quantity of gold and silver to the people, crying out "Largesse."[41]

The same thing occurred at the coronation of Marie de Médicis on 13 May 1610,[42] when care was taken to make a distribution as soon as the mass was over. Let us look closely at "the modern forms observed at the anointing and coronationof the kings of **14**
France, developed expressly to serve at the anointing of King Louis XIII in the year 1610." The successive moments of the ritual are meticulously detailed. "Largesse" was shouted at the moment of enthronement, just after the unction and mass. After crowning the king and seating him on the throne, the archbishop of Rheims declared him the **13**
"mediator between the clergy and the people, just as the clergy is the mediator between God and men":

39. Rabelais, *Gargantua and Pantagruel,* book 5, chap. 33.

40. Ibid., chap. 50; see "Texts on the Gift," no. 12, below.

41. Godefroy, *Cérémonial français,* 2:20.

42. Ibid., 1:581.

> Monsieur of Rheims removed his miter, and, after great reverence and honor were shown to that lord by the king, he kissed him, and then said aloud: *Vivat rex in aeternum.*
>
> After him, all the other peers also kissed the king, the ecclesiastics first, and also said: *Vivat rex in aeternum.*
>
> And then all the people cheered him, and cried, "Long live the king," sounding trumpets, oboes, and all manner of instruments. And my lord monsignor of Rheims began the *Te Deum laudamus,* accompanied by organs and other music.
>
> And during that joy and public acclamation, in the nave of that church, and outside on the square before the great portal as well, largesse of a good many gold and silver coins was made. They were usually minted with the representation and effigy of that lord, with the day and year of his anointing and coronation, or with some other figure, as it pleased his lord. And a number of coins of regular currency were also distributed.[43]

An equivalence seems to be established between the oil and holy water dispensed through religious power and the money then scattered by the king. The grace that has descended from on high is transmuted: it is oil on the king's head, and it becomes gold in the heralds' hands. A favor granted by the highest Authority descends to the people. The archbishop performing the unction and the king scattering coins are merely the mediators of that grace. The scattered coins are evidence of life; they confirm the "Long life!" that is shouted as acclamation. There is no more striking image of this than the one presented by Sergey Eisenstein—an image that borders on hallucination—in the
11 scene of anointing in the film *Ivan the Terrible.* The "modern forms" established for the anointing of Louis XIII were repeated up until the anointing of Charles X.[44] Even very ancient customs are maintained, as the chroniclers in particular note: birds were regularly set free as an aerial and living form of the *sparsio.*[45]

Are we so sensitive to these forms because we know how the story will end? In reading the accounts of witnesses, we find that many royal fetes in the eighteenth century turned out badly. People's hearts were no longer in them. Here, for instance, is a contemporary account of the fetes of February 1745.

> The goal of M. le prévôt of merchants was to provide the public, that is, the Paris bourgeoisie, with entertainment, a place to come to dance and amuse themselves. But that was not to the bourgeoisie's taste. Since people entered from all sides, as if into covered halls, there was a miserable confusion. The place was filled only with riff-raff of the worst sort, who threw all sorts of things off the buffets: tongues, brains, bread, turkey legs. And catch as catch can! This caused quite a stir. The large sym-

43. Ibid., 1:52–76. A painting by Jacques Stella, executed prior to 1642, represents Louis XIII as Titus, distributing liberalities from a high terrace. Richelieu, whose coat of arms figures in the painting, is escorting the king. A small group of figures, harmoniously composed, beseech him or gather the royal gifts from the ground. There is no sign of an unseemly battle. In the foreground, dancing figures distract a bit of the attention from that scene; as a result, the predominant feeling produced is that of the idyll. There is no disorder. The *sparsio* is dignified and quiet. For a discussion of this painting, now at the Fogg Art Museum in Cambridge, Massachusetts, see Anthony Blunt, "La libéralité de Louis XIII et de Richelieu," *Revue de l'Art* 11 (1971).

44. A discussion of this ceremony can be found in the collection entitled *Couronne poétique de Charles X* (Paris, 1825), with texts by Lamartine, Hugo, Soumet, etc. See Françoise Waquet, *Les fêtes royales sous la Restauration ou l'Ancien régime retrouvé* (Geneva: Droz, 1981).

45. Recall the cloud of birds evoked in the saturnalia poem by Statius. At the anointing of Louis XVI in 1775, letting birds go was interpreted as a symbol of freedom: "Fowlers liberated a great number of little birds which, in regaining their freedom, signifed the outpouring of the sovereign's favors on his people. And never were men as truly free as they are under the reign of an enlightened, just, and beneficent prince." Dom Gobet, *Journal historique du sacre et couronnement de Louis XVI roi de France* (Paris, 1775), 49–50. In Paris, the responsibility for freeing birds fell to fowlers, in return for their privileges. See the editorial note in *Chronique de la Régence et du règne de Louis XV ou Journal de Barbier* (Paris: Charpentier, 1857) 5:103–4.

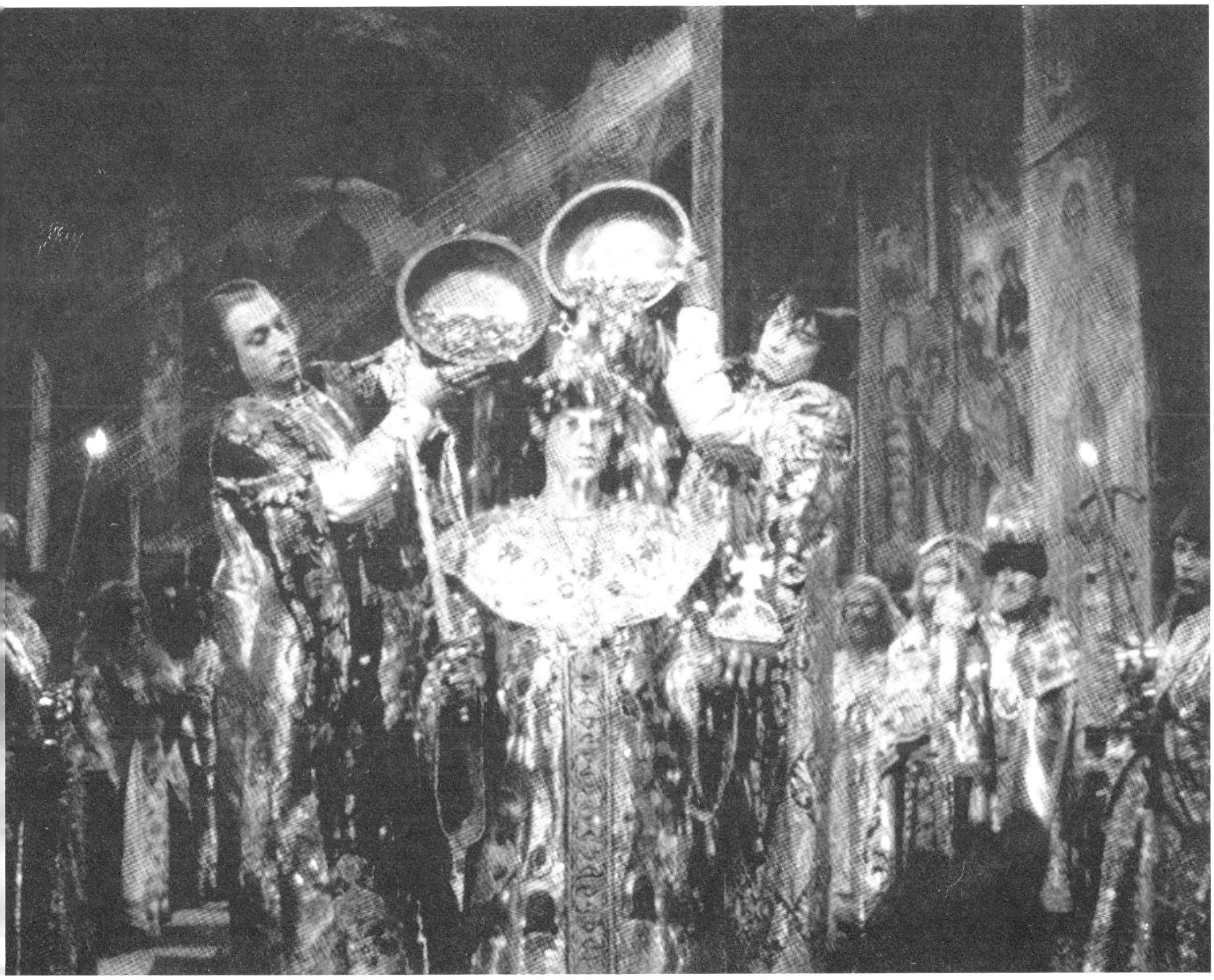

11. Sergey Mikhaylovich Eisenstein, *Ivan the Terrible: The Shower of Gold.*

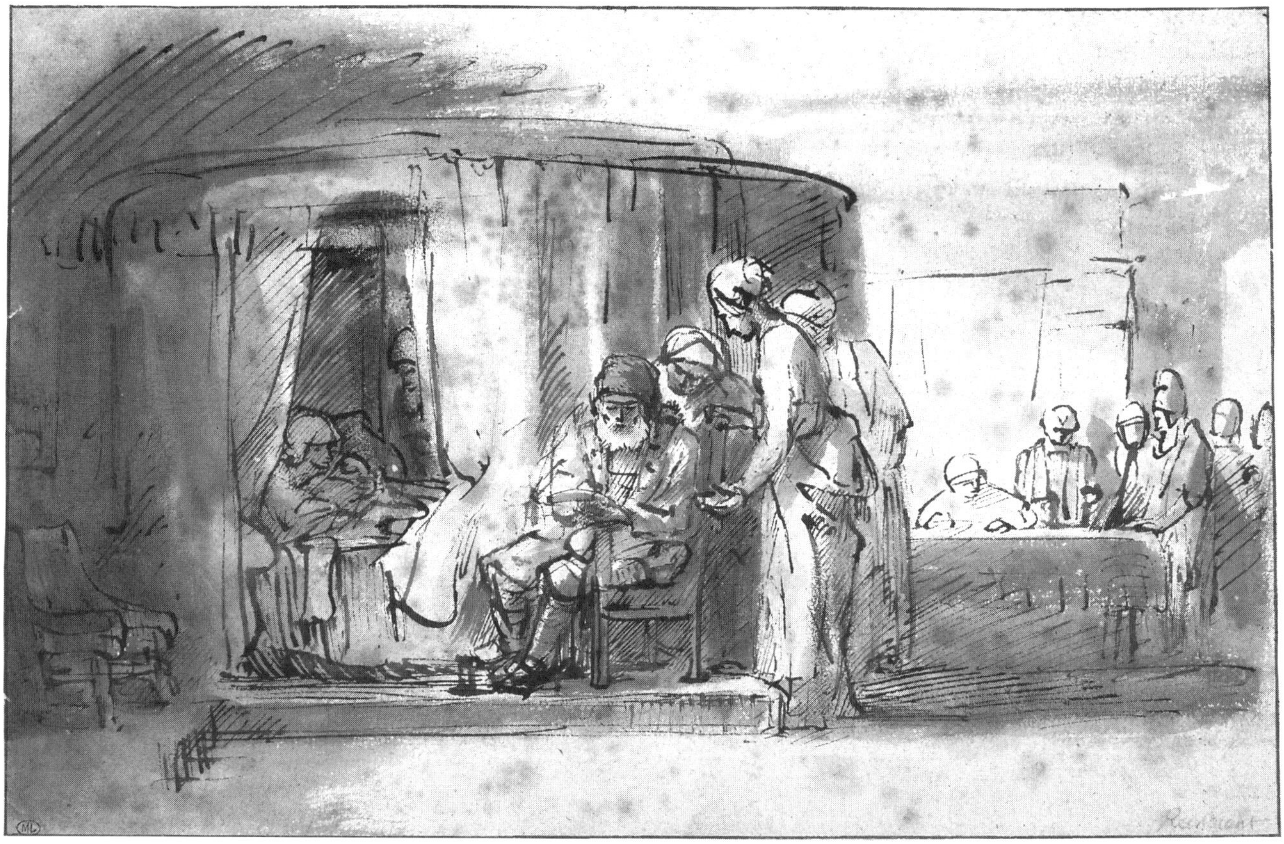

12. Rembrandt, *The Naming of John the Baptist,* Louvre Museum.

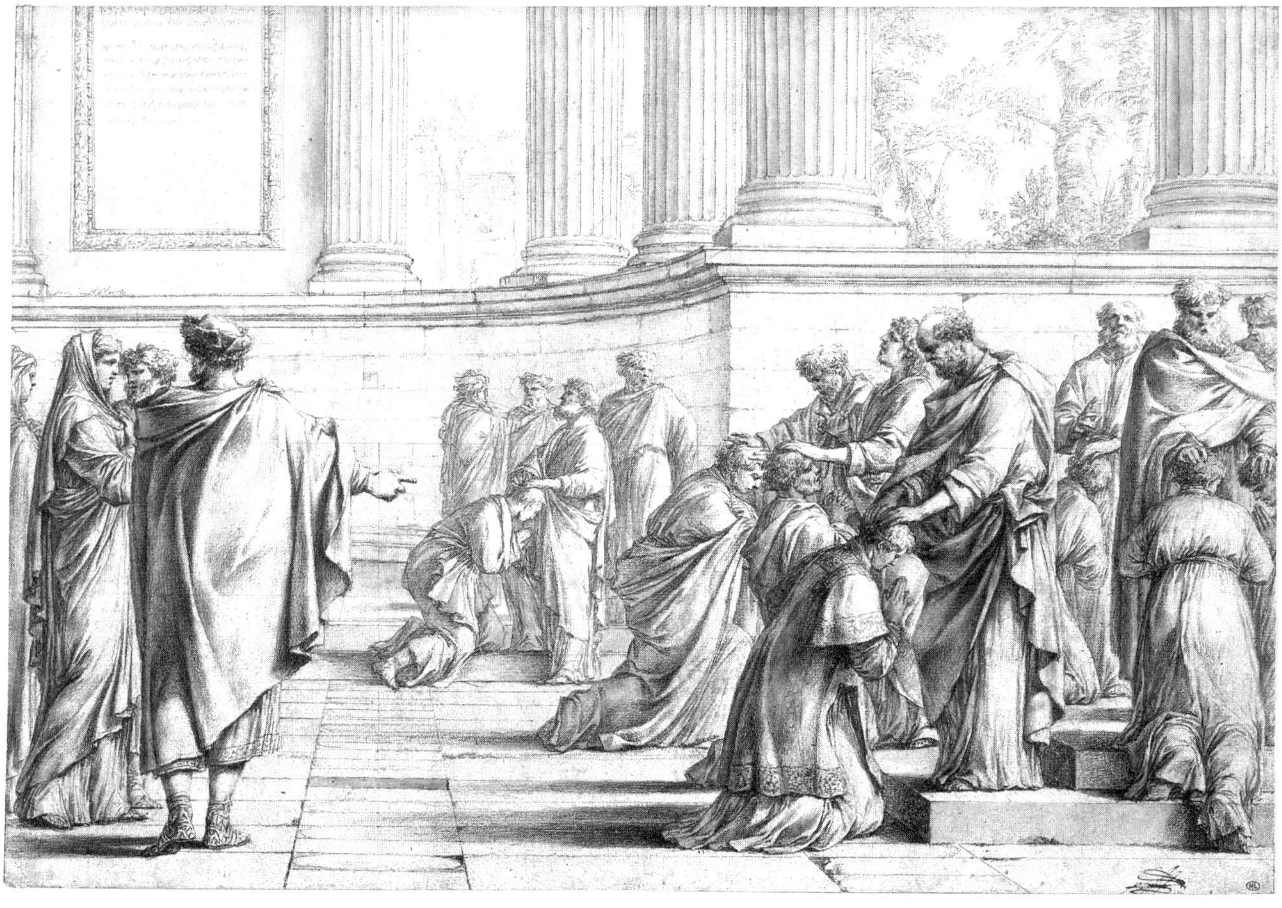

13. Laurent de La Hyre, *Laying Hands on the Seven Deacons,* Louvre Museum. A vertical gift legitimizing the horizontal gift. The twelve apostles consecrate the seven deacons, who will serve tables in "the daily ministration" (Acts 6:1–6).

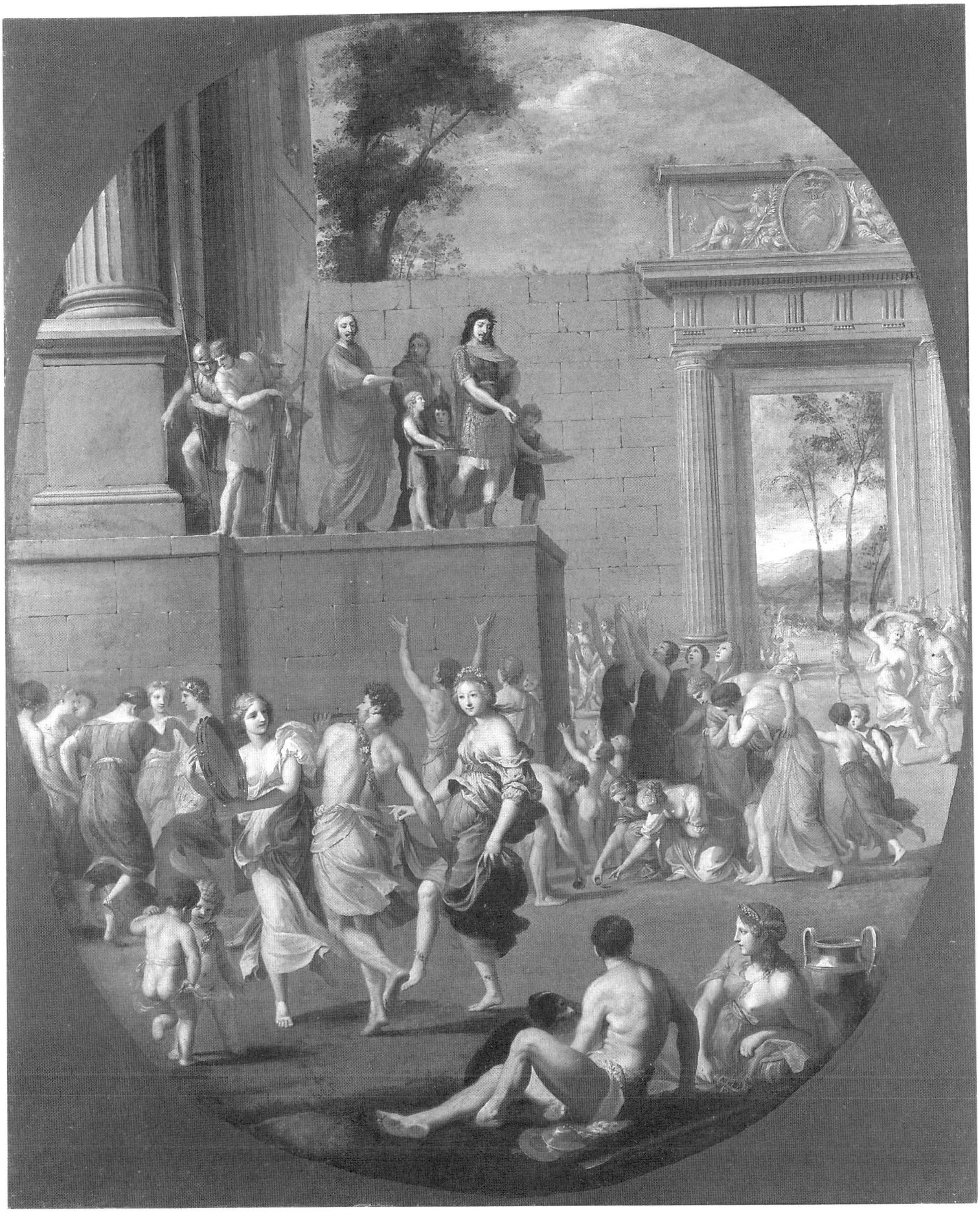

14. Jacques Stella, *The Liberality of Titus (Louis XIII and Richelieu)*, Cambridge, Fogg Art Museum.

phony, which was quite good, played quadrilles, but no one danced, except once in a while a gang of urchins in a circle. A shoemaker's wife or a seamstress would have felt dishonored to have danced there.[46]

When a son was born to the dauphin in September 1751, there was the "usual" tumult among the people to gather up the money thrown them. But no one shouted, "Long live the king!" Louis XV put a halt to public festivities (they were very expensive) and decided to use the money he would have spent to "marry off six hundred girls in Paris."[47] On 30 May 1770, the fireworks set off on Place Louis XV for the marriage between Marie Antoinette and the dauphin provoked a deadly scuffle.[48] At the coronation of Louis XVI, the largesse was parsimonious: "French guards fought over the largesse given to the people, and the officers, who had not foreseen such baseness, were ashamed to see it perpetrated by their soldiers."[49] During the Restoration, public festivities were met with great irony by the liberal journalists and caricaturists, and especially by those, like Charlet, who were nostalgic for Bonaparte.

Let us now turn to the concluding chapters of Stendhal's *Le rouge et le noir,* for a final evocation of classic noble largesse. Julien wants to go from his prison to the guillotine without being humiliated by the bourgeois of Verrières as he passes: "There is one means remaining to earn some consideration in their eyes, and that is to throw gold coins at the people as I go to face the ultimate punishment. My memory, associated with the idea of *gold,* will be resplendent for them."[50] Julien's plan is carried out by Mathilde de la Mole. To remain faithful to the great idea she has formed of the sixteenth century and of her illustrious ancestor Boniface de la Mole, she gives a princely sepulchre to the remains of her decapitated lover:

> Mathilde followed her lover to the grave he had chosen. A great number of priests escorted the coffin and, unbeknownst to all, alone in her draped carriage, she held on her lap the head of the man she had loved so much.
>
> Arriving in the middle of the night at the highest point of one of the tall mountains of the Jura, twenty priests celebrated the service for the dead in that little cave, magnificently illuminated by an infinite number of candles. All the residents of the little mountain villages that the convoy had traversed followed it, attracted by the oddity of that strange ceremony.
>
> Mathilde appeared among them in long mourning clothes and, at the end of the service, she had several thousand five-franc coins thrown to them.
>
> Remaining alone with Fouqué, she wanted to bury the head of her lover with her own hands.
>
> Fouqué almost went mad with sorrow.
>
> Through Mathilde's attentions, that wild cave was decorated with marble, which had been sculpted in Italy at great cost.[51]

46. *Journal de Barbier,* 4:18–19.

47. Ibid., 5:102–4.

48. "This spectacle was more like a city under siege than a wedding celebration." Bachaumont, *Mémoires secrets* (London, 1777), 5:144. This scuffle prefigures that which occurred at the celebration of Nicholas II's coronation in 1896, where more than a thousand people died in the crowd invited to Khodynka to receive gifts. Both events were later interpreted as dark omens.

49. According to a document cited by Maurice Renard in *Notre-dame royale* (Paris, 1927), 140.

50. Stendhal, *Le rouge et le noir* (The red and the black), vol. 2, chap. 36.

51. Ibid., chap. 45.

Largesse has taken a dark turn. It has become an extravagant posthumous wedding. In the end, the old aristocratic world survives in this "chronicle of 1830" only in the form of a ceremony of ostentatious mourning in the middle of nature. The ritual symbol of fecundity has taken on a sense of archaism and sterility.[52]

52. On the largesse and "seigneurial beneficience" of central Europe as they were known at the beginning of the twentieth century, see Joseph Roth's short story "Die Büste des Kaisers" (Stuttgart: Reclam, 1969).

CHAPTER TWO

Fortune

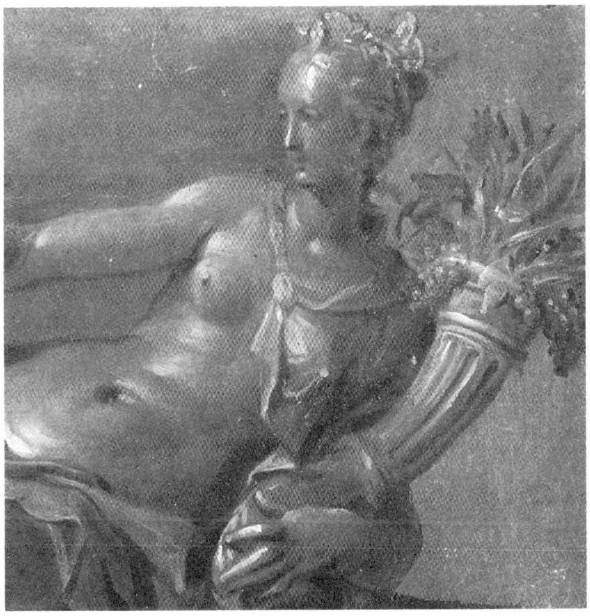

Who Pays for the Fete?

From the philosopher's perspective, princely magic has no validity and its prestige must be undermined. Only a naive view of the act of largesse can lead people to fall into the trap of believing it inexhaustible. Spectators can remain in awe only if their eyes stay fixed on the hands of the clever jongleur, the giver: treasures rush forth as if he were their source, as if he were sharing himself with the crowd. What an illusion! People simply allow themselves to be deceived when they believe that abundance is innate and that it immediately satisfies cravings. Reflection leads to questions. What are the antecedents and consequences, what comes before and what follows after? Although *largitio* seems to flow from a spring, we need to ask: How are its resources accumulated? Where did these riches that liberality scatters come from? How were they acquired? What will the consequence of the goods distributed be for those who give and for those who receive? What advantage will those who accepted them, who rushed in to seize them, enjoy from them? Did they know they would have to fight for them, steal for them, subdue for them? You were expecting a gift? In its place, you get nothing but disorder! Misers who refused to let go of anything and who shirked their duties are disgraced, but spendthrifts who shone for a moment but proceeded to their ruin are open to ridicule. The satiric poets—Horace and Persius—warned ambitious men who hoped to attain glory by means of largesse that they would bear the cost. Classical ethics continually raised these questions, taking up Aristotelian and Ciceronian formulas.[53]

The debate goes back a long time. Ulysses arrived naked among the Phaecians, but left laden with gifts. The gifts of hospitality (like the more modest *apophorèta,* which guests take away with them at the end of a banquet) are costly for the generous hosts. On the eve of Ulysses' departure, Alcinous proposes to add more gifts to those that have already been prepared. He slips in a remark that speaks volumes:

> My lords,
> ever my company, sharing the wine of Council,
> the songs of the blind harper, hear me further:
> garments are folded for our guest and friend
> in the smooth chest, and gold
> in various shaping of adornment lies
> with other gifts, and many, brought by our peers;

53. Aristotle, *Ethica Nicomachea* 4. Compare Cicero, *De officiis* 2.55–60: "There are two kinds of men who give amply, the one extravagant and the other liberal. The extravagant, with their banquets, their public distributions of meat, their gladiatorial performances, their spectacular provisions of games and of wild animals in combat, pour out their money on things for which they will be remembered briefly, if at all. The liberal, however, out of their resources, ransom captives from bandits, or assume their friends' debts, or help them finance their daughters' marriages, or give them assistance in acquiring or enlarging their property. . . . [Theophrastus] is expansive in his praise of the personal provision of magnificent public events and he considers the harvest of riches to lie in having the resources for such expenditure." But, adds Cicero, Aristotle observes that "those things are gratifying to boys and to weak women, to slaves and to those free men that are most like slaves. . . . On the other hand, any suspicion of avarice must be avoided." Cicero, *On Duties,* English translation by Margaret Atkins (Cambridge: Cambridge University Press, 1991), 84–85. The notion of the gift is the object of long discussions in Seneca's treatise *De beneficiis.* The distinction between prodigality and liberality is taken up again by Thomas Aquinas: "Prodigalitas semper est peccatum, non principaliter propter guantitatem, sed propter inordinationem dandi" (Prodigality is always a sin, not primarily because of the quantity of what is given, but because of the disorder in the act of giving). *Summa theologica* 2–2^{e}.117, 118, 119.

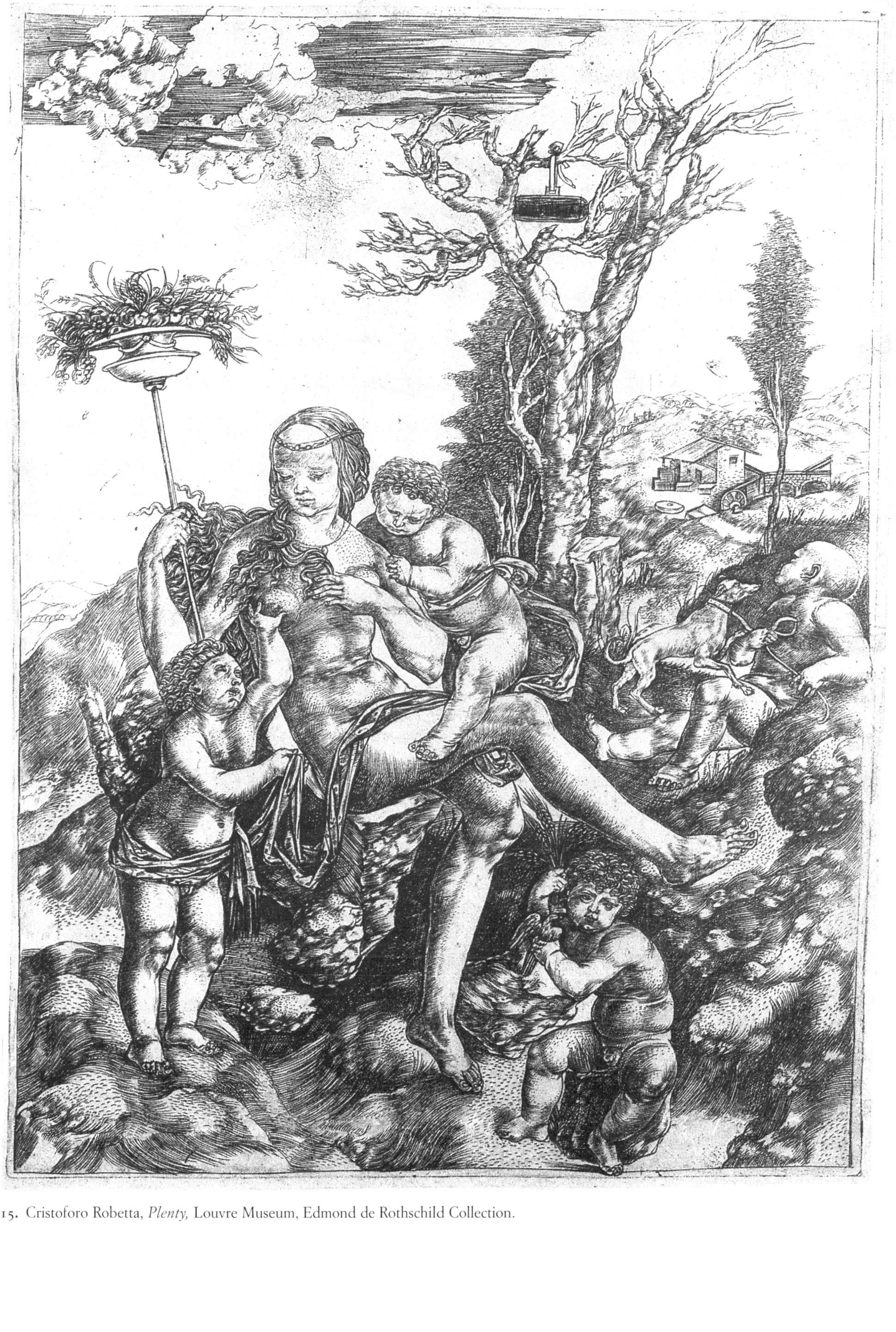

15. Cristoforo Robetta, *Plenty,* Louvre Museum, Edmond de Rothschild Collection.

> let each man add his tripod and deep-bellied
> cauldron: we'll make levy upon the realm
> to pay us for the loss each bears in this.[54]

We might therefore consider the other side of all the scenes of largesse already evoked. If we are to believe Flavius Josephus, the conspirators who overcame Caligula became resolved in their designs when they saw people protesting taxes and being subjected to bloody repression at the circus itself.[55]

From La Boétie to the *Encyclopédie,* an entire aspect of the antiabsolutist argument consisted in denouncing the exactions by means of which the prince accumulated the substance for his largesse. Behind largesse there lay raids, pillaging, and fiscal abuse. "Tyrants would distribute largess, a bushel of wheat, a gallon of wine, and a sesterce: and then everybody would shamelessly cry, 'Long live the King!' The fools did not realize that they were merely recovering a portion of their own property, and that their ruler could not have given them what they were receiving without having first taken it from them" (La Boétie).[56] "The worst Roman emperors were those who gave the most: Caligula, Claudius, Otho, Vitellius, Commodus, Elagabalus, and Caracalla" (Montesquieu).[57] In the *Encyclopédie,* we find an article entitled "Missilia," attributed to Jaucourt: "Those sorts of largesse . . . always led to a great deal of disorder. Those who gave them ruined themselves; those herded in to participate in them sometimes lost their lives. True largesse is tax relief. Making gifts to people who are being crushed by fees is clothing them with one hand and ripping off their skin with the other."

At his accession to the throne, the king received the gifts of joyous advent from his vassals, accompanied by the "gratuitous gift" of the clergy (which was solicited under still different circumstances). For the first two orders of the state, these gifts implied a confirmation of their privileges. But the clergy did not like forced sacrifices. According to the "Germanist" theory of the eighteenth century, the king was originally the first among equals, elected and designated by his peers. The hypothesis of that primitive equality of noble chiefs finds support in the late survival of the symbolic system of exchange, of gifts and return gifts, that is, in the escalation characteristic of the ancient potlatch. Criticism of the monarchy, even before the prerevolutionary period, denounced these exchanges as a dupe's bargain, for which the third estate paid the cost. The bourgeoisie of the ancien régime learned to give an exact accounting of income and expenses, though certain financiers of common origin, who sought to be admitted into the aristocracy, practiced noble spending. But the obviousness of the deficit, which announced the French Revolution, put an end to the era of ostentatious luxury and prestigious largesse.

And what was the consequence of the gesture of largesse among those to whom it
17 was directed? Violence and brawls, the disabused observer replies. Only a flatterer such as Statius (who lived off the emperor's gifts) could have found that melee joyous. Contempt for such scenes of violence is a constant theme in the writings of the Stoics. To

54. Homer, *The Odyssey,* English translation by Robert Fitzgerald (Garden City, N.Y.: Doubleday, 1963), 13.7–15 (p. 229).

55. Flavius Josephus, *Jewish Antiquities* 19.1; see n. 25 above.

56. Etienne de la Boétie, *The Politics of Obedience: The Discourse of Voluntary Servitude,* English translation by Harry Kurz (Montreal: Black Rose, 1975), 70. See "Texts on the Gift," no. 15, below.

57. Montesquieu, *De l'esprit des lois* 5.18.

dissuade ambitious men, Epictetus uses this image: "Someone scatters nuts and figs. Children scramble and quarrel for them; but not men, for they think them trifles." Money, a praetorship, and a consulate "are mere figs and nuts." Epictetus does not reject fortune, as, for example, when a fig happens to fall by chance *(apo tukhès)* into the fold of his tunic. "But if I am to stoop and throw down a rival, or be thrown down by another, and flatter those who succeed, a fig is not worth this, nor is any other of those things which are not really good, and which the philosophers have persuaded me not to esteem as good."[58]

Thus, an observer to the scene of the gift sees the figure of the dispenser of liberalities take on a strange resemblance to that of Fortune. Giving is a blind act of dispensation that always remains inadequate or disproportionate, never in keeping with popular expectations and greed. If there is one ancient text that might have stayed in Rousseau's memory as he described the battle of the peasants on the grounds of La Chevrette, it is letter 74 from Seneca to Lucilius.[59] Fortune personified is represented in the role of Caesar, scattering gifts haphazardly to the circus audience. And those who are expecting her favors, those who wish to "make their fortune," are like foolish men who try to get their hands on objects of little value:

> Picture now to yourself that Fortune is holding a festival, and is showering down honours, riches, and influence upon this mob of mortals: some of these gifts have already been torn to pieces in the hands of those who try to snatch them, others have been divided up by treacherous partnerships, and still others have been seized to the great detriment of those into whose possession they have come. Certain of these favours have fallen to men while they were absent-minded, others have been lost to their seekers because they were snatching too eagerly for them, and, just because they are greedily seized upon, have been knocked from their hands. There is not a man among them all, however,—even he who has been lucky in the booty which has fallen to him,—whose joy in his spoil has lasted until the morrow.
>
> The most sensible man, therefore, as soon as he sees the dole being brought in, runs from the theatre; for he knows that one pays a high price for small favours. No one will grapple with him on the way out, or strike him as he departs; the quarrelling takes place where the prizes are. Similarly with the gifts which Fortune tosses down to us; wretches that we are, we become excited, we are torn asunder, we wish that we had many hands, we look back now in this direction and now in that. All too slowly, as it seems, are the gifts thrown in our direction; they merely excite our cravings, since they can reach but few and are awaited by all. We are keen to intercept them as they fall down. We rejoice if we have laid hold of anything; and some have been mocked by the idle hope of laying hold; we have . . . paid a high price for worthless plunder with some disadvantage to ourselves.[60]

The brawls are savage. The urgent advice given by Seneca is to walk away from the game. "Let us withdraw": *secedamus.* "Let us therefore withdraw from a game like this,

58. Epictetus, *Discourses,* 4.7, English translation by Thomas Wentworth Higginson (New York: Walter J. Black, 1944), 305–6.

59. *The Epistles of Seneca,* English translation by Richard M. Gummere (Cambridge and London: Harvard University Press and William Heinemann, 1962). In this letter, Seneca says that we must embrace the *honest (honestum)* and avoid falling to the power of Fortune and the discretion of others. See "Texts on the Gift," no. 4, below. In the reverie I have cited at length, Rousseau lays claim to the same principle, declaring he does not want to combine "*honest* things and a monetary price, which degrades the nobility they have and taints the disinterest in them." The same vocabulary is used in both cases.

60. Ibid., 2:117–19. It is possible Rousseau was familiar with the French translation of this letter in the Pintrel edition, which was revised by La Fontaine (Paris: Barbin, 1681).

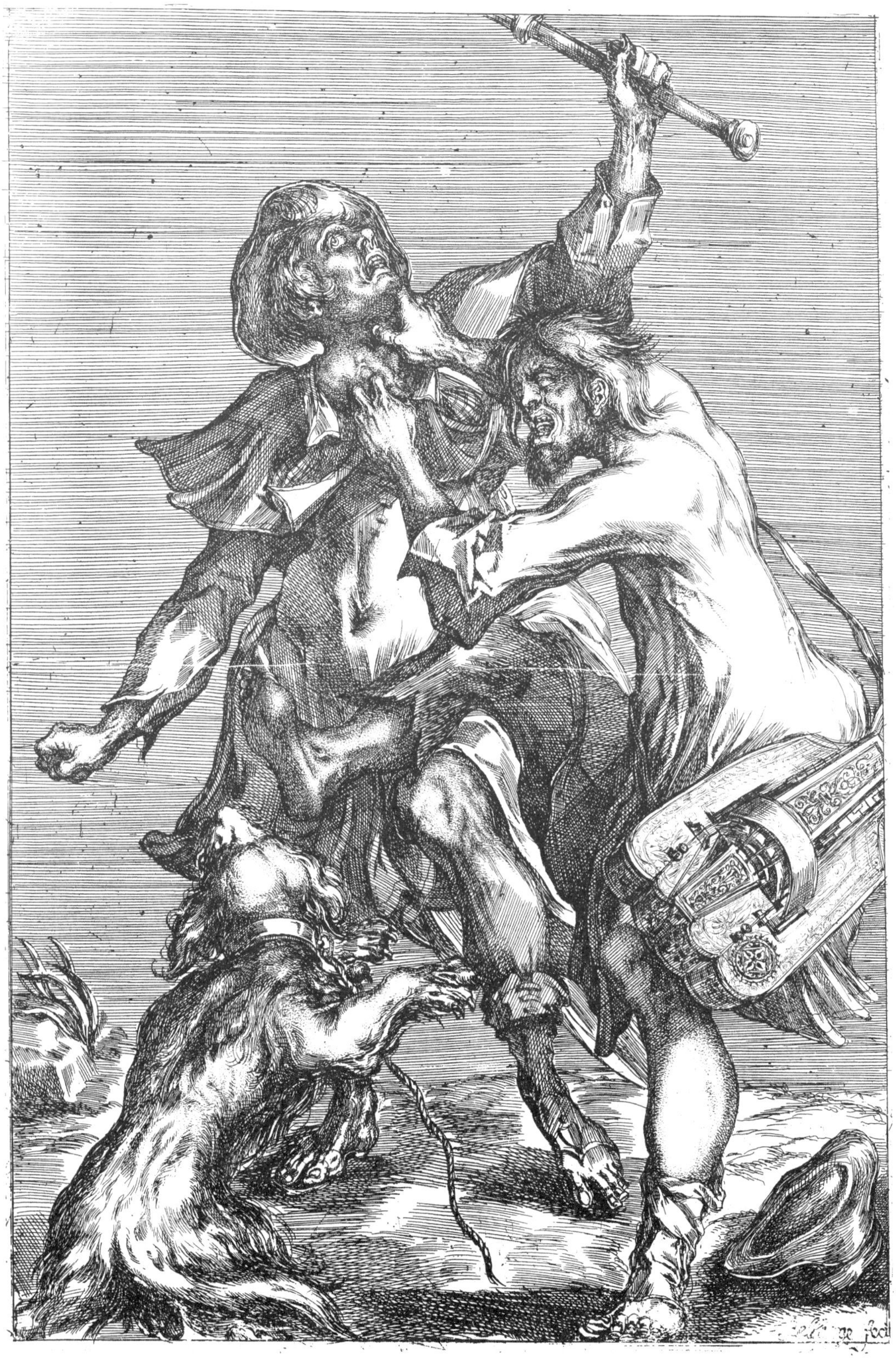

16. Jacques Bellange, *Beggars' Brawl,* Bibliothèque Nationale.

and give way to the greedy rabble; let them gaze after such 'goods,' which hang suspended above them [*bona ista pendentia*] and be themselves still more in suspension [*pendeantur*]" (Seneca, letter 90). This double act of suspension nullifies all enjoyment, all true possession. The gifts thrown out in such a way seem to announce abundance. At first, they belonged to no one, and everyone had an equal right to them. But there is never enough for all. This is no longer crude primitive equality, where nature supplied all the needs of a humanity that was still untamed. This is greedy competition, which elicits violence and fraud. It is the war of all against all.

In a poem by Boethius in book 2 of his *Consolation of Philosophy* (a book whose influence on Western culture was capital), the spectacle is the same, but more universal and more abstract.

> What though Plenty pour her gifts
> With a lavish hand,
> Numberless as are the stars,
> Countless as the sand;
> Will the race of man, content,
> Cease to murmur and lament?
>
> Nay, though God, all-bounteous, give
> Gold at man's desire
> Honours, rank, and fame—content
> Not a whit is nigher;
> But an all-devouring greed
> Yawns with ever-widening need.
>
> Then what bounds can e'er restrain
> This wild lust of having,
> When with each new bounty fed
> Grows the frantic craving?
> He is never rich whose fear
> Sees grim Want forever near.[61]

The agitated crowd has become the "human race," a collective being, a starving, craving monster, opening *(hiantem)* its insatiable mouth beneath the horn of plenty that pours out its treasures. There are many images of desire and of its violence: among these, hunger and thirst occupy an important place. An oral drive endlessly demands satisfaction. Yet true nourishment is rare. In certain representations, Fortune hold sheaves of corn like Cybele, but to no avail. The overflowing horn she carries is that of the she-goat Amalthea, whose milk nourished Jupiter as a child; but it is no use. What Fortune gives, she also takes away indiscriminately. She leaves men hungry.[62]

Fickle, blind, smiling and cruel in turn, Fortune reigns over the world. Virtue does not submit to her: she remains indomitable. She looks on the folly of others, on their insatiable appetite, as a spectator; she does not wish to possess anything but her own freedom. She counts on the force of will. Those who are in possession of themselves

61. Boethius, *The Consolation of Philosophy* 2.2, English translation by H. R. James (London and New York: Routledge and Sons and E. P. Dutton, n.d.).

62. In place of the mythological horn of plenty, we now have Santa Claus's sack; Santa is the benign version of old Saturn in the Golden Age.

expect no gift from the outside and do not place their hopes in the generosity of Fortune: "Fortune exerts no right over an ordered life" (In mores Fortuna jus non habet) (Seneca, letter 36). "Well then, if you succeed in being master of yourself, you will possess something that you will never consent to lose and that Fortune cannot take away from you."[63]

A Digression on Organized Plunder

Seneca looks down from the bleachers on the scene unfolding on the ground. Foolish
17 men are snatching at goods, plundering. But the struggle is of dubious value, and the plunderers are troubling themselves for nothing. The philosopher confined himself to simply naming Fortune, who conducts the games from above him. He is not interested in her, he avoids turning to look at that deceitful figure. He depicts only the battle.

He might have found subject matter for other descriptions. For the greedy sometimes vary their pleasures. Is it absolutely necessary to scatter gifts haphazardly? The potentate can dispense them without wearing himself out. He can have treasures and food placed at a good distance from the competitors. At the sign, they fling themselves on the loot. The less vigorous are torn to pieces. This was an amusement that Emperor Augustus offered himself. The prince had everything prepared, but he remained off to the side. Organized plunder (*direptio* in Latin) was a pure spectacle for him.[64] Is this merely a feature of the mores of imperial Rome? Not at all. This game undoubtedly enjoyed enough popular favor to persist. The same practice was retained throughout the Middle Ages on carnival days and during other fetes, in the form of *cocagnes,*[65] treasure hunts, and so on. Exquisite dishes were spread out on trestle tables. Help yourself! *E aperto a tutti quanti: Viva la libertà.*[66] It is not impossible that "ritual plunder," long maintained by custom in Italy, was a more anarchical version of this.[67]

One proof that the custom had taken root is that Louis XIV engaged in the same game. We are somewhat astonished to read the following scene, related by Félibien, of the fete at Versailles on 18 July 1668: "After their majesties had been in this charming place for some time, the king abandoned the tables to the plunder of the people behind them; and the destruction of such a lovely arrangement served once more as an agreeable entertainment for the whole court, because of the eagerness and confusion of those who demolished the marzipan castles and the mountains of jam."[68] The elegant prose of an official writer does not manage to mask the perverse element mingled in with this form of entertainment.

63. In his early writings, Saint Augustine had appealed to the notion of fortune. Later, in his *Retractationes,* he criticized himself for having used that notion, saying it is better to speak of our incomprehension of the paths of providence.

64. Fabia's "Missilia" gives a very good account of its history (n. 14 above).

65. Naples was long the legendary homeland of the *cocagne*—which involved racing for a buffet or for an artificial volcano showering down meats and macaroni. Today's society goer is familiar only with a very innocuous version of it, though it is still called a *slaughter* in the jargon of professional guests.

66. These words are taken from Lorenzo da Ponte's libretto of *Don Giovanni.* Don Juan pronounces them as he ushers in guests to his fete at the end of the first act of the opera (scene 21). It is he who will behave as a predator.

67. They were carried out with great violence by the common people against the goods of church dignitaries who had recently died or had been promoted to the papacy. This violence, often directed against Jews at the same time, was not accepted by the authorities, but leniency was observed in repressing it. This disorder often took place during an interregnum. See Carlo Ginzburg, "Pillages rituels au Moyen Age et au début des Temps modernes," in *Normes et déviance: Rencontres internationales de Genève, 1987* (Neuchâtel: Baconnière, 1988).

68. Molière, *Oeuvres,* ed. E. Despois and P. Mesnard (Paris: Hachette, 1881), 6:618.

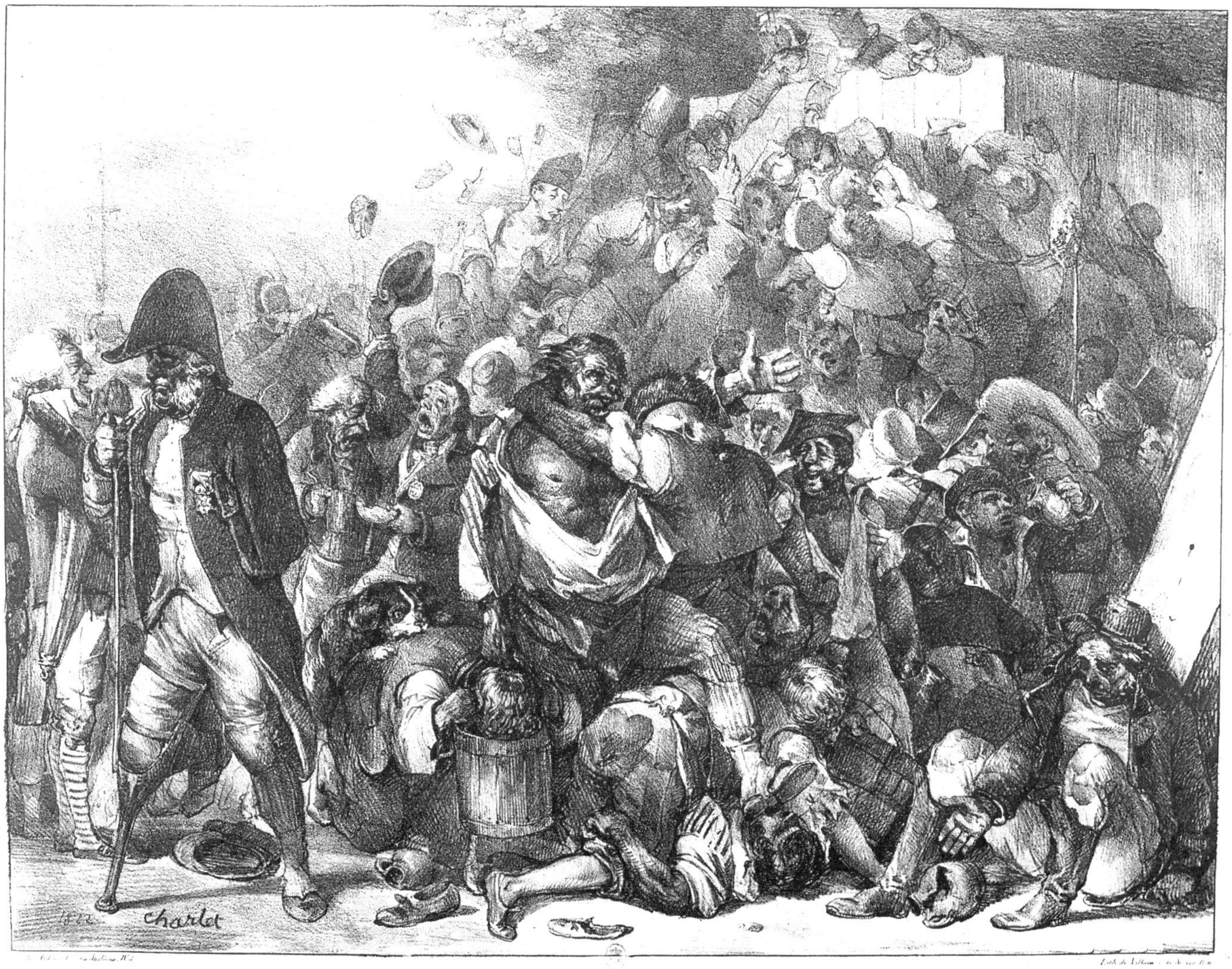

. Nicolas-Toussaint Charlet, *Public Festivities,* Bibliothèque Nationale.

The perversity of the spectacle of *direptio* is fully in evidence in Sade. In *Histoire de Juliette* (1797), we find an episode where the viceroy of Naples offers his debauched guests the spectacle of a popular *cocagne.* Under the windows of the palace, the crowd breaks loose to snatch the food being offered. A mechanical device installed by the viceroy makes the platform collapse. Hundreds die. From the balcony, cries of erotic transport from the "whore" Clairwil echo in response.[69]

We see the same aggressivity in Sylvain Maréchal's play *Le jugement dernier des rois* [The last judgment of kings] (1793). Here, the social roles are reversed. In this violently antimonarchist caricature, the pope and the kings of Europe are confined on a desert island by the sansculottes. The Parisian public is treated to the spectacle of a universal deportation of highnesses. Given only the bare necessities, the princes provide for their own destruction. First, they fight over a piece of bread. A large barrel of biscuits is taken to them, and all hell breaks loose. Maréchal's stage directions are precise: "The ground is strewn with the debris of chains, scepters, crowns; mantles are in tatters. . . . The sansculottes wanted to enjoy from afar the confusion of kings reduced to starvation." The author no doubt sought to caricature a truth put forward by the jurisconsults of the Enlightenment: states, which is to say, princes, live among themselves in the same relation of competition as do individuals in the state of nature, before the establishment of social conventions.[70] In Maréchal's play, a volcanic eruption—the arbitrary furor of nature—brings the spectacle to an end.[71]

Several great nineteenth-century texts turned to the recent past to evoke the popular plundering organized by the masters of the world. One of the most striking examples is the short story by Herman Melville entitled "Poor Man's Pudding and Rich Man's Crumbs" (1854). A stranger to London is there the day after the victory at Waterloo. A banquet at the town hall has brought together the victorious kings. The next day, the poor are invited to get their own hands on the leftovers of the feast. The stranger, guided by an obliging bureaucrat, joins the band of poor people:

> The walls swept to and fro, like the foliage of a forest with blazonings of conquerors' flags. Naught outside the hall was visible. No windows were within four-and-twenty feet of the floor. Cut off from all other sights, I was hemmed in by one splendid spectacle—splendid, I mean, every where, but as the eye fell toward the floor. *That* was foul as a hovel's—as a kennel's; the naked boards being strewed with the smaller and more wasteful fragments of the feast, while the two long parallel lines, up and down the hall, of now unrobed, shabby, dirty pine-tables were piled with less trampled wrecks. The dyed banners were in keeping with the last night's kings; the floor suited the beggars of to-day. The banners looked down upon the floor as from his balcony Dives upon Lazarus.[72]

The distribution was to be orderly, with blue tickets being issued, but that does not last long. The stranger is soon dragged into the cataclysmic whirlwind of poor people who leap on the pitiful remains with a furor that turns into revolt:

69. D. A. F. de Sade, *Histoire de Juliette,* beginning of part 6, in *Oeuvres complètes* ed. J.-J. Pauvert (Paris: Au cercle du livre précieux, 1966), 9:399–401. See "Texts on the Gift," no. 5, below.

70. This is one point on which Montesquieu and Rousseau agree.

71. See the text by S. Maréchal and the songs from the performance published by Riccardo Carnesecchi, "La sovranità in scena fra Piovoso e Termidoro: Fortune e censure," *Musica e storia* (Venice: Il Mulino, 1993), 1:53–147.

72. Herman Melville, "Poor Man's Pudding and Rich Man's Crumbs" (1854), in *The Piazza Tales and Other Prose Pieces, 1839–1860,* vol. 9: *The Writings of Herman Melville* (Chicago: Northwestern University Press and the Newberry Library, 1987), 299.

> The last dish had been seized. The yet unglutted mob raised a fierce yell, which wafted the banners like a strong gust, and filled the air with a reek as from sewers. They surged against the tables, broke through all barriers, and billowed over the hall—their bare tossed arms like the dashed ribs of a wreck. It seemed to me as if a sudden impotent fury of fell envy possessed them. That one half-hour's peep at the mere remnants of the glories of the Banquets of Kings; the unsatisfying mouthfuls of disembowelled pasties, plundered pheasants, and half-sacked jellies, served to remind them of the intrinsic contempt of the alms. In this sudden mood, or whatever mysterious thing it was that now seized them, these Lazaruses seemed ready to spew up in repentant scorn the contumelious crumbs of Dives. (301)

The stranger, though merely a witness, finds himself in tatters at the end of his initiation into the hell of the charity fete.

The popular battle is certainly similar in the *sparsio* and in organized plunder: whether the gifts fall from above or are left about, the expected response is the same. Theft is allowed when goods are momentarily without owners, but these goods do not escape destructive hoarding for long. Only the position of the "benefactor" has changed: the princes in Melville's story do not throw anything to the people. They do not even show themselves: they leave their leftovers and go on their way. The battle takes place in their absence, and they know nothing about it. No one takes pleasure in it, except perhaps the forces of law and order, who naively believe that charity has been provided. Of course, the ethics of the modern age finds such a spectacle unacceptable. The scandalized narrator expresses this view, asking his guide: "Would not . . . something to do, and be paid for, be better?" If only full employment and the "abolition of pauperism" could eliminate such brutal fetes.

Charles Fourier's utopia presents a plan for a more perfect society, where *harmony* will supplant the unjust *civilization* in which we live: it presents a spectacle of orderly euphoria and satisfaction, the reverse side and corollary of the revolting scene narrated by Melville. The great Babylonian crusade in *Le nouveau monde amoureux* ends with a pie fight, where everyone finds something to feast on. After legitimizing and recording all of love's appetites, Fourier is careful not to omit all the pleasures of the mouth.[73] But how did it happen that he felt the desire to borrow the forms of the crusade and of the battle for his imaginative work?

To indulge in the full measure of buffoonery, Alfred Jarry shows us the amusements that celebrate Ubu's coming to power. First, there is a *sparsio,* followed by a second competition, a treasure hunt (a kind of *direptio*). A first bloody battle, for money thrown at the feet of Ubu and Ma Ubu, is followed by the scuffle and tumult of contestants who run through the court to seize a chest of gold. These two variants of the princely gift end in ridicule.[74]

Is it merely his imagination, his erudite memory, that leads Félicien Rops to images
of *sparsio?* His *Satan Sowing the Chaff*—a giant sower walking through Paris in wooden 18
shoes and disseminating the bodies of women—cleverly revives the ancient gesture and links it to the myth of Capital, Sin, and (who knows?) even the Pox. When fin de siècle eroticism assumes an apocalyptic aspect, it dresses up an immense skeleton and lets it perform perverse largesse. It glorifies an infernal Fortune.

73. Charles Fourier, *Le nouveau monde amoureux,* ed. S. Debout-Oleszkiewicz (Paris: Anthropos, 1967). See "Texts on the Gift," no. 7, below.

74. See "Texts on the Gift," no. 8, below.

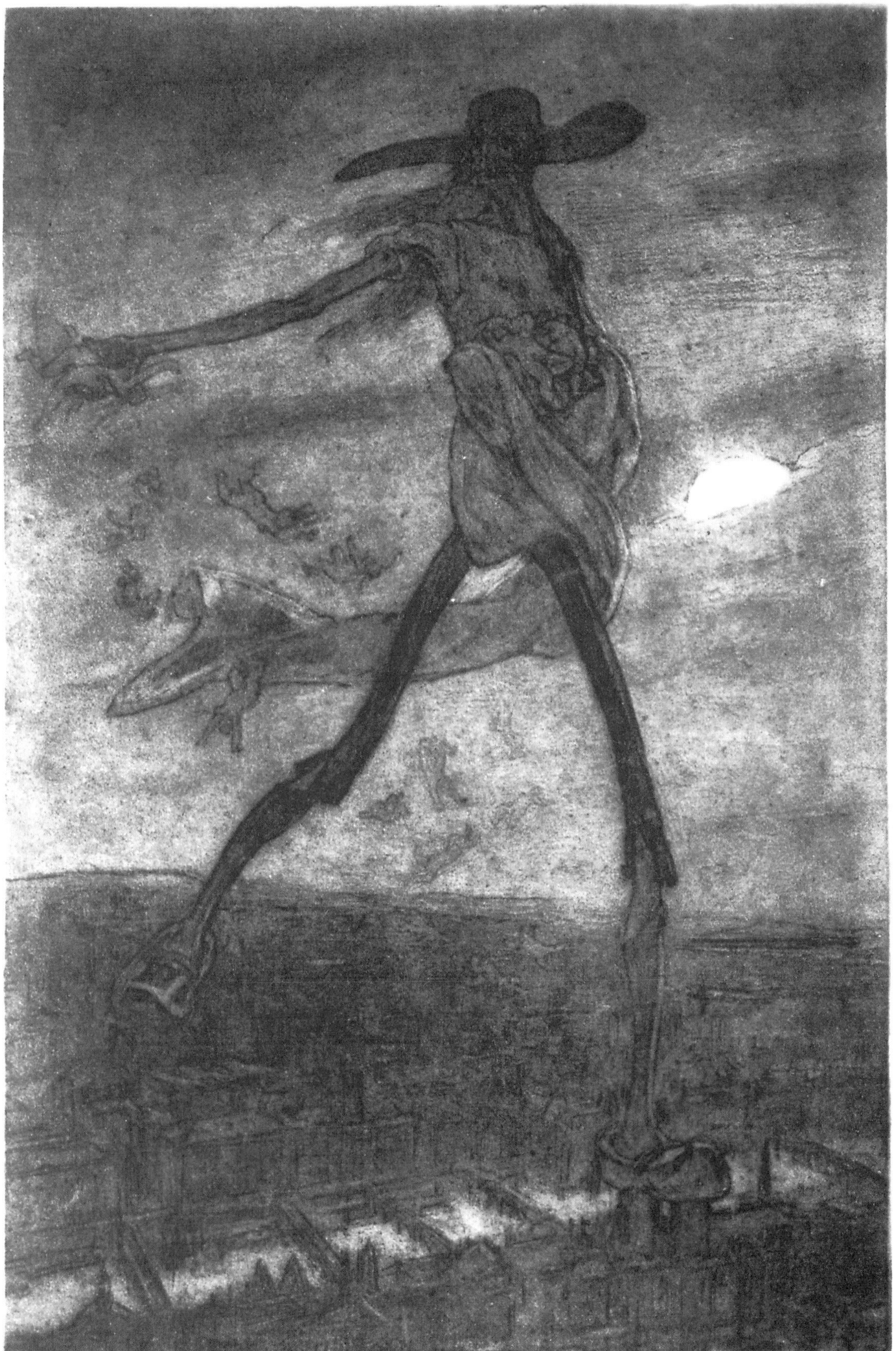

18. Félicien Rops, *Satan Sowing the Chaff,* Bibliothèque Nationale.

Fortune as Dispenser

The representations of this unforeseeable power, which both makes amends and ravages, raises up and brings down, illuminates and darkens, can only be diverse. To give Fortune a particular shape entails a perpetual inventiveness based on a few great models that have prevailed throughout the ages, beginning with antiquity.[75]

She always bears the name "Fortune," but she is never the same. Despite the fact that abstraction is its dominant feature, the art of the emblem can still invent strong images; it makes good use of the omnipresence and variability of Fortune. And variety affects not only the look and guises of Fortune, but also the domains over which she reigns. There is good Fortune and bad. She can be surrounded by cupids or she can flirt with death. She is a seductress and a bad mother, despite her occasional resemblance to representations of nature, or Ceres. She is sometimes a bit of a whore. She is mistress of
the wheel of fortune, the wheel of time, which inevitably becomes the torture wheel. She **21**
surges up from the foam and is borne on a conch like Venus. She resembles Isis in the sail she holds to the wind. Sometimes she stands as navigator at a capricious helm, sometimes she balances on the sphere (both the world and changeableness). Fortune, who
smiles on the audacious, is the sister of opportunity: She can be seized only by a single **20**
lock of hair. She is the queen of ancient lotteries and modern casinos.[76] She piles wealth on the sleeper, and flees whoever pursues her.

In a beautiful drawing by Farinati, Mercury (who is Art in every sense of the term), **19**
stands on the shoulders of Fortune and directs her, even as he allows himself to be led along by her. Such is the sensible representation of a combined power—chance at the service of intelligence—that assures success. This drawing reminds us that taming Fortune is not impossible: if we are to believe a famous passage from Machiavelli, such is the task of geniuses, valorous men, "golden boys." "I am well persuaded, that it is better to be impetuous than cautious. For Fortune is a woman who to be kept under must be beaten and roughly handled; and we see that she suffers herself to be more readily mastered by those who so treat her than by those who are more timid in their approaches. And always, like a woman, she favours the young, because they are less scrupulous and
fiercer, and command her with greater audacity."[77] But success is rare. A drawing by **22**

75. The cult of Fortune in Rome and Latium (in particular in Praeneste, today Palestrina) goes back to ancient times. A large number of modifiers differentiated between kinds of fortune: *publica, privata, equestris, muliebris, virilis,* etc. Fortune occupies a place in Pliny the Elder's depiction of the world (see "Texts on the Gift," no. 9, below). On the images of Fortune, see Alfred Doren, "Fortuna im Mittelalter und in der Renaissance," *Vorträge der Bibliothek Warburg* (1922–23) 2:71–144; Lucie Galactéros de Boissier, "Images emblématiques de la Fortune: Eléments d'une typologie," in *L'emblème à la Renaissance* (Paris: CDU and SEDES, 1982), 79–125; see also the texts by Lucie Galactéros de Boissier, Yves Giraud, and Claude Bérard in *Fortune,* catalog of the exhibit of the Musée de l'Elysée, ed. Florian Rodari (Lausanne, 1981), bibliography.

76. Until the eighteenth century, Fortune and Nature were often opposed: Fortune confounds all our plans, while Nature imposes a strict law, an inflexible path of cause and effect. Beginning in the eighteenth century, the figure of Fortune fades away. She is no longer an opposing power. The unforeseeable is resorbed into the calculation of probabilities. Calculation takes randomness in its charge and resituates it within Nature the gambler.

77. Niccolo Machiavelli, *The Prince,* trans. Hill Thompson (New York: Heritage Press, 1954), chap. 25, p. 178. Machiavelli does not use the image of *sparsio,* but in this famous chapter, the affinity between *largitio* and the flowing of a spring extends to Fortune itself, which is compared to an overflowing river: "I would liken her to one of those wild torrents which, when angry, overflow the plains, sweep away trees and houses, and carry off soil from one bank to throw it down upon the other" (174). Let us recall that Machiavelli devoted two of his *Capitoli* in verse to Opportunity and Fortune. Beside more traditional allegorical figures, we also find the same image of the overflowing torrent.

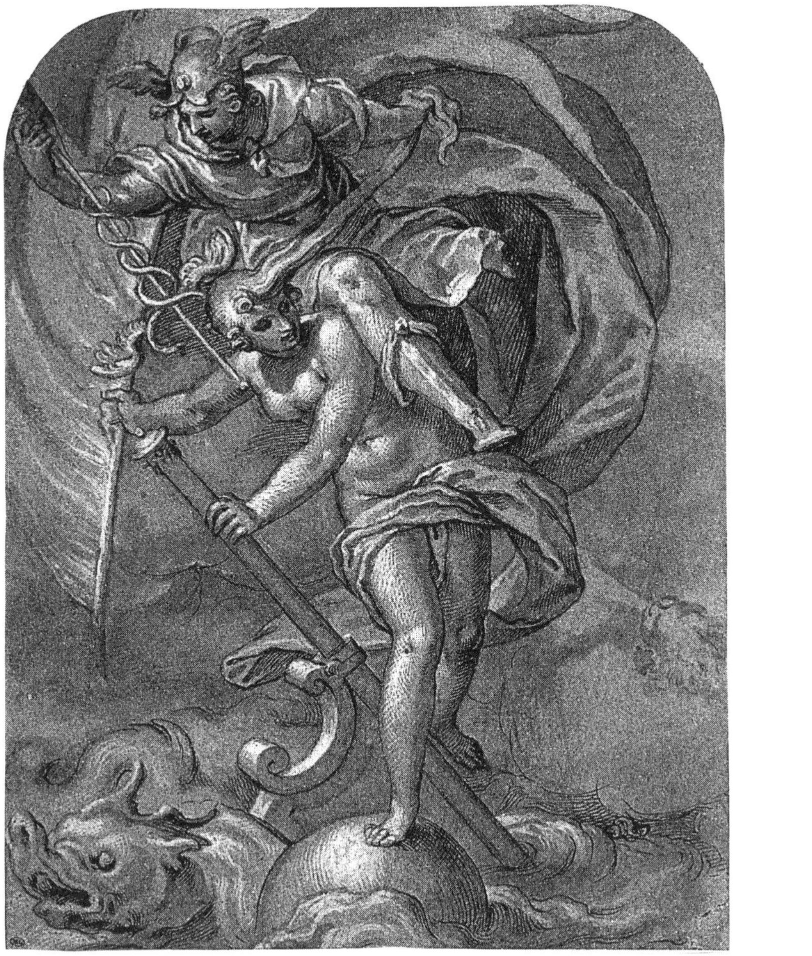

19. Paolo Farinati, *Mercury and Fortune,* Louvre Museum.

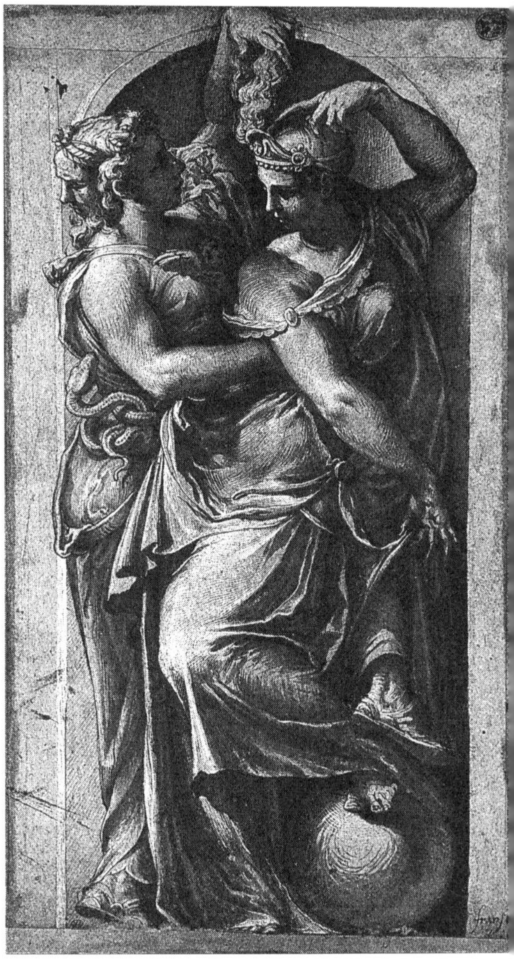

20. Francesco Salviati, *Prudence Seizing Opportunity,* Louvre Museum.

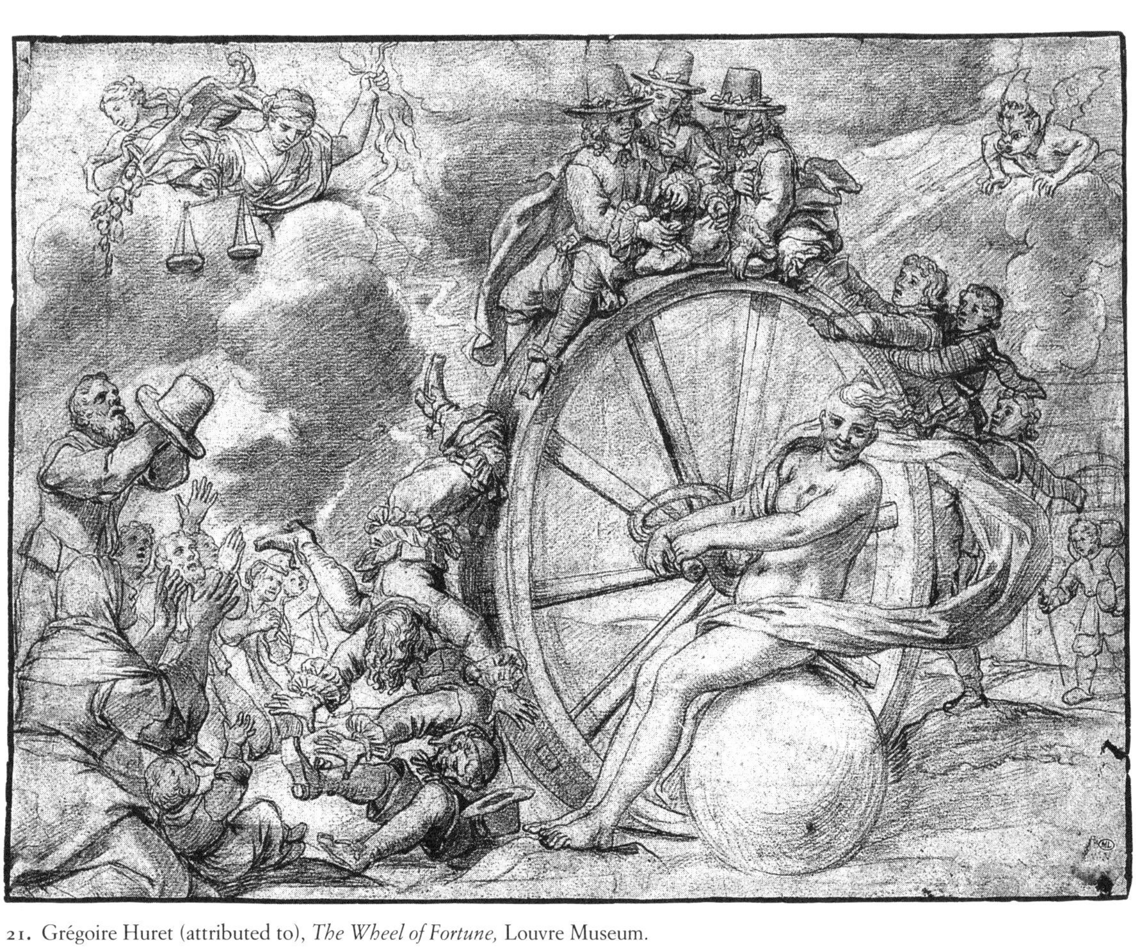

21. Grégoire Huret (attributed to), *The Wheel of Fortune,* Louvre Museum.

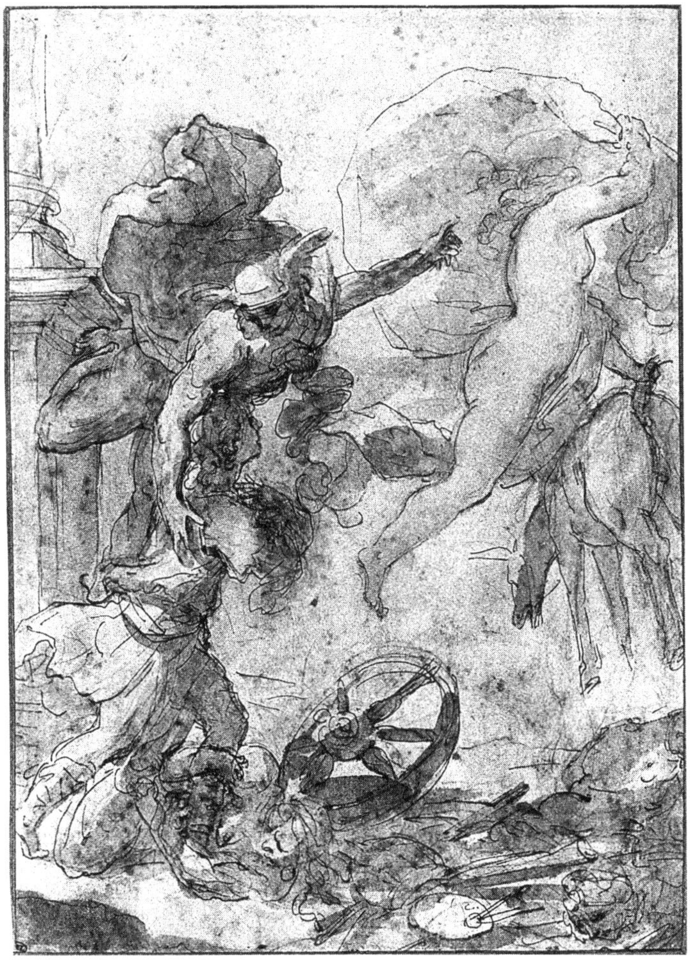

22. Salvator Rosa, *Fortune,* Louvre Museum.

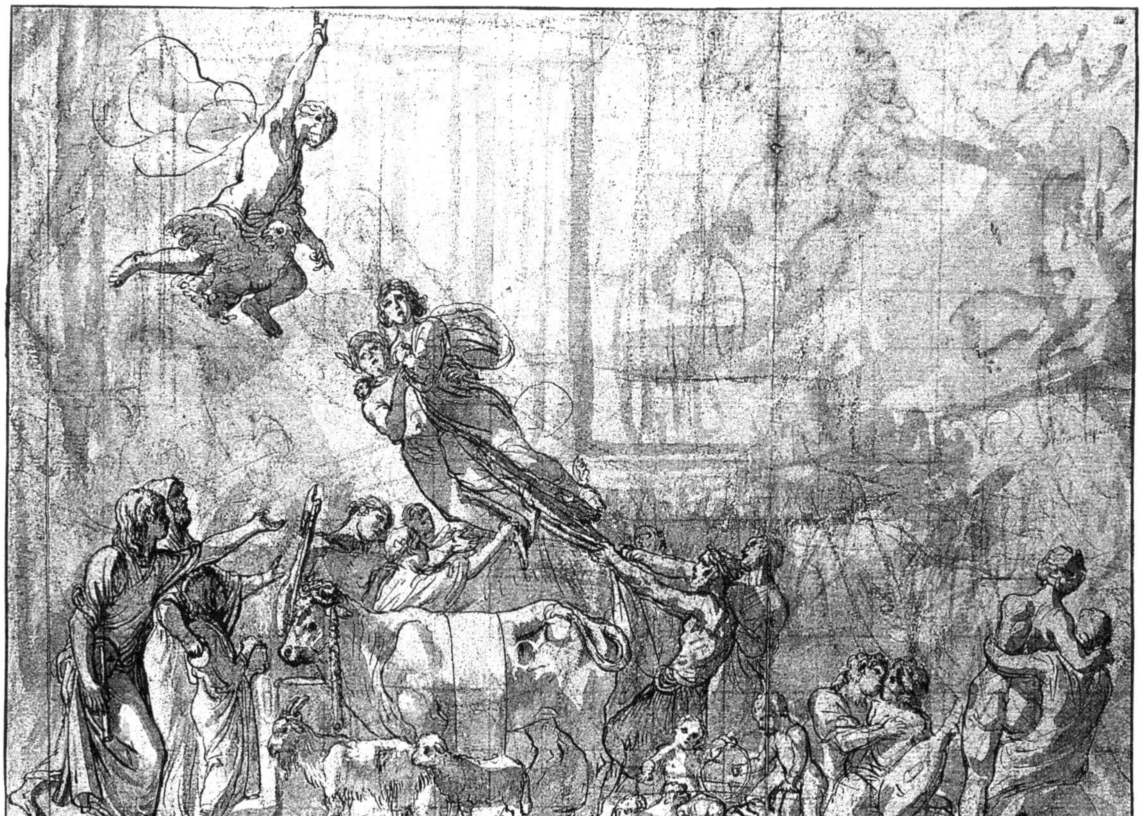

23. Adam Elsheimer, *Il Contento,* Louvre Museum.

Salvator Rosa shows Fortune taking flight, picking up an ass by the tail, and flying toward glory: she is escaping the serious artist, supported by Mercury, who tried in vain to obtain
23 her favors. *Indignum Fortuna fovet.* Fortune coddles those without merit. A strange work by Adam Elsheimer presents another scene of flight, in which incongruity is expressed through a different fable: on the order of Jupiter, Fortune, identified this time with happiness *(il Contento),* is abducted by Mercury from among men. Their gifts and propitiatory sacrifices are useless: they attempt to hold her, but to no avail. While lovers exchange their last kisses, she returns to the dwelling of the gods.[78]

How many battles at the feet of Fortune could we find in paintings, drawings, and engravings of the classical centuries? I do not know. An inventory of this theme can only be imagined.

I shall confine myself to one example that makes the gesture of *sparsio* quite obvi-
25,24 ous. It is to be found in an engraving by Jan Harmensz Muller and in the model by Cornelisz Van Haarlem (at the Museum of Art and History in Geneva). There you see Fortune lavishing boundless wealth on one side and extending an empty hand on the other. On one side, a shower of treasures; on the other, categorical refusal. The wind sweeps over the treasures, picking up in a single gust the scarf and the lock of hair belonging to the deity, who is perched on the globe and pedestal. Full purses, coins, chalices, and emblems of every sort of power and glory are falling to the ground. The artist has placed you at such a distance that these favors appear as mere playthings, as a momentary downpour. Is that little winged trumpet really glory? Is that tiny gonfalon really a military command? Is that bauble a scepter? Do people really fight over so little? In the crowd of Fortune's favorites, some carry away their prey in all haste; others have already put on the miter or the crown. Some are preparing to receive with open hands. But, in the same camp, some have arrived too late and are about to be denied the goods that seemed within their reach. They crawl, topple over, push back or block their competitors, climb over bodies lying in front of them, all for a doubtful result. It is mass confusion; but, on a more distant plane, an appearance of order is just barely emerging from it. Now turn toward the unfortunate souls: one character is still imploring, vainly extending his hands toward the pirouetting deity. Two or three others look reproachfully at the goddess who is ignoring them. As for the rest, they are prostrate, their arms shielding their heads, sitting isolated in their regret, lowering or closing their eyes, their gaze fixed on the void. They are not fighting. The efforts of the unfortunate souls are directed against themselves. But the grief and desolation are no less spectacular than the greed, pride, and struggling on the other side. Even as the artist dynamically uses every

78. See Keith Andrews, *Adam Elsheimer: Il Contento* (Edinburgh: Board of Trustees of the National Gallery of Scotland, 1971). In this study, the probable source for the drawing is given as Mateo Aleman's *Guzman d'Alfarache* (book 1, chap. 7), where first Fortune and then Pleasure appear: "In the past, the Egyptians, a very superstitious people, made the mistake, among others, of adoring Fortune, believing that there exists a divinity by that name. They celebrated a holiday for her on the first day of the year with sumptuous banquets and opulent feasts, to show their gratitude for past riches and to beg her to continue to bestow them in the future. They believed this goddess had everything at her disposal and had supreme command over it, giving and taking away everything at will." Pleasure, first sent among men by Jupiter, becomes their only god. On the advice of Apollo, Jupiter sends Mercury, then intervenes himself. "Since men were clinging to the tunic of Pleasure *(il Contento),* through a clever strategem, he pulled it away and left its brother Displeasure *(el Descontento su hermano)* in its place and in its own clothing." This story can be read as a variant of the myth of Astrée, who returns to heaven at the end of the Golden Age.

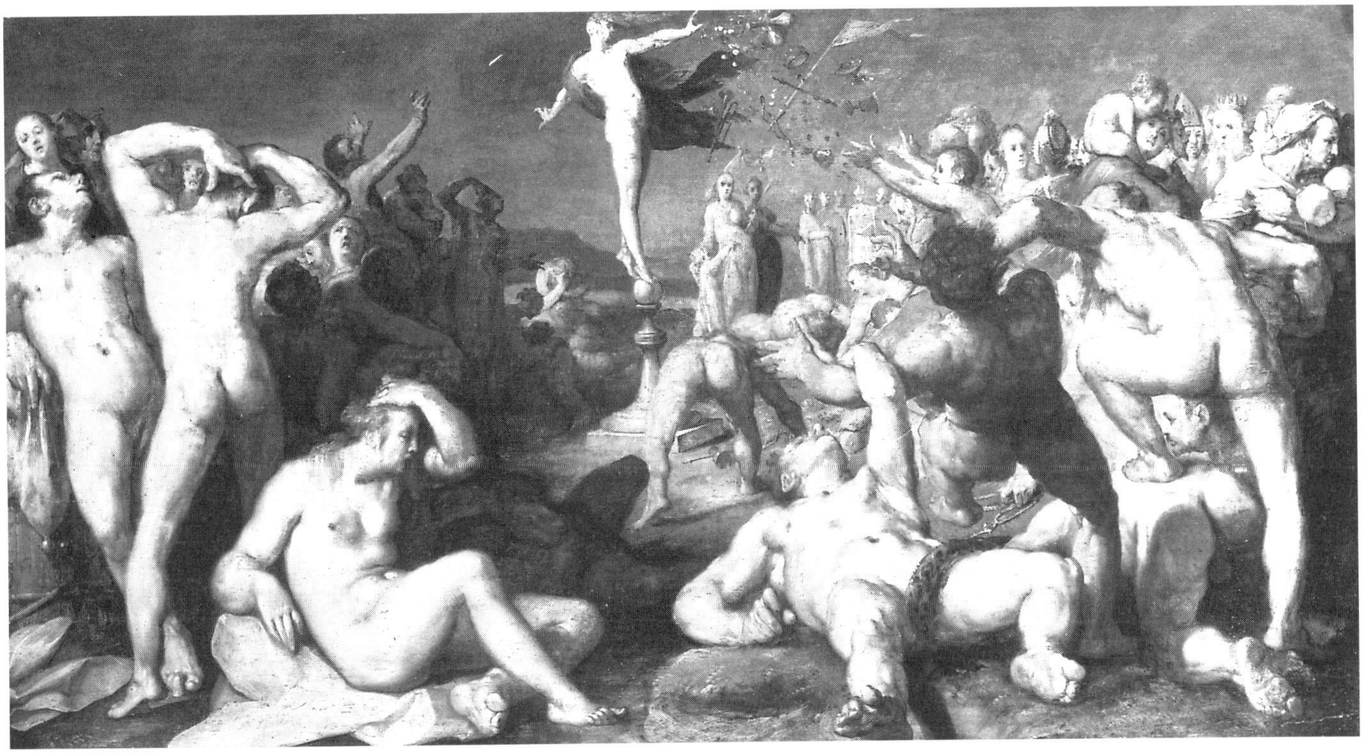

24. Cornelisz Van Haarlem, *Allegory of Fortune,* Museum of Art and History, Geneva.

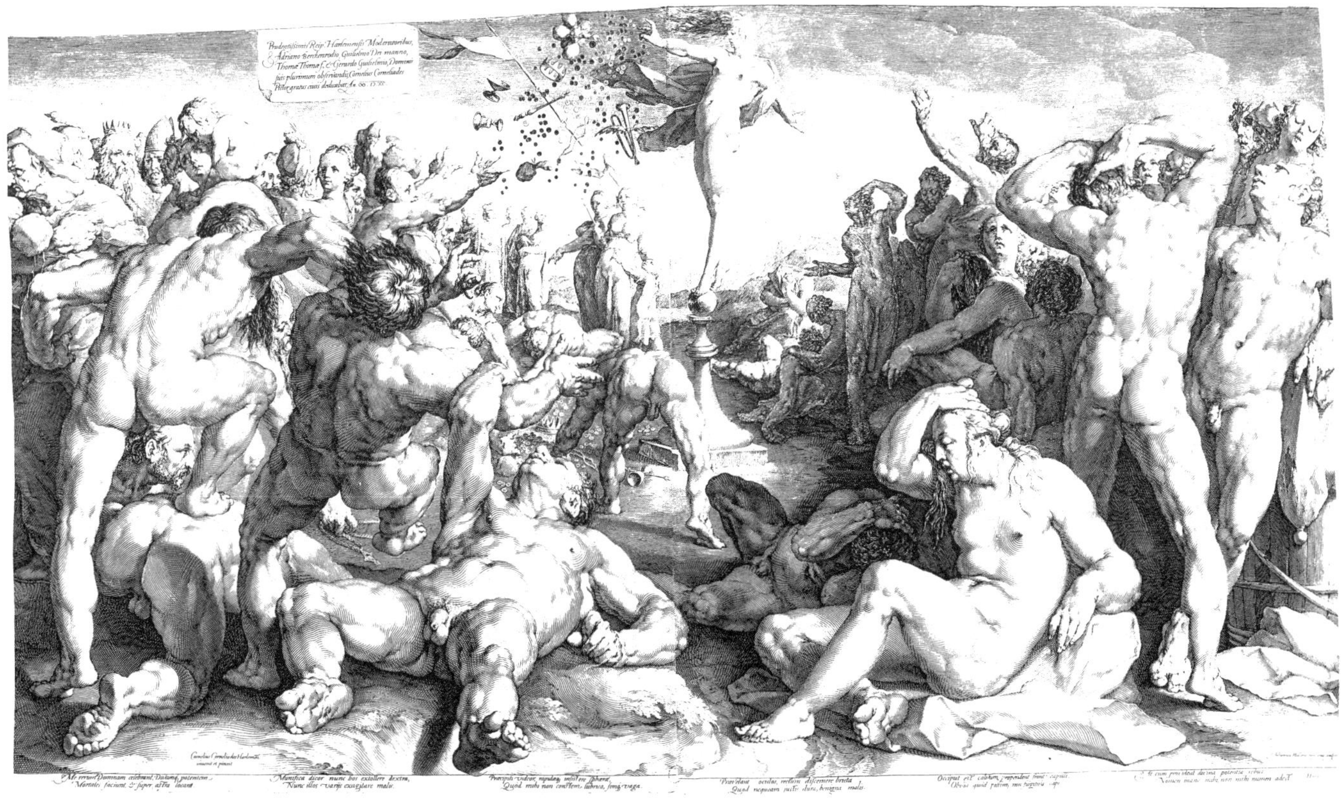

25. Jan Harmensz Muller, *Blind Fortune Distributing her Wealth,* Bibliothèque Nationale.

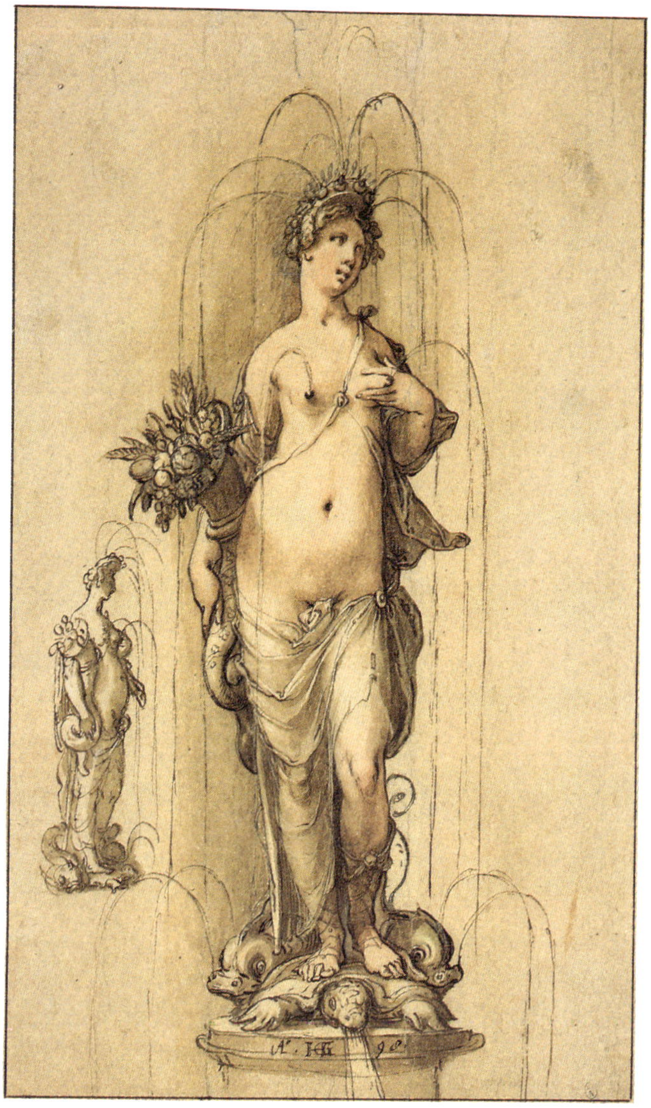

26. Hendrick Goltzius, *Allegory of Plenty,* Louvre Museum.

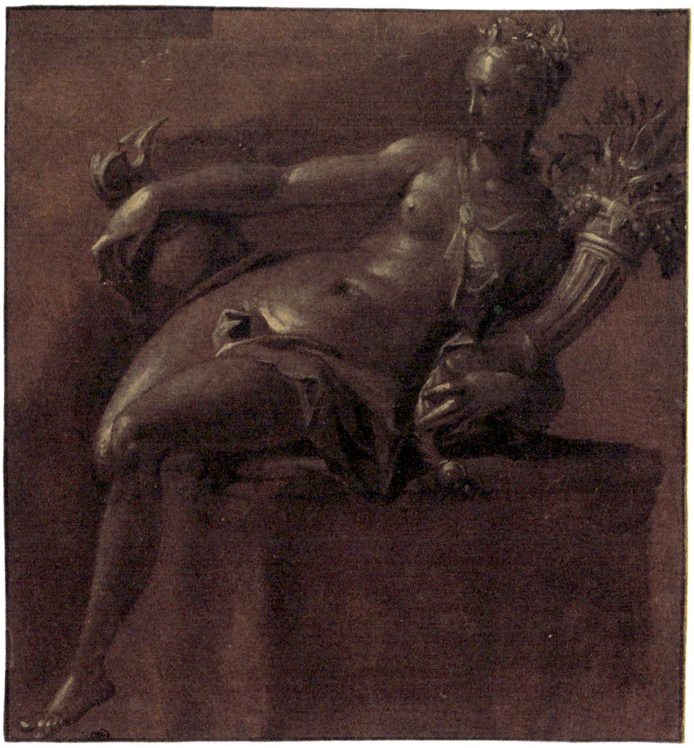

27. Hubert Gerhard, *Naiad Holding a Horn of Plenty,* Louvre Museum.

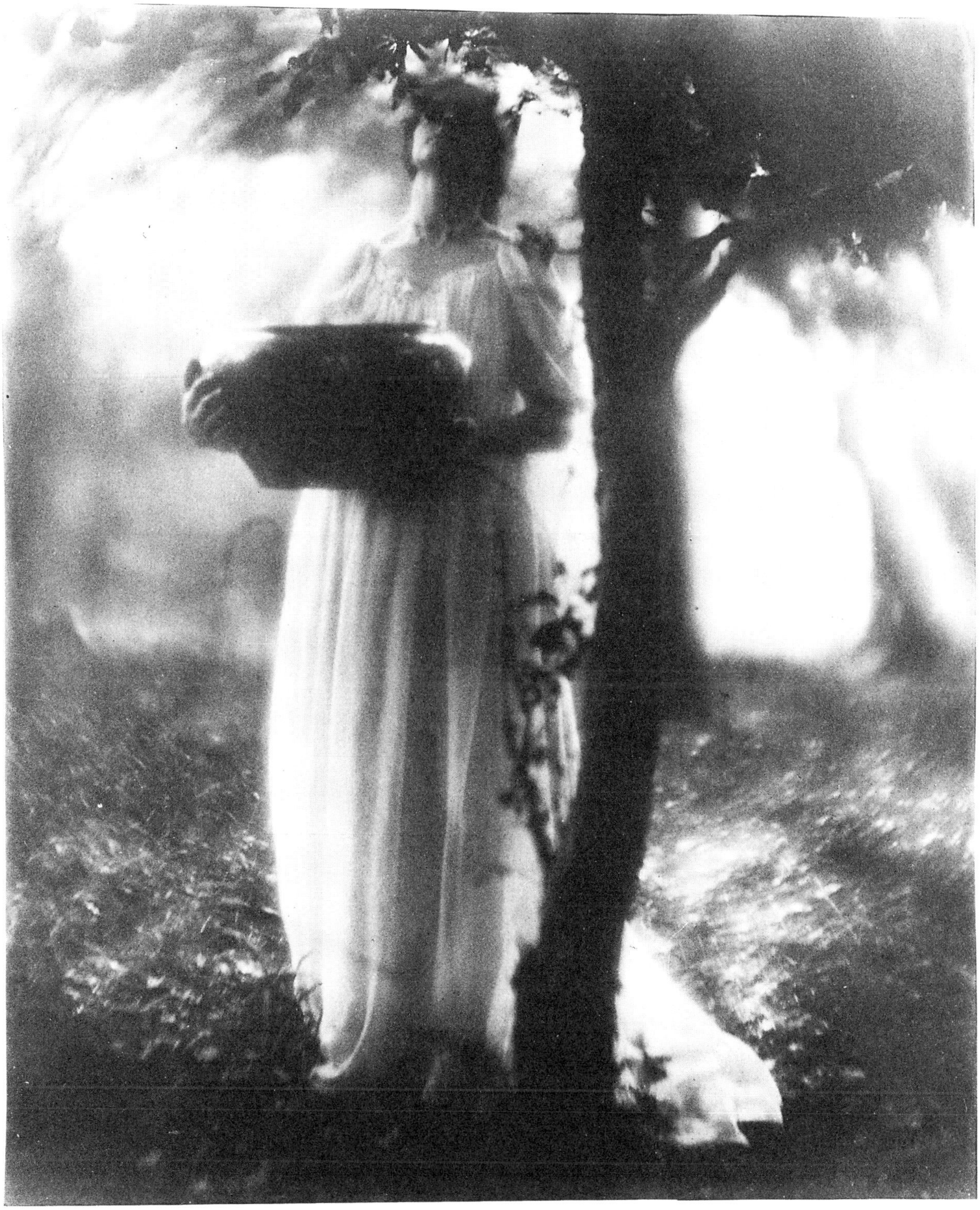

28. Georges H. Seeley (1852–1934), *The Offering,* Orsay Museum. Tinted silver proof. George Seeley belonged to the Photo-Secessionist group. This symbolist work, probably dated 1907, evokes the memory of the sacred offering, just as the music of the same period evoked "forgotten offerings."

corner of the space, he calculates the arrangement of the two antithetical groups so as to balance them. On each side, you can see three large nude bodies in the foreground, each as tormented as the others. And you may sense a peculiar correspondence between the mannerist technique and the subject treated. To show the irrevokable arbitrariness of Fortune, her seductive grace, her caprice and indirection, and the violence she provokes, the painter's inventiveness and the engraver's mastery have multiplied the effects of perspective, of vanishing points, foreshortening, torsions, obliques. Muscles in relief suggest *écorché.* Fortune throws her wealth skyward: her hands are raised, but the falling baubles and the battle on the ground offer a counterpoint to this upward motion. The execution is so skillful that it confers a dancing eloquence, a spiraling exuberance on the masses of bodies it shapes and chisels. This eloquence is both excessive and vain; the nonsensical nature of the covetousness awakened by Fortune is revealed through an exposure of anatomies. Bodies show their backsides and nether regions—buttocks, scrotum, sex organs. They were naked when they coveted, and they remain naked after the lots are drawn and there is nothing more to expect. The black and white of the engraving (as opposed to the colored model) does not convey a sense of lack; for even in the painting, everything is expressed in the lines, and the meaning of the work is not conveyed through the color, which would have suggested a kind of richness. The elegant precision of the lines neutralizes the risk of their becoming lost in smoke. Thus, the brutal illusionism of representation becomes a reflection of the illusory gifts distributed by Fortune. In its palpable unreality, the image leads us to understand that Fortune is only a dream.

And that leads to a reflection on this moment in sixteenth-century art. In the virtuosity that cast its spell over the mannerists, it seems that the artist's hand hazards a stroke only to immediately conceal it, offers the image only to reject it. Mannerism exhibits and holds back all possible gifts, so well, in fact, that the sharp precision of the lines almost makes you dizzy. It becomes a way of avoiding the risk of dissolution. Such is the case
26,27 when artists such as Goltzius or Gerhard draw allegorical figures of Plenty as fountain projects. The attributes associated with the figures become ornaments. Plenty uses the water that flows from her breasts, the fruit she holds, to adorn herself rather than spreading it around. The fruit and grain packed into the horn are her jewels, the water is lacework to make her more beautiful. They are not goods to be lavished on others, not something that generosity would abandon to the hunger and thirst of strangers.

24 I have just spoken of obliqueness in describing Cornelisz Van Haarlem's *Fortune.* This trait is expressed in many ways in mannerist art. Hence, when Goltzius abandons mythology in favor of scenes depicting reality, he takes as his theme the oblique maneu-
29,30 vers of an old woman and an old man in love. The old man offers gold to the cavalier who wanted to go away with the young woman; the old woman does the same to the girl who wanted to leave with her gallant. The young man, tempted by the old woman, and the young girl, solicited by the old man, both glance obliquely at this gold. They turn and move away from their companions, more suitable mates, in order to accept (or so we imagine) a cold, venal love. They are on the point of letting go of life in favor of gold.

Rubens, however, could never let go of life. He was the painter of overabundant life, the master of largesse, "where life flows and churns without end," in Baudelaire's admirable expression.[79]

Precious Vases, Maleficent Contents

In the work of art by Cornelisz Van Haarlem, we caught a glimpse of crowns that had 24
fallen to the ground. In Jacopo Ligozzi's extraordinary *Triumph of Death,* we rediscover 32
these crowns, along with miters, now in the foreground (the artist was also a marvelous painter of flowers). Warriors have battled to the death. The same figure of death has brought both of them down, and the insignia of powers both spiritual and temporal lie about abandoned. Death, in its gaunt furor, is the only one left standing; in the sky, a skull blowing destruction functions as a second figure of death. The skull reinforces both the angels of the storm and a maleficent star, which might be called Absinthe, like the star of the apocalypse. A completely different power has taken the place of Fortune. We cannot know what bygone gifts gave rise to the symbols of authority. Those gifts are now lost in confusion. We see how the story ends.

Abandoned treasures, a detail in the last images evoked, can also acquire the dignity
of a principal theme—that of *vanity*—in an entire aspect of the artistic labors of painters 33
and engravers. For decades, under the double patronage of Fortune and Death (the random and the peremptory), this motif was consistently reproduced. The transition from the inequitable distribution of Fortune to the eternal deprivation represented by Death is entirely comprehensible.

Let us now pass through the gallery of vanities. Certain works of art found there could be subtitled "How Gifts End." What becomes of riches when it is pride, coquetry, and sensuality that have seized possession of them?[80] The ties to one's possessions come undone in every possible manner: either the object becomes tainted or breaks (some objects are as fragile as soap bubbles), or the possessors move beyond frivolity and, seized by melancholy, touched by conversion, or vanquished by adversity, let go of them. The legendary character most often associated with these images is Mary Magdalene, the reformed sinner who recognizes the nothingness of earthly pleasures and ornaments. Her carnal beauty remains; she may still have at her side testimony to her long error, mirrors and jewels that were given to her as the wages of sin. But she has renounced everything she condemns (or maligns) as superfluous: she has rendered unto death that which is death's. And the sensible presence of death—the skull—forbids renewed access to the vanities of the world. Through mortification, everything perishable has been handed back to Fortune. There is now place only for the total gift to the absolute power—a power that does not allow itself to be touched, but has promised to give itself absolutely in return. Visible vanity, the vanity of the visible, is the preliminary for the greatest possible exchange of gifts. According to the language of mystics, that exchange is union, or at least the threshold of union. "Son, you must give yourself utterly and keep nothing of yourself."[81]

79. See Yves Bonnefoy, "Baudelaire contre Rubens," *Le nuage rouge* (Paris: Mercure de France, 1992), 9–88.

80. See the catalog *Les Vanités dans la peinture au XVIIe siècle: Méditations sur la richesse, le dénuement et la rédemption,* ed. Alain Tapié (Caen and Paris, 1990–91).

81. Thomas à Kempis, *De imitatione Christi* 3.27.1: "Fili, oportet te dare totum pro toto, et nihil tuiipsius esse."

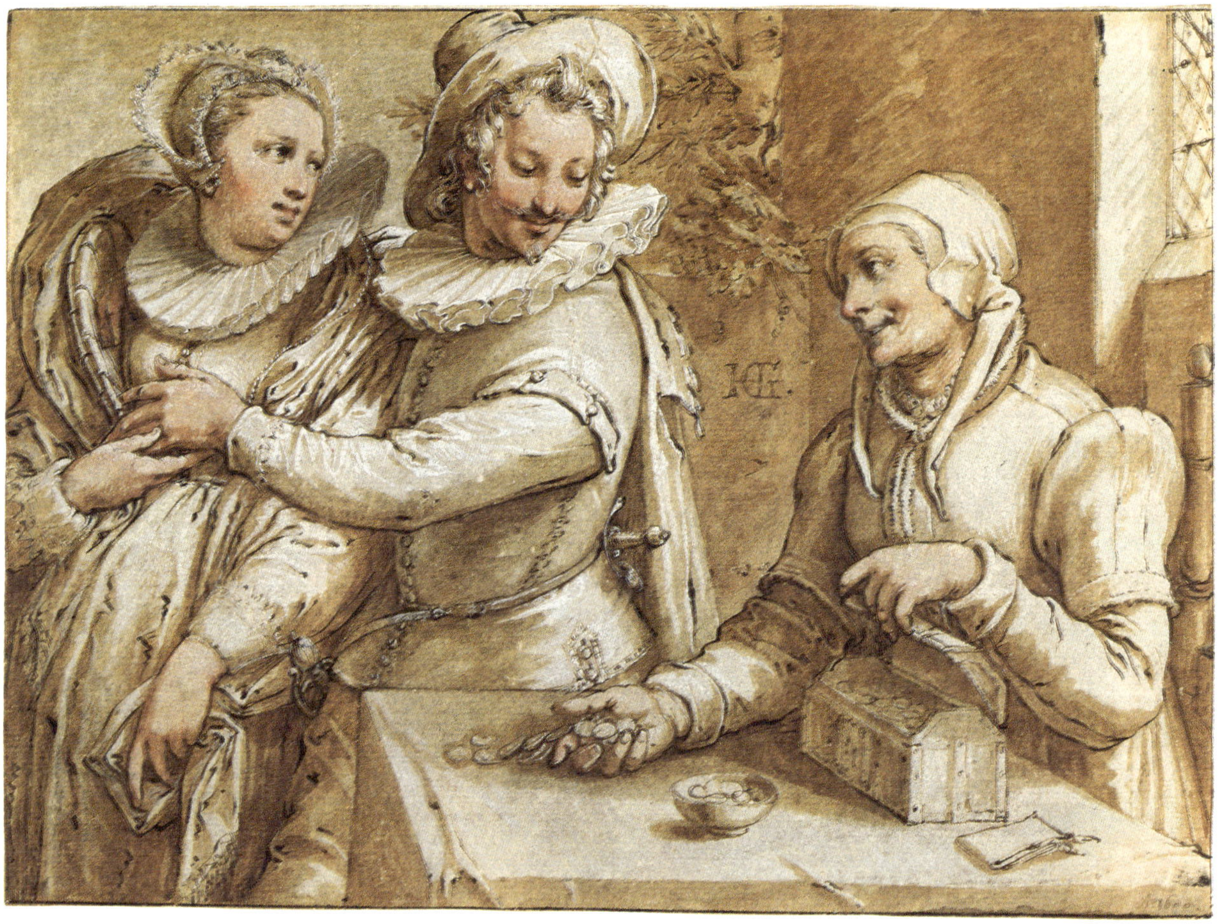

29. Hendrick Goltzius, *Old Woman in Love,* Louvre Museum, Edmond de Rothschild Collection.

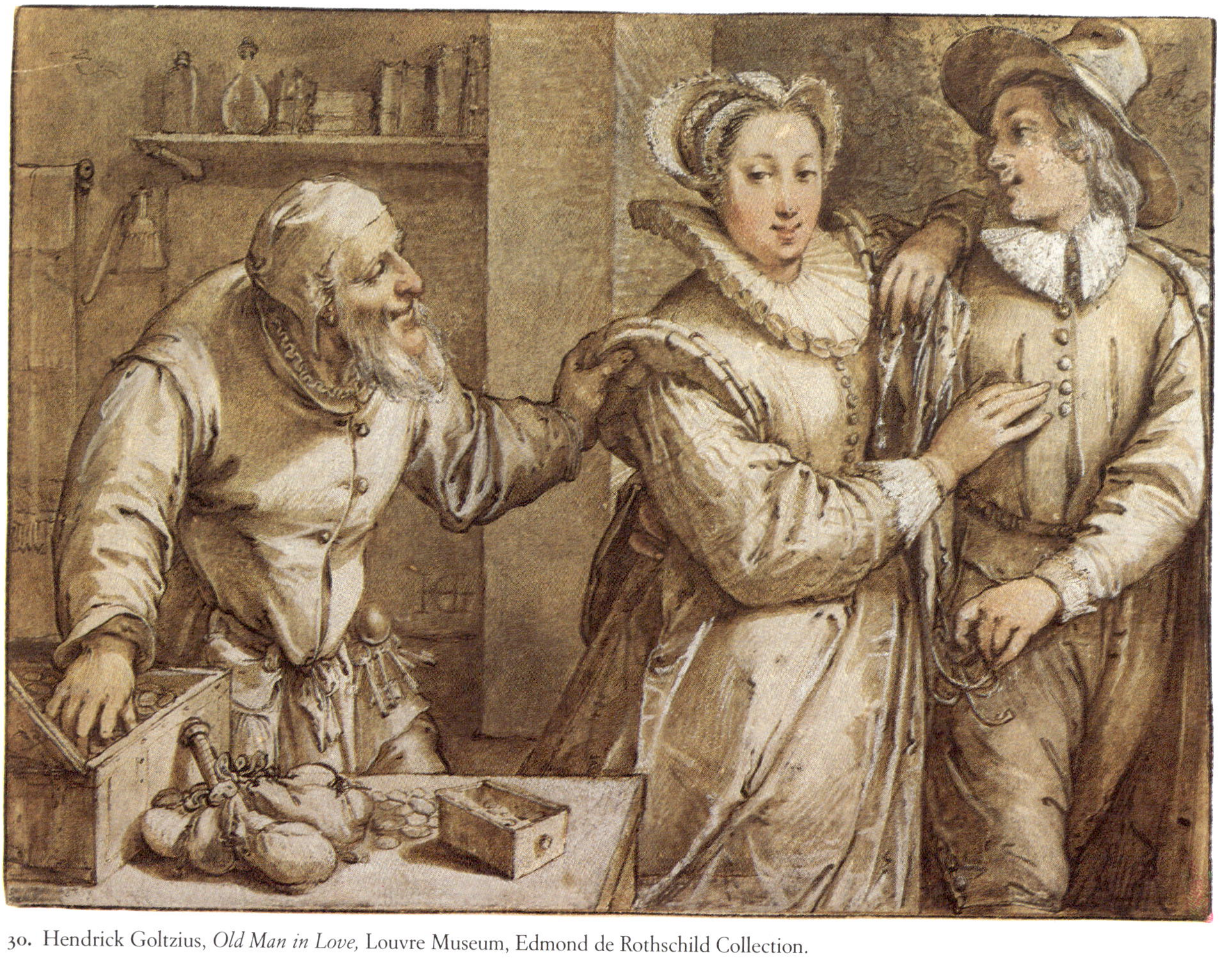

30. Hendrick Goltzius, *Old Man in Love,* Louvre Museum, Edmond de Rothschild Collection.

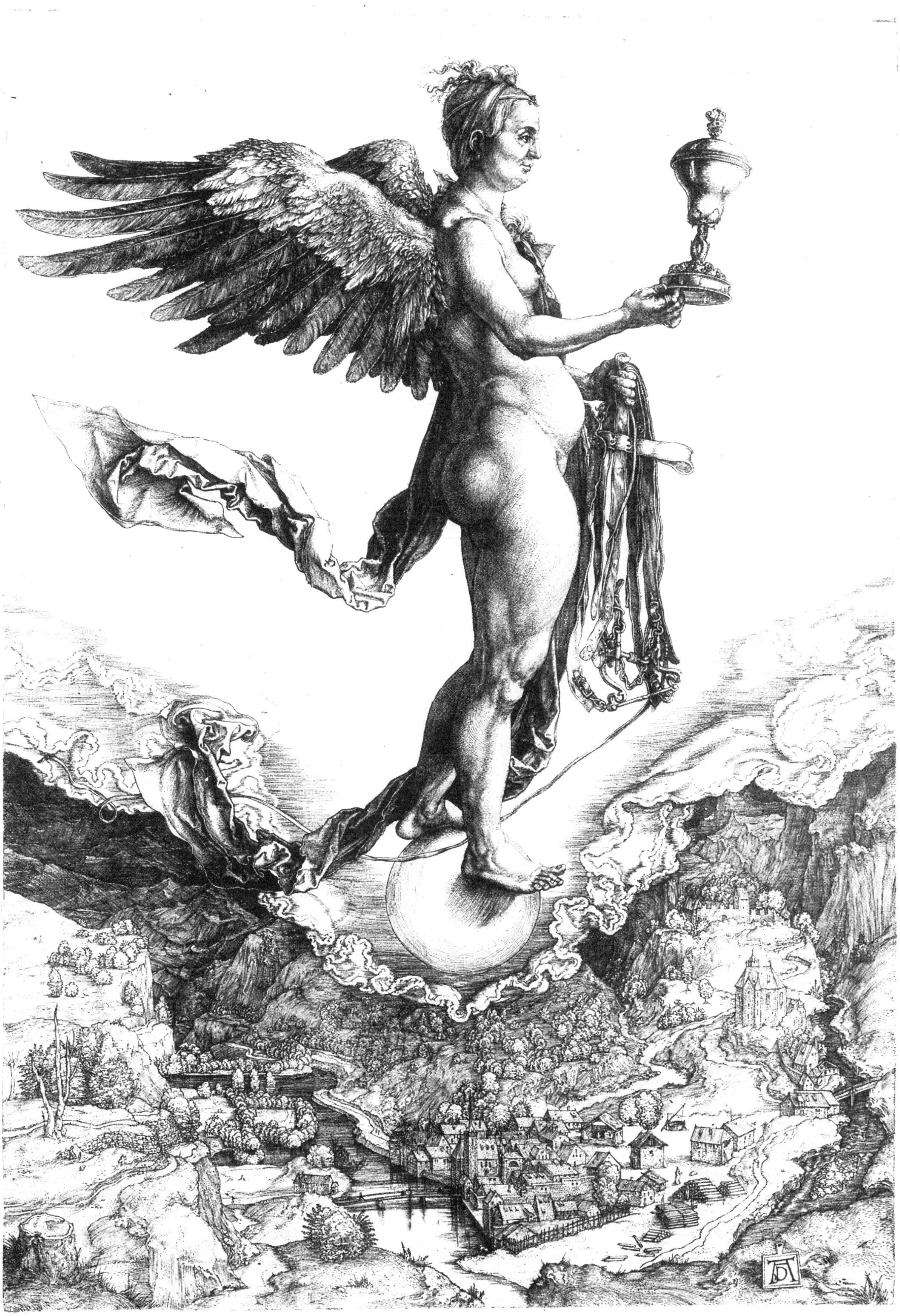

31. Albrecht Dürer, *Large Fortune* (*Nemesis*), Louvre Museum, Edmond de Rothschild Collection.

In the system of allegorical signs, only the form of an attribute need change for the
31 entire identity of a figure to be read differently. For example, when Dürer places a precious closed vase in the hands of a female character standing on a sphere and dominating a mountain landscape from the air, he certainly does not forbid us from thinking of Fortune. Yet the closed vase is not a fitting symbol for the prodigality of Tyché, since its content must necessarily be limited. The fact that it is no longer the open and inexhaustible horn of plenty is not a matter of indifference. We understand that this meditative figure is Nemesis, who comes to bring just retribution to human actions. In her left hand, she carries the bit and reins that will curb violent men; in her right, she holds the sober reward of the virtuous.[82]

36 When the sphere, the lock of hair, and the veil also disappear from the image, the bearer of the closed vase is most probably Psyche or Pandora. Psyche must bring a little water from the Styx to Venus, her persecutor: it is not a true gift but a required ordeal and tribute. Pandora, fashioned by the order of Zeus, receives the gifts of all the gods; she is herself the maleficent gift they make to the human race, to take revenge for Prometheus's ruses in stealing fire. In the myth recounted by Hesiod,[83] Pandora, imprudently accepted by Epimetheus, lifts the cover of a jar and all the evils escape. Henceforth, men will suffer on account of them. In their excellent study, Dora Panofsky and Erwin Panofsky have shown how the illustrators of the myth belatedly substituted a box for the jar; they also demonstrate how the versions have varied since antiquity.[84] It is as if the image attempted to gather together in the smallest possible space the quintessence of the *concealed,* the deadly *content* that ought to have been left alone, forbidden, under
34 cover. The gesture of Pandora (or, according to the version put forth by Erasmus, of Epimetheus, who forgot the warning he had received) is not *sparsio,* the sowing to the wind of coveted and deadly riches, but rather the fatal opening of a receptacle that should have been kept closed. The content, as if it were an element that could no longer remain secret, escapes and spreads irrepressibly, even though there was no manifest intention in the gesture of opening. The gesture is an accident. (Some have attributed it to curiosity, but the first account does not mention this.) The gods, through the intermediary of their creation, thus succeed in "hiding what gives life to men." In the case of the woman-gift, no more than a movement was required to lift the cover and reveal the evils contained in the vase: immediately, the primitive resources of life become hidden. It is a fatal revelation, and Epimetheus reflects upon it with eternal regret. In contrast to the welling up of the spring of largesse, this is a diffusion of misfortune.

37 That gift should not have been accepted. And how many others likewise! The category of the deadly gift clearly takes shape before us. Such gifts catch their recipients in the trap of appearance. That trap is all the more perilous in that the proprieties of
28 civilization prescribe that gifts be offered and accepted: brews of hospitality, ostentatious gifts.

82. See the catalog *Fortune;* and Galactéros de Boissier, "Images emblématiques de la Fortune."

83. Hesiod, *Work and Days,* ll. 57–101, and *Theogony,* ll. 570–90.

84. Dora Panofsky and Erwin Panofsky, *Pandora's Box* (London, 1956).

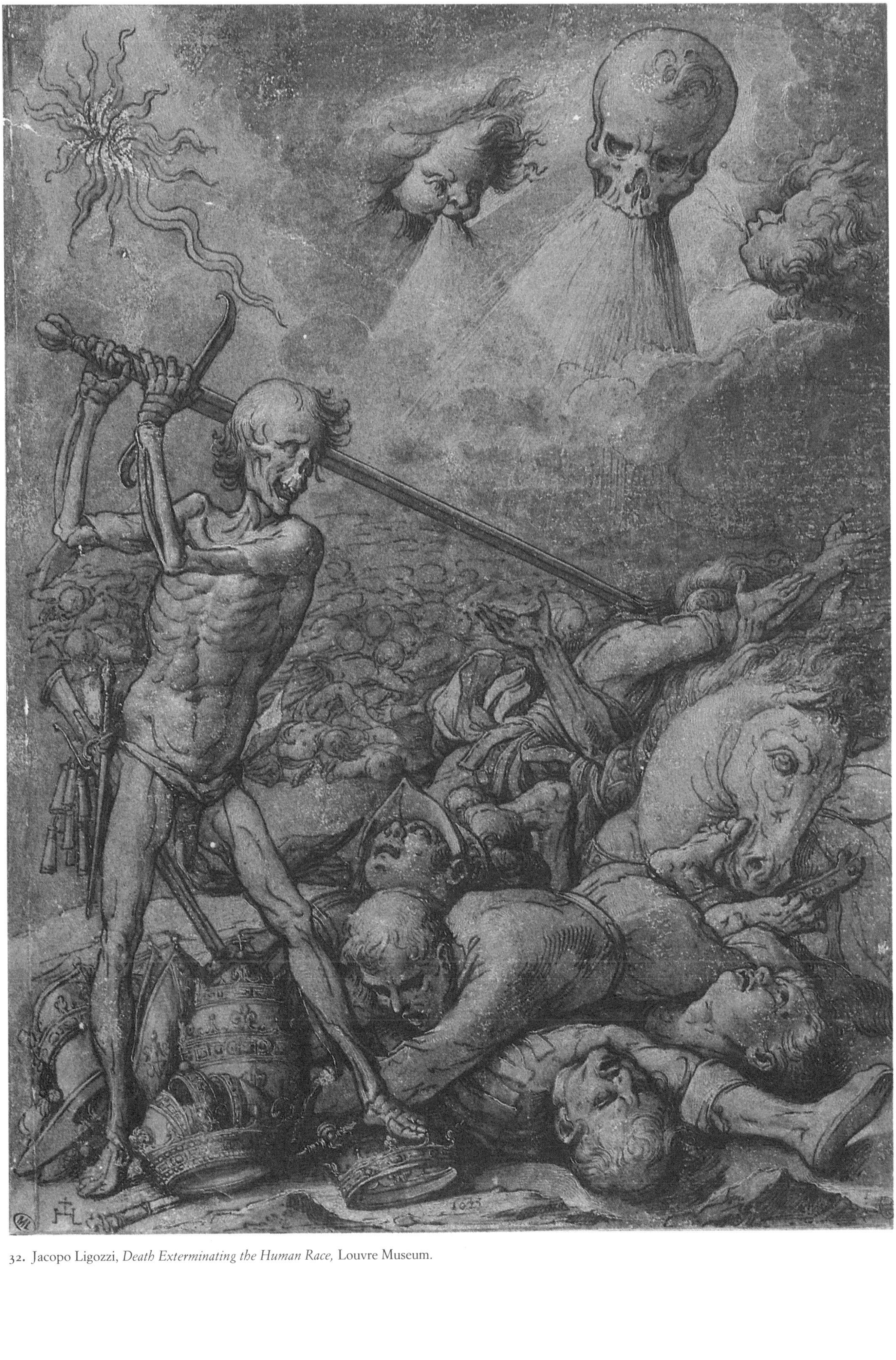

32. Jacopo Ligozzi, *Death Exterminating the Human Race,* Louvre Museum.

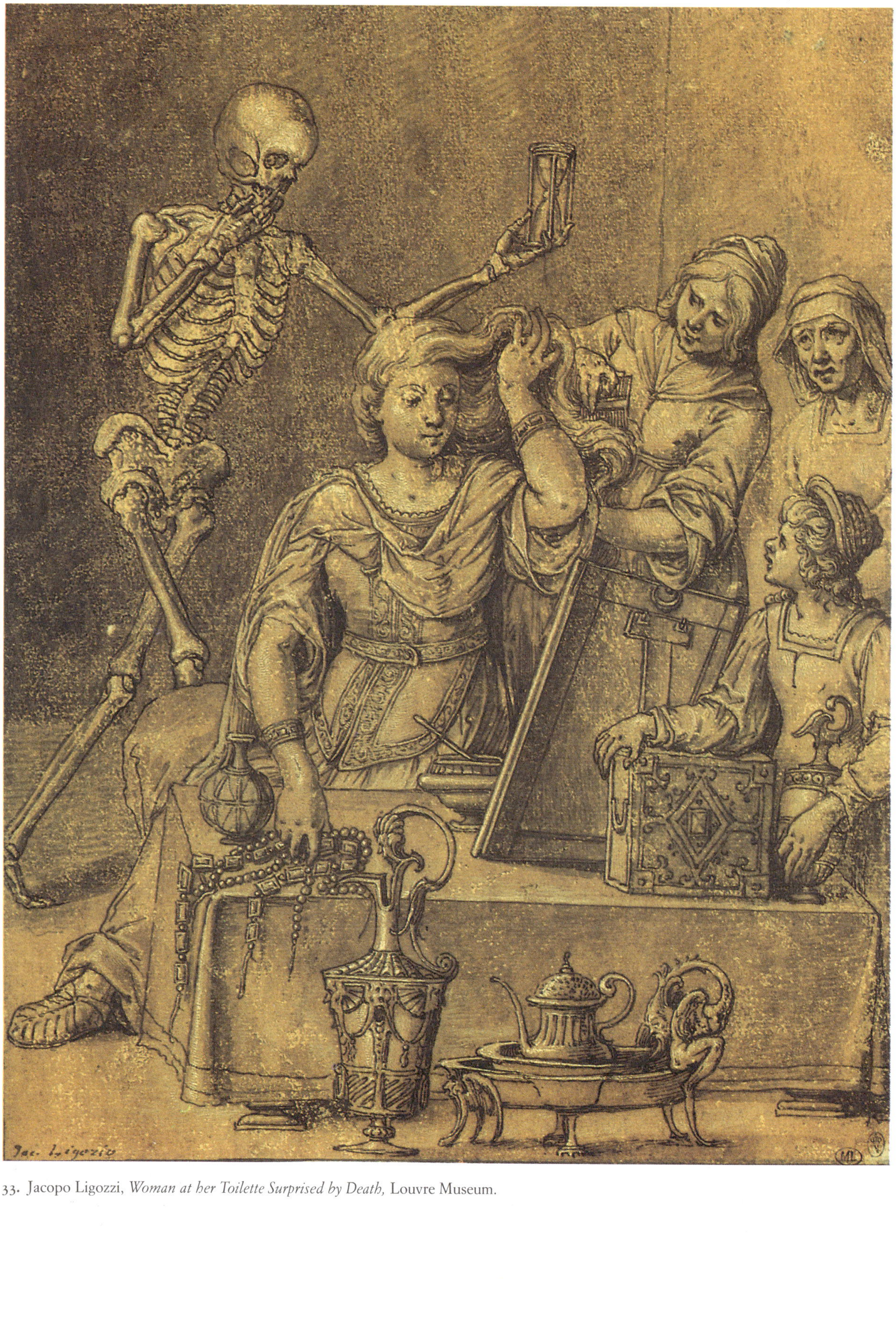

33. Jacopo Ligozzi, *Woman at her Toilette Surprised by Death,* Louvre Museum.

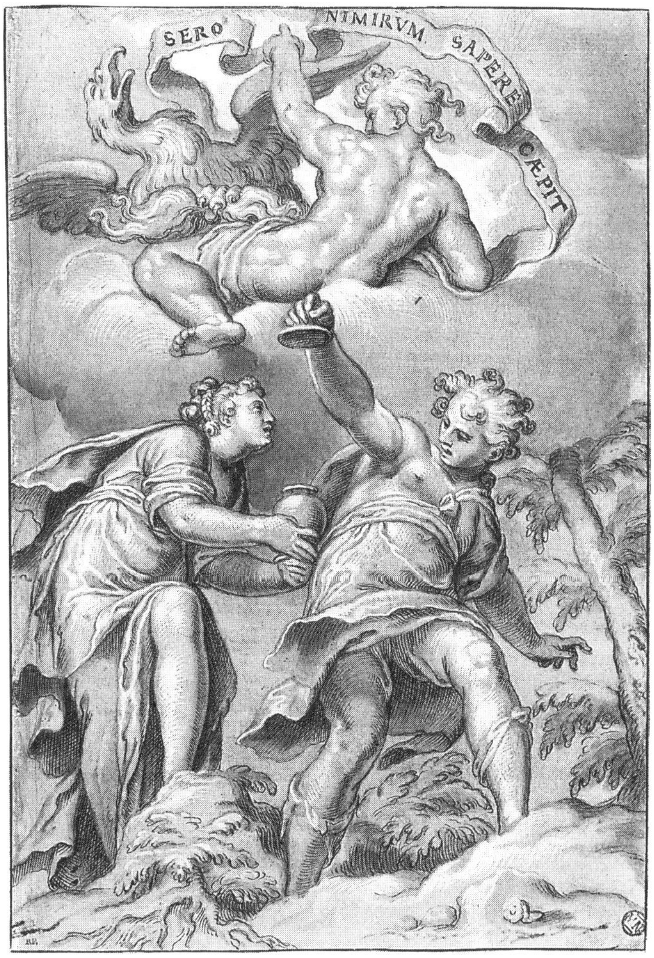

34. Paolo Farinati (after), *Epimetheus Opening Pandora's Box,* Louvre Museum.

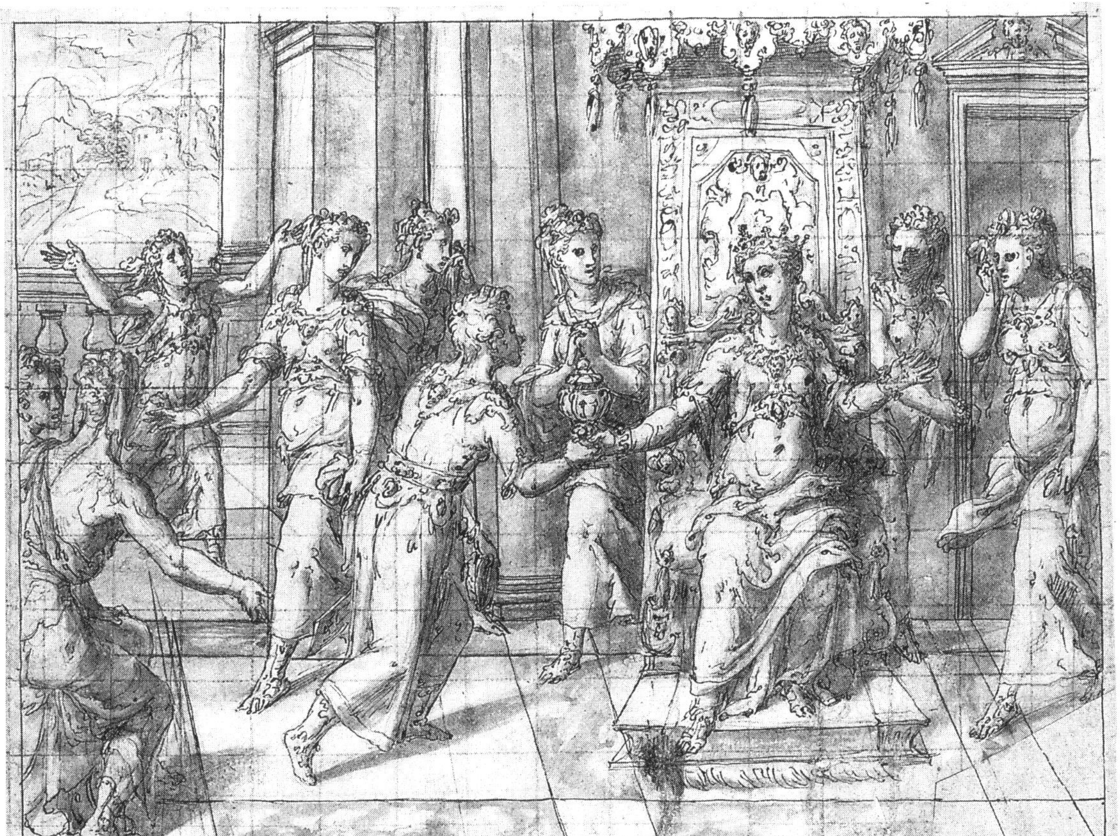

35. Ottavio Semino, *Sophonisba Receiving the Hemlock,* Louvre Museum.

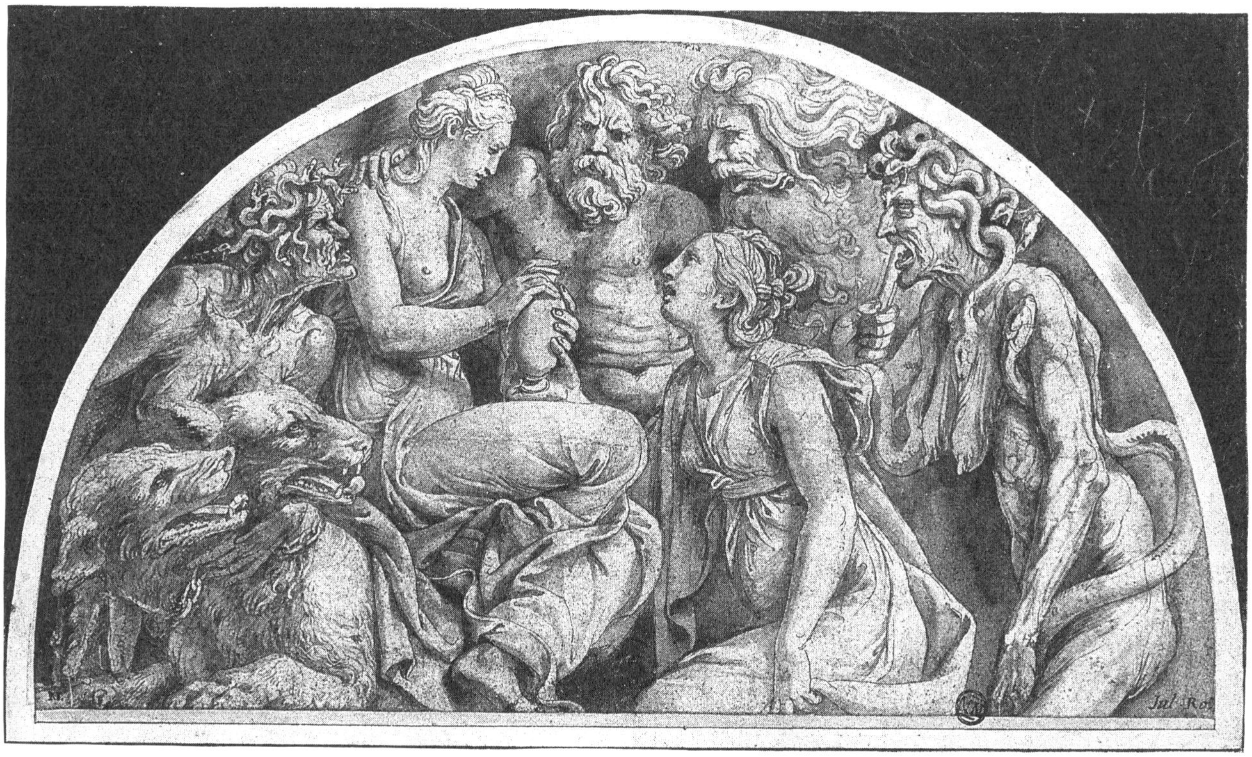

36. Giulio Romano, *Psyche Receiving the Vase of Prosperine,* Louvre Museum.

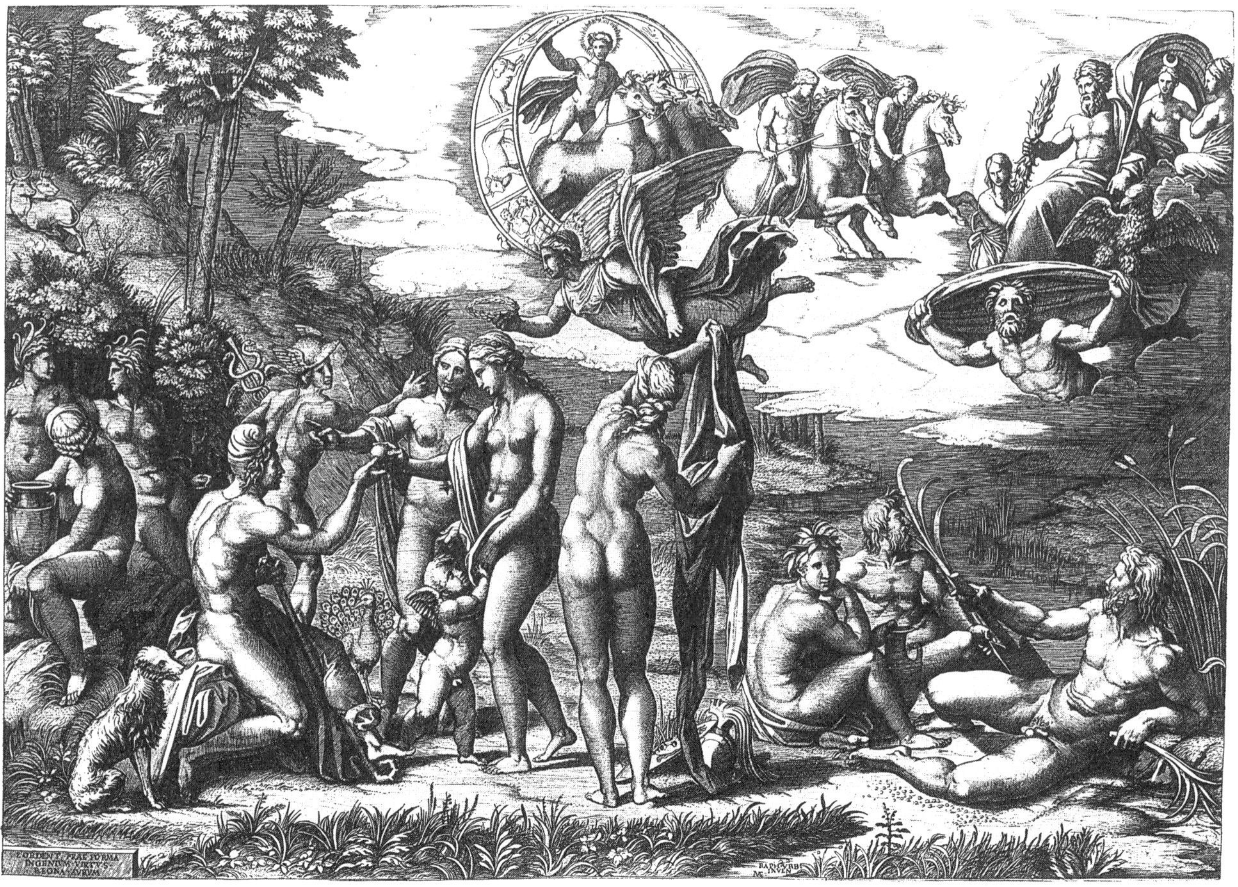

37. Marcantonio Raimondi, *The Judgment of Paris,* Louvre Museum, Edmond de Rothschild Collection.

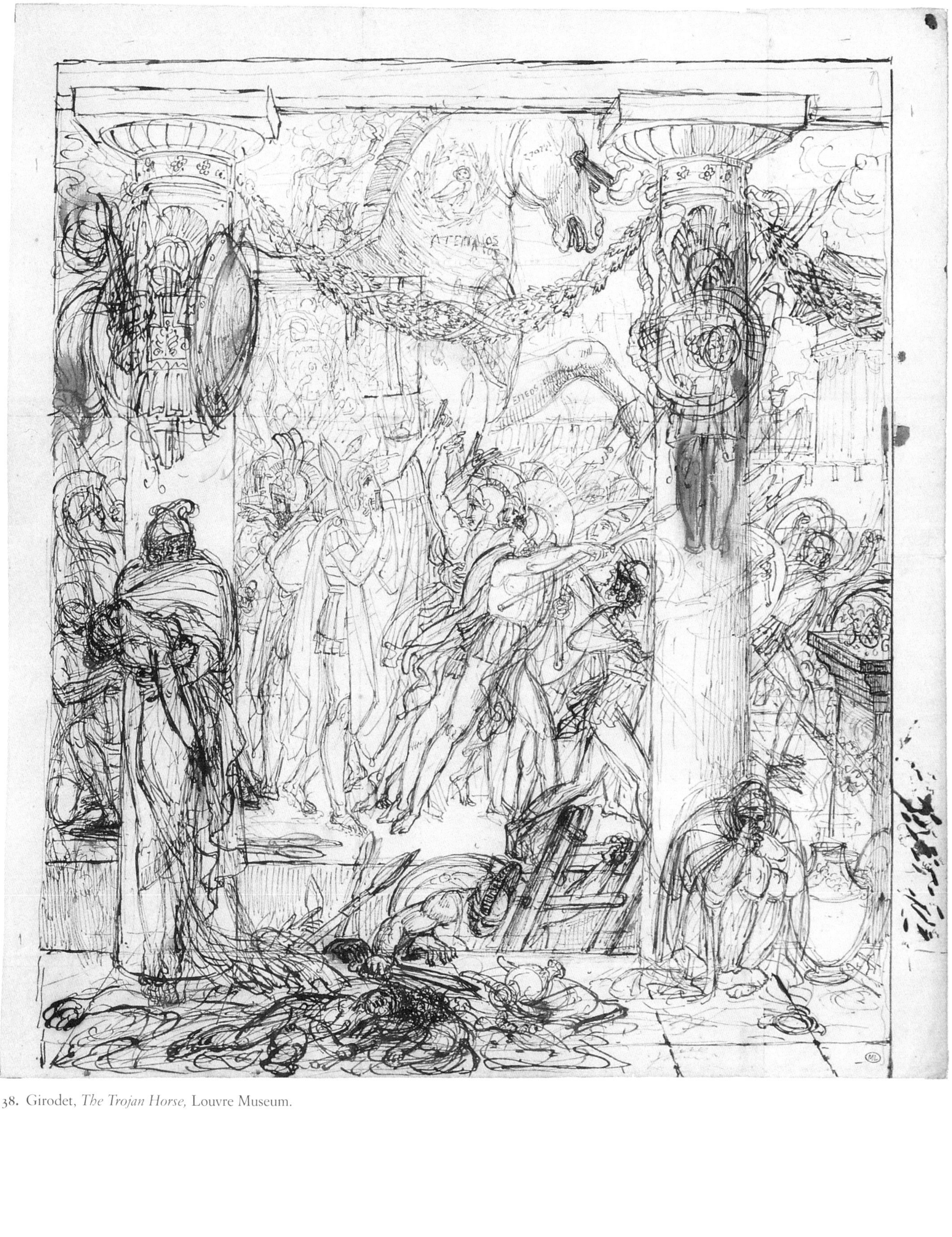

38. Girodet, *The Trojan Horse,* Louvre Museum.

38 In Troy, no one wanted to heed the advice to refuse the horse offered by those cunning Greeks, whom one must fear even when they are bearing gifts, *et dona ferentes.*[85] The beautiful, gigantic statue also has a maleficent content. The city will perish because of it.

Ulysses, warned of peril by Hermes, receives a magic herb from him. He can thus drink with impunity from the welcoming cup extended by the magician Circe.[86] If he had not been protected by the *antidote,* he would have taken on the shape of an animal, like his companions. The gift of hospitality was the worst poison. A divine gift was needed to nullify its effect.

The homonymy, or rather, the semantic duality, in ancient Germanic languages of *Gift, gift*—a word designating both gift and poison—has long been discussed by etymologists, and then by sociologists. The polysemy of other terms relating to the gift has also been signaled: for example, the Greek *dosis* is the act of giving, but it is also the "dose" of a lethal substance.[87] One example of this is suggested by an episode in the Roman conquest of Africa, made illustrious by Renaissance and baroque theater and repeated endlessly. The poison offered to Queen Sophonisba by her spouse Masinissa was the ultimate means for avoiding captivity in Roman hands. The success of this theme in the sixteenth and seventeenth centuries lay in the fact that it assured the fusion between
35 the motif of the gift and that of Stoic suicide. Sophonisba receives of her own free will the poisoned cup that allows her to safeguard her freedom. In the face of destiny, the gift that assures the possibility of putting an end to existence is one of the most eloquent oxymorons possible. In accepting the gift that allows her to give herself death, Sophonisba belongs only to herself, to the very end. She thus escapes her captors and tormentors. In narrative, in tragedy, this is the gift of the denouement. At the end of Malraux's *Condition humaine* [The human condition], the gift of cyanide is another example of a gesture that, in giving access to voluntary death, allows one to escape the punishment prepared by the political enemy. A lethal gift becomes a gift of liberation.

85. It is Laocoön who cries: "Timeo Danaos et dona ferentes" (Beware of Greeks bearing gifts). Virgil, *The Aeneid* 2.48.

86. *The Odyssey* 10.281ff. An entire category of popular fables concerns deadly gifts. In *L'histoire du soldat,* which C.-F. Ramuz borrows from a Russian story collected by Afanasyev, the soldier unwisely accepts a magical book offered by the devil in exchange for his violin. The violin, which is the happiness of the soul, can be recovered only by giving the devil all the money the book has earned.

87. We might also add the double sense of words such as *pharmakos* and *philtron,* which has long been noted. In the story of Tristram, the fatal philter was a gift destined for the husband of Isolde. See Marcel Mauss, "Gift, gift," in *Mélanges Charles Andler* (Strasbourg, 1924), 243–47; "Essai sur le don" (1923–24), *Sociologie et anthropologie,* with an introduction by Claude Lévi-Strauss (Paris: PUF, 1950), 255; Emile Benveniste, "Don et échange dans le vocabulaire indo-européen," *Problèmes de linguistique générale* (Paris: Gallimard, 1966), 315–26; "Donner et prendre," *Vocabulaire des institutions indo-européennes,* 2 vols. (Paris: Minuit, 1969), vol. 1, sec. 2, pp. 65–121. Derrida examines these works in *Donner le temps.*

CHAPTER THREE

Charity

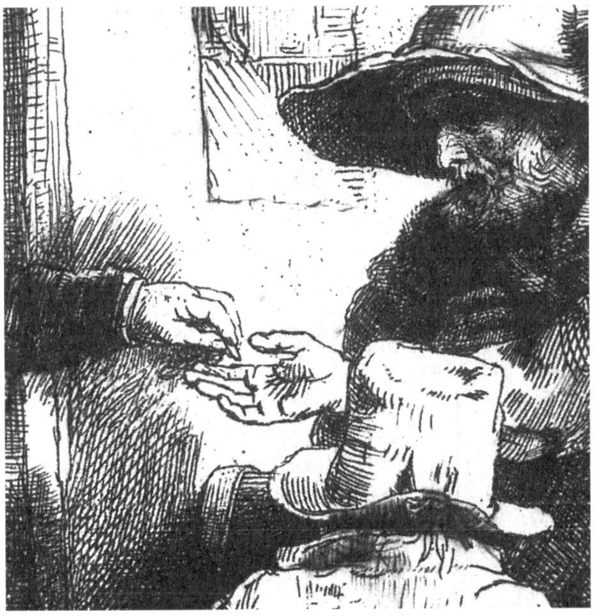

The World Is a Benefit

Renaissance humanism inclined toward syncretism and linked the giving God of the Hebrew Bible to the Platonic demiurge and to the god-benefactor of Stoicism.

Seneca's treatise *De beneficiis,* where the question of the gift is treated exhaustively, sees God as the supreme example of disinterested beneficence. We would do well to consider that work, which Diderot said he had read three times in succession, moistening the pages "with a few tears" even on the fourth reading.[88] For the philosopher, God's liberal gifts are an opportunity to set before us the entire earthly landscape and the full expanse of the heavens. Seneca composed a vast enumerative tableau (or hypotyposis, to adopt the term used by teachers of rhetoric). During the neo-Stoic age, that is, in the years surrounding 1600, landscape painting no doubt drew inspiration from it. Eighteenth-century physicotheology continued to develop the same arguments in a more applied manner. Seneca asks:

> Was it too small a thing that Nature gave when she gave to us herself? "God gives no benefits," you say. Whence, then, comes all that you possess, all that you give, all that you withhold, all that you hoard, all that you steal? Whence come the countless things that delight your eyes, your ears, your mind? . . . Whence all the trees yielding their varied fruits, all the healing plants, all the different sorts of foods distributed throughout the whole year, so that even the slothful find sustenance from the chance produce of the earth? Whence, too, the living creature of every kind, some born upon dry and solid ground, others in the waves, others that descend through the air, in order that every part of Nature's domain might pay to us some tribute? Whence the rivers—these that encircle the fields in the loveliest curves, those that, as they flow on in their vast and navigable courses, provide a channel for commerce. . . . If anyone had made you a gift of but a few acres, you would say that you had received a benefit; and do you say that the illimitable stretches that the earth opens to you are not a benefit? If anyone has presented you with money, and, since this is a great thing in your eyes, has filled your coffer, you will call it a benefit. God has planted in the earth countless mines, has drawn forth from its depths countless rivers that over the lands where they flow carry down gold; silver and copper and iron in huge store have been buried in all places, and he has given to you the means of discovering them . . . yet do you say that you have received no benefit? If you should receive the gift of a house that was resplendent with marble and a ceiling gleaming with gold or decked out with colours, you would call it no commonplace gift. God has built for you a huge mansion that need not fear conflagration or ruin, a house in which you see, not flimsy veneers thinner than the very blade by which they are sawn, but virgin masses of most precious stone, whole masses of a substance with such a variety of markings that the tiniest fragments of it fill you with wonder, and a ceiling gleaming in one fashion by night, and in another by day—yet do you say that you have received no gift?[89]

Whatever name is given this exclusive power—Nature, Liber, Hercules, Mercury, Destiny, Fortune—it is the universal gift giver.

The lesson is twofold. First, how can we not feel gratitude when we receive such gifts? But, second, if we imitate the gods, if we are beneficent like them, why should we expect gratitude? A god is adequate unto himself. God, nature, and the sun give freely, without asking to be paid in return *(sine praemio, sine mercede),* without seeking to bind or obligate their beneficiaries. The duty of the truly beneficent man is exactly the same.

88. Denis Diderot, *Essai sur les règnes de Claude et de Néron,* in *Oeuvres complètes* (Paris: Club français du livre, 1972), 13:537–45.

89. Seneca, *De beneficiis* 4.5, in *Moral Essays,* English translation by John W. Basore (Cambridge and London: Harvard University Press and William Heinemann, 1958), 211–15.

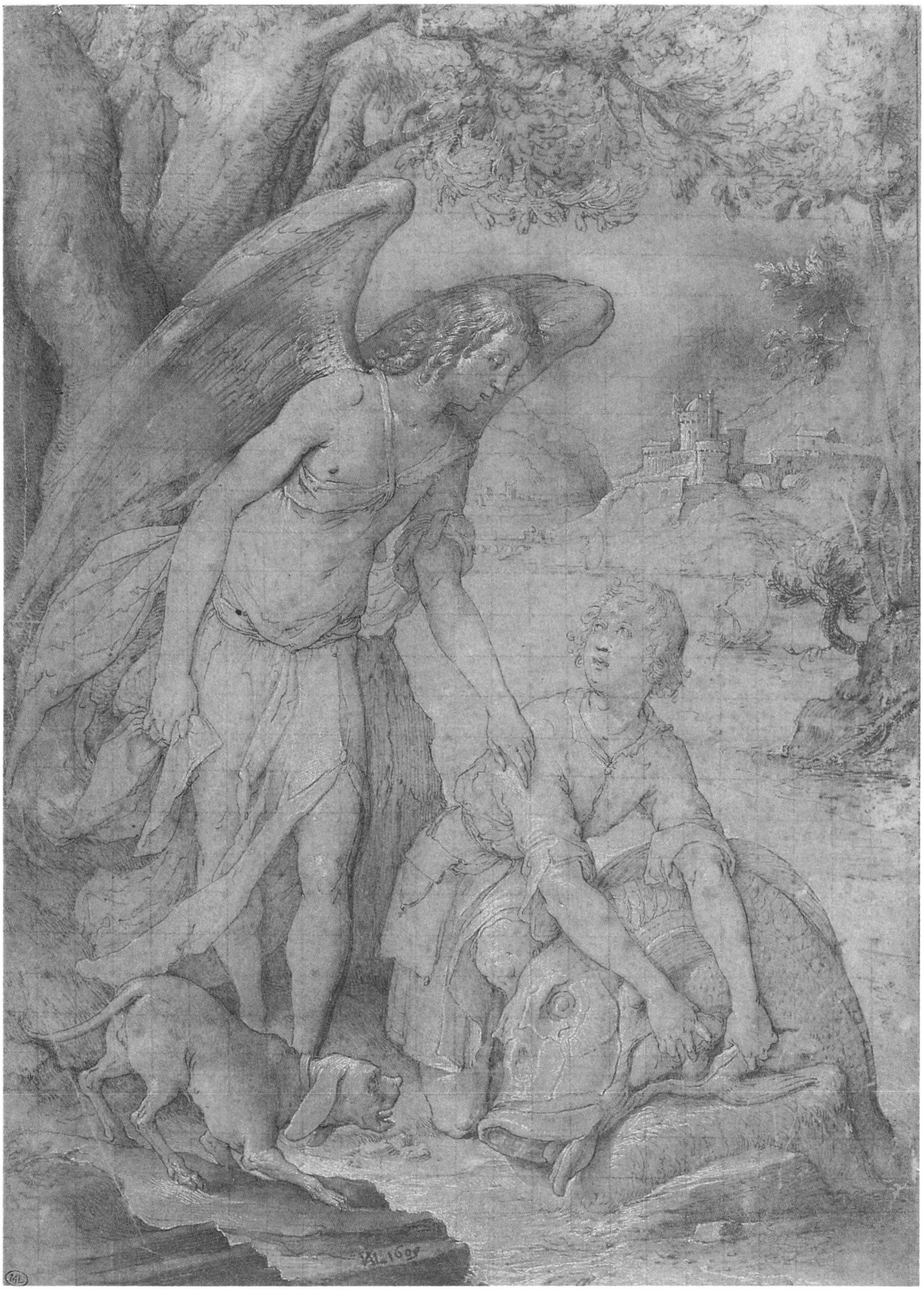

39. Jacopi Ligozzi, *Tobias and the Angel,* Louvre Museum. "The gall is for anointing a man's eyes when white patches have spread over them. . . . The eyes will then recover" (Tobit 6:9)

"Why, then, does he give?" Seneca asks. "For fear that he should fail to give, for fear that he should lose an opportunity of doing good. . . . That which has gain as its object cannot be a benefit."

Let us understand that, in the spirit of ancient morality, giving, especially giving unconditionally, is more honorable than repaying a debt or expecting a gift in return. Friendship places everything in common, to the point that bequeathing the burden of a family to one's most beloved friends is equivalent to offering them an opportunity for true glory. Such is the story of Eudamidas, who, in dying, gave his two friends the responsibility for feeding his mother and marrying off his daughter. This exemplary testament,
96 which Poussin depicted in a painting, is glossed by Montaigne: "If, in the friendship I speak of, one could give to the other, it would be the one who received the benefit who would oblige his friend. For, each of them seeking above all things to benefit the other, the one who provides the matter and the occasion is the liberal one, giving his friend the satisfaction of doing for him what he most wants to do. . . . Eudamidas bestows upon his friends the kindness and favor of using them for his need. He leaves them heirs to this liberality of his, which consists of putting into their hands a chance to do him good."[90]

In fact, the highest gift one can give is the gift of oneself in one's entirety to a single friend. Montaigne regrets the fact that Eudamidas designates two friends rather than one. "For this perfect friendship I speak of is indivisible: each one gives himself so wholly to his friend that he has nothing left to distribute elsewhere."[91]

There is a kind of gift implying friendship that takes on a singular importance. That is the gift that occurs assymetrically, from a student to a teacher, which is then reciprocated by the teacher to the student. Recall the wonderful example reported by Seneca at the beginning of *De beneficiis* (1.8):

> Once when many gifts were being presented to Socrates by his pupils, each one bringing according to his means, Aeschines, who was poor, said to him: "Nothing that I am able to give to you do I find worthy of you, and only in this way do I discover that I am a poor man. And so I give to you the only thing that I possess—myself. This gift, such as it is, I beg you to take in good part, and bear in mind that the others, though they gave you much, have left more for themselves." "And how," said Socrates, "could it have been anything but a great gift—unless maybe you set small value upon yourself? And so I shall make it my care to return you to yourself a better man than when I received you." By this present Aeschines surpassed Alcibiades, whose heart matched his riches, and the wealthy youths with all their splendid gifts.

Aeschines's gift of himself to Socrates, as it is formulated here, can serve as a model for other gifts. It indicates the possibility of a total consensual alienation—the offer of all one *is,* for lack of *having* something else to give. (In psychoanalytic terms, is this a successful transference?) It finds its counterpart in Socrates' promise to return a better being. What is here the relation between the disciple and the master becomes, in Rousseau's *Social Contract,* the relation between the individual and society as a whole: every individual gives himself "entirely" to "the whole community" (1.6) in order to be returned to himself, having received in exchange the status of citizen.[92] The individual

90. Michel de Montaigne, *Essays* ("On Friendship"), in *The Complete Works of Montaigne,* English translation by Donald M. Frame (Stanford: Stanford University Press, 1957), 141–42. The source is Lucian's *Toxaris.*

91. Montaigne, *Essays,* 141.

92. Rousseau explicitly uses the verb *donner* (to give) in defining the fundamental contract. "Each one gives himself entirely"; "Each giv[es] himself to all."

gains "civil liberty and the ownership of everything he possesses" (1.8). He has been educated in reason and in freedom. Rousseau extends the gift, followed by restitution, to the political realm. In Seneca, it remained at the level of a relation of friendship. But Rousseau attempts to present as reciprocal and symmetrical a relation that is, in fact, still marked by the asymmetry between the individual and the collective.[93]

God's Gifts and Men's Gifts

In Genesis, God creates man and woman in his own image and tells them: "Of every tree of the garden thou mayest freely eat" (Genesis 2:17). The gift of subsistence occurs on the sixth day, in the final moment of the first account of creation. In the biblical
narrative that follows, the companion given to man offers him the forbidden fruit to eat, 1
which she has tasted at the instigation of the serpent. And when God calls upon Adam, who has covered his nakedness, he answers: "The woman whom thou gavest *to be* with me, she gave me of the tree, and I did eat" (Mulier, quam dedisti mihi sociam, dedit mihi de ligno, et comedi). In a style where, of course, repetition is far from the exception, the repetition of the verb "give" still produces a dizzying effect: the cause of evil goes back to the first gift, if only because that gift is freedom—the supplementary divine gift—which theology attributes to the human creature. (Let us recall, however, that it is Pauline and Augustinian theology that confers an ontological meaning on Adam's disobedience, seen from the eschatological perspective of redemption.) For Renaissance syncretism, this is an opportunity to link Eve to Pandora.[94] Paternal gifts become deadly gifts, and paradise is lost by the first couple. The debt will be paid by God himself. The good news of the Gospels speaks of a new gift: "For God so loved the world, that he gave his only begotten Son" (Sic enim Deus dilexit mundum, ut Filium suum unigenitum daret) (John 3:16). He gave him out of love for the world, in a distant echo of Abraham, who was ready to give his only son out of obedience to the call that put him to the test.

It is not my intention to inventory or comment on the many gifts that stand out as 95
landmarks of biblical history, which have already elicited a meticulous exegesis: the promise and gift of the land of Canaan, the gifts of Melchizedek rejected by Abraham,
the engagement gifts for Rebekah, the gift of the Ten Commandments on tables of stone, 42
the gift of manna in the desert, the legal transfer of a corner of the field so that poor people and strangers can glean it, gifts from the Queen of Sheba to Solomon, the
heavenly gift of food to the prophets, gifts and festivities that annually celebrate Esther's 45
victory over the enemies of the Jews, the possessions the family of Tobias offered the angel Raphael (who refused them), the gifts of the Magi. . . . The God celebrated by the Psalms is a god of largesse: "The eyes of all wait upon thee; and thou givest them their meat in due season. Thou openest thine hand, and satisfiest the desire of every living thing" (Psalm 145:15–16).

The reader of the biblical text soon learns to distinguish between God's gift—bene- 39

93. The Rousseauist lawmaker takes up in part the pedagogical role of Socrates in the account reported by Seneca.

94. On the theme of *Eva prima Pandora,* see Panofsky and Panofsky, *Pandora's Box.*

fit, satiety, forgiveness, benediction—which descends vertically, and men's offerings in return, the honor shown to God out of love, obedience, and sacrifice, a gift that ascends vertically. The covenant returns to God the love God has for men. These two movements call out to each other, and religious discourse owes its extraordinary attraction to its evocation of this double movement. In addition, the law prescribes justice and compassion (*tsedaks* and *hessed*), the gifts men owe one another, in a horizontality of mutual aid and exchange. But the "horizontal" and the "vertical" orientations are inseparable from each other. In the Hebrew Bible, and then in the Gospels, the aid the good man provides to others has the value of a gift made to God, and will be reciprocated sooner or later as a favor from Him.

"Give Me to Drink"

The Psalms and the books of the prophets seem to retain the memory of the scene in
91 which the angel helps Hagar and her child (Genesis 21:14–19), and the scene where
40 Rebekah offers a drink to the messenger of Abraham: "And the servant ran to meet her and said, Let me, I pray thee, drink a little water of thy pitcher. And she said, Drink, my lord: and she hasted, and let down her pitcher upon her hand, and gave him drink" (Genesis 24:17–18). In a literal reading at least, this is merely generous hospitality. Yet it is the model for the verses in Psalm 107:4–6 and in this passage from Isaiah: "Ho, every one that thirsteth, come ye to the waters, and he that hath no money; come ye, buy, and eat; yea, come, buy wine and milk without money and without price" (Isaiah 55:1).[95] This text, among others (e.g., Isaiah 41:18), is in turn the model elaborated in one of the Hymns of the Master of Justice,[96] and in the story of the woman of Samaria. Jesus meets the woman of Samaria at Jacob's well and repeats to her the words of Abraham's servant: "Give me to drink." The woman of Samaria is astonished at this request made by a Jew, that is, by a stranger. Jesus answers: "If thou knewest the gift of God, and who it is that saith to thee, Give me to drink; thou wouldest have asked of him, and he would have given thee living water" (John 4:7–10). The one who first asked for the (horizontal, symmetrical) gift of hospitality reveals that he is in fact the one who dispenses the (vertical, asymmetrical) gift of salvation. Whoever drinks of that water shall never thirst again (John 7:37–38).

Behind the word "largesse," we discovered the Latin *largus, largitio,* and with it, waves and an abundance of churning and running water. We have seen the ostentatious *sparsio* develop one of the meanings of that abundance. In fact, however, Saint Jerome's Latin translation of the Bible uses words from that family only rarely. Once, in Psalm 112:9, we find the verb *dispersit* (*eskorpisen* in the Septuagint), used in the sense of scattering goods. It is modified by the expression *dedit pauperibus.* The passage is rendered in the King James Bible as: "He hath dispersed, he hath given to the poor."[97] The image

95. I am attempting here to summarily follow the thread of a motif (the spring, the fountain), which numerous interpreters, both orthodox and heterodox, have embraced. Madame Guyon, the quietist mystic, devoted a book to this subject, the *Torrents spirituels* (1704), which goes so far as to make every soul a spring or torrent.

96. "Hymn O," *La Bible: Ecrits intertestamentaires,* ed. André Dupont-Sommer and Marc Philonenko (Paris: Gallimard, "Bibliothèque de la Pléiade," 1987), 264–69.

97. The psalm praises the good man. The King James Version reads: "A good man sheweth favour and lendeth" (Psalm 112:5). A note preceding the passage in Le Maistre de Stacy's French translation declares: "This good man, of whom it is said that his posterity will be powerful on the earth, is properly speaking of the good man par excellence, Jesus Christ himself, the head and father of all good men."

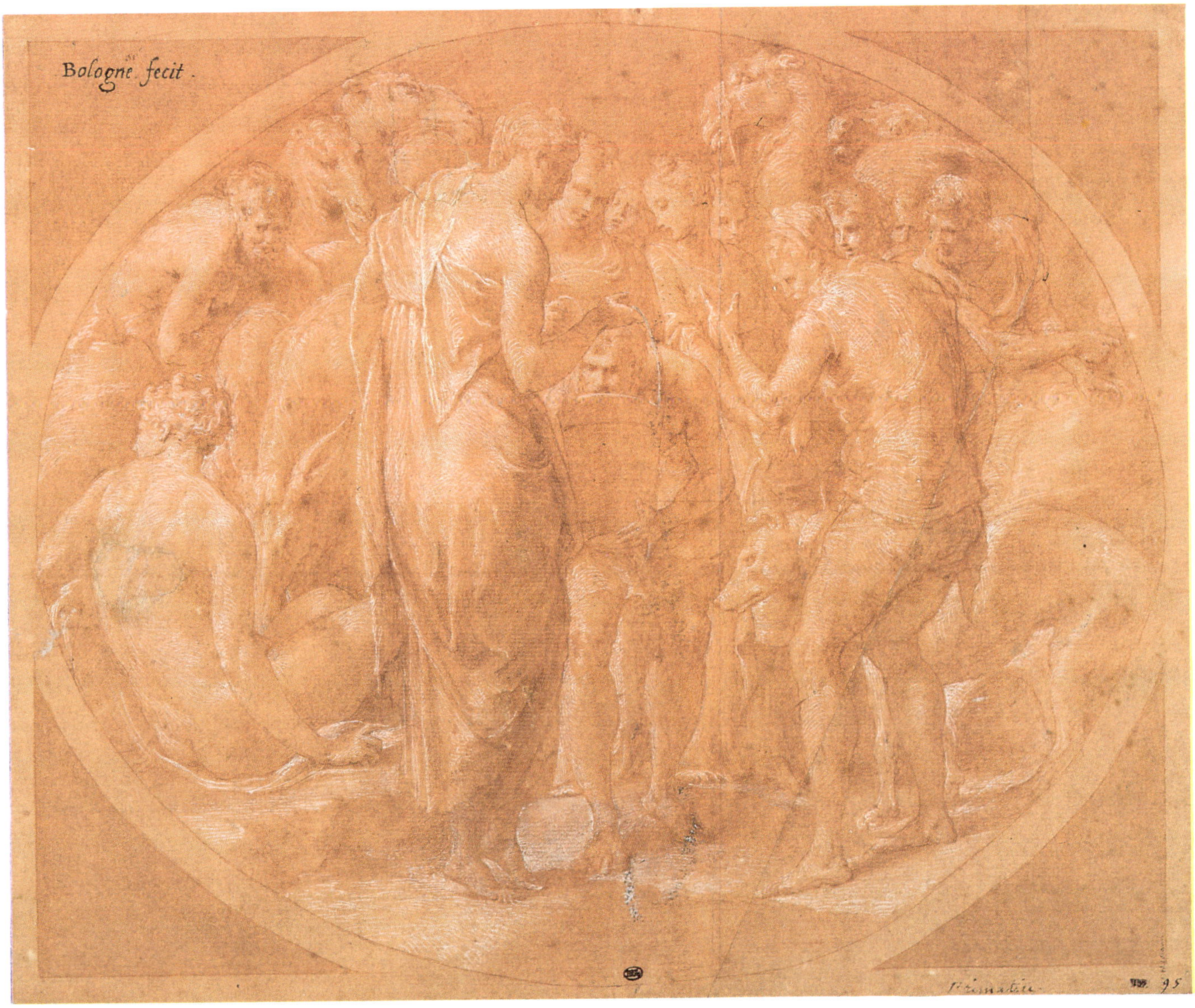

40. Primaticcio, *Eliezer and Rebekah,* Louvre Museum.

of living water, in the most striking use made of it in the Bible, is applied not to the wealth and riches given, but rather to the spring that wells up in those who give to the
49-57 poor and who are righteous. The spring is internal, and it is the reward for charity. In a passage from Isaiah 58:7–11, which serves as the foundation for all later texts on the works of mercy, we read, in the King James Version:

> *Is it* not to deal thy bread to the hungry [that we fasted], and that thou bring the poor that are cast out to thy house? when thou seest the naked, that thou cover him; and that thou hide not thyself from thine own flesh? . . . And *if* thou draw out thy soul to the hungry, and satisfy the afflicted soul; then shall thy light rise in obscurity, and thy darkness *be* as the noon day: And the Lord shall guide thee continually, and satisfy thy soul in drought, and make fat thy bones: and *thou shalt be like a watered garden, and like a spring of water, whose waters fail not.* (My emphasis)

In this internal spring, we make out the echo not only of the request made to Rebekah, but also of the spring that rose up from the earth in the Garden of Eden, as recounted in Genesis, even before the mention of the four rivers.[98] We are reminded of the water
41 that, to satisfy the people's thirst in the desert, gushes forth from the rock struck by Moses (Exodus 17:5–6),[99] water alluded to in Psalms 107:35 and 114:8.[100]

The water given to the thirsting people in the account of the exodus takes on a "symbolic" sense when it wells up in the man who gives to the indigent. As latecomers to the text, we have learned to give a "spiritual" sense to what first occurred "literally," in external space. We venture to interpret the striking of the rock allegorically, adding a tropological and moral sense to the historical sense of the account. In Isaiah, then in numerous gospel texts derived from it (including the pericope of the woman of Samaria), the light or spring that wells up within the charitable person is considered the divine
43 return gift, the very presence of God.[101] Hence the invitation to give alms to the humble is associated with the promise of an inestimable reward in another place and time. The merciful act performed in an individual's history (the historical sense of the narrative) finds a counterpart in the unquantifiable parity corresponding to it in the economy of salvation (the anagogical sense of the promise). The "horizontal" gesture of charity toward the poor and humble is repaid through the "vertical" outpouring of divine grace, and through the righteous man's ascent to the kingdom of heaven.

45 The "bread of affliction" in the Jewish Passover, which is shared in memory of servitude, and of the exodus to freedom, and of the gift of the law, becomes, at the Last Supper of the Gospels, a sharing in the very body of God incarnate. The gift God makes of himself to men (and what reward is not promised them "on high") is grafted onto the gift men make among themselves, in memory of the captivity from which they have been delivered. This first gift is even obliterated by the second. Painters, always dedicated to

98. "But there went up a mist from the earth, and watered the whole face of the ground" (Genesis 2:6).

99. "And the Lord said unto Moses, Go on before the people, and take with thee of the elders of Israel; and thy rod, wherewith thou smotest the river, take in thine hand, and go. Behold, I will stand before thee there upon the rock in Horeb; and thou shalt smite the rock, and there shall come water out of it, that the people may drink."

100. "He turneth the wilderness into a standing water, and dry ground into watersprings"; and the god of Jacob "turned the rock *into* a standing water, the flint into a fountain of waters."

101. Revelation takes up this spiritual sense: "And he shewed me a pure river of water of life, clear as crystal, proceeding out of the throne of God and of the Lamb. In the midst of the street of it, and on either side of the river, *was there* the tree of life" (Revelation 22:1–2). This time, the material water of the first two narratives springs forth in the heavenly Jerusalem, among the last things. An anagogical journey is completed.

manifesting the incarnation, even at the risk of being taken for guiltily "carnal," have had the task of recalling the human gesture of sharing, the materiality of the food shared, on the horizontal tabletop prepared for the celebration of Passover.[102] They must justify themselves by offering enough support for an allegorical reading.[103]

But must the gesture of giving be offered to view? Not if we heed one of the injunctions of the Sermon on the Mount, which insists on the discretion the faithful must show in carrying out good works, if they are to receive their heavenly reward:

> Give to him that asketh thee, and from him that would borrow of thee turn not thou away. . . . Take heed that ye do not your alms before men, to be seen of them: otherwise ye have no reward of your Father which is in heaven. . . . But when thou doest alms, let not thy left hand know what thy right hand doeth: That thine alms may be in secret: and thy Father which seeth in secret himself shall reward thee openly. . . . Lay not up for yourselves treasures upon earth, where moth and rust doth corrupt, and where thieves break through and steal: But lay up for yourselves treasures in heaven, where neither moth nor rust doth corrupt, and where thieves do not break through nor steal: For where your treasure is, there will your heart be also. (Matthew 5:42, 6:3–4; 6:19–21)

At first glance, the image of the incorruptible treasure does not resemble that of the thirst-quenching spring. But springs and treasures have in common the characteristic of plenty. Both overflow. It is not simply a play on words to note that there is a wave *(unda)* in the endlessly repeated *abundantia,* in the verbs *abundare* and *superabundare,* which the Vulgate associates both with the perfect justice reigning among the disciples (Matthew 5:20) and with the gift of grace. In Romans 5:15–20, we read that "the gift of grace . . . hath abounded in many" and above all, that "where sin abounded, grace did much more abound."[104] And the gift granted by heaven is too abundant not to be redistributed. The apostles who have received can give in their turn—and just as freely—thus proving the truth of the master they embrace. The principal proofs—gifts of charity—are healings: "Heal the sick, cleanse the lepers, raise the dead, cast out devils: freely ye have received, freely give" (Matthew 10:8).

The Works of Mercy

Figural means of expression are many and varied. Spiritual overabundance, emblematized by water and the irrigated garden, can also take human shape, in the figure of the **46,48**
nursing mother. Such is the theological virtue of charity, incarnated in the nursing breast surrounded by happy children, which paintings exalt even in the paradoxical image of **47**
Roman charity—the daughter nursing her prisoner father.[105] The image is paradoxical

102. See Walter Magass, *Semiotik einer Tischordnung* (Linguistica Biblica, 25/26, 1973). The author studies the ritual of the banquet and insists on the symmetry between giving, taking, and sharing. Stoic thought was oriented toward a reflection on these gestures. Giving, receiving, and returning were the allegorical meanings of the three Graces, according to Seneca, who drew his authority from Chrysippus (*De beneficiis* 1.3). See the study by Edgar Wind, "Seneca's Graces," in *Pagan Mysteries in the Renaissance* (New York: Penguin, 1967), 26–35.

103. On this important point, see the catalog of the exhibit *L'allégorie dans la peinture: La représentation de la charité au XVIIe siècle,* texts by Alain Tapié et al. (Caen, 1986).

104. The Greek text uses the noun *perisseia* and especially the verbs *perisseuo* and *huperperisseuo.*

105. Christian iconology, particularly in the seventeenth century, made reference to a story told by Valerius Maximus, a pagan author from the first century of the Common Era. His narrative refers explicitly to pictural representation, the only appropriate means, he declares, for inciting the requisite admiration for the heroism of filial devotion. See "Texts on the Gift," no. 10, and *L'allégorie dans la peinture* (bibliography).

in that it reverses the natural course of time: it returns an old man to the destitution of childhood and regenerates him. It has rightly been linked to Saint Bernard's meditation on Mary, who is both the daughter and the mother of God. When the painter represents the act of nursing by Roman charity, he teaches that maternal love and filial piety are one and the same love. (Less troubling is the medieval emblem of the pelican—another figure for charity—nourishing her young with her own blood.) The daughter's gift of the breast to her father takes on a perverse meaning only if the libidinal level alone is perceived, because of an excess of literal flesh or the viewer's incapacity to read the scene allegorically.[106] Greuze barely escapes this peril through the energy of his lines, but still makes natural reality prevail.

49 In Caravaggio's *The Seven Works of Mercy,* the young woman offering her breast to her father represents two merciful works: feed the hungry and visit prisoners. At the top of the painting, above the intertwined angels, the Madonna and Child (perhaps added after the fact by the painter) contemplate the scene. The Virgin's face, it appears, is tilted toward the group composed of the prisoner father and his daughter. The gaze of the large angel is also directed toward them. Illuminated by the torch of the priest preparing to bury a dead body, the young woman is like the bright source of mercy. Prominent signs establish movement in this impressive work of art: the angel's right hand is dropping almost vertically, in an authoritarian gesture that could be either benediction or injunction; his left arm and hand extend upward, indicating the place of the promise beyond the painting. The angel imposes verticality from its position at the top of the painting, while the works of mercy are performed in the horizontal space of the nocturnal city.

The Sermon on the Mount recommends that the performance of good works be kept secret. But the teacher also recommends we not place our light under a bushel: "Let your light so shine before men, that they may see your good works, and glorify your father, which is in heaven" (Matthew 5:16). Which of the two precepts should we heed? Must we avoid showing ourselves to others and glorifying ourselves before them? Or must we, on the contrary, make our example shine? It is easy to imagine that, during the Christian centuries, those who mistrusted representation embraced the recommendation to secrecy, the invitation not to call attention to the gesture of giving alms. And that, in defending images against iconoclasm, others invoked verses that appealed to the idea of shining a light before men and spreading the Father's glory. When the imperative for spreading the faith through sensible means prevailed—during the Counter-Reformation, for example—churches and oratories were filled with images of saints offering their lives, being martyred, and then receiving the crown of martyrdom offered by the angel. Plays representing the giving of alms, presented at ceremonies by bishops and saints (Carlo Borromeo, Toma of Villanueva) were also performed in places of honor inside religious

106. In the iconological repertoire, the spurting of milk recalls Juno and the myth of the origin of the Milky Way. The breast that has dried up, on the other hand, is taken sometimes as an the emblem of heresy, at others as an emblem of melancholy. Serodine, a painter from Ascona after the manner of Caravaggio, depicted a beautiful figure of a woman musician vainly pressing her breast; the reading of this figure is still a matter of dispute.

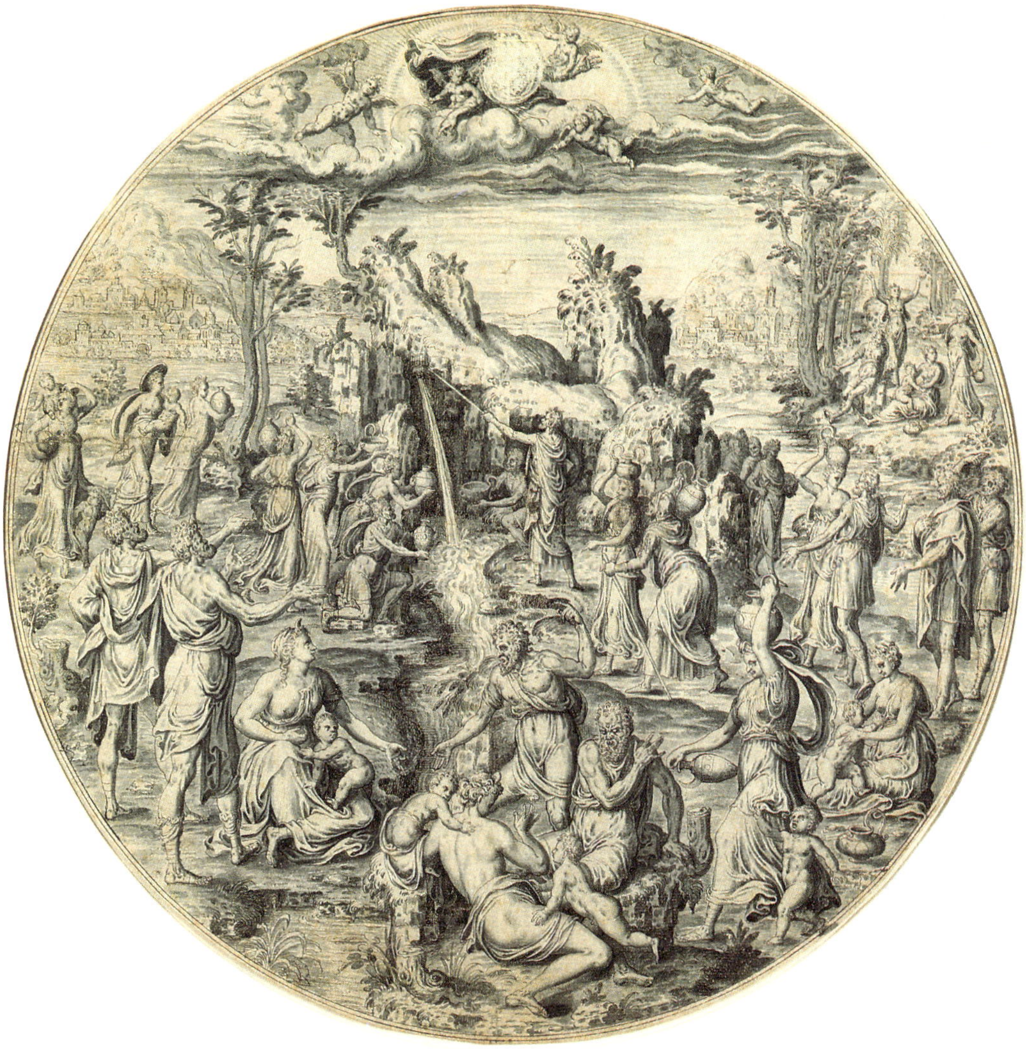

41. Frans Floris, *Moses Smiting the Rock,* Louvre Museum, Edmond de Rothschild Collection.

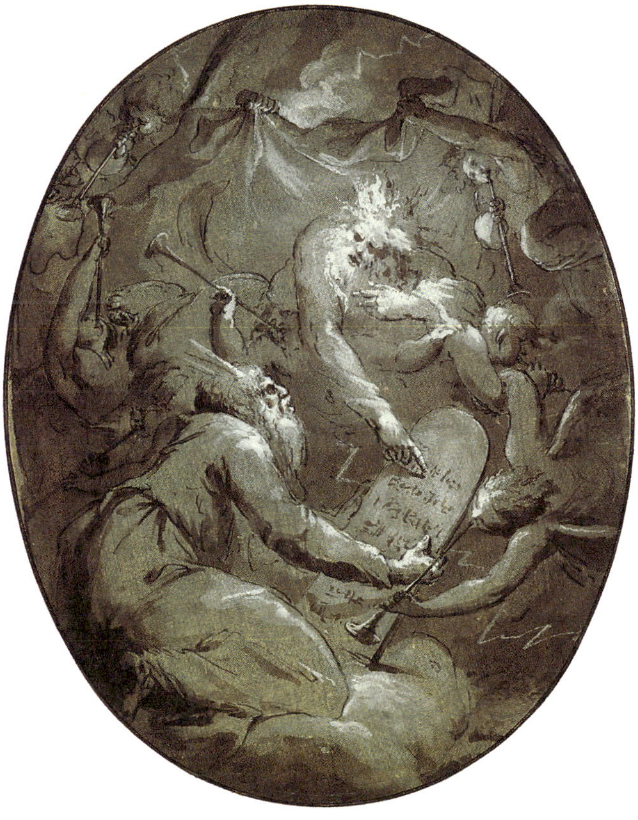

42. Jean-Jacques Lagrenée the Younger, *God Giving Moses the Ten Commandments,* Louvre Museum.

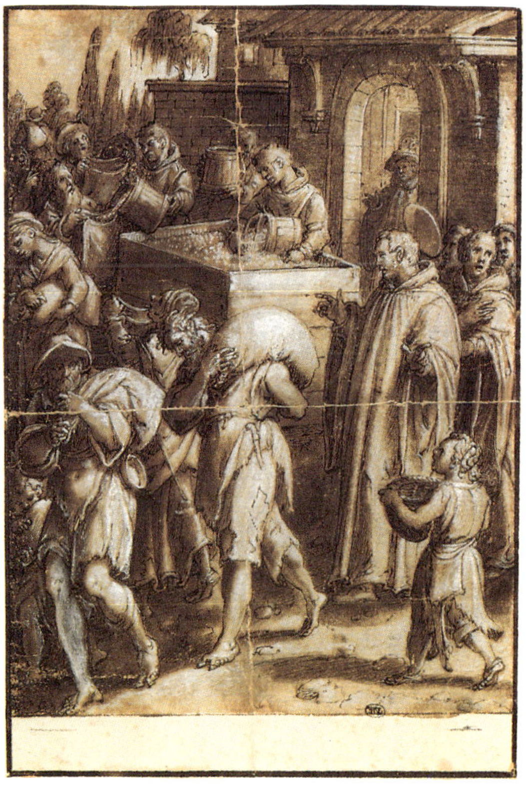

43. Jan van der Straet (Stradanus), *Saint John Gualbert Distributing Grain to the People,* Louvre Museum.

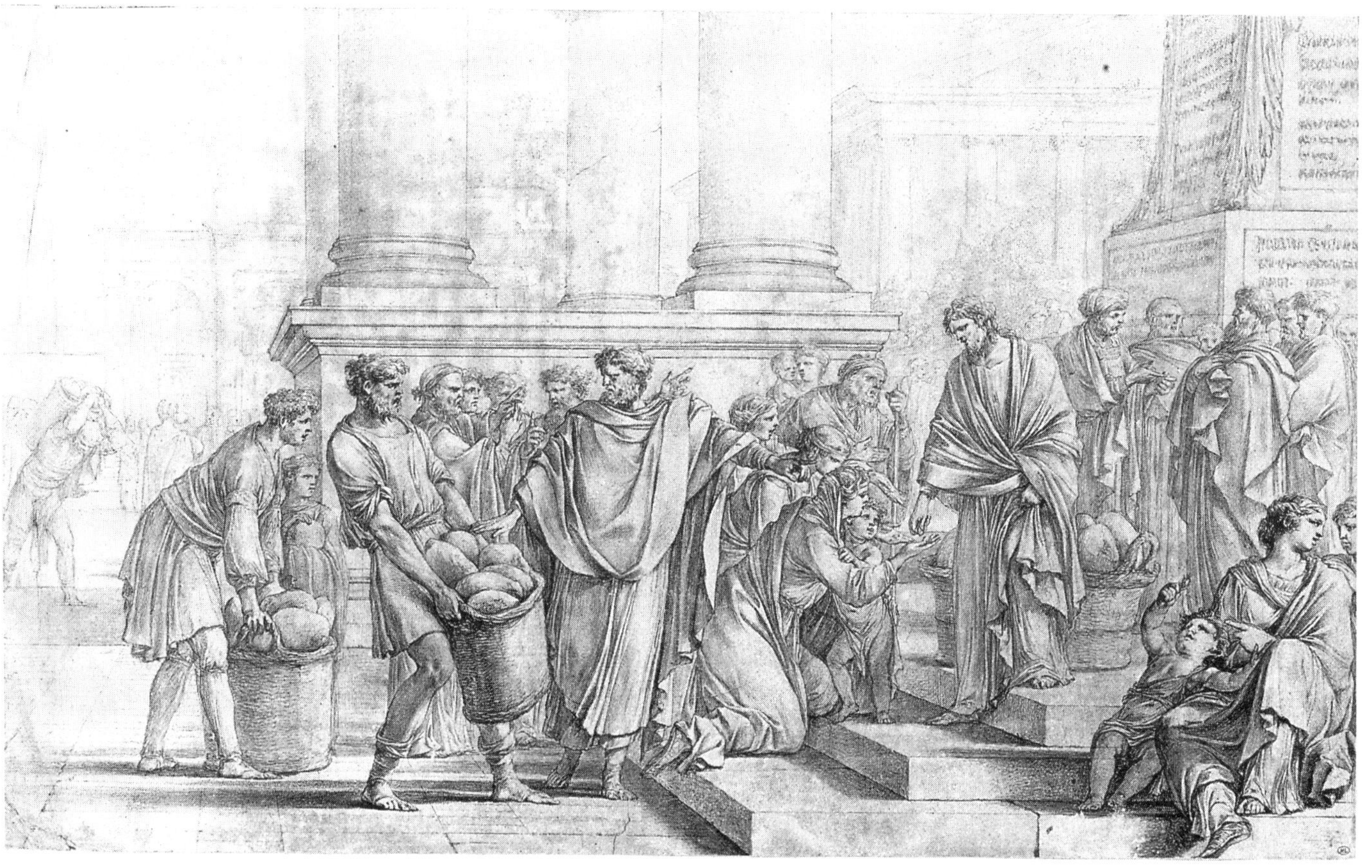

44. Laurent de La Hyre, *The Community of the First Christians,* Louvre Museum.

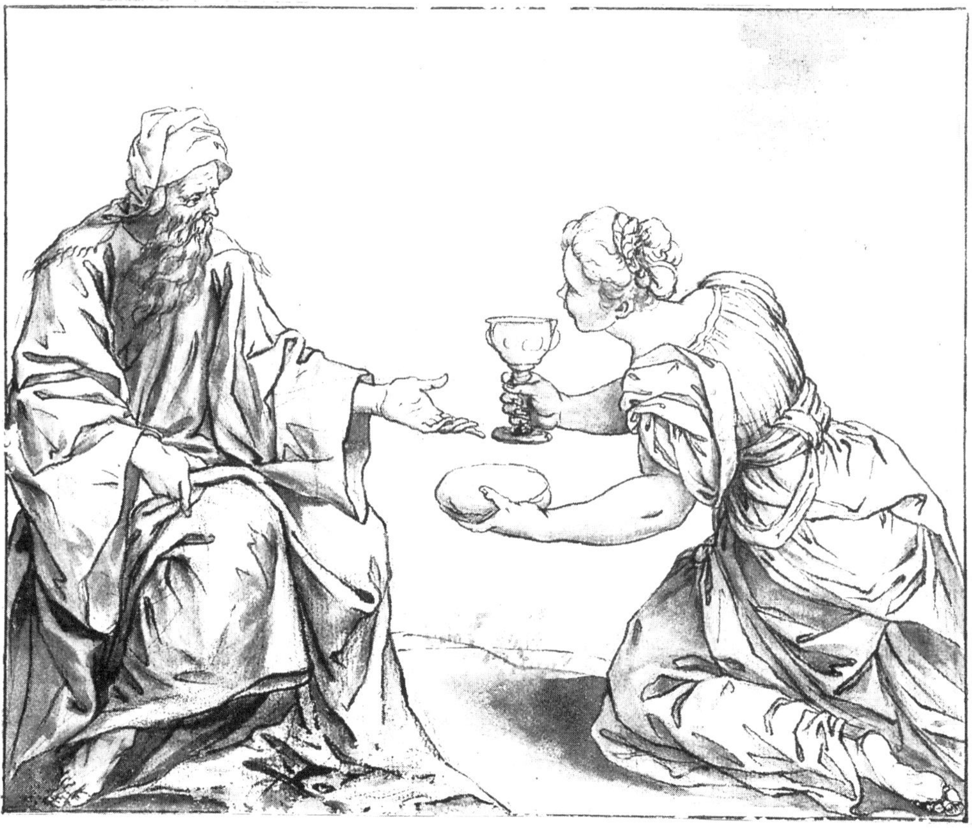

45. Sebastian de Herrera Barnuevo, *Elijah and the Widow of Zarephath,* Louvre Museum.

buildings. Caravaggio's painting, though it included odd effects of occultation and superimposition, belongs to the category of works that did not fear to offer secret gifts to view.[107]

In enumerating the works of mercy, ecclesiastical authors drew inspiration from 51-57
Christ's sermon on the Mount of Olives, which prophesied of Judgment Day. Six works are mentioned:

> Then shall the King say unto them on his right hand, Come, ye blessed of my Father, inherit the kingdom prepared for you from the foundation of the world: For I was an hungred, and ye gave me meat: I was thirsty, and ye gave me drink: I was a stranger, and ye took me in: Naked, and ye clothed 50
> me: I was sick, and ye visited me: I was in prison, and ye came unto me. Then shall the righteous answer him, saying, Lord, when saw we thee an hungred, and fed *thee?* or thirsty, and gave *thee* drink? . . . And the King shall answer and say unto them, Verily I say unto you, Inasmuch as ye have done *it* unto one of the least of these my brethren, ye have done *it* unto me. (Matthew 25:34–40; see also Isaiah 59:6–11)

Burying the dead became the seventh work of mercy, based on the example given by Tobit: "In the days of Shalmanesar, I had done many acts of charity to my fellow-countrymen: I would share my food with the hungry and provide clothing for those who had none, and if I saw the dead body of anyone of my people thrown outside the wall of Nineveh, I gave it burial" (Tobit 1:15–17).[108] In bidding farewell, the angel Raphael confirms the power of alms, in words that religious preachers would often evoke in the seventeenth century: "Better give alms than hoard up gold. Almsgiving preserves from death and wipes out every sin. Givers of alms will enjoy long life" (Tobit 12:9–10).[109] To console the old Tobit, whose story is so much less troubling than that of Job, the angel acted as intercessor for his works and prayers before the Almighty. And, after the long ordeal of blindness, Tobit recovered his sight through the attentions of Tobias, and 39
looked upon this beloved son, who he had believed was dead.

With the expression "give us . . . ," the beseeching prayer is directed to the one who holds within his power all material and spiritual goods (daily bread, peace, etc.). Since everything men possess must be recognized as a gift from God, men must thank him by performing favors and must share among themselves what has been given to them. The economy of the gift is a circuit that must not be interrupted. One of the definitions of sin (the creature's preference for itself) condemns precisely what, through human greed, 64
causes the circuit to be interrupted and dries up the source of new divine gifts. In the seventeenth and eighteenth centuries, especially during consecutive years of poor crops, the preachers and teachers of the monarchy returned to this theme insistently. Bossuet,

107. The works of mercy were often treated by seventeenth-century French painters, especially in the circle of the Le Nain brothers. See Jacques Thuillier, catalog of the exhibit *Les frères Le Nain* (Grand Palais, 1978–79; Réunion des musées nationaux, 1978).

108. I cite from the Revised English Edition of the Bible with the Apocrypha. See also Matthew 8:22, where Christ commands: "Follow me, and let the dead bury their dead."

109. See Irénée Noye's article devoted to the works of mercy in the *Dictionnaire de spiritualité* (Paris: Beauchesne, 1976); and esp. Léon Lallemand, *Histoire de la charité,* 4 tomes in 5 vols. (Paris: 1902–12); this considerable opus, marred by a polemic with a religious bias, was the first to speak of the "confinement of the poor" in reference to the police operation of 1656–57; Michel Foucault's *Histoire de la folie* borrows a great deal from Lallemand. See also the collection *La charité: L'amour au risque de sa perversion,* ed. Odile Gandon (Paris: Autrement, "Série morales," no. 11, 1993).

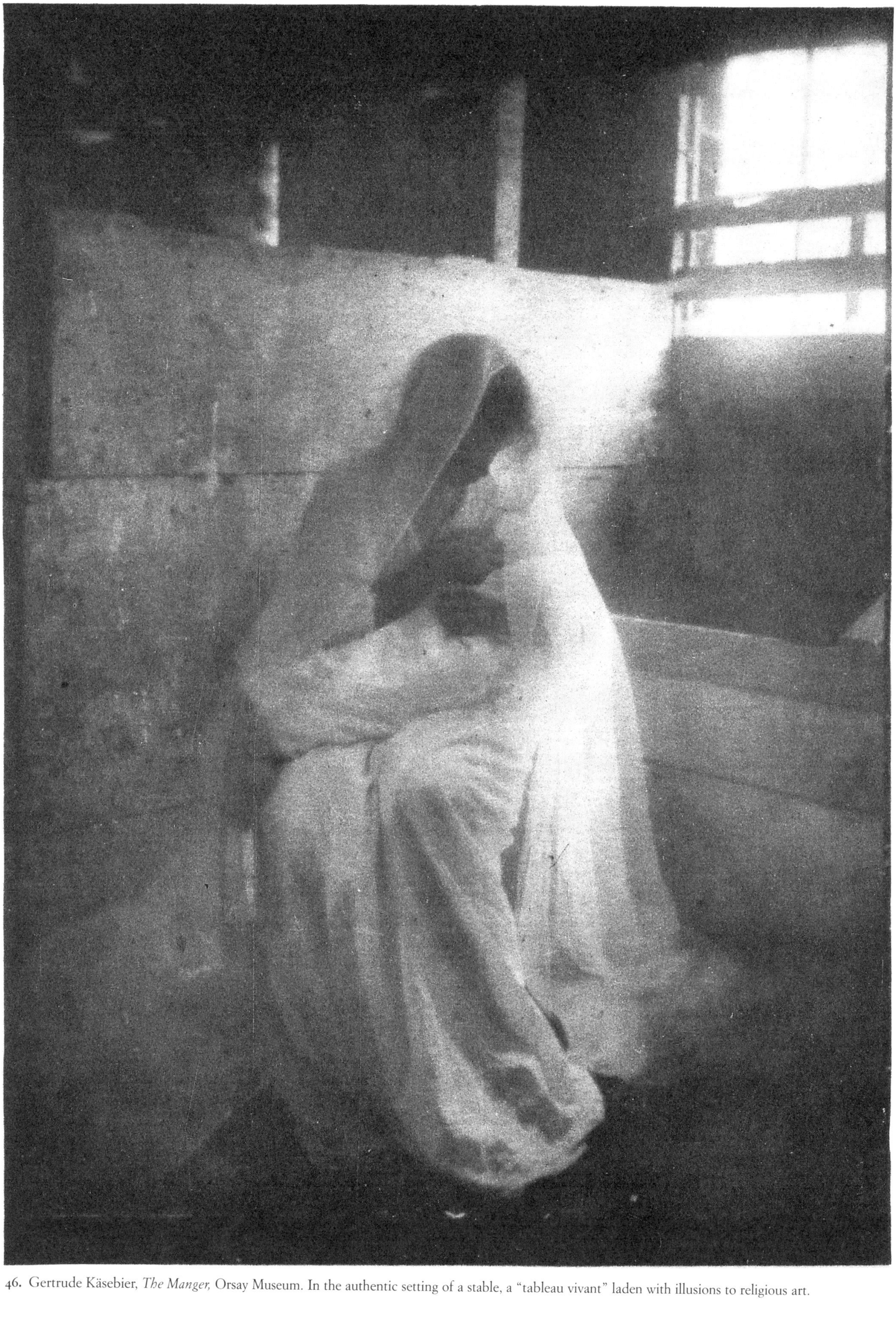

46. Gertrude Käsebier, *The Manger,* Orsay Museum. In the authentic setting of a stable, a "tableau vivant" laden with illusions to religious art.

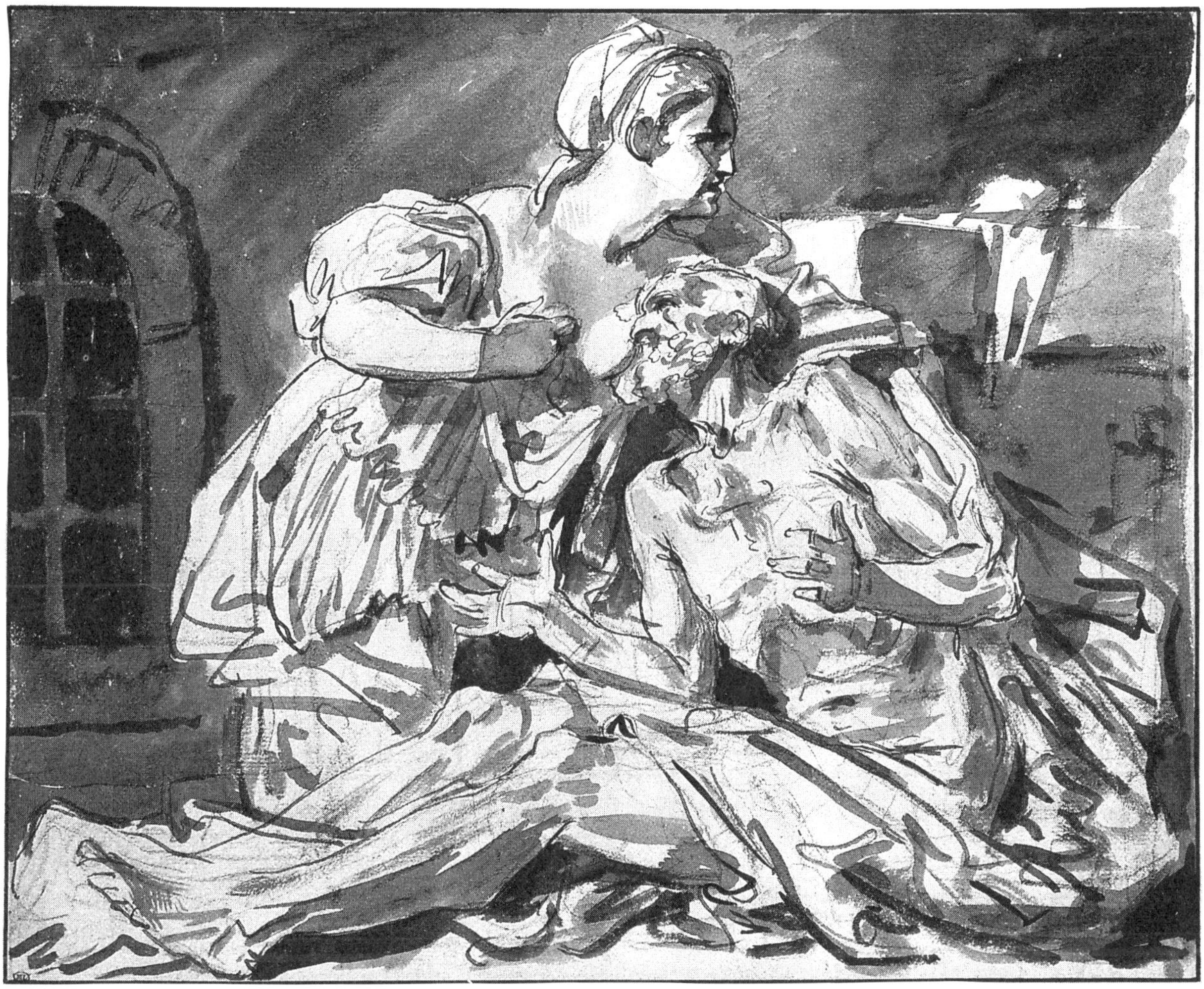

47. Jean-Baptiste Greuze, *Roman Charity,* Louvre Museum.

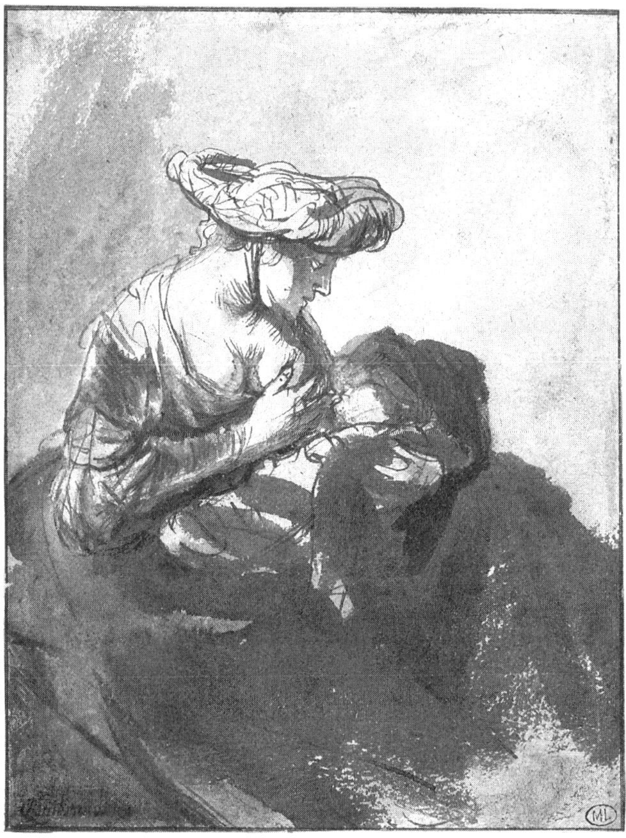

48. Ferdinand Bol, *Woman Nursing a Child,* Louvre Museum.

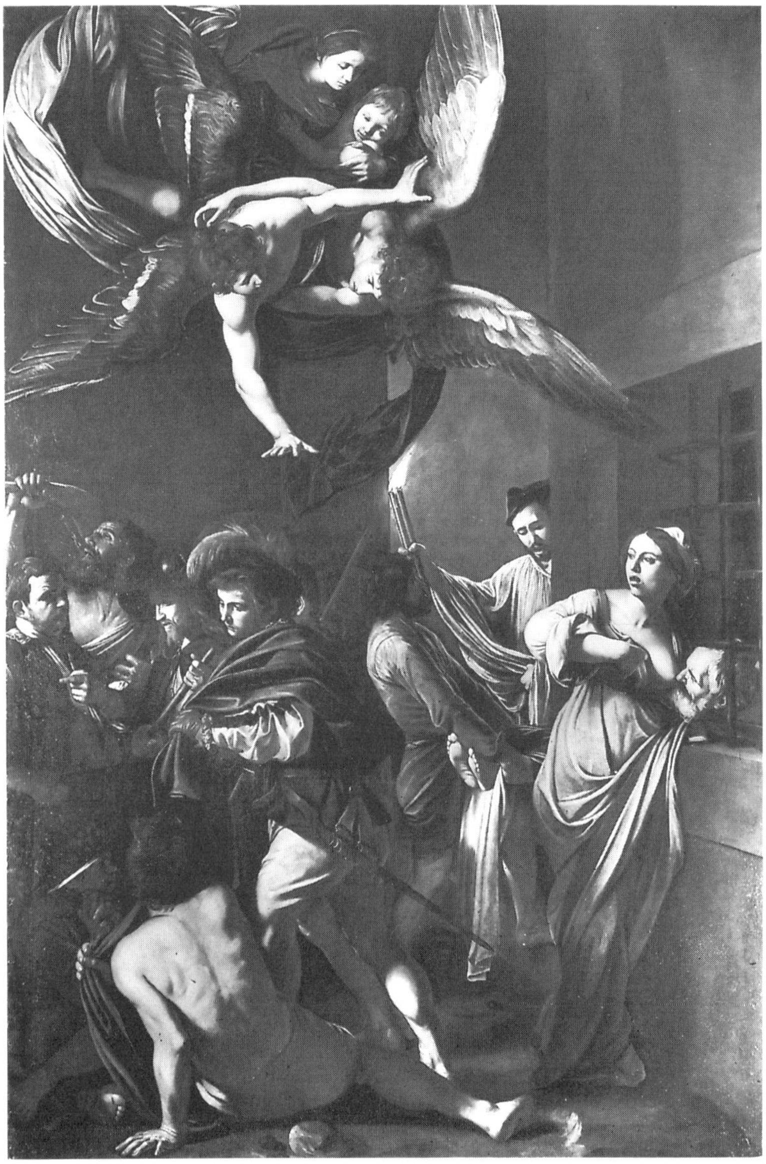

49. Caravaggio, *The Seven Works of Mercy,* Church of the Pio Monte della Misericordia, Naples.

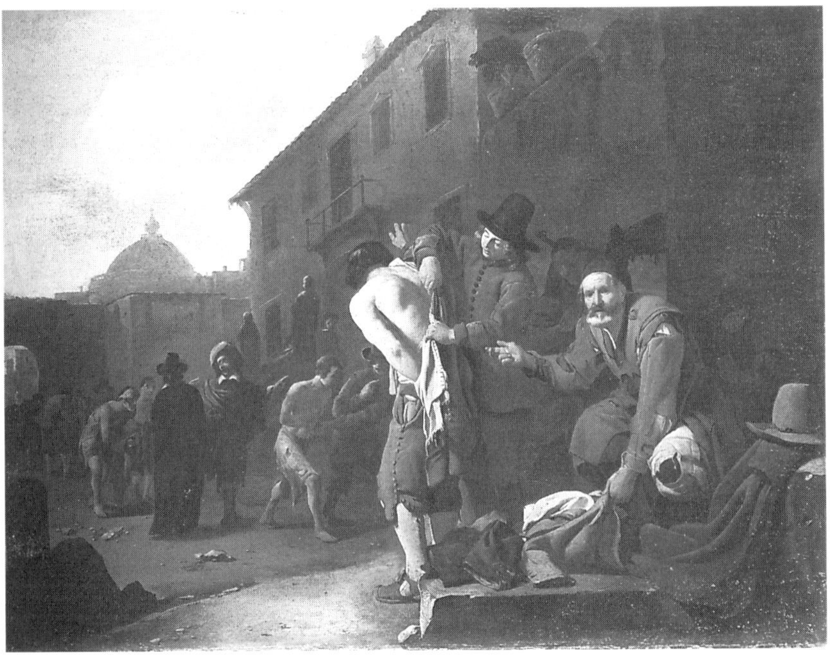

50. Sweerts, *Clothe the Naked,* Rijksmuseum, Amsterdam.

Massillon, and Fénelon vehemently admonished the court and powerful men on behalf of the hungry.[110] In contrast, the sacred orator repaid the beneficence of the powerful with the treasures of his eloquence. Funeral orations never failed to celebrate the charity of those who had been magnanimous and willing to help.[111]

The Poor

Alms are a gift of compassion *(éléèmosynè).* They assign a particularly important 82
role to the poor. Since salvation is to be awarded to the compassionate, it must be attained through the object of compassion: the humble, the sick, and the poor, in whom God is present. The gift that heaven will repay a hundredfold must be conveyed through the poor and humble. (We find analogous precepts in Islam, which echo those found in the Hebrew Bible.)

There were beggars before Christianity. They could be found on the bridges of Rome. The most ancient Greek texts (e.g., *The Odyssey*) mention beggars who were acknowledged as such: Iros in Ithaca, for example. Posted at the gates of royal palaces, they protected their territory. There were also philosophers such as Diogenes, who assumed the role of beggar on public roads. People gave as the mood struck them, most often a small coin *(stips),* but did not use the act as a pretext for assigning any particular merit to themselves.[112]

In an entire aspect of its teachings, Christianity commanded its servants to "bring in hither the poor, and the maimed, and the halt, and the blind" (Luke 14:21) to public feasts. By that means, poverty became the object of a new interpretation and, in many ways, of a new social behavior. Jewish law and Christian theological discourse in some sense *invented* "the poor man." The notion, of course, corresponds to a certain reading of poverty and not to the appearance of destitution itself, which all societies have known

110. See "Texts on the Gift," nos. 20 and 21, below.

111. "Look into this great heart, for it is what remains of the ancient greatness of the innocent man, the inclination that leads the magnanimous man never to receive except with difficulty, and always to give with pleasure. . . . That was the dominant inclination in Henrietta: she received thanks for her benefits only awkwardly, and was never known to refuse favors; even though her wit was capable as no other of providing that liberality so common to the powerful, which consists only in obliging words, she was persuaded that the powerful, who are made in God's image, should speak only in their acts. She loved to give to everyone for the sake of liberality; she loved even more to give to the poor, for the sake of religion; among them, she preferred poor converts, for the sake of Catholicism." Jules Mascaron, "Oraison funèbre d'Henriette d'Angleterre," in *Recueil des oraisons funèbres,* new ed. (Paris: J. Desaint, 1740), 127–29.

112. According to Seneca, the wise man does not feel compassion, which is a kind of sadness, a sorrow of the soul. He offers his help without feeling pity. "The wise man . . . will not suffer pity, because there cannot be pity without mental suffering. All else which I would have those who feel pity do, he will do gladly and with a lofty spirit; he will bring relief to another's tears, but will not add his own; to the shipwrecked man he will give a hand, to the exile shelter, to the needy alms (*stipem*); he will not do as most of those who wish to be thought pitiful do—fling insultingly their alms and scorn those whom they help, and shrink from contact with them—but he will give as a man to his fellow-man out of the common store. . . . And he will not avert his countenance or his sympathy." Seneca, *De clementia* 2.6.1–2, in *Moral Essays* (441–43), see n. 89 above. In another treatise, *De vita beata* (25), Seneca declares that whether he is in an extremely wealthy home or on the bridge of Sublicius among the poor who hold out their hands for alms (*ad stipitem*), it is all a matter of indifference to him. For Aristotle, Cicero, and Seneca, the charitable offering is an act that links friends. Small gifts are not charity. "Some services are too small to have the right to be called benefits. . . . Who ever called a morsel of bread a benefit *(stipem),* or tossing anyone a copper, or enabling him to get a light" (*De beneficiis* 4.29, p. 217). The term *eléèmosynè* was adopted late in Greek and in Latin, very probably to correspond to notions that were Hebrew in origin.

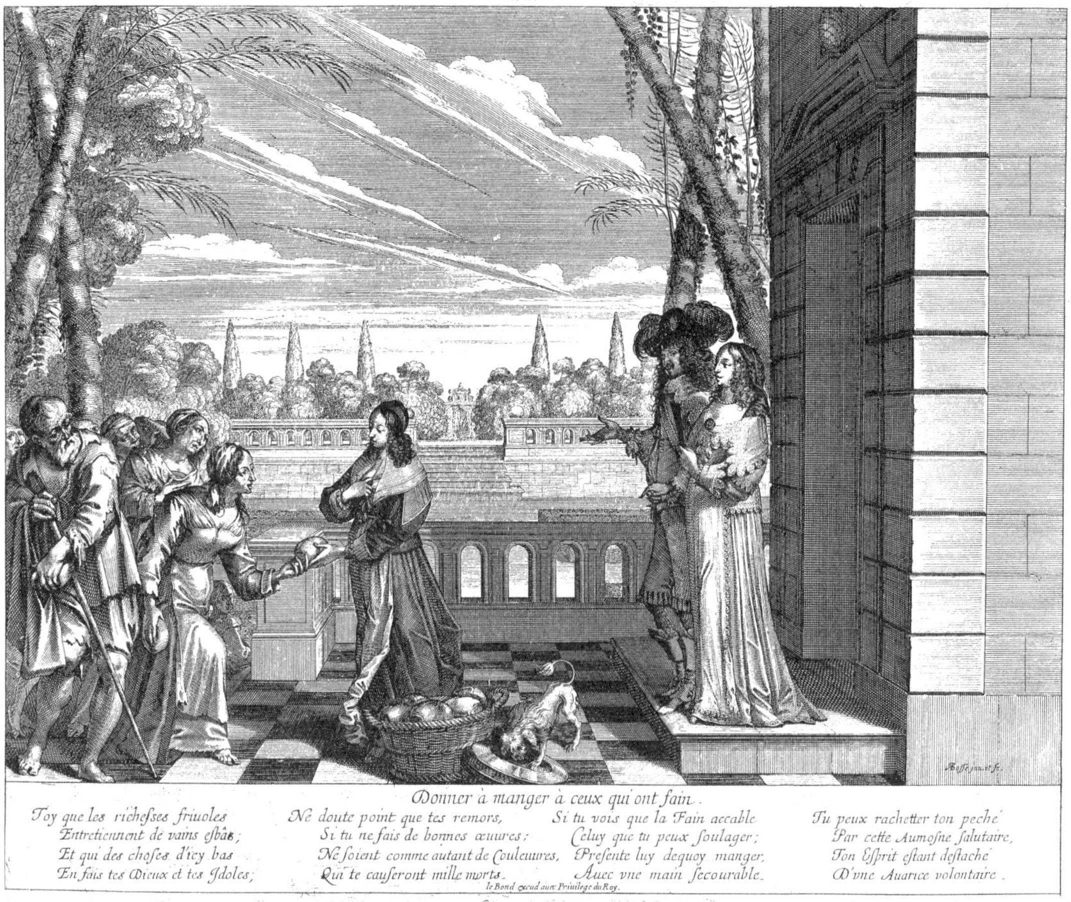

51. Abraham Bosse, *Feed the Hungry,* Louvre Museum, Edmond de Rothschild Collection.

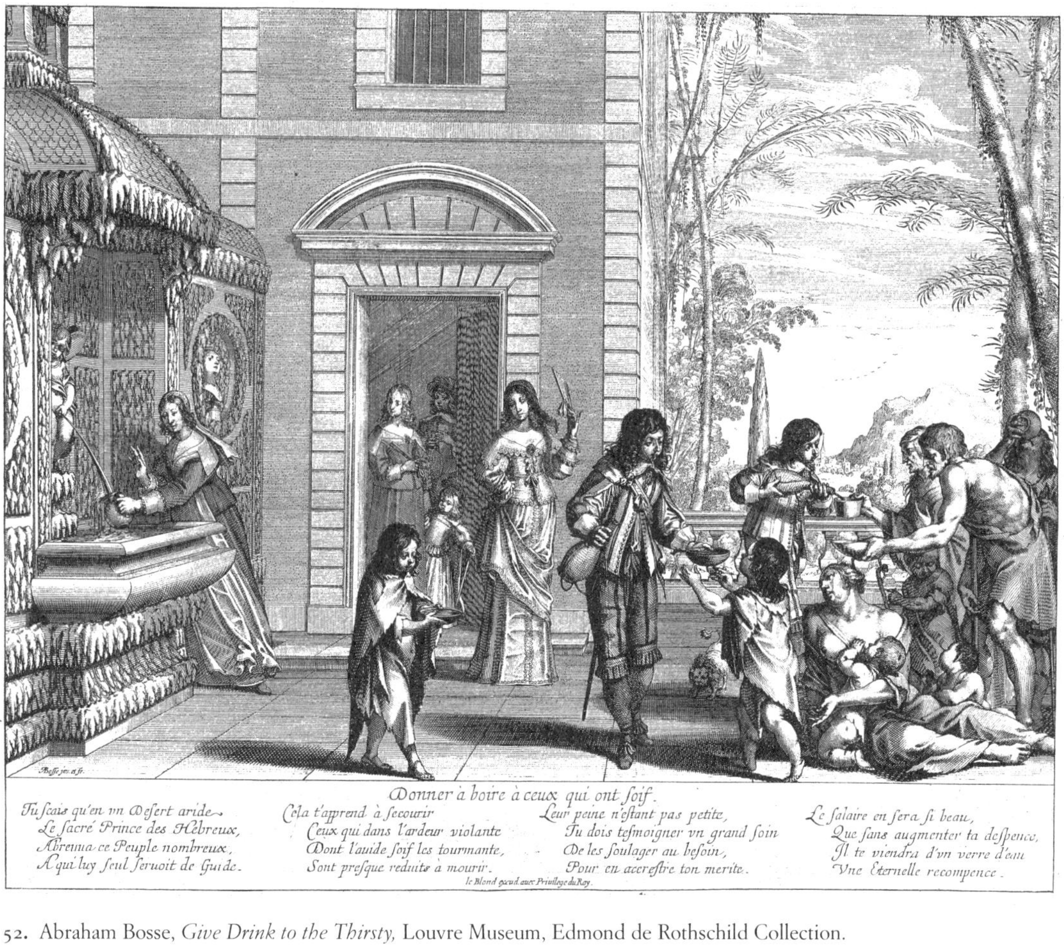

52. Abraham Bosse, *Give Drink to the Thirsty,* Louvre Museum, Edmond de Rothschild Collection.

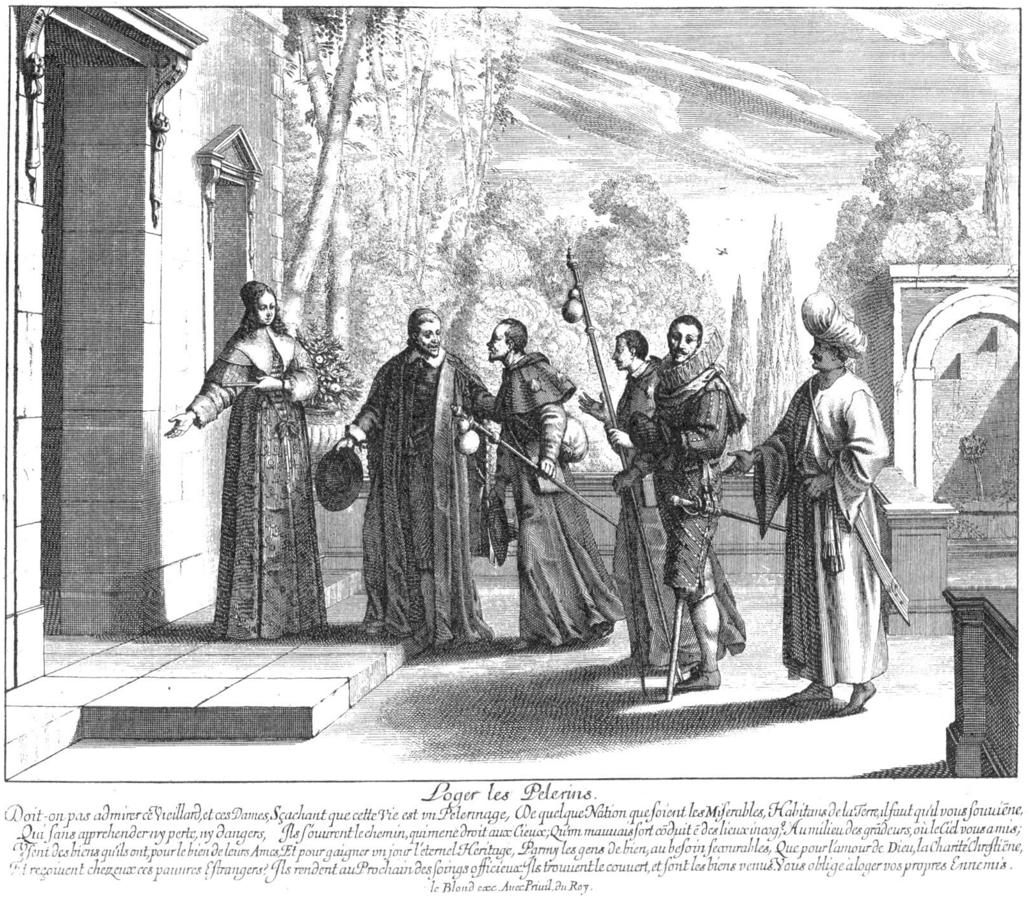

53. Abraham Bosse, *Give Lodging to Pilgrims,* Louvre Museum, Edmond de Rothschild Collection.

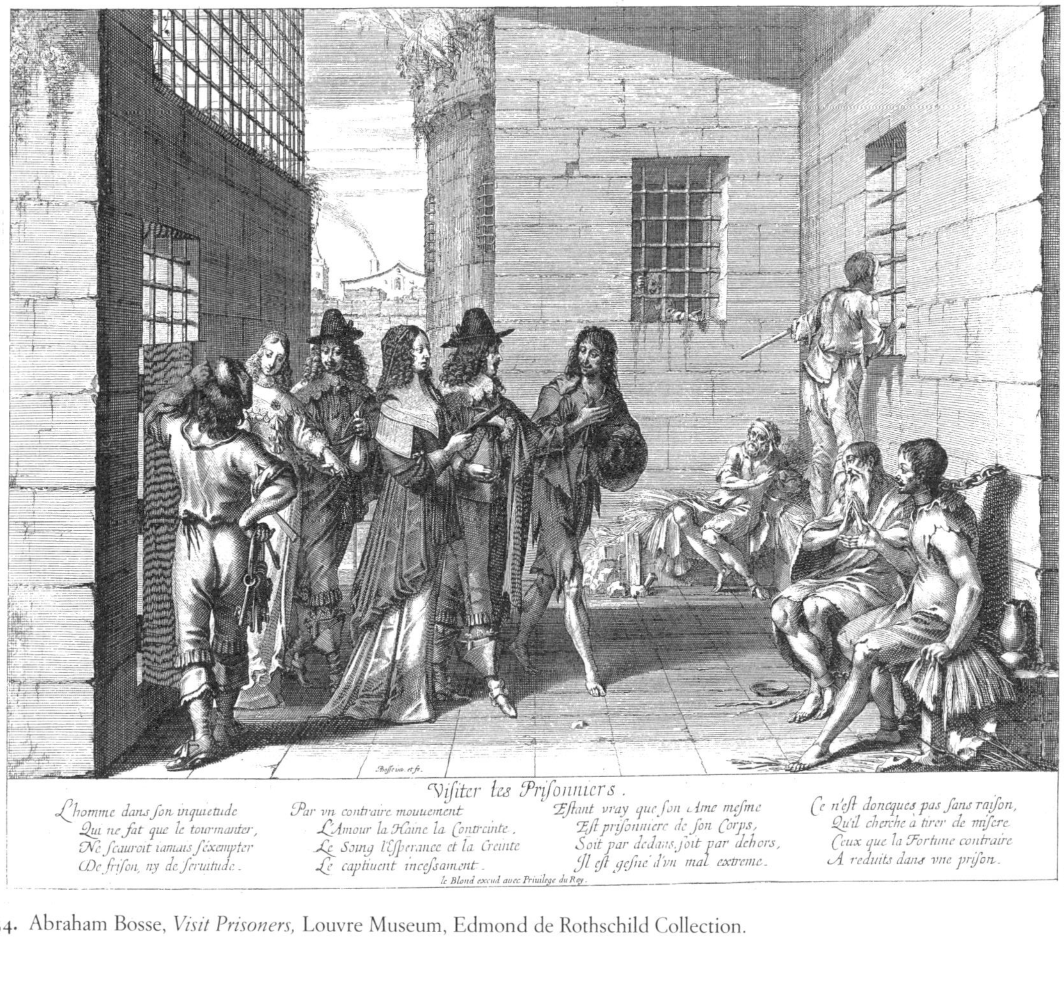

54. Abraham Bosse, *Visit Prisoners,* Louvre Museum, Edmond de Rothschild Collection.

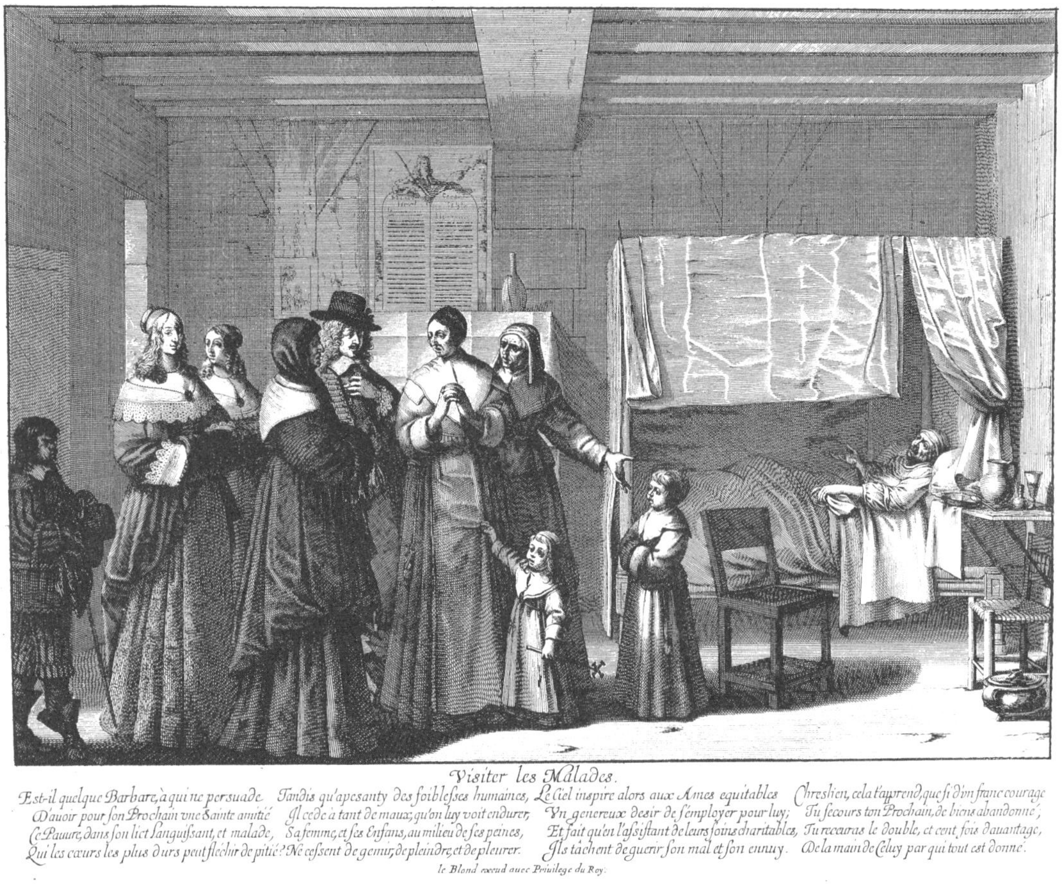

55. Abraham Bosse, *Visit the Sick,* Louvre Museum, Edmond de Rothschild Collection.

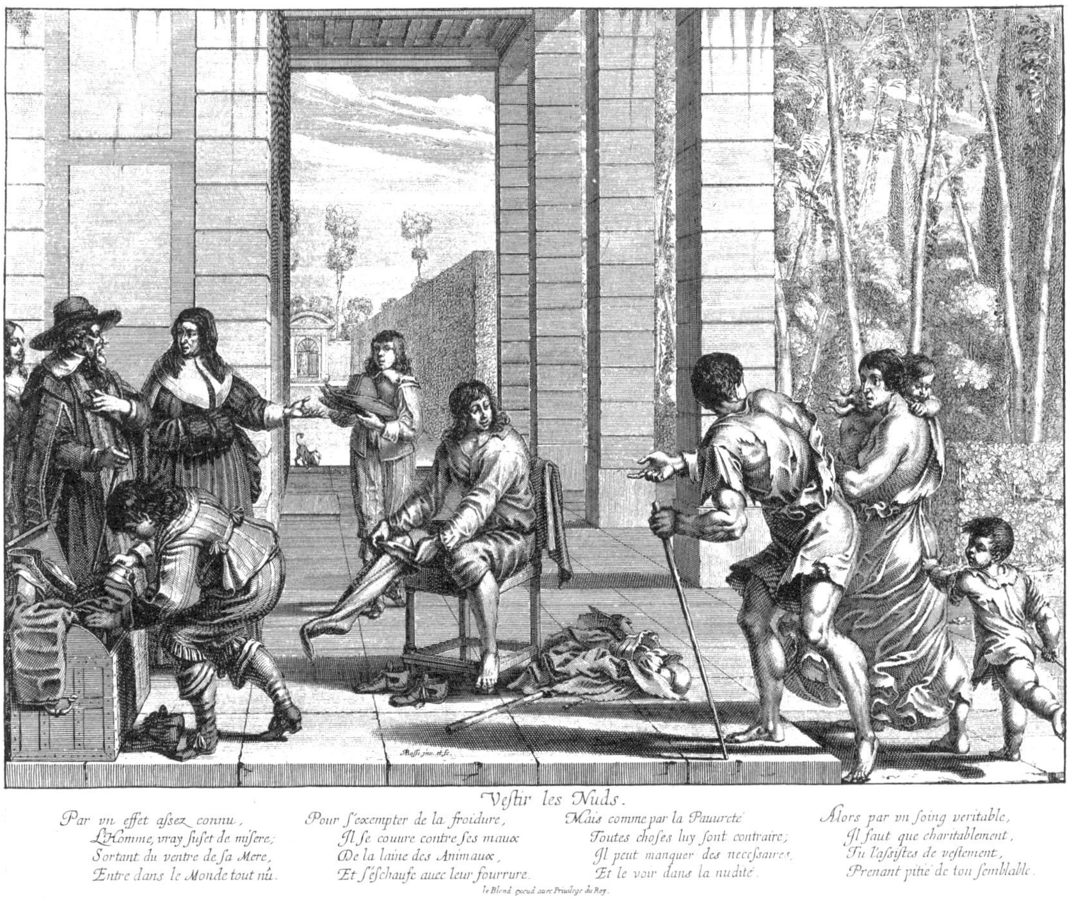

56. Abraham Bosse, *Clothe the Naked,* Louvre Museum, Edmond de Rothschild Collection.

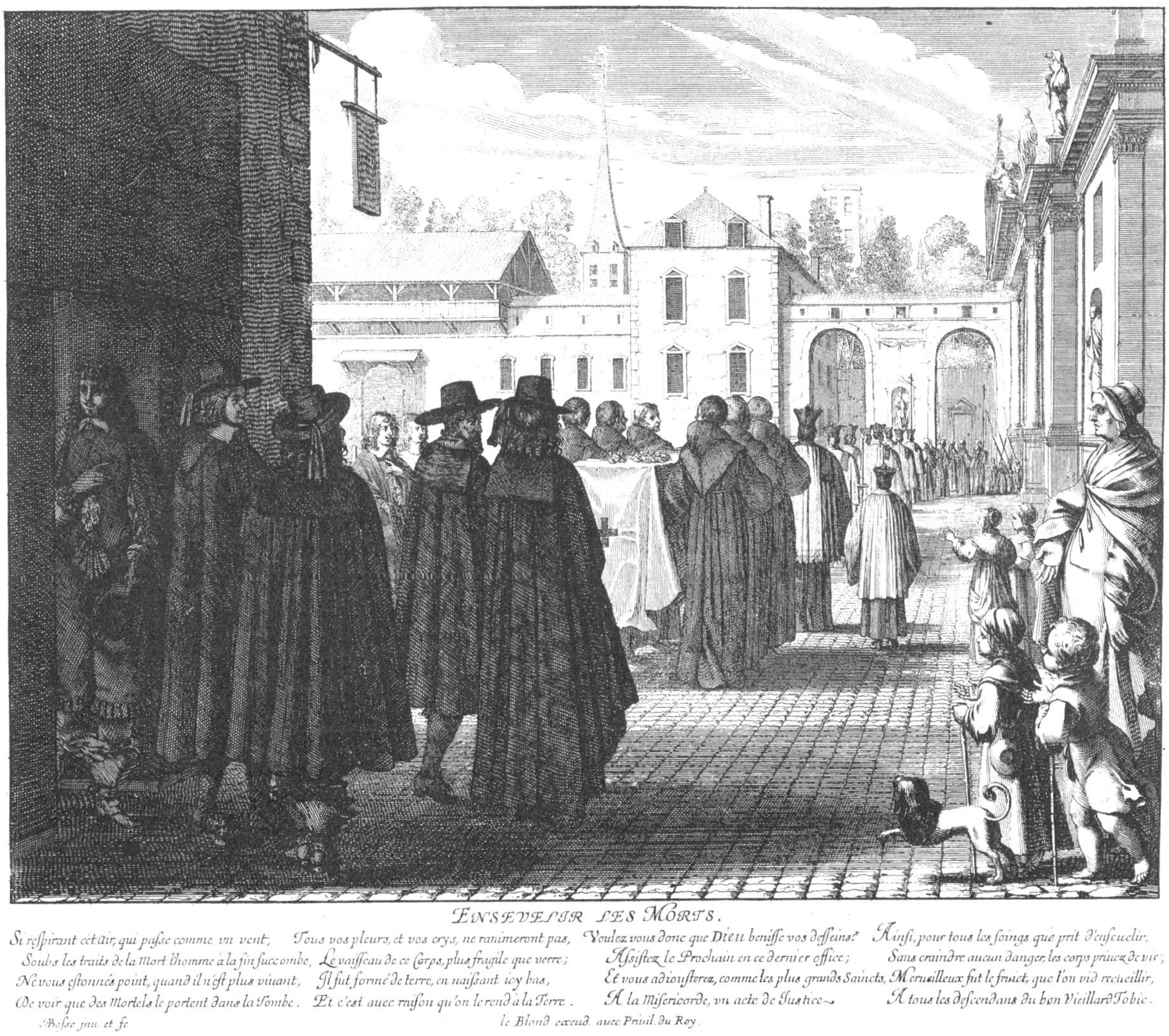

57. Abraham Bosse, *Bury the Dead,* Louvre Museum, Edmond de Rothschild Collection.

as a result of war and famine. Such a reading demanded a certain attention and played a considerable role in history, even though it did not lead to actual relief for marginals and the destitute. The theological exaltation of the poor awakened the consciousness of a duty, without, however, leading to the alleviation of the general conditions of indigents in the eras most marked by faith.[113] At the very least, hagiography produced many wondrous images showing the signs of heavenly favor that would reward those who served the poor.

58 In an admirable painting by Zurbarán, the roses that appear suddenly in Casilda's apron, in place of the bread she had hidden there, give a force of real presence to her piously deceitful excuse. Legend tells us that this daughter of a caliph, who had secretly converted to Christianity, was attempting to dissimulate from her father the food she was giving to Christian prisoners. The gift to the poor elicited the divine gift, which marked her as chosen and confirmed her conversion: the sign perfumed and exquisitely adorned the charitable princess.[114] Casilda's soul was occupied with thoughts of bread for the poor, and, through transubstantiation, the armful of roses bore witness to the fact that thinking of the subsistence of the poor is the same as thinking of God, who is omniscient in his grace. The poor serve as a means for revealing virtues and provide the opportunity for the floral signs that the painting puts to such good use. In fact, the miracle of the roses rewards Casilda for her boldness and for the gift of her own life, which underlies her act of compassion.[115]

Even beyond the charity given to the poor, the legends of saints manifest a familiarity with other supernatural gifts of flowers: as he is about to be martyred, Dorotheus meets the unbeliever Theophilus, who asks him to send fruits and flowers from paradise. At the instant of Dorotheus's decapitation, Theophilus sees a floral shower falling upon him: the sign is irrefutable, and he converts. Flowers from paradise remained a constant motif from that time on, finally finding expression in the romantic imagination. This time, they were associated with the power of dreams, and offered no evidence of the real existence of paradise. Rather, they elicited a question that remained unanswered. "If a man could pass through Paradise in a dream," wrote Coleridge, "and have a flower presented to him as a pledge that his soul had really been there, and if he found that flower
60 in his hand when he awoke—Ay! and what then?"[116] *The Dream,* a very beautiful painting by Balthus, depicts a sleeping woman and an odd character running toward her with
59 a flower in his hand (in a companion piece, *The Golden Fruit,* the character is holding a piece of fruit). Is he an angel or a demon? Does his gift come from paradise?[117] It is not up to the painter to decide the question.

113. Among the recent histories of poverty, see esp. Bronislaw Geremek, *La potence ou la pitié,* French translation from the Polish by J. Arnold-Moricet (Paris: Gallimard, "Bibliothèque des histoires," 1987). On preaching, see also Bernard Groethuysen, *Origines de l'esprit bourgeois en France,* vol. 1: *L'église et la bourgeoisie* (Paris: Gallimard, 1927), 178–94.

114. The story of Casilda includes episodes similar to those attributed to Elizabeth of Hungary, whose historical existence is more certain (1207–31). Elizabeth is the saint who placed a leprous child in her bed. Her husband lifted the blanket, and discovered with surprise the divine Child. Murillo represented Elizabeth of Hungary caring for victims of ringworm (Madrid, Prado). See Louis Réau, *Iconologie de l'art chrétien* (Paris: PUF, 1958) 3:417–21.

115. "Le miracle des roses" is the title of one of Jules Laforgue's *Moralités légendaires.* In this ironic and sorrowful text, the author may be knowingly proposing his personal variation on the hagiographical theme of Casilda.

116. Quoted by John Livingston Lowes, *The Road to Xanadu,* rev. ed. (London, 1930), 341, from Coleridge's posthumous collection *Anima poetae.* Borges speaks of this note of Coleridge's in *Other Inquisitions,* English translation by Ruth L. C. Simms (Austin: University of Texas Press, 1964), 10–11.

117. According to Jean Leymarie, Balthus was inspired by an English romantic poet. Coleridge perhaps? See *Balthus* (Geneva: Skira, 1978).

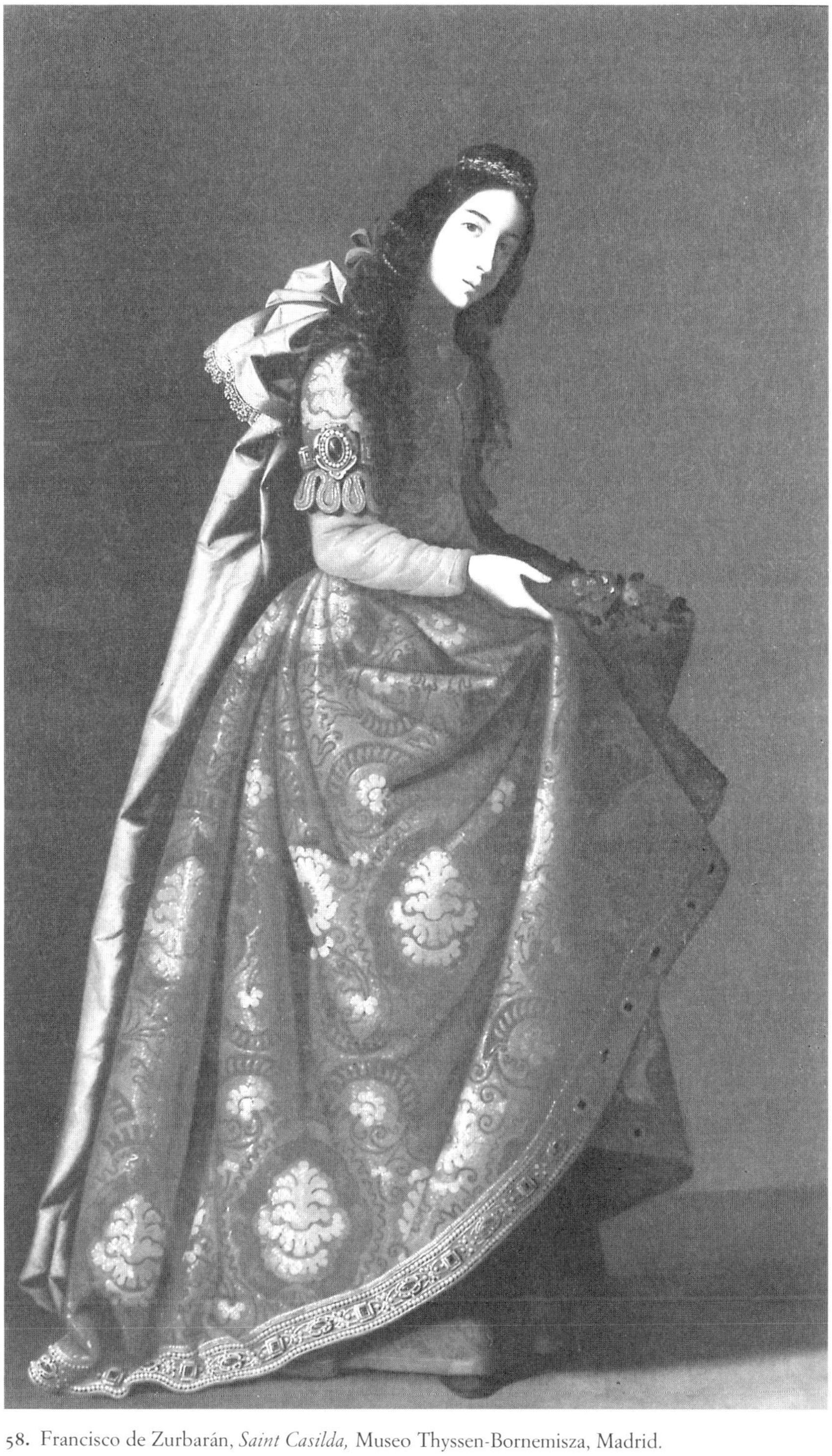

58. Francisco de Zurbarán, *Saint Casilda,* Museo Thyssen-Bornemisza, Madrid.

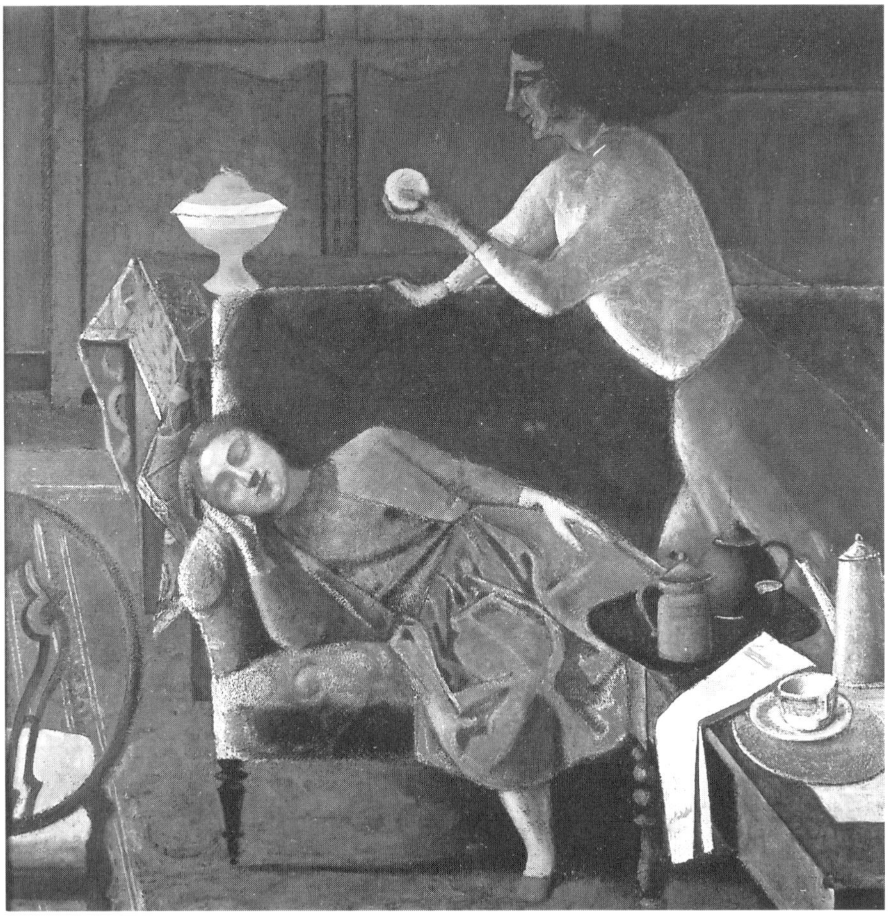

59. Balthus, *The Golden Fruit,* private collection.

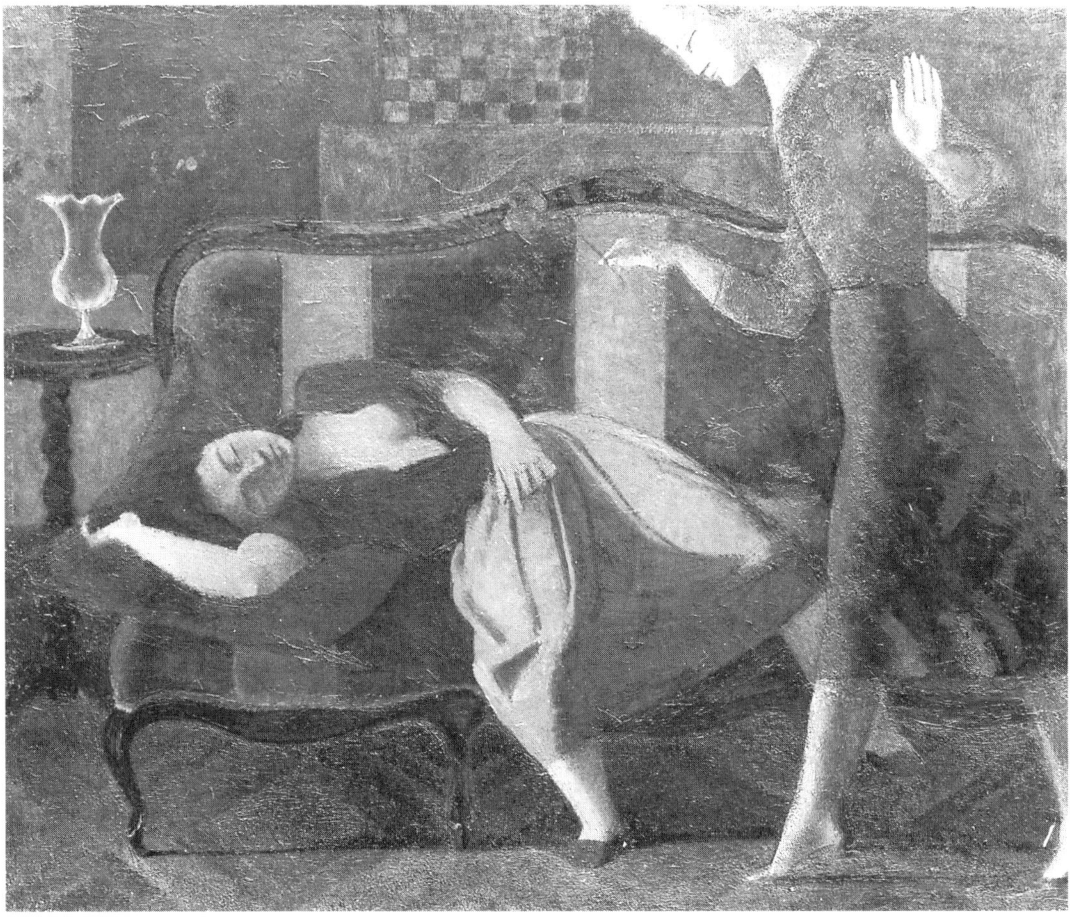

60. Balthus, *The Dream,* private collection.

The heightened dignity of the poor and the exaltation of the charitable gift gave
rise to a whole new set of problems. The images of the poor became more diverse and
produced an entire casuistry of poverty. For poverty is both a moral postulate and a
social condition. According to a radical version of the imperative, the true charitable gift
is a gift from one poor person to another. Most sanctified figures of charity, in fact, are
those who have become poor voluntarily, who have renounced all worldly goods, have 61
given everything away (Saint Alexis, Saint Francis of Assisi). They wished to be poor to 80
imitate the poverty of Christ and of the apostles. They had read that "it is easier for a
camel to go through a needle's eye, than for a rich man to enter into the kingdom of
God" (Luke 18:25). Often, they gave everything to a devout community, and they knew 82
from the story of Ananias and Sapphira, reported in Acts,[118] the punishment from heaven
that awaited hypocrites who did not give the entire amount they had promised. Often
as well they became beggars or seekers. Christ was thus doubly present, first in those
who imitated him in his acts of charity, and then in those who received that charity: the
poor and sick. They tried to imitate God inasmuch as God is the one who gives; as a 65
result, they identified those who received with God. And although this was not an occa-
sion to establish a holy equality among various conditions, it was at least an opportunity
to establish an equality in misfortune. The blind Gloucester in *King Lear,* roaming over
the heath, gives a purse to the fool (in fact, his son Edgar):

> Here, take this purse, thou whom the heavens' plagues
> Have humbled to all strokes; that I am wretched
> Makes thee happier; Heavens, deal so still!
> Let the superfluous and lust-dieted man,
> That slaves your ordinance, that will not see
> Because he does not feel, feel your pow'r quickly;
> So distribution should undo excess,
> And each man have enough.[119]

This would seem to imply that the poor man is expected to conserve, in his very obscurity, a virtue of patient innocence and purity: in some sense, he is required to prove that he is the victim of an undeserved fate, that he is enduring a Passion, and that he is thus the legitimate witness to the salvation of those who grant him his subsistence.

This results in a necessary discrimination. In fact, the role the "poor man" must
play in the economy of the salvation of charitable souls makes the distinction between
the good poor and the bad all the more indispensable. There are the worthy poor, who
hide their indigence and who have lost their honest means of existence; and there are
the unworthy poor, the lazy, the malingerers, the drunks, the gamblers, the debauched.
The good poor are the widows and orphans, those whom misfortune has chased off their 44
lands. Ruth is one of the models for that "honest" poverty. The bad poor, in contrast, 80
are tramps who make a career out of begging and who swindle in every way possible. 16

118. Acts 5:1–11. The primitive community (which resembles that of the Essenes) has just been described in these words: "Neither was there any among them that lacked: for as many as were possessors of lands or houses sold them, and brought the prices of the things that were sold, and laid *them* down at the apostles' feet: and distribution was made unto every man according as he had need" (Acts 4:34–35).

119. William Shakespeare, *King Lear,* 4.1.67–74.

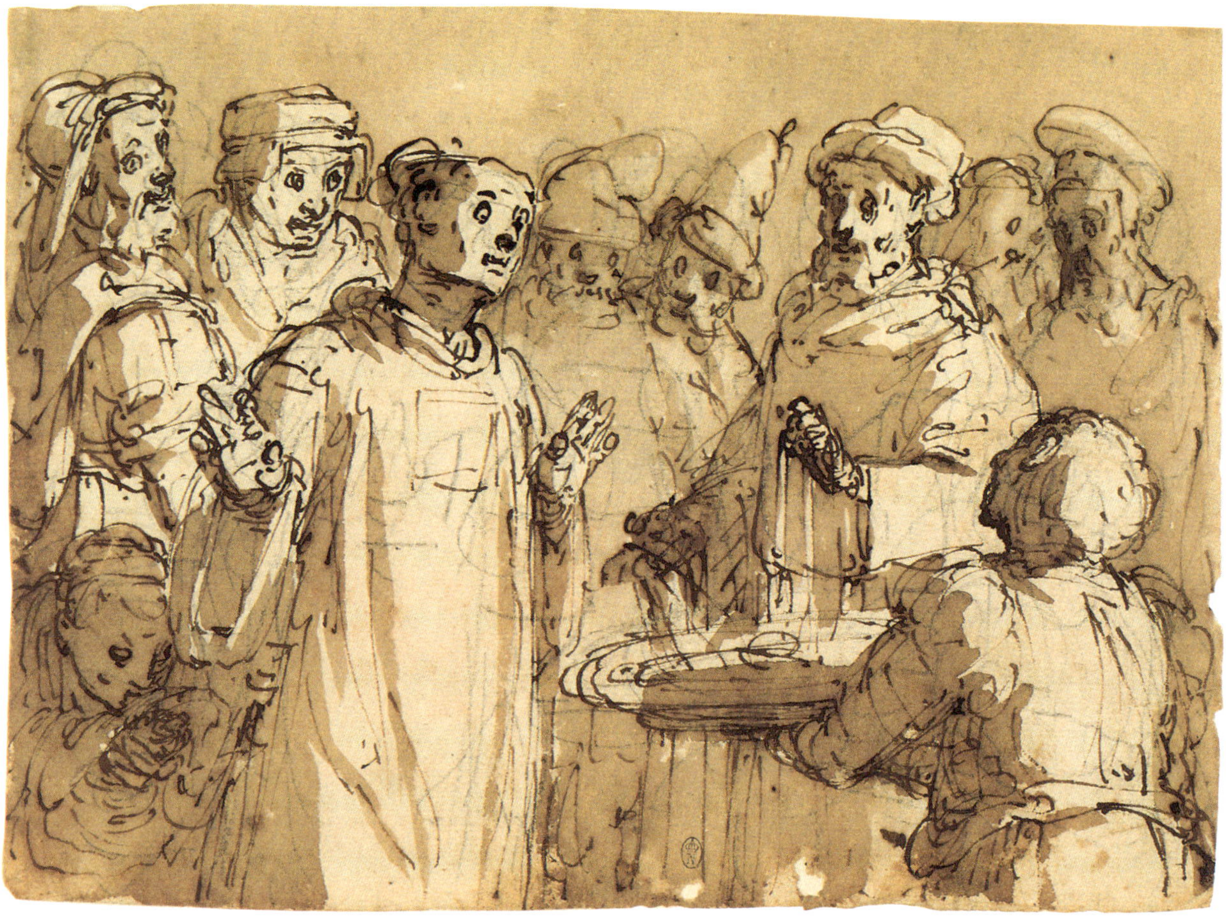

61. Giulio Benso, *Saint Leonard of Limoges Refusing Presents,* Louvre Museum.

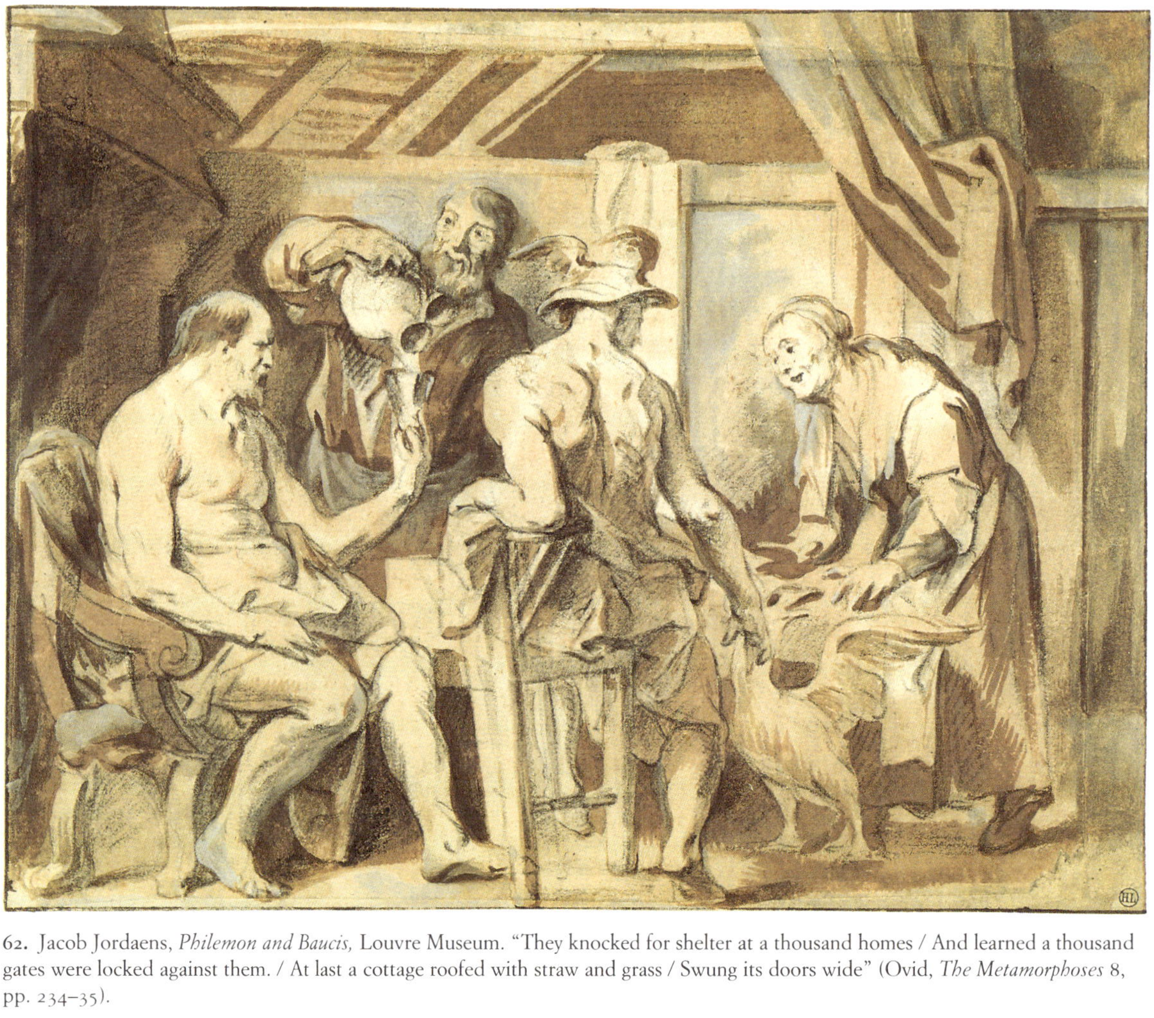

62. Jacob Jordaens, *Philemon and Baucis,* Louvre Museum. "They knocked for shelter at a thousand homes / And learned a thousand gates were locked against them. / At last a cottage roofed with straw and grass / Swung its doors wide" (Ovid, *The Metamorphoses* 8, pp. 234–35).

Among them are many children of Saturn, whose pleas one must take care not to heed. These are people who frighten: thieves, acrobats, pilferers, deserters. Among that gaudy **66**
band of marginal beggars are those who have betrayed the duty of piety: religious men whom the devil has seduced, pilgrims gone astray, hermits unfaithful to their vows who have become gyrovagues.

In a world that discriminates in such a way, Rembrandt appears to be a great excep- **63**
tion. In his compassionate look at the poor, he never distinguishes between the cohorts of good and the cohorts of evil. He is familiar with every grimace of the human face, but he does not ridicule or reprove anyone. There is only a single reality, rife with splen- **82**
dor and misery; no borderline separates the profane from the religious, the earthly from the spiritual, the biblical world from the ordinary universe. The same door welcomes all, whether it is the door where a family of beggars in rags presents itself today, or the door the Good Samaritan of the gospel parable had the injured man enter, when he paid the **65**
other man's share. Sarah gives Hagar to Abraham in an interior scene, simple and sub- **95**
lime. In Rembrandt's universe, the gift is simple and without grandiloquence, because it is one of the constitutive elements of that very universe, beginning with relation between light and dark.[120]

As urban Europe developed, the administration of charity became more orderly, and contrived to help only "Christ's poor," not "the demon's poor."[121] Beginning in the sixteenth century, this was one of the great concerns of religious institutions and municipalities. To suppress the delinquency associated with beggary, the "manual" distribution of alms was forbidden in various places: the works of mercy were to be practiced inside establishments reserved for that purpose, and individuals' contributions were to go to these hospitals. The Parisian police operation of 1656–57, designed to better assure "the confinement of the poor," was accompanied by severe penalties punishing alms given in public.[122]

This explains how a satirical and burlesque image of poverty could, for more than three centuries, be set against a devout image of charity. It is as if a certain anxiety had to be expressed, and then exorcised through laughter. Artists, often living from hand to mouth themselves, could in that way feel some sympathy for vagabonds, without excluding the most undesirable of them, namely, those who imitated every form of evil and

120. See Georg Simmel, *Rembrandt: Ein kunstphilosophischer Versuch* (Leipzig: Kurt Wolff, 1917), 141–95.

121. The expression is taken from Père Guevarre, one of the apologists for treating poverty in hospitals. See Lallemand, *Histoire de la charité,* 4:215–59 (n. 109 above).

122. Blaise Pascal had the idea of "two-penny coaches" to offer collective aid to the poor of Blois. But he preferred to give alms personally. Marguerite Périer, Pascal's sister, wrote: "He never refused alms to anyone, even though he possessed little, and the costs he was obliged to pay because of his infirmities exceeded his income. . . . He sometimes cried out: 'If my heart were as poor as my spirit, I would be very happy; for I am exceedingly persuaded of the spirit of poverty, and that the practice of that virtue is a great means for assuring salvation.' All these words led us to examine ourselves and sometimes to seek general regulations that would provide for all necessities, and we proposed them to him. But he did not find them good, and told us that we were not called upon as a group but as individuals; and that he believed the manner of serving the poor that was most agreeable to God was to serve them in poverty, that is, according to one's own power. . . . It is not that he found the establishment of general hospitals bad; but he said that these great undertakings were reserved for certain persons whom God destined for them, and whom he led there almost visibly; but that it was not the shared vocation of everyone, as the individual and daily assistance of the poor was." From "La vie de Monsieur Pascal," in Blaise Pascal, *Oeuvres complètes,* ed. Jean Mesnard (Paris: Desclée, 1964), 1:626–67. In one of his masterpieces *(San Toma de Villaneuva faisant l'aumône),* Murillo glorifies such "individual" assistance.

made beggary itself an art. Art lovers could make fun of this ragged and deformed world, which merited only laughter and not compassion. Jacques Bellange, an artist issuing from mannerism, sometimes engraved slender flame girls—saints, that is—and at other times
16 atrocious beggars' brawls. The grimaces and convulsive gestures of the beggars approached the demonic: like the crutch in Samuel Beckett, a long flute became a weapon that one beggar brandished against another.

A certain aggressivity, which we saw at work in the *sparsio,* thus persisted and spread, though somewhat at the margin of societies spiritually governed by the Church. That, in any case, is the sense we can assign to the picaresque, which developed on Spanish soil in the sixteenth century. In the admirable *Vida de Lazarillo de Tormes,* the young *pícaro*'s first master is a mean, double-dealing blind man with countless resources for extorting alms and gifts. Lazarillo, his scapegoat, finds a way to run away and take revenge at the same time. On a day of torrential rain, with the streets impassable, Lazarillo orders the blind man to jump. But he points him in the wrong direction: the blind man knocks his head against a post. Lazarillo thus commits an act that is the object of one of the great biblical curses: "Cursed *be* he that maketh the blind to wander out of the way" (Deuteronomy 27:18). Other figures, who can afford the high life, are less decidedly rascals than is Lazarillo's blind man.

66 And ambiguities sometimes remain. Where is the smiling clubfooted boy depicted by Ribera headed? Toward some den of thieves, to be among fortune-tellers, pickpockets, and infirm people who pick at their sores? Or toward a road where passersby who meet up with him can attain salvation if they take pity at his courage and respond to the note he is holding in his hand: "Give me alms for the love of God" (Da mihi elimosinam propter amorem Dei)?

For the Love of Humanity?

In ancient society, the practice of beneficence established a network of obligations and debts, which the benefactor did not expect to see discharged so quickly. The act of giving without being paid in return placed a man almost among the ranks of the divine. The poet Rabirius evokes the triumvir Marc Antony, after his defeat at Actium, crying out: "I no longer have anything but what I gave away." Seneca admired this and commented: "One must count as true possessions our goods that, given away, have changed names, becoming forever benefits."[123] The idea is fixed with a line from Martial: "The only riches you will always possess are those you have given away" (Quas dederis, solas semper hebebis opes). Only the god of the Stoics could give without expecting anything in return; for them, that expectation would have been a lack incompatible with divine perfection.

In contrast, the Christian who gives alms, if he has taken the promises of Scripture too literally, makes heaven indebted to him. Wages *(misthos)* are promised in return for

123. Seneca, *De beneficiis,* 6.3: "The wealth that you esteem, that, as you think, makes you rich and powerful, is buried under an inglorious name so long as you keep it. It is but house, or slave, or money; when you have given it away, it is a benefit" (p. 369).

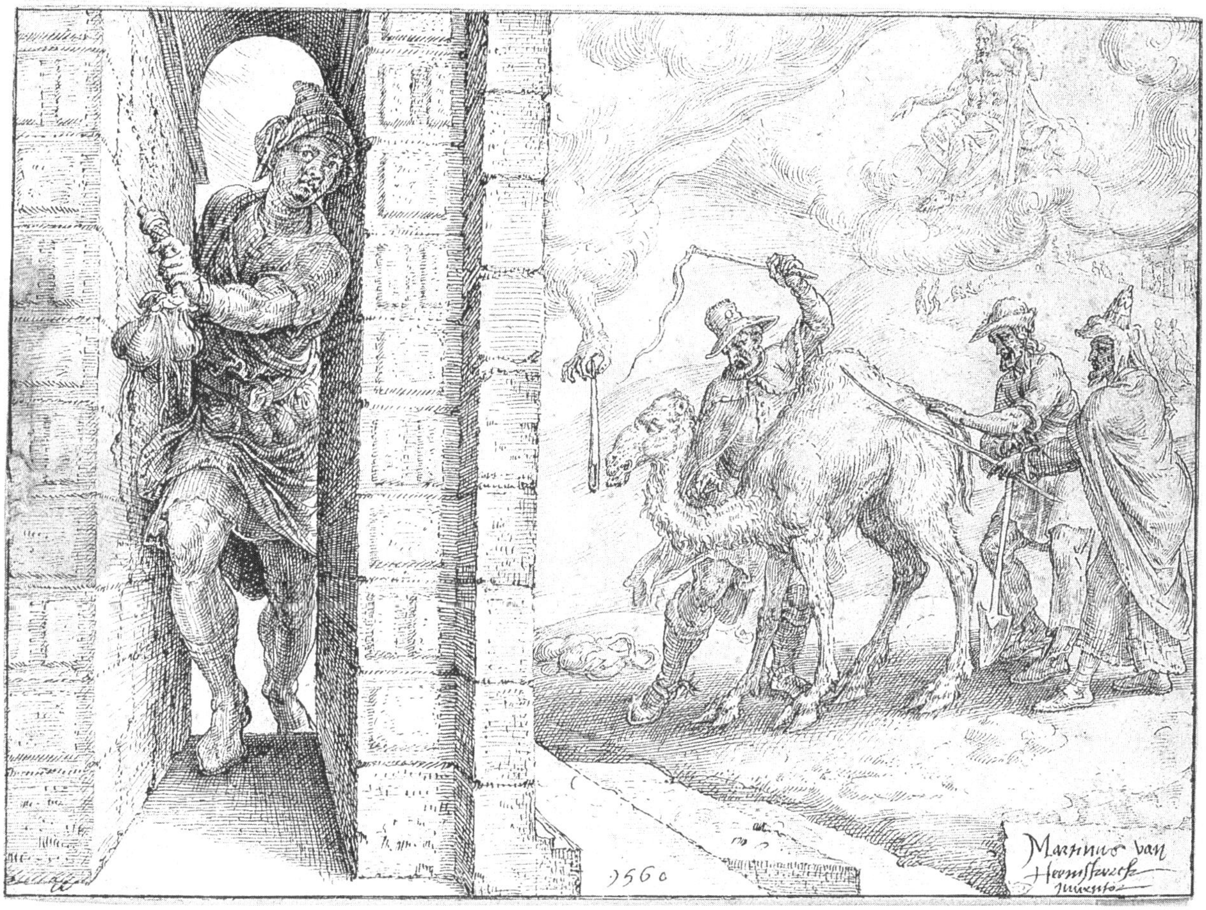

63. Maerten van Heemskerck, *The Parable of the Rich Man,* Louvre Museum, Edmond de Rothschild Collection.

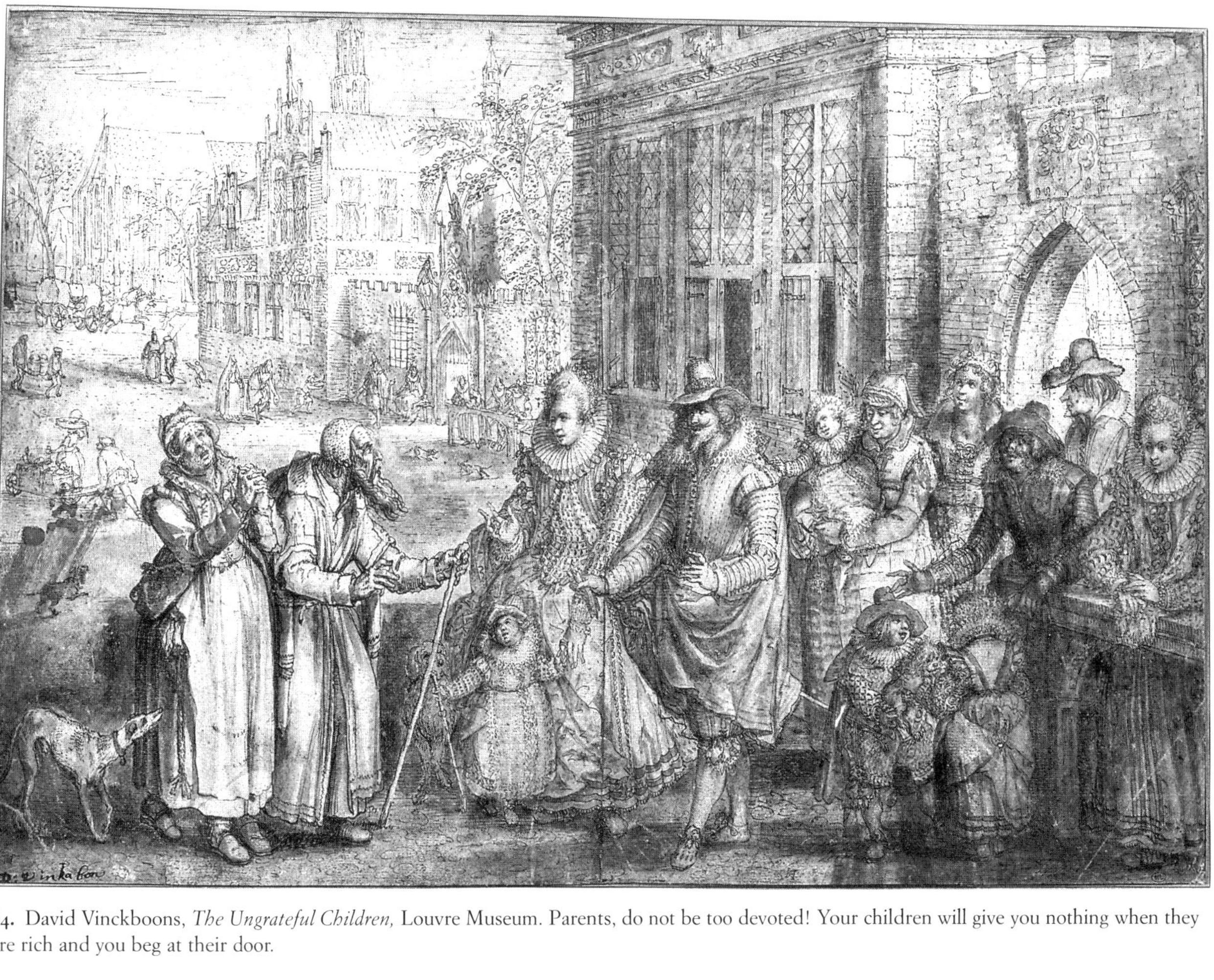

64. David Vinckboons, *The Ungrateful Children,* Louvre Museum. Parents, do not be too devoted! Your children will give you nothing when they are rich and you beg at their door.

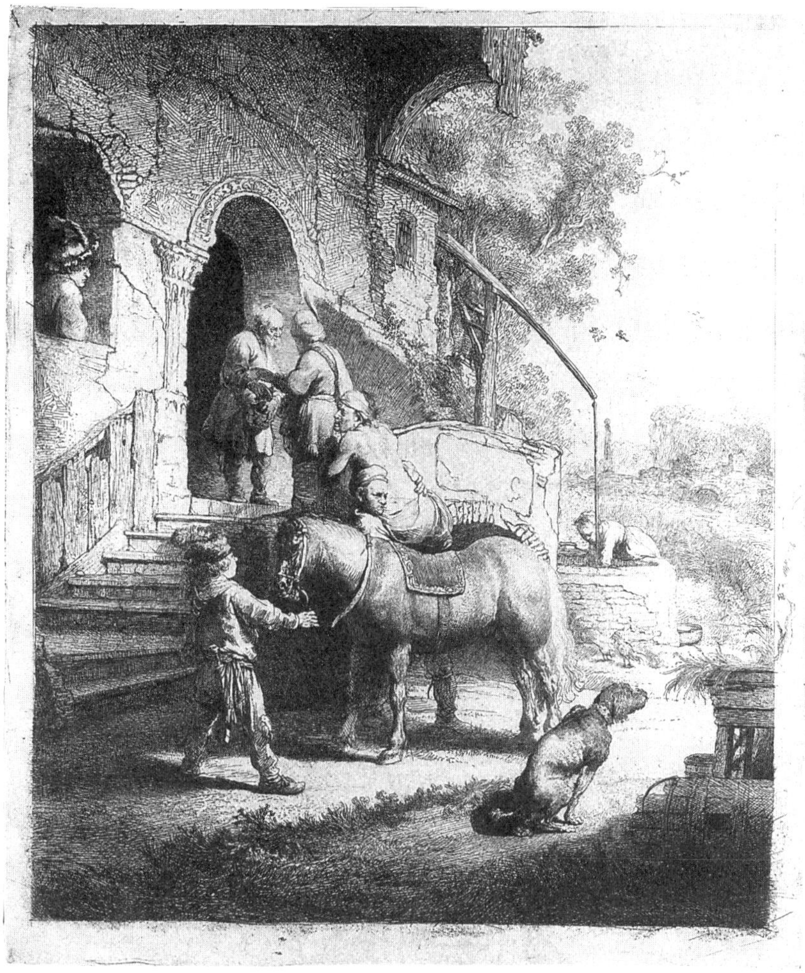

65. Rembrandt, *The Good Samaritan,* Louvre Museum, Edmond de Rothschild Collection.

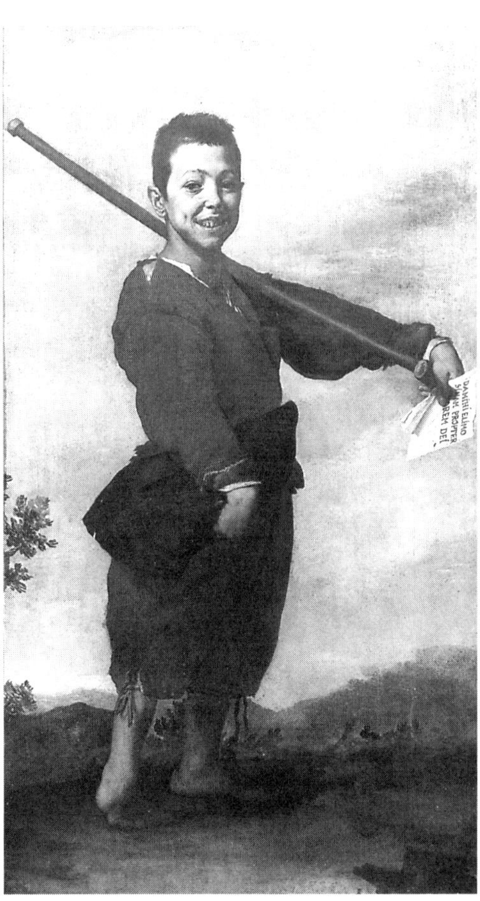

66. Ribera, *The Clubfoot,* Louvre Museum.

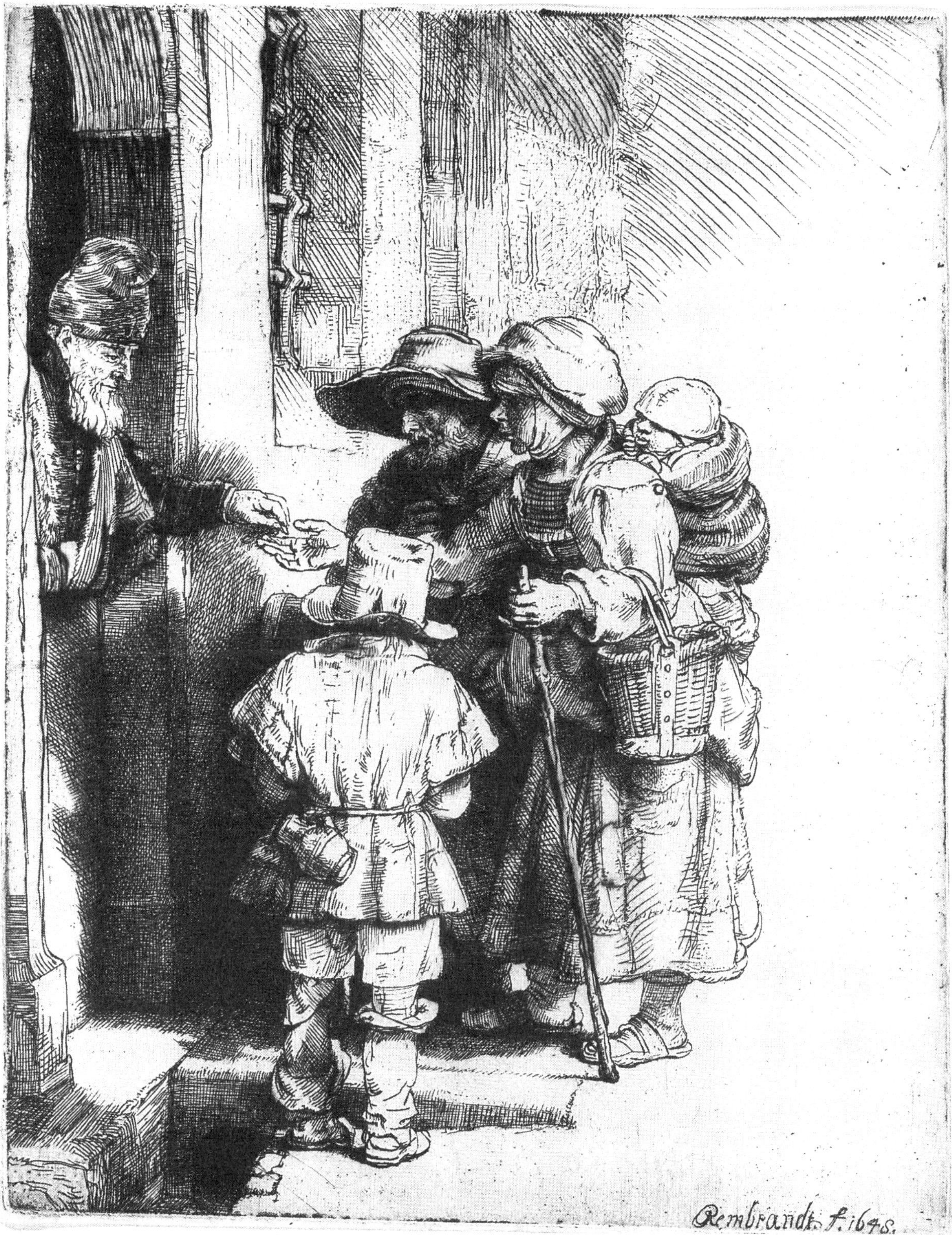

67. Rembrandt, *Family of Beggars Receiving Alms,* Louvre Museum, Edmond de Rothschild Collection.

his alms. He accumulates a treasure. Must one despair of seeing the triumph of the pure gift, the gift without compensation, the gift given without consideration for one's own interest? Would it not be preferable to imitate the Stoic god by giving without expecting anything in return, either from men or from heaven? To give without expecting "tit for tat," without striking a bargain where those who worked to relieve human suffering would be remunerated with future happiness?

The philosophy of the Enlightenment culminates in a categorical imperative that is not accompanied or enforced by a promise of reward. Let us recall Kant's Latin phrase: "Omnes quantum potes juva" (Help others as much as it is in your power). The imperative is unconditional: it is imposed independently of the happiness that might come to the one who accepts it.

In fact, the philosophy of the Enlightenment merely renewed a debate whose elements were outlined in a few enigmatic and searing strokes in the famous "scene with the poor man" in Molière's *Dom Juan.* This scene alarmed religious censors, and for good reason, since the very meaning of alms is called into question. The libertine hero finally gives a twenty-franc piece to a poor man who had asked for alms in heaven's name. But in doing so, he gives the gesture an entirely different finality: "For the love of humanity."[124] The formula Dom Juan uses is disinterested, and might very well correspond to the imperative for a very pure morality. But it is only one of the postures of this hero, this *gambler.* He is drowning in debt. He squanders whatever he possesses and has little regard for other people's money. He gives when it pleases him to give, for his own pleasure: it costs him nothing, and it can be replaced with beautiful words. When the poor man (using the traditional formula) proposes himself as the intercessor for heaven's gifts, Dom Juan retorts that the bargain is largely conjectural: the pitiful appearance of the poor man places the solvency of heaven in doubt. He is, however, ready to conclude a different bargain with the poor man: in return for the alms granted, he enjoins him to curse, that is, to become his accomplice in his challenge to divine authority. Frightened by the peril of blasphemy and refusing to bend to the will of the "great lord and evil man," the poor man refuses to receive a gift at such a price. The final gift, "for the love of humanity," is a beau geste, a cavalier gesture that Dom Juan happens upon. In it, an *aesthetic* aspect of the gift makes its appearance, an aspect destined for a great future.

No one loses his honor in the exchange, not the petitioner with his conformist piety nor the petitioned in his outrageous impiety.[125] The gift implies neither an acquiescence to "heaven," nor a scandalous negation of it; it posits a different object of love, which is universal and "philosophical." At least, such an object is posited in words, though it is not certain whether Dom Juan cares any more for humanity than he does for heaven. What gives this brief scene from Molière all its importance is the possibility it reveals of excluding any vertical dimension: the love of humanity situates the gift exclusively in the horizontal dimension.

And since an aesthetic attitude exists, why not consider its caricatural aberration? Why not look to the nineteenth century and Madame Bovary? That peasant's daughter,

124. See "Texts on the Gift," no. 22, below.

125. See Michel Serres, "Conclusion," *Hermès I, La communication* (Paris: Minuit, 1968), 233–45.

prisoner of bourgeois mediocrity, dreams of an aristocratic, passionate existence. Her spending leads to her ruin. In the coach that brings her back for the last time to Yonville from Rouen, she throws a last five-franc coin at the horrid blind man. A moment before, Homais had given him five centimes, and had asked for one back in change! For Emma, compassion and charity are not at issue: "Emma, overcome with *disgust,* threw a five-franc coin over her shoulder to him. It was her entire fortune. For her, it seemed *beautiful* to throw it away in that manner." [126] Through that last act of prodigality, Emma concedes that the absurdity of destiny has won the game. The final exorbitant gift places all Emma's existence under the sign of chimerical largesse. Pathetically, she attains only the ridiculous, when her ambition was to realize the beautiful.

The philosophy of the Enlightenment dissociated the question of poverty and the appeal to charity. It made poverty a problem of politics and government. A displacement came about that established a duty for society at large, setting aside considerations of salvation and dissuading people from using alms or houses of charity as the principal remedies. Montesquieu was particularly clear on the subject: "A man is not poor because he has nothing, but because he does not work. . . . However many alms are given to a man naked in the streets, they do not fulfill the obligations of the state, which owes all its citizens an assured minimal existence, food, suitable clothing, and a way of life that is not injurious to their health. . . . In Rome the hospitals contrive for everyone to be comfortable, except those who work, those who are industrious, those who cultivate the arts, those who have land, and those who are in business." [127] At most Montesquieu concedes that, even in rich nations, "short-term help" is necessary for workers in a "branch of commerce" that is experiencing difficult times. These, however, would be momentary measures to keep the people from suffering, or from revolting. Montesquieu clearly points to the movement set in place during the French Revolution, which momentarily placed "*public* assistance" in competition with *private* acts of charity. We know that private organizations continued to have resolute adherents in the nineteenth century, because they called for the gift of oneself, a disinterested devotion, a dedication of one's entire existence, whereas legal measures were imposed in an impersonal and distant manner. Private charity became a rallying point for those nostalgic for the religious order. In *L'envers de l'histoire contemporaine* (The other side of contemporary history), Balzac imagines a secret society moved by faith alone and led by an admirable woman, Madame de la Chanterie, whose motto is borrowed from Acts 10:38, *Pertransit benefaciendo.*

This might come as a surprise: in the "ethical conclusions" of *Essai sur le don* (1924), Marcel Mauss claimed that social security and the new state mechanisms for redistributing wealth suggested a return to an economy of the gift. That economy preceded commodity economies, where goods are bought and sold at a "fair price," using money, credit, and so on. Did Marcel Mauss wish to return to archaic modes of production? It would be just as accurate to say that he had in mind the establishment of social relations where the obligation for a return gift and for generalized exchange would supplant the granting of charity. It is important to note that when society assumed the burden of poverty at the end of the eighteenth century, it began by challenging the privileged role

126. Gustave Flaubert, *Madame Bovary,* pt. 3, chap. 7.

127. Montesquieu, *De l'esprit des lois,* 23.29.

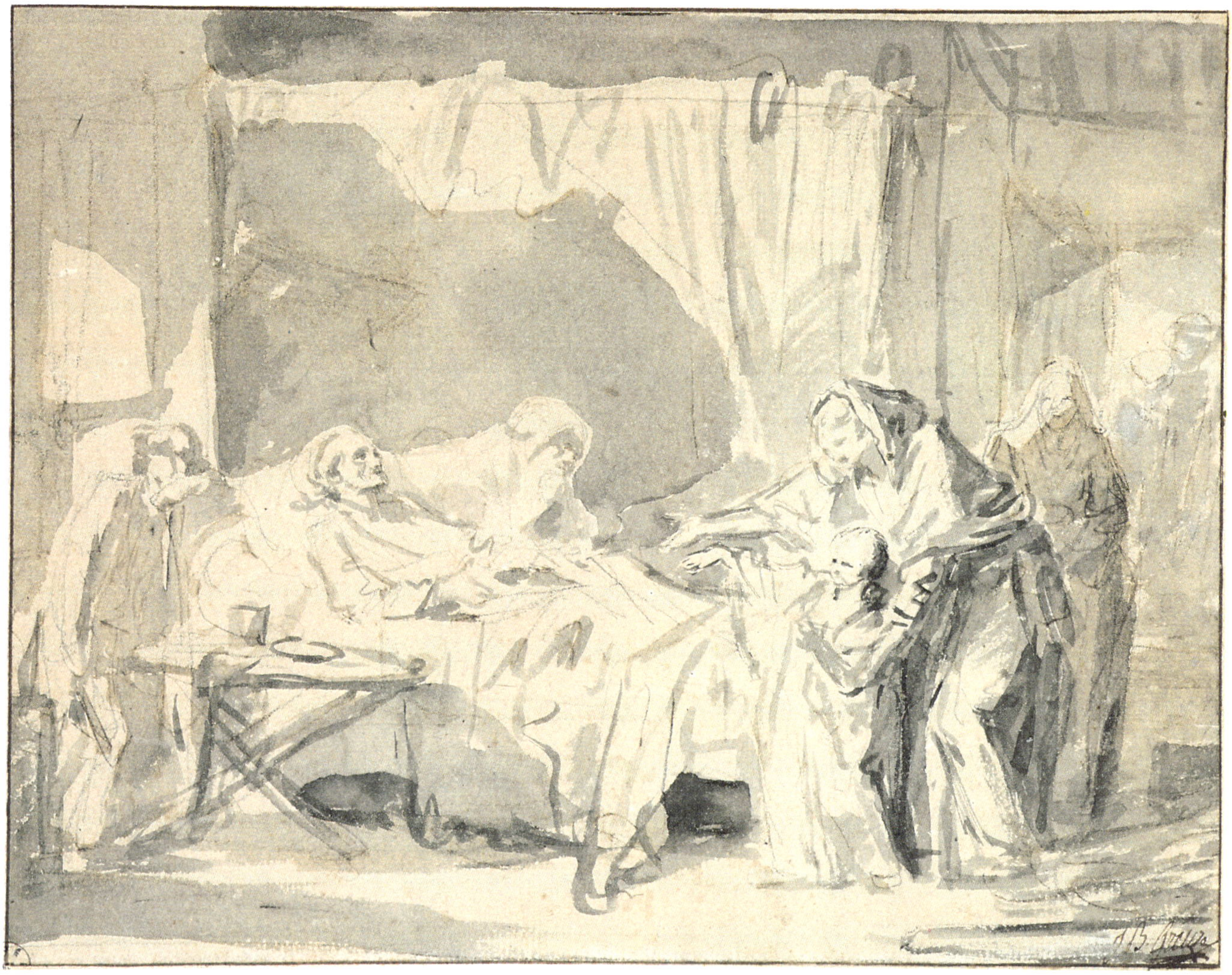

68. Jean-Baptiste Greuze, *The Lady of Charity,* Museum of Fine Arts, Agen.

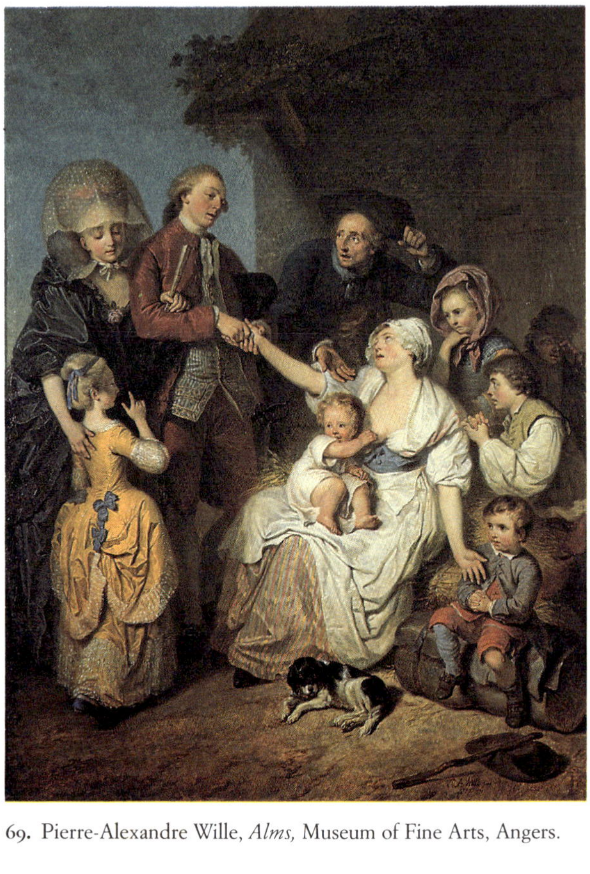

69. Pierre-Alexandre Wille, *Alms,* Museum of Fine Arts, Angers.

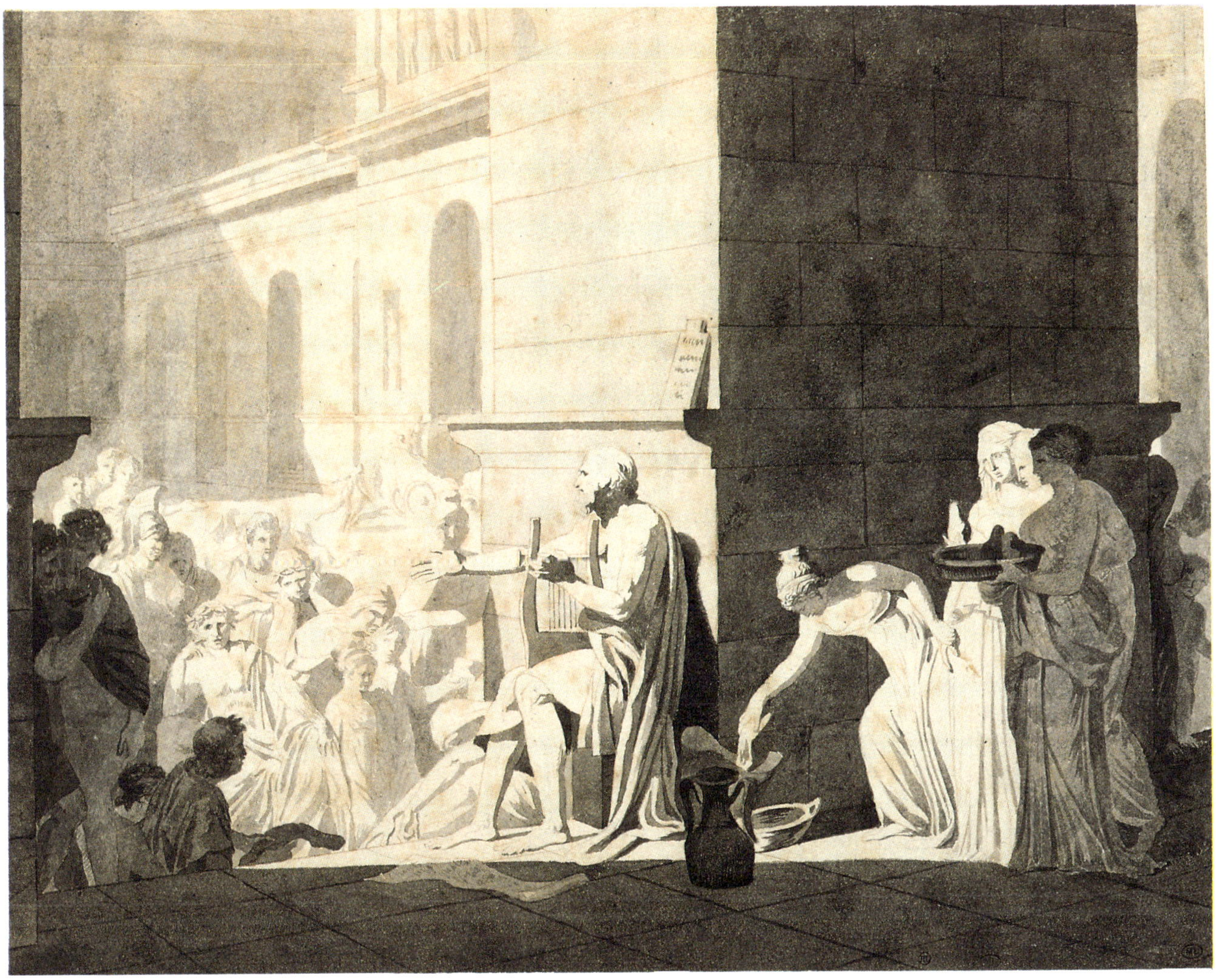

70. Jacques-Louis David, *Homer Reciting His Poems,* Louvre Museum.

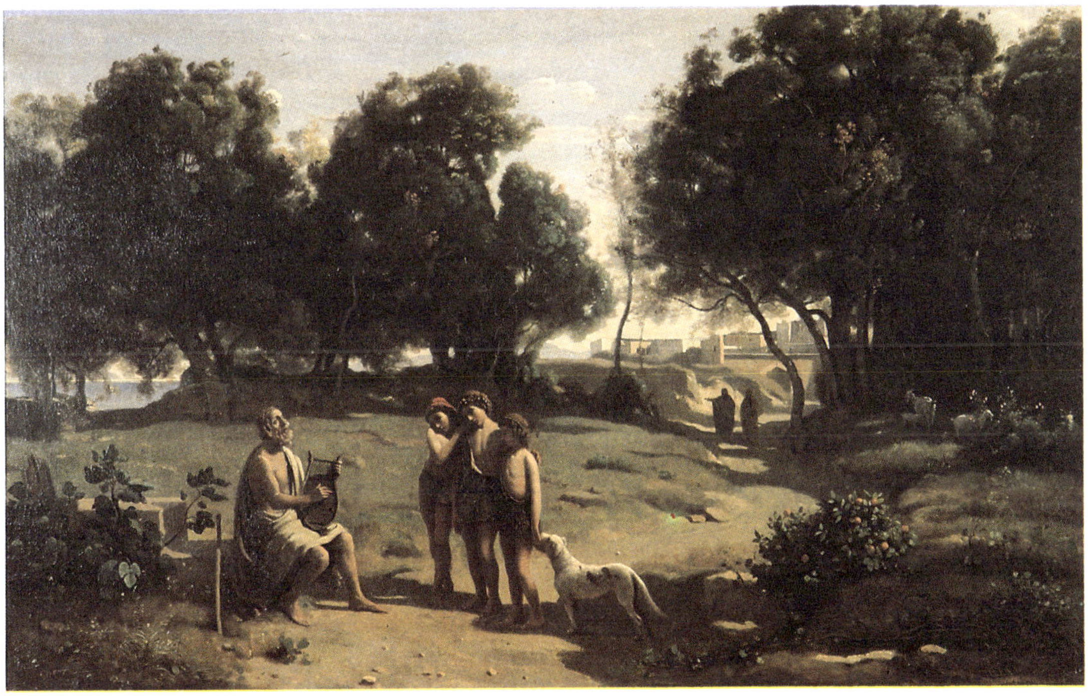

71. Jean-Baptiste Camille Corot, *Homer and the Shepherds,* Museum of Fine Arts, Saint-Lô. Homer was thrown onto the bank. The shepherds who listen to him will give him generous alms: "'Prends, et puisse bientôt changer ta destinée!' / Disent-ils. Et tirant ce que, pour leur journée / Tient la peau d'une chèvre aux crins noirs et luisants / Ils versent à l'envi, sur ses genoux pesants, / Le pain de pur froment, les olives huileuses, / Le fromage et l'amande, et les figues mielleuses." ("Take it, and may your destiny soon change!" / They said. And taking from a goatskin with black and shining pelt, / Its contents for the day, they vied with one another, / To pour onto his heavy knees, the purest wheat bread, oily olives, / Cheese and almonds, and figs as sweet as honey.) André Chénier, *L'aveugle* (The blind man), 45–50. In David's watercolor (fig. 70), the gifts are brought by the group of women on the right.

in that area of charitable orders that made appeals for gifts and compassion. These gifts were judged insufficient, humiliating, arbitrary, and without reciprocity. The only similarity between the ostentatious potlatch and the almost abstract social measures discussed by Mauss is reciprocity. He calls for a disciplining of commodity society through full employment, the redistribution of revenues, and "lifetime security"; he does not call for a return to the rivalrous generosity of "primitive," precommodity societies. Melville's short story, cited earlier, satirizes the London charity ball; like Montesquieu, what the narrator demanded for the poor was "remunerated work." That was also the practice Voltaire applied in Ferney, making the fact known throughout Europe. Mauss went further, wishing to establish a generalized exchange that would not be limited merely to "the payment of a salary."

In truth, the great minds of the Age of Enlightenment, as they waited for political reforms that would put a check on poverty, practiced and encouraged individual benefi-
68 cence in the form of philanthropy.[128] They took up the activities that had belonged to the "ladies of charity" of the preceding century, but in an entirely secular manner. The reference to religion was toned down. The "belle âme" was driven by the desire to manifest himself, in order to be recognized by his peers: he assured himself of his own virtue through the admiration shown him by those moved by his example. And, at the same time, deep within himself, a sensitive man could avail himself of his acts of charity as proof of his own goodness: his beneficence allowed him to be self-satisfied. As Rousseau said in an almost provocative manner: "When I give a gift, I give myself pleasure."[129] In that way, the gift reflects back on the giver without the intermediary of transcendent intercession. In the preceding century, the Jansenist moralists expressed the wish that charity would not "stop" at creatures but would "move on" to God. It is nearly the same for Rousseau and his disciples, but for one considerable difference: now beneficence "moves" narcissistically to the deified self. Hence, at the end of the eighteenth century, the practice of beneficence not only assumed an ostentatious and spectacular character, it also became marked by a touch of aestheticism, almost a hedonism of emotion. The theatrical side of authentic beneficence lends itself to fraudulent imitation. Do we need to recall the strategy of the great seducers? Lovelace (in Richardson's *Clarissa*) and Valmont (in Laclos's *Liaisons dangereuses*) both resort to putting on an act, offering help to needy homes; and they reap the blessings of gratitude, thus awakening the sympathy of the virtuous women they wish to conquer.[130] Wearing the halo of beneficence, they meet with less resistance.

128. The word *bienfaisance* (beneficence) entered the *Dictionnaire de l'Académie* in 1762. The noun was of recent invention. Voltaire attributed its creation to the abbé de Saint-Pierre, a utopian thinker always on the lookout for means of perfecting oneself.

129. Rousseau, *Les rêveries du promeneur solitaire,* sixth reverie, in *Oeuvres complètes* (Paris: Gallimard, "Bibliothèque de la Pléiade," 1959), 1:1054. The sixth reverie is a reflection on alms and charity, in the personal case of Jean-Jacques. Rousseau expressed himself on the subject on many occasions: in *La nouvelle Héloïse,* in *Emile,* and in his correspondence. I have examined this subject in "Don fastueux et don pervers" (n. 5 above). This aspect of Rousseau's thinking (where very "paternalistic" attitudes often manifest themselves) cannot be detached from the rest of his philosophy.

130. Choderlos de Laclos, *Les liaisons dangereuses,* pt. 1, letter 21, in *Oeuvres complètes,* ed. Laurent Versini (Paris: Gallimard, "Bibliothèque de la Pléiade," 1979), 45–47, and note 1202–3. For anyone seeking literary examples of edifying beneficence, I recommend the first canto of *La pitié* (1802) by Jacques Delille. The modern reader will smile at it or become indignant, but Delille did not have an ironic intention.

In such a climate of sensitivity, we can understand how the scene of beneficence (or 69
of welcoming hospitality) could have given rise to historical tableaux, in the manner of Greuze's idyllic realism. An ancient paradigm—Philemon and Baucis welcoming the 62
gods into their modest home—remains present in the memory of neoclassicism: the poor also give! These paintings and engravings take the place of the allegories celebrating the works of mercy. The figure of the benefactor grows in stature, but without ever leaving the profane register or the antique fable.

The figure of the beggar also grows in stature; previously, he had usually remained confined within genre painting. There were numerous depictions in French painting of Belisarius,[131] from the moral novel by Marmontel: Justinian's general, disgraced and blind, has the child who guides him hold out his helmet to collect the small offerings of passersby. In a touching moment, a soldier recognizes the beggar as his old general. The subject, already treated in the seventeenth century (in a painting by Van Dyck and a play by Rotrou) experienced an extraordinary revival in the arts at the end of the eighteenth century: these paintings are emblematic of a genre I shall call *heroic alms.* The genre, which lent itself to neoclassical interpretations both in poetry and in painting, presents great men in misfortune, or sometimes, old friends who have fallen into poverty. These are poor people by accident, not by essence. Their archetype is Ulysses, disembarking naked on the island of the Pheacians and putting off the moment when he reveals his name. So it is with Chénier's *Beggar* and with his *Blind Man,*[132] who is none other than Homer himself, thrown onto an island by the greedy sailors who had taken him aboard (according to a legendary narrative by Pseudo-Herodotus).[133] After the emotional moment of gifts made to the supplicant who seems to be a poor man, the essential moment occurs when his true identity is *recognized.*[134] He is not a "true" beggar, but an equal, or,
in the case of Homer, a demigod. In André Chénier and in David, the great poet sur- 70
passes his hosts in generosity: he offers them the sublime song in return. The poet, in 71
making the gift of song, thanks an entire people for the fruits offered the stranger he had been on the bank. In Chénier's poem, the final celebration around Homer, the divine beggar, transfigures indigence into sovereignty and celebrates an (entirely imaginary) "consecration," where poetry becomes the supreme authority and the dispenser of glorious largesse.[135]

131. Of them, the paintings by David and Gérard are the most famous. We would also need to discuss the figure of the prisoner, especially that of Florestan in *Fidelio.* Beethoven gives striking grandeur to the first scene of act 2, where Leonora/Fidelio and Rocko descend into the underground passage, dig the prisoner's grave, and secretly give him bread and wine. Here, we can recognize four of the traditional works of mercy: visiting prisoners, burying the dead, feeding the hungry, and giving drink to the thirsty. Florestan calls down the rewards of heaven upon his benefactors. But Florestan's deliverance is a Passover in the horizontal, political dimension.

132. In *Le mendiant,* Chénier recalls *The Odyssey* and imitates it. But it is now a "bourgeois" story where a well-off landowner finally recognizes an old friend (a "guest") in the unfortunate soul taken in by his daughter. The friend had been a victim of misfortune and had become unrecognizable.

133. One of the great paintings of Corot's earlier period—*Homer and the Shepherds*—owes its inspiration to Chénier or harks back to the same legendary source.

134. On recognition in literature, see Terence Cave, *Recognitions: A Study in Poetics* (Oxford: Clarendon Press, 1988).

135. See Paul Bénichou, *Le sacre de l'écrivain, 1750–1830* (Paris: José Corti, 1973).

CHAPTER FOUR

Poetry

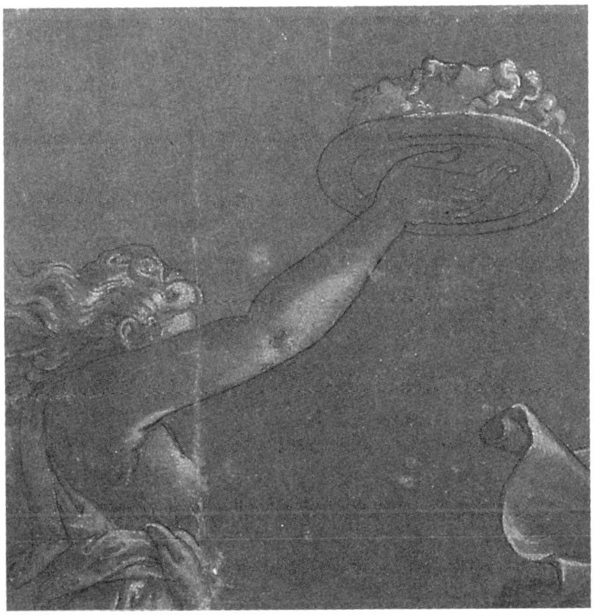

Wordsworth

In casting a soft light on the imploring face of unfortunate noblemen, heroic alms prepared minds for the reverse image: the heroization of the beggar and the vagabond, who are ennobled by their very exclusion. All earlier theological elaborations, which announced the presence of Christ in "the poor man," may have contributed toward that heroization. The Christ of romanticism was a poor man, a "sansculotte," before being an intercessor.[136]

72 At the turn of the nineteenth century, when police measures against the poor, too visible on public roads, were gaining force in England, leading to the confinement of the indigent in workhouses and industry houses, compassionate voices demanded they be allowed to roam about in freedom.[137] Wordsworth's "The Old Cumberland Beggar" (written in 1798 and inserted into the *Lyrical Ballads,* 1800) ends with a supplication addressed to political leaders. In this plea, the beggar appears as the person who maintains the living memory of a community's past. He is also the one who, unseeing, almost blind, lives in the eye of nature, in its dazzling proximity:

> Few are his pleasures: if his eyes have now
> Been doomed so long to settle upon earth
> That not without some effort they behold
> The countenance of the horizontal sun,
> Rising or setting, let the light at least
> Find a free entrance to their languid orb.
> And let him, *where* and *when* he will, sit down
> Beneath the trees, or on a grassy bank
> Of highway side, and when the little birds
> Share his chance-gathered meal; and finally,
> As in the eye of Nature he has lived
> So in the eye of Nature let him die![138]

In the poem, the beggar has become a figure of nature, who must be left in his natural place. The gift the poet requests on his behalf is not so much alms as the right to freely receive the light of the sun. The beggar, deprived of a place to sleep, is in fact a citizen of the real world; he belongs to the immensity of earthly space. In an early poem by Wordsworth, "An Evening Walk,"[139] the apparition of a sad beggar woman and her two children gives way in the speaker's eyes to that of a pair of swans surrounded by their young. The contrast between the happiness of natural creatures and human misery is striking. In interrupting the poet's rapture of contemplation, the beggar woman and her children, threatened by death, leave a blot of unhappiness on the landscape. But the interruption does not last; the poet's gaze quickly moves on to something else. By that very fact, the impoverished group has the privilege of acquiring (but in a negative way)

136. See Frank P. Bowman, *Le Christ romantique* (Geneva: Droz, 1973), and *Le Christ des barricades, 1789–1848* (Paris: Cerf, 1987).

137. At the very least, we should mention George Crabbe's very moving *Village* (1783).

138. William Wordsworth, "The Old Cumberland Beggar," in *Poems,* ed. John O. Hayden (New York: Penguin Books, 1977) 1:262–68. See "Texts on the Gift," no. 24, below.

139. Ibid., 1:83–85.

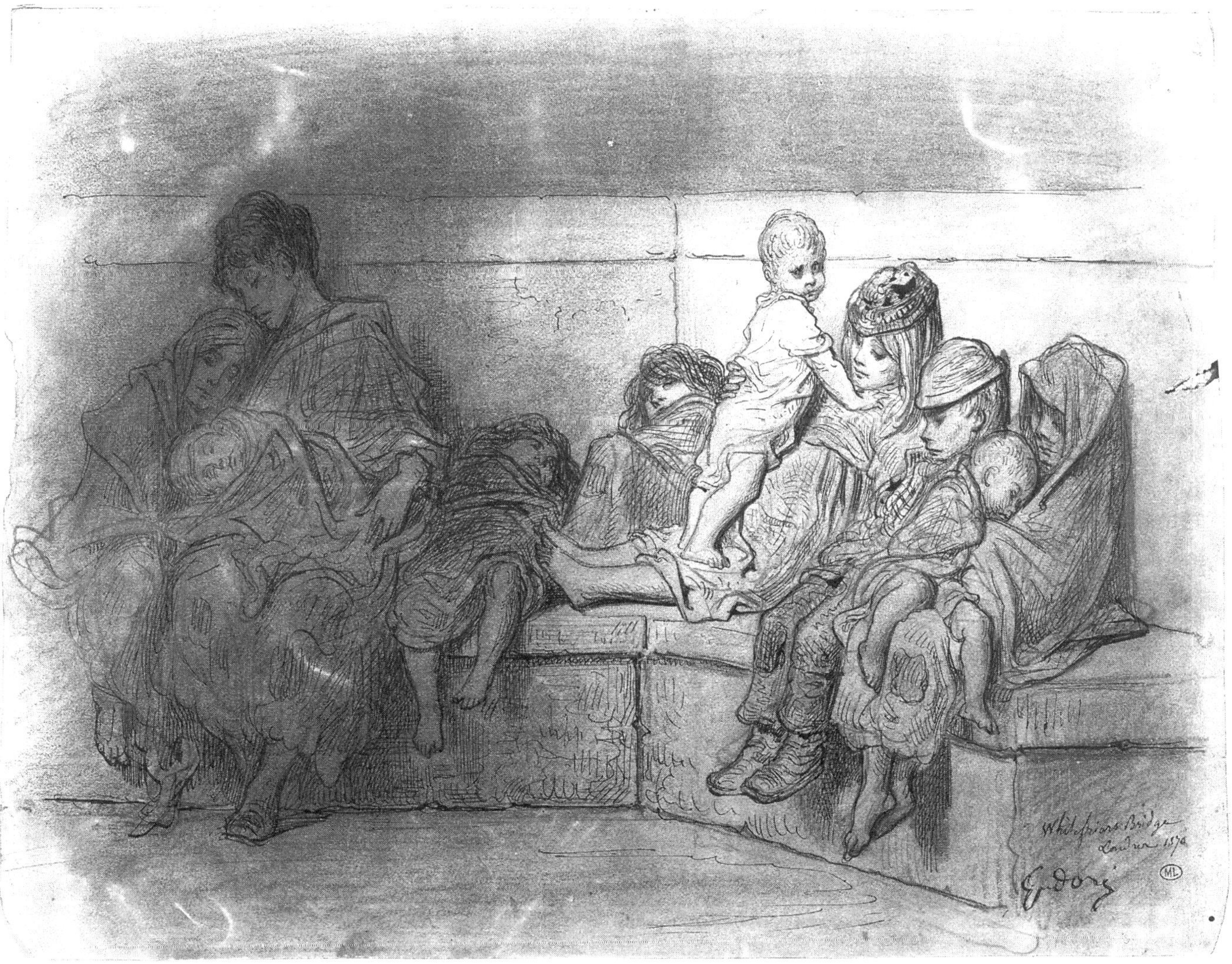

72. Gustave Doré, *Whiterfiors Bridge,* Louvre Museum, Orsay Museum Collection.

the same *transitory* importance as the great objects exalted in his reverie on natural beauty: trees, the lake, the evening light. A completely different aspect of poverty ap-
73 pears in another poem, "Beggars."[140] Wordsworth confers an almost supernatural beauty on some gypsies encountered along the road: the mother is tall and might have been "fit person for a Queen / To lead those ancient Amazonian files; / Or ruling Bandit's wife among the Grecian isles." Not far away, boys who bear a resemblance to her are playing with grace and skill.

> Yet *they,* so blithe of heart, seemed fit
> For finest tasks of earth or air:
> Wings let them have, and they might flit
> Precursors to Aurora's car
> Scattering fresh flowers; though happier far, I ween
> To hunt their fluttering game o'er rock and level green.

To make the poet pity them, they plaintively claim to be orphans. Indignant over this lie, he refuses to give them alms, which he had earlier given their mother. But even as he condemns their "moral depravity,"[141] he sees them as creatures that, if they had wings, "might flit / Precursors to Aurora's car / Scattering fresh flowers." Amazing! In the poet's imagination, the poor, and in this case, even the "bad poor," "the demon's poor," become dispensers of largesse, genies holding the horn of plenty in the procession led by a deity of the air. They make the gesture of *sparsio* (perfectly evoked with the verb "scatter") proper to caesars, *évergètes,* and kings (either directly or through the intermediaries of heralds). The seductiveness of these little acrobats makes them children of Hermes. Wordsworth also wrote the "Sequel to 'Beggars' Composed Many Years After,"[142] in which the final image is the "immortal bloom" of these blithe liars. They have been protected by the "Spirits of beauty and grace." Their earthly tribulations end in an apotheosis. Géricault recorded more disheartening scenes of England, which are implacably deprived of any religious transcendence. Sunk down on a bakery's door-
74 step, an old beggar, holding out his hand, has come to the end of the road.[143] Perhaps he once lived in the eye of nature and played on the heath, but the London pavement has long since become his home and his tomb. We have reached rock bottom in our fall.[144]

A dynamic of ascension analogous to that found in Wordsworth reappears in Victor Hugo. The beggar's hole-pocked coat, held up to the welcoming hearth fire, is transformed into a celestial vault where stars are shining:

> Son manteau, tout mangé des vers, et jadis bleu,
> Etalé largement sur la chaude fournaise,
> Piqué de mille trous par la lueur de braise,
> Couvrait l'âtre, et semblait un ciel étoilé.
> Et tandis qu'il séchait ce haillon désolé
> D'où ruisselait la pluie et l'eau des fondrières,

140. Ibid., 1:516–17, 2:365–66. In this poem, Wordsworth transformed a story his sister had recounted to him into a first-person account.

141. Wordsworth, *Poems,* 2:975–76.

142. Ibid., 2:365–66.

143. See the catalog of the *Géricault* exhibit, commissioned by Sylvain Laveissière and Régis Michel (Paris: Réunion des musées nationaux, 1991–92).

144. On taking flight and falling, see Peter Greenaway, *Le bruit des nuages* (Paris: Réunion des musées nationaux, 1992) [*Flying Out of This World* (Chicago: University of Chicago Press, 1994).]

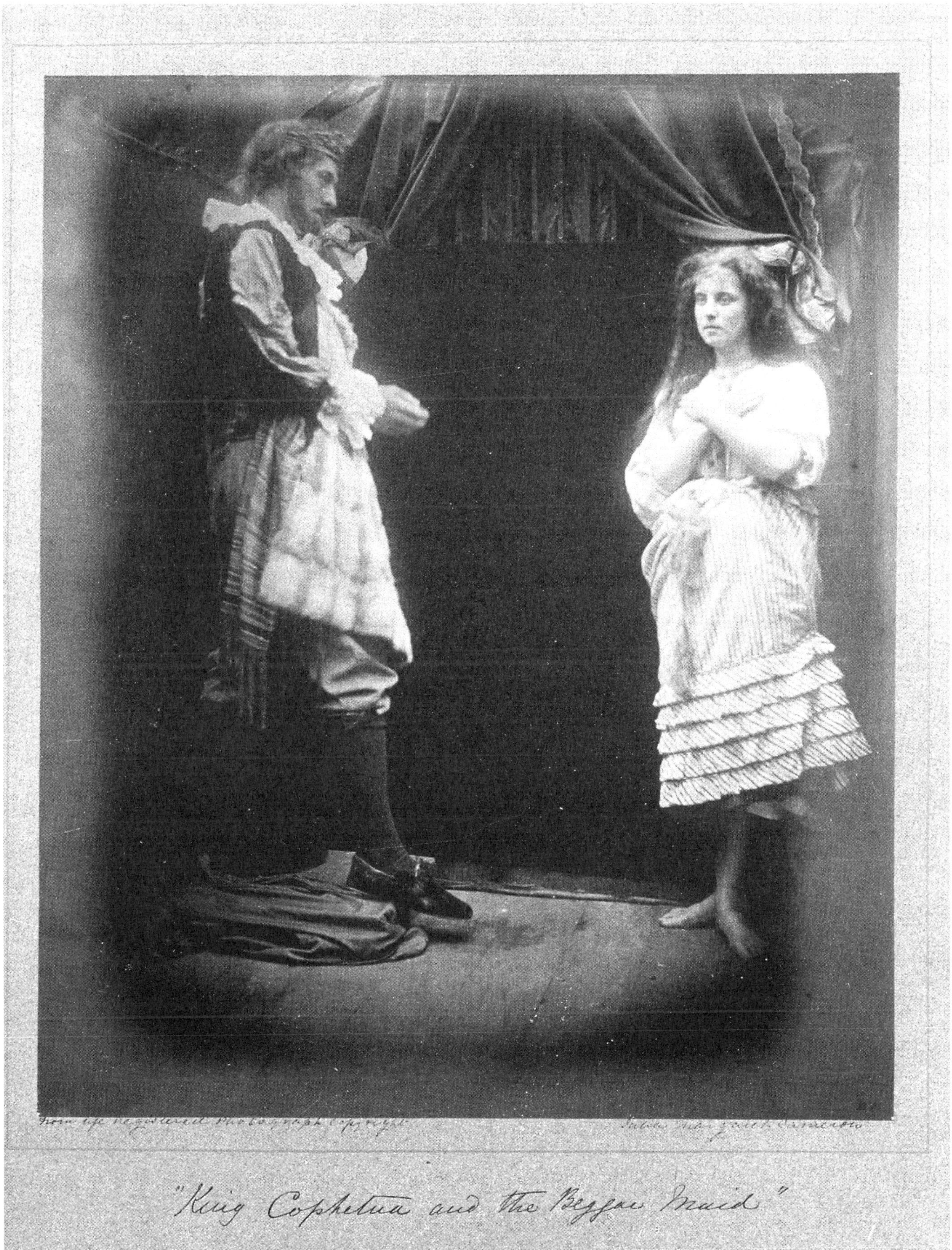

73. Julia Margaret Cameron, *King Cophetua and the Beggar Maid,* Orsay Museum. Copy dedicated to Maria Jackson, Virginia Woolf's grandmother. The tableau vivant illustrates Tennyson's "The Beggar Maid": "Her arms across her breast she laid; / She was more fair than words can say: / Barefooted came the beggar maid / Before the king Cophetua. . . . Cophetua sware a royal oath: / 'This beggar maid shall be my queen!' "

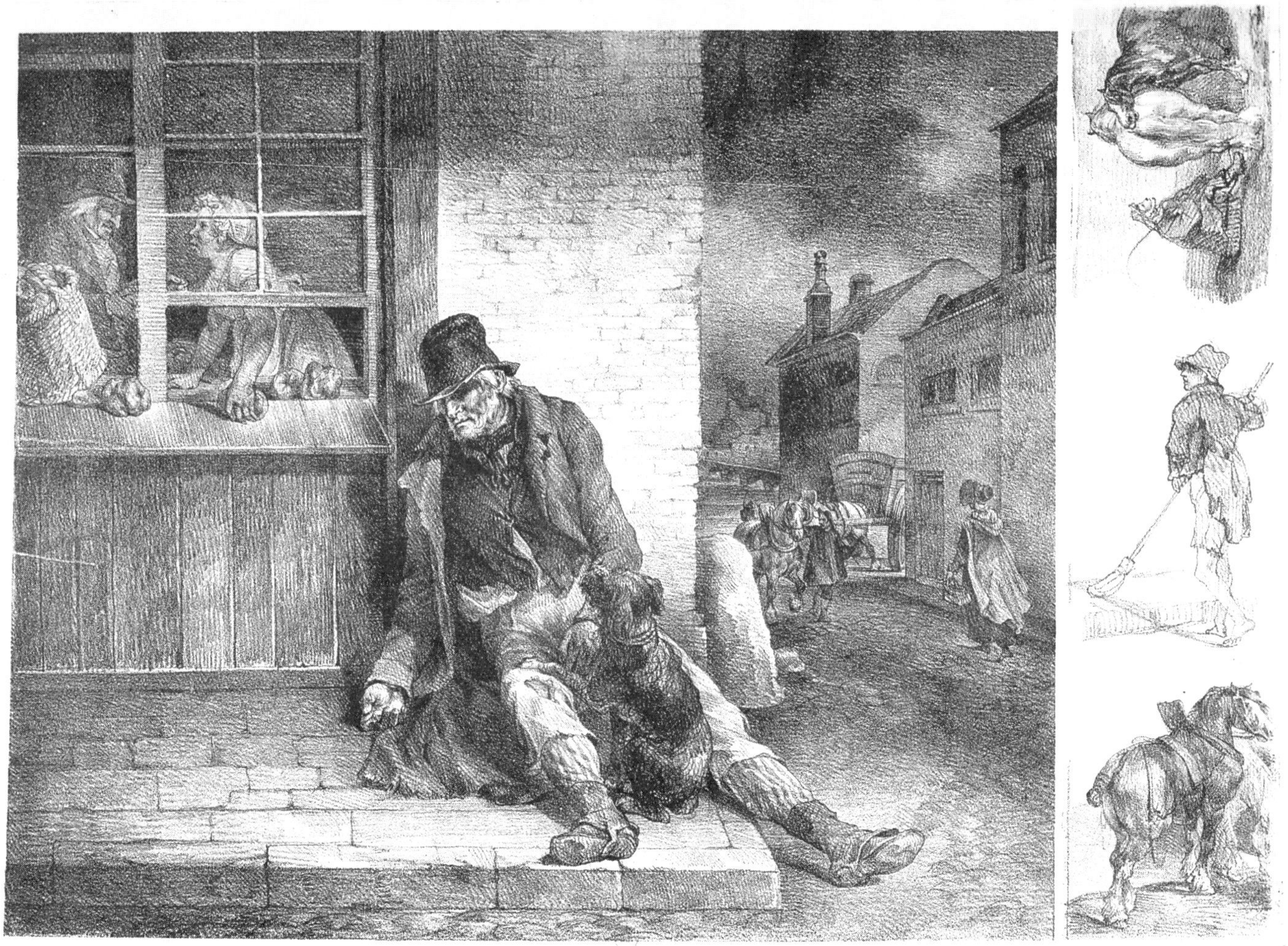

74. Théodore Géricault, *The Old Beggar,* Bibliothèque Nationale.

> Je songeais que cet homme était plein de prières,
> Et je regardais, sourd à ce que nous disions,
> Sa bure où je voyais des constellations.[145]

In Wordsworth, a mysterious communication was established between the poet and the graceful scamps to whom he refused alms: a reconciliation, almost an identification, came about through the virtue of beauty. In Hugo, author of "Plein ciel" (Open sky), the poor man's coat unfurls a sky, and the poor man himself, "full of prayers," becomes the poet's humble allegorical double, just as clowns, exiles, and acrobats later become those of Baudelaire.

What Is Thrown (or Not) Out the Window

In a poem composed when he was an adolescent, Baudelaire evokes the street musician's hurdy-gurdy, whose melody, rising up to the poet's bedroom, reminds him of a friend. Absorbed by the sweetness of the memory, he does not give the musician a coin. He denies him this modest largesse, he does not even think of it: "Le pauvre s'en fut tristement. . . . —Et j'ai laissé les vitres closes, / Ingrat, pour qui m'a fait ainsi / Rêver de si charmantes choses." [The poor man went away sadly. . . . —And I left the windows closed, / Ungrateful toward the one who made me thus / Dream of such charming things.][146]

There is something even worse than keeping the window closed and refusing to give alms: namely, throwing a flowerpot out the window onto the "modest ambulatory fortune" of a "bad glazier," to punish him for not carrying in his sack colored glass that would make life beautiful to behold.[147] In this allegorical fable, the poet repeats the gesture of ancient *sparsio, projecting* onto it all the aggressivity that so often animated it. Into the streets of the big city, the common people threw rubbish, excrement, love letters, and coins (see Hogarth, for London in the eighteenth century). Just to be agreeable, I might decipher the symbolic meaning of these objects using the modern dictionary of psychoanalysis. This has the merit of suggesting that not everything thrown is largesse, and that all largesse is related to expulsion and has an "anal" symbolic charge. We thus discover that a paradoxical and perverse kind of inspiration can emerge from the theme of *blocked* alms. In a prose poem, Baudelaire sees an impoverished old acrobat at a fair; his booth stands a bit to the side and is not attracting anyone. The narrator sympathizes with the pathetically motionless character to the point of feeling his own "throat constricted by the terrible hand of hysteria." He considers offering him alms, but does not manage to

145. Victor Hugo, "Le mendiant," (1854), in *Les contemplations.*

"His coat, worm-eaten, and once blue, / Spread out upon the burning furnace, / Pierced by a thousand holes by light of glowing embers, / It covered the hearth, and seemed a starry sky. / While he was drying that sorry rag / The rain and pothole water dripping from it, / I thought, this man is full of prayers, / And looked at his rough coat, deaf to what we were saying, / And there saw constellations." In older poems, Hugo addresses the rich and invites them to practice charity, elaborating the entire classical argument in accordance with the spirit of the Restoration: both earthly happiness and a future life are to be secured in an *ultimately* advantageous bargain.

146. Baudelaire, *Oeuvres complètes,* ed. Claude Pichois, 2 vols. (Paris: Gallimard, "Bibliothèque de la Pléiade," 1975), 1:200–201. All subsequent references to Baudelaire refer to this edition.

147. Baudelaire, "Le mauvais vitrier," in *Le spleen de Paris,* 1:285–87.

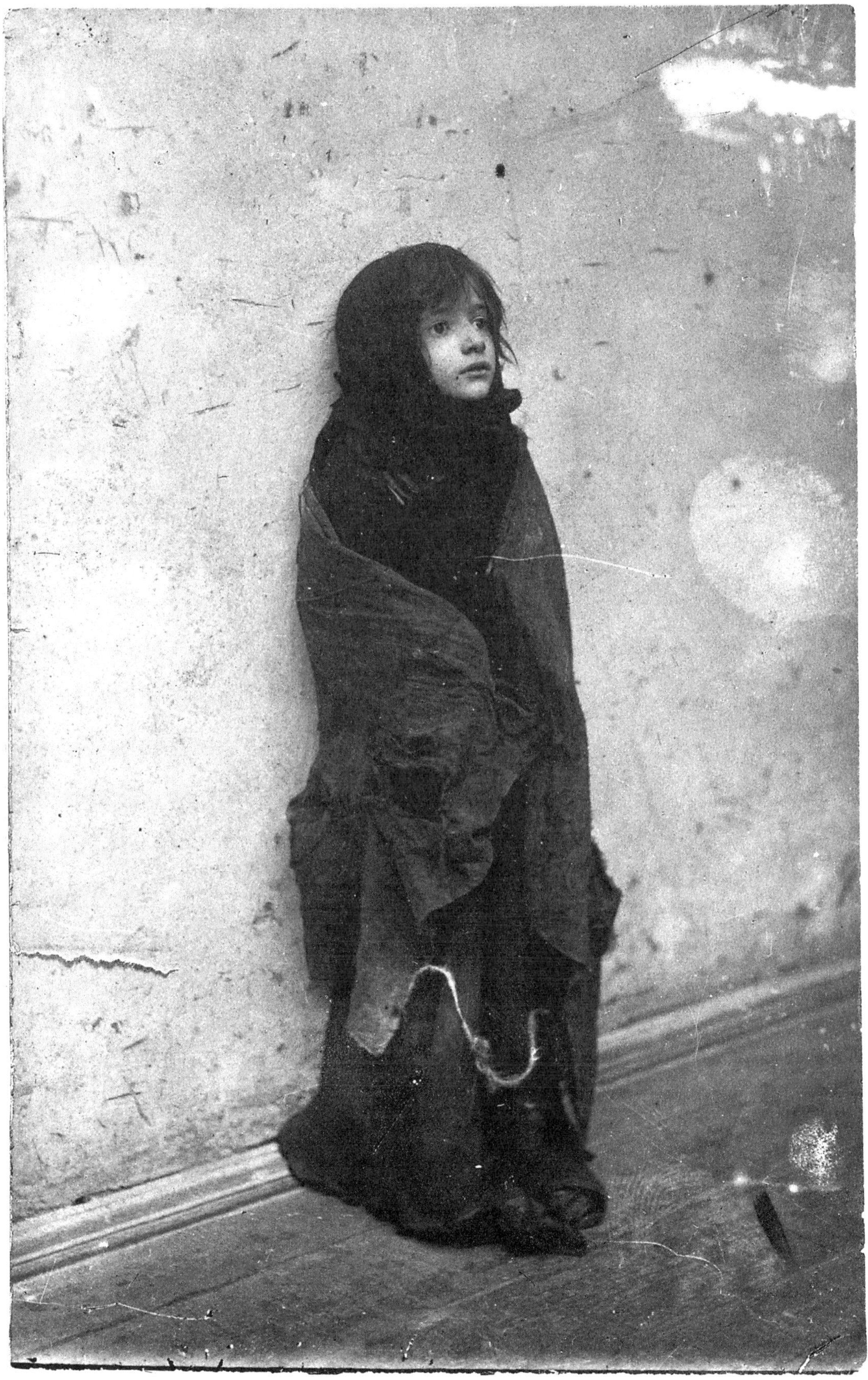

75. Anonymous photographer, *Little Girl against a Wall,* Orsay Museum. The photograph was taken in the Jewish quarter of Warsaw between 1913 and 1922.

do so. Inhibition prevails: "Finally, I had resolved to put some money on one of his boards as I passed, hoping he would guess my intention, when a great surge of people, caused by some unknown disturbance, dragged me far from him."[148]

Mallarmé was not familiar with Baudelaire's poem about the hurdy-gurdy man when he himself wrote "Plainte d'hiver" (Winter lament), but we discover exactly the same attitude in this prose poem, it too an early work. The grieving dreamer hears a barrel organ playing under his window; he is moved, and yet, deliberately, he does not open the window or throw out the smallest alms to the musician. This odd similarity suggests that, among writers of the second half of the nineteenth century, the cult of art found that *insulting the beggar* was a particularly seductive emblem for marking its rejection of any interference from received morality:

> A barrel organ was playing its song languidly, melancholically, under my window. It was playing in the great avenue lined with poplars, whose leaves had seemed dreary to me, even in springtime, ever since Maria had passed that way one last time, accompanied by candles. An instrument for the sad, truly it is: the piano sparkles, the violin casts warmth on frazzled nerves, but the barrel organ, in the twilight of memory, made me dream a desperate dream. Now it was murmuring a happy, vulgar tune, an old-fashioned, banal tune, which lightened the heart of the suburbs: How is it that the ritornello reached my soul and made me cry, as if it had been a romantic ballad? I savored it slowly and *did not throw a penny out the window* for fear of troubling myself and realizing that the instrument was not playing itself. (Emphasis mine)[149]

In another prose poem— "Pauvre enfant pâle" (Poor pale child)—the street musi- **75**
cian is also deprived of any sign of sympathy as he stands beneath the window of a lovely bourgeois home. While he sings, the shutters remain closed. His disheartening destiny, the subject of the poem, will be revolt, crime, the guillotine. He will become the scapegoat who *will pay* for the writer of the cruel poem:

> Poor pale child, why cry at the top of your lungs, why shout your shrill and insolent song in the street? It is lost among the cats, lords of the rooftops. For it will not pass through the shutters of the second floor, and you know nothing of the heavy curtains of pale incarnate silk there. . . .
>
> Not a penny falls into the wicker basket held by your long hand, hanging hopelessly from your pants: you'll turn bad, and one day you'll commit a crime.
>
> Your head is still erect, but it wants to leave you, as if it knew something in advance, as you sing in what is becoming a menacing manner.
>
> It will bid you farewell, that head, when you pay for me, and for those worth less than me. You came into the world toward that end, no doubt, and you'll go hungry from now on. We'll see you in the papers. Oh! Poor little head![150]

Once more, an identification is established between the poet and the beggar, but it is unlike what we saw in Wordsworth and Hugo. The poet too is the one for whom no window opens, whom no one heeds and no one pays. He too is waiting for alms. The

148. In this text, the source of Baudelaire's sympathy lies in his allegorical interpretation of the real scene, which authorizes him to read the present downfall of the acrobat as his own future as a "man of letters . . . whose stall the oblivious world no longer wishes to enter." See "Le vieux saltimbanque," 1:295–97; and Jean Starobinski, *Portrait de l'artiste en saltimbanque* (Geneva: Skira, 1970; Paris: Flammarion, "Champs," 1983).

149. Stéphane Mallarmé, *Oeuvres complètes,* ed. H. Mondor and G. Jean-Aubry (Paris: Gallimard, "Bibliothèque de la Pléaide," 1945), 270–71.

150. Ibid., 274–75.

76 head separated from the little singer anticipates that of John the Baptist, whose decapitation, in Baudelaire's Herodias cycle, figures the destiny of the "genius" who hopes to return to his chimera.[151]

In other poems, Mallarmé imagines alms granted to the poor, but they are linked to such provocative and perverse conditions that the alms given are burdened with as much negativity as those that are denied. He exhorts the poor man to purchase a blade, or, rather than "buying bread," to "extract some bizarre sin from the precious metal." The poor man is enjoined not to secure his all-too-precarious existence, but rather to squander the "loot" by seeking "superfluous" pleasures and rare sensations. "I hate useful alms," declares the poet. In this case, the end is to not receive (or give), in opposition to the traditional version of charity.[152] And at the same time—the reader is a witness to this—there is a simulacrum of poetic proselytism addressed to the beggar. Let him become the poet's brother, but a brother in his escape from daily reality, in the pleasure *given* by tobacco, wine, opium, debauchery. There is no more conclusive manner to challenge the "dominant" economic morality. A little later, Nietzsche will denounce Jewish and Christian compassion as "slave morality."

The same reversal that transforms the gift into an evil spell can be found in Mallarmé's "Les fleurs" (The flowers). Nature (an early version of the poem referred to God) is praised, as in a psalm. The first stanza of the poem, in this initial version, should be read as a variation on the gesture of largesse. Everything begins with the profusion of the purest gift:

> Des avalanches d'or du vieil azur, au jour
> Premier, et de la neige éternelle des astres,
> Mon Dieu, tu détachas les grands calices pour
> La terre jeune encore et vierge des désastres.[153]

Yet nature (or God) is praised in particular for creating for the poet's use flowers that bear death within them—and for expressly *giving* them to him so that he may return to nothingness. Let us read the first version, where the emphasis is more clearly blasphemous:

> Hosannah sur le cistre et dans les encensoirs.
> O mon Père, hosannah du profond de nos limbes!
> A jamais hosannah dans l'or des jours sans soirs,
> Par l'azur des rayons et le frisson des nimbes!

151. Mallarmé, "Cantique de saint Jean," *Oeuvres complètes,* 49. See also *Poésies,* with a preface by Yves Bonnefoy, ed. Bertrand Marchal (Paris: Gallimard, "Poésie," 1992), 83.

152. Mallarmé had a clear knowledge of the tradition, as an early poem (1869) attests. It is entitled *On donne ce qu'on a* [One gives what one has]: "Le riche au pauvre, au froid automne, / Jette l'or où brille l'espoir: / Le mendiant lui fait l'aumône avec sa prière du soir! / L'Aube de sa paupière rose / Sur l'églantier épand ses pleurs: / L'églantier donne à l'aube éclose / Ses chants d'oiseau et ses senteurs" [The rich man to the poor, in the cold of autumn, / Throws gold that shimmers with hope: / The beggar gives him alms with his evening prayer! / The Dawn with its pink eyelids / On the wild rose scatters its tears: / The wild rose gives the blooming dawn / Its birdsong and its scent). In this text, written in his eighteenth year, the poet goes out of his way to establish exact relations of reciprocity. A gift in exchange for a gift. "Each gives the little he has!" In a less naively generous moment, he will become aware of disparity and asymmetry. The gift of nothing. The gift without return.

153. Mallarmé, "Les fleurs," *Oeuvres complètes,* 33. "Avalanches of gold from the old azure, on the first / Day, and of eternal snow from the stars, / My God, you detached great chalices for / The earth, still young and virgin of disasters."

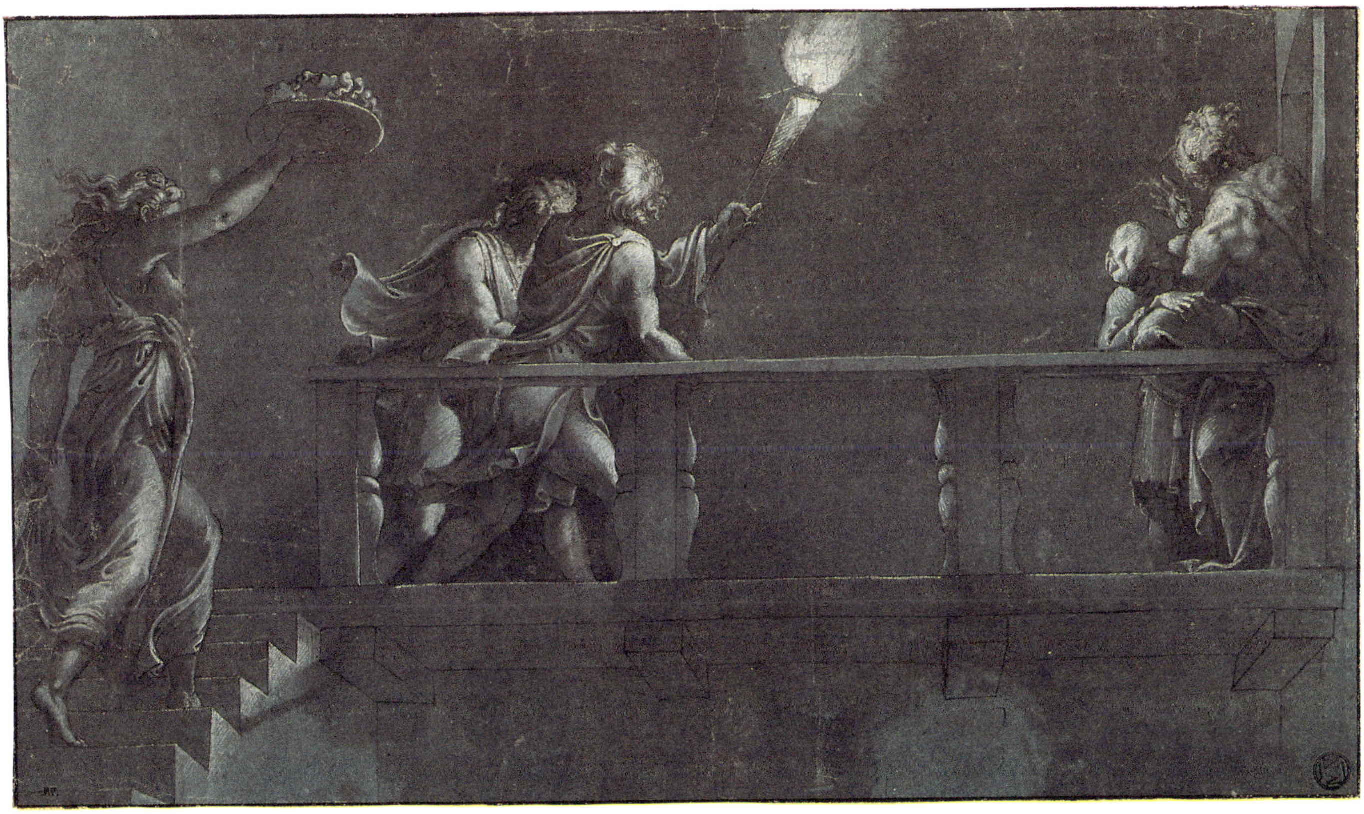

76. Giulio Romano (school of), *Salome Carrying the Head of John the Baptist,* Louvre Museum.

Car, n'oubliant personne en ton charmant effort,
Tu donnas, lui montrant son devoir sans mensonge,
De fortes fleurs *versant* comme un parfum la Mort
Au poète ennuyé que l'Impuissance ronge.[154]

In the final version, the psalm of gratitude celebrates the "calices balançant la future fiole, / De grandes fleurs avec la balsamique Mort" (chalices balancing the future phial, / Of great flowers with balsamic Death). Thanks are expressed to the giving power for the euthanasia it offers the poet.

Prodigality and Poetry: Goethe

Dishes are also thrown out the window. But they are not thrown as a gift to the itinerant singer; instead, a child throws them in order to break them. This prank is recounted by Goethe at the beginning of *Poetry and Truth.* The memory is so old that he suspects the story he heard regarding the scene has become confused with his own reminiscence. With each piece of crockery thrown and broken, his young visitors encourage him: "Noch mehr!" (More, more!) And he throws out even more dishes. The whole household goes out the window. Freud devoted a brief study to this scene, proposing we read the gesture as a symbolic expulsion of a brother who had recently been born. This interpretation is plausible in Freud's view because it is suggested and corroborated by a similar fantasy on the part of one of his patients, who had spoken of the same gesture in evoking his jealous resentment toward the newborn rival who had stolen his mother's affection. That is conceivable. But the relentlessness of the throwing, and, especially, the act of casting out ever more objects, establishes a dynamic scene that cannot be accommodated merely by the fratricidal meaning Freud attributes to it, which is a bit too univocal. Freud is intent on interpreting the sense of *what is thrown,* the unwanted brother.[155] But he does not seem to make very much of the crescendo of successive throws. This crescendo, however, belongs to the set of complex meanings of largesse, and what largesse implies about joyous destruction and endlessly recreated abundance. (Think of the ritual of the new year in certain parts of southern Italy, where broken dishes mark thc passagc to a new temporal space.) As it happens, this escalating action of *sparsio* is staged several times in Goethe's work. In a few famous instances, the meaning of the scene in full calls into question art itself or, more precisely, a certain practice of art. Let us recall three characters: Philina (in *Wilhelm Meister's Apprenticeship*), Pandora (in the uncompleted play that bears her name), and the "boy charioteer" (in the first act of the second *Faust*).

154. Ibid., 1423. "Hosannah on the cittern and in the censer. / O my Father, hosannah from the depths of our limbo! / Forever hosannah in the gold of days without evenings. / By the azure of rays and the quivering of haloes! / For, forgetting no one in your charming effort, / You *gave,* showing him his duty without lies, / Strong flowers *pouring* out like perfume Death / To the bored poet whom Impotence eats away."

155. The Freudian interpretation is not without a certain pertinence if we concede that, in the figure of his greatest love—Nathalie—Wilhelm Meister finds both the androgyne warrior (Clorinda in Tasso's *Jerusalem Delivered*) and the image of Stratonice (the "father's wife," according to the famous story by Plutarch), that is, the two figures that haunted his adolescent imagination. Among the recent commentaries on this novel, see Pietro Citati, *Goethe,* English translation by Raymond Rosenthal (New York: Dial Press, 1974).

Philina is the blond actress who whiles away her life at the mercy of caprices and pleasures of the moment. Wilhelm sees her for the first time when she stands, her hair undone, *at the window* of an inn, looking out on the square of a little town where acrobats have come to set up their stage. Wilhelm had bought a bouquet of roses from an itinerant merchant girl. Philina, who notices Wilhelm from her window, orders the little boy who serves as her hairdresser to request part of the bouquet. The gift of roses is granted to the young woman. Soon Wilhelm is welcomed into the actress's bedroom. There he sees another character, the actor Laertes, *pouring (schütten)* an entire package of grilled almonds into her lap. Philina offers Wilhelm a lovely little powder knife *(Pudermesser)* with the inscription: "Think of me" *(Gedenke mein).* Wilhelm asks for permission to make a return gift *(ein Gegengeschenk).* The little company leaves in a barouche to have lunch at the mill. There they again find theater, this time among country people (miners) turned occasional actors. On the road, Philina distributes largesse:

> Laertes had brought round the coach, and they commanded a very gay excursion. To every beggar, Philina threw out money from the window, giving along with it a merry and friendly word. . . .
>
> Philina . . . urged them to a quick return homewards, that they might arrive in time for seeing the performance of the rope-dancers in the evening. On the road back she continued her lavish generosity, in a style of gaiety reaching to extravagance; for at last, every coin belonging to herself or her companions being spent, she threw her straw hat from the window to a girl, and her neckerchief to an old woman.[156]

Wholly into the joy of the moment, living entirely on the surface of existence, Philina is prodigal with both her heart and her body: she expects gifts and she redistributes them. Her behavior is unpredictable, but she is incapable of imposture. She does not think of the future. Her misogynous companion, Laertes, sees her as "another genuine Eve, the great mother of womankind."[157] Philina, who is so often seen "en négligé" and who considers everything a pretext for song, is the (almost too obvious) allegorical figure for a gracious and facile art that is expended carelessly.

Goethe's Pandora is only very distantly related to that frivolous Eve. Epimetheus, 34
watching her return to heaven after a brief union, remembers her for the dowry of sovereign poetry she brought him. The vase does not contain unknown evils, as popular versions of the legend have it; rather, in a flow of steam, it lets loose a swarm of divine images that human beings cannot hold on to:

> I welcomed her, sweet wife, with drunken senses.
> And then approached her mysterious dowry,
> The earthen vessel with its well-turned form,
> It stood there closed. The lovely beauty advanced,
> Broke the seal placed on it by the gods, raised the cover.
> Then, rushing over the edges, a cloud boiled forth,
> Light, rising, as if an incense smoke
> Wanted to thank the Uranians. And gaily,
> From this flow of steam a star flashed up,

156. J. W. von Goethe, *Wilhelm Meister's Apprenticeship,* English translation by Thomas Carlyle, vol. 3 of *Goethe's Works* (New York: International Publishing, 1901), 113–15.

157. Ibid., 119.

Then another; more followed, bursting forth.
I raised my eyes, and already, floating on the cloud
A loving and diverse world, the images of gods.
. . . .
At the same time, the growing human mob, the choir of novices
Assembled round me as for a feast.
With joyous eye fixing the graceful figures of air
They pressed, seeking to seize them, but the spirits,
Quick to flee, escaped the earthly hands held out,
And, rising and falling, disappointed all in their pursuit.[158]

Such was Epimetheus's happiness, and such is henceforth his unappeasable torment, since Pandora herself has left his home to return to the immortals. Pandora's physical perfection was an ephemeral gift, and the fleeting images she offered are now nothing but an object of regret and melancholic reflection.

Is that the case for all poetry or only for poetry that fleetingly offers the illusion of a purity foreign to life? Goethe tried to respond to that question through the multiple voices of his characters. At the beginning of the second *Faust,* Mephistopheles is at once scriptwriter, stage director, and prompter at the great carnival unfolding at the court of the emperor. A chariot drawn by four winged horses appears suddenly in the parade. An attractive adolescent holds the reins *(Knabe Lenker);* Plutus, the god of riches, an incarnation of Faust himself, occupies the place of honor in the chariot. "Und seine reine Lust zu geben / Ist grosser als Besitz und Glück" [His pure pleasure in giving is greater than possessions and good fortune].[159] This full-cheeked god, wearing a turban and driven through the parade, suggests Mantegna's figures of Roman triumph, or the
77 allegorical figure depicted by Holbein. Plutus, wrote Lucian, never dwells in a single place.[160] He weighs so much that he cannot walk by himself; he must be transported from one home to another. This is a good pretext for carrying him about with great pomp. Holbein, however, also imagined an antithetical procession in honor of poverty: mania followed by melancholia. The carnival in the second *Faust* deliberately revives one of the genres that marked Renaissance ostentation: the "mask," the entrance or parade in disguise. Ronsard in particular wrote poems for celebrations and masquerades of this kind. And when a *rich* subject calls for a song of praise, it tends to take on the appearance of a parade.[161]

158. J. W. von Goethe, *Pandora,* in *Goethes Werke* (Hamburg: Christian Wegner, 1958), 5:335–36.

Die holde Braut empfing ich mit berauschtem Sinn.
Sodann geheimnisreicher Mitgift naht' ich mich.
Des irdenen Gefässes hoher Wohlgestalt.
Verschlossen stand's. Die Schöne freundlich trat hinzu,
Zerbrach das Göttersiegel, hub den Deckel ab.
Da schwoll gedrängt ein leichter Dampf aus ihm hervor,
Als wollt' ein Weihrauch danken den Uraniern.
Und fröhlich fuhr ein Sternblitz aus dem Dampf heraus
Sogleich ein andrer; andre folgten heftig nach.
Da blickt' ich auf, und auf der Wolke schwebten, schon
Im Gaukeln lieblich, Götterbilder, buntgedrängt. . . .
Indessen hatte sich das frische Menschenchor,
Das Chor der Neulinge, versammelt mir zum Fest.
Sie starrten froh die muntern Luftgeburten an
Und drangen zu und haschten. Aber flüchtiger
Und irdisch ausgestreckten Händen unerreich—
Bar jene, steigend jetzt empor und jetzt gesenkt,
Die Menge täuschten stets sie, die verfolgende.

159. J. W. von Goethe, *Faust, Part One and Part Two,* English translation by Charles E. Passage (Indianapolis, New York, and Kansas City: Bobbs-Merrill, 1965), 1.1.946–47 (p. 196) [translation modified].

160. Lucian, *Timon,* 20.21.

161. Such is the case for his great song of praise *L'or* [Gold].

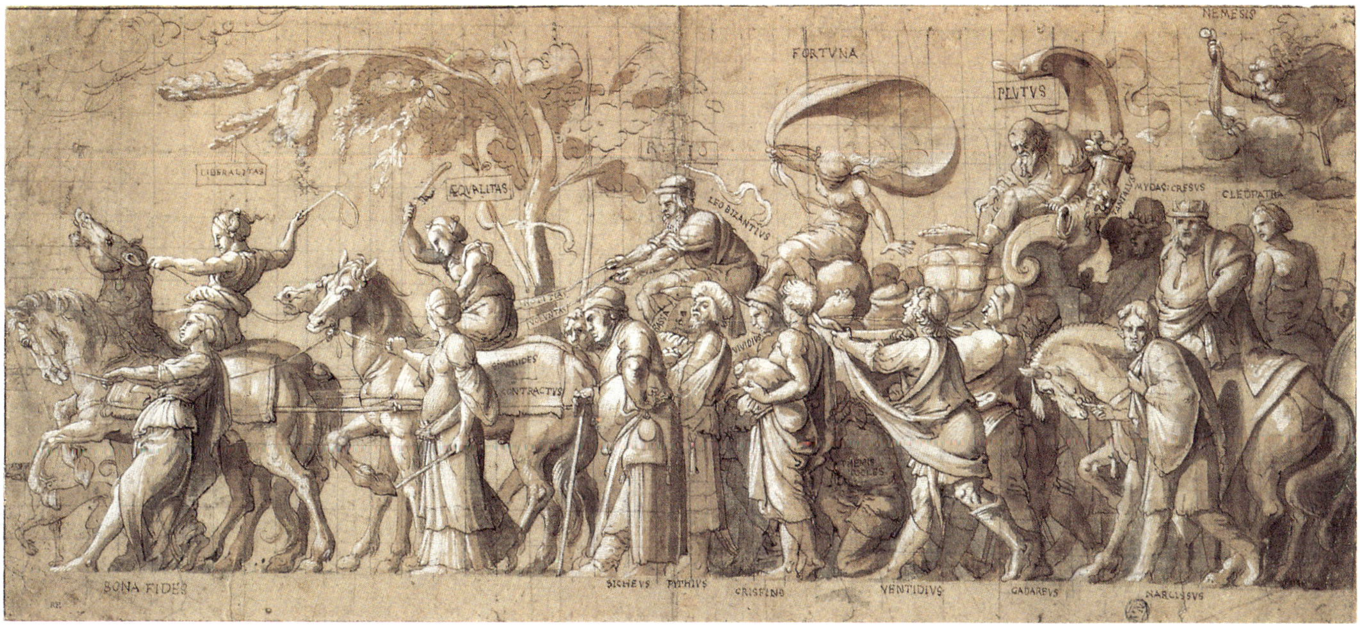

77. Hans Holbein the Younger, *The Triumph of Wealth,* Louvre Museum; and detail.

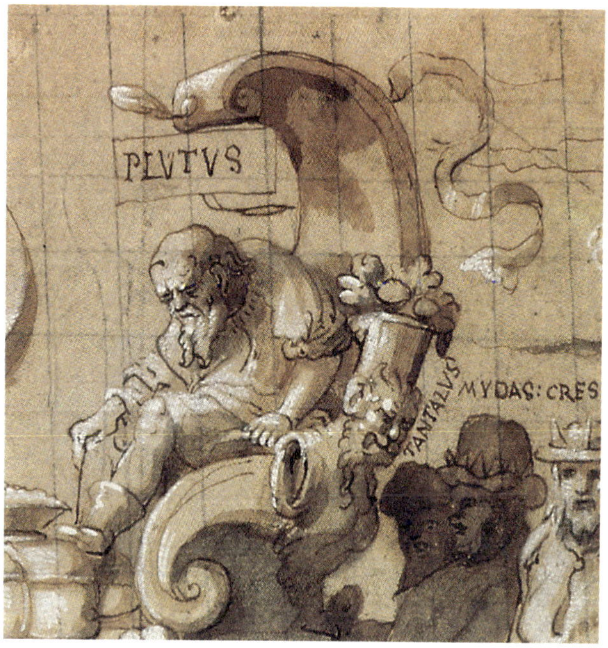

77, detail

"We are allegories," declares the boy charioteer, and he is not long in revealing his identity:

> My names are Lavishness and Poetry.
> I am the poet who achieves his ends
> When he his inner substance most expends.
> I too have riches infinite, and here
> I look upon myself as Plutus's peer.
> I deck his dances, I am his banquet's pride,
> And what he lacks for, I provide.[162]

What are his powers? Invited to manifest them, he immediately complies. With a snap of his fingers, he brings forth necklaces, gold buckles, rings, and sparks. The crowd fights over them. But, in the hands of the greedy possessors, everything decomposes, falls apart, and slips away. The herald comments on the spectacle:

> How this dear crowd does grab and rush!
> The giver is half stifled in the crush.
> He snaps forth gems as in a dream
> And all grab for their flash and gleam.
> And now these are new tricks I see:
> What each one grabs so eagerly
> Proves actually a sorry prize:
> No sooner caught than off it flies.
> The pearls come loose and slip their strand
> And beetles wriggle in his hand;
> The poor oaf flicks them off for dead
> And there they buzz around his head.
> Others, instead of solid things,
> Catch butterflies with wanton wings.
> For all his promises, the bold
> Rogue gives what only *gleams* like gold.[163]

Recall the circus games Seneca imagined given by Fortune, and the *missilia* thrown out to the battling crowd. We find the same confused melee here, and the same final nothingness of the distributed wealth. But here the *sparsio* has become the very act of poetry. The question is, then: Can poetry be possessed? Or is it the flame that can never be fixed in one place? Goethe leaves us in uncertainty. Are the jewels the charioteer disperses the image of poetry in general, which we must accept as a "beautiful appear-

162. Goethe, *Faust,* 2.1.961–67. "Bin die Verschwendung, bin die Poesie; / Bin der Poet, der sich vollendet, / Wenn er sein eigenst Gut verschwendet / Auch ich bin unermesslich reich! / Und schätze mich dem Plutus gleich, / Beleb' und schmück' ihm Tanz und Schmaus, / Das, was ihm felt, sa teil' ich aus."

163. Ibid., 978–94 (pp. 197–98).

> Wie greift und hascht die liebe Menge!
> Fast kommt der Geber ins Gedränge.
> Kleinode schnippt er wie ein Traum,
> Und alles hascht im weiten Raum.
> Doch da erbel' ich neue Pfiffe:
> Was einer noch so emsig griffe,
> Des hat er wirklich schlechten Lohn,
> Die Gabe flattert ihm davon.
> Es löst sich auf das Perlenband,
> Ihm krabbeln Käfer in der Hand.
> Er wirft sie weg, der arme Tropf,
> Und sie unsummern ihm den Kopf.
> Die andern statt solider Dinge
> Erhaschen frevle Schetterlinge.
> Wie doch der Schelm so viel verheisst
> Und nur verleiht, was golden gleisst!

ance"? In that case, after their moment of fascination, human beings' stupidity would consist in not accepting poetry's lack of solidity, in rejecting it because it is not a thing, and in not divining that there is an essence *(Wesen)* under the outward appearance. Or is Goethe targeting only a certain type of poetry, more clearly defined with the romantic excesses of Euphorion, the later incarnation of the charioteer, the son sired by Faust and conceived by the shadow of Helen of Troy? Euphorion is Byron's allegorical double, destined for Icarus's fate, that is, destined to fall from the sky in full frolic. That kind of poetry would be unauthentic and deceptive, like Mephistopheles's worthless money or the blazing metallic wealth that Plutus—in the same carnival parade[164]—brings forth from his coffers: an insolvent poetry, a bouncing check. The response (one possible response) is given when Plutus descends from the chariot and liberates the charioteer, returning him to solitude, far from the fete:

> Off to your sphere now, straight!
> Here it is not! Wild, checkered, and unclear
> Are those deformed shapes crowded round here.
> Only where clear in clarity your gaze,
> On self rely, to self belong, by ways
> Where nothing pleases but the good and fair
> In solitude—go found your kingdom there.[165]

It is clear that poetry, even when it is prodigal, is not made to be yoked to the chariot of riches; it is not designed to distribute its goods indiscriminately to the crowd. Such was already the injunction that Seneca addressed to his disciple Lucilius, through the great image of Fortune, mistress of the public games: "Let us withdraw!" The poet is now the recipient of the same ethical precept.

But this time, he is not to turn away from fortune to devote himself to virtuous asceticism: rather, he is to construct a world through language. The riches of art cannot consist in the illusionism of prodigality. As long as he throws his trinkets to the multitude, the charioteer is no different from Nero, the great star of *sparsio* and of the *bel canto,* who believed that Rome was losing an artist when the fatal blow struck him down. The fulfillment of poetry, the expectation of a clear world, impose a higher morality.

164. The scene is repeated as a parody in Bulgakov's *Master i Margerita* (chap. 12), a very free variation on the Faust theme.

165. Goethe, *Faust,* 2.1.1078–84 (p. 200). "Nun frisch zu deiner Sphäre! / Hier ist sie nicht! Verworren, scheckig, wild / Umdrängt uns hier ein fratzenhaftes Gebild. / Nur wo du klar ins holde Klare schaust. / Dir angehörst und dir allein vertraust. / Dorthin, wo Schönes, Gutes nur gefällt. / Zur Einsamkeit!—da schaffe deine Welt."

CHAPTER FIVE
New Children's Battles

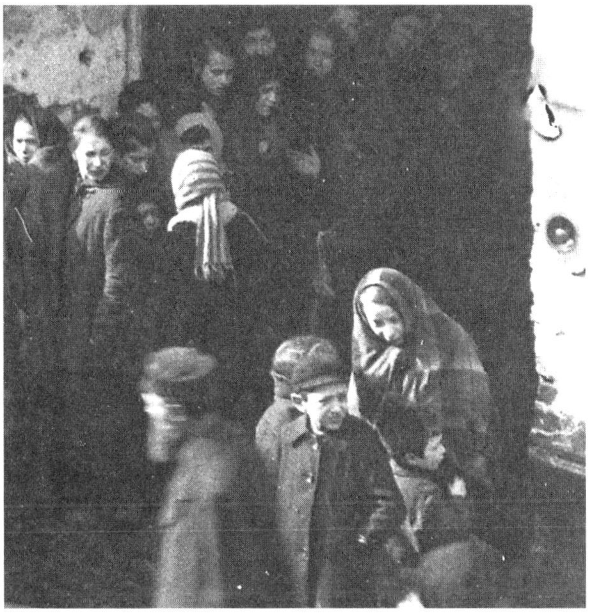

Baudelaire did not like Rousseau. He had read him with enough attention, however, not to remain indifferent and not to cling to hostility on principle, as he did toward Voltaire, the antipoet. In Baudelaire's critical texts, in his intimate journals, and in *Spleen de Paris,* Rousseau was both a model and an adversary. For a time, Baudelaire imagined giving the collection of his prose poems a Rousseauian title: *Le promeneur solitaire.* He noted on a list of possible projects: "On Jean-Jacques—sentimental and vile author." [166] The avowed Rousseauism of George Sand definitively situated Rousseau among those who, refusing to believe in hell and sin, placed undue confidence in nature and in their own feelings. Jean-Jacques, who "got high without hashish," had "a superlative idea of his own moral value." [167] He deified himself. Baudelaire's criticism was that Rousseau confused imagining virtue, having a sensation of moral goodness, with possessing a true "practical aptitude for virtue." In other words, his criticism targeted the confusion between aesthetics and ethics. "He completely confuses dreams with actions, and his imagination, overheated by the enchanting spectacle of his own mended and idealized nature, substitutes that fascinating image of himself for the real individual he is, so poor in will, so rich in vanity. As a result, he ends up decreeing his apotheosis in the clear and simple terms that, for him, contain a whole world of abominable pleasures: *I am the most virtuous of men!*" [168]

Baudelaire develops this critique of Rousseau in narrative form in his prose poem "Le gâteau" (1861),[169] where we discover a peculiar, perhaps semiconscious, strategy. Baudelaire echoes two famous passages from Rousseau, reworking and reinterpreting the motifs, which are easily recognizable: the exalting ascension to the mountains (*La nouvelle Héloïse,* pt. 1, chap. 23) and the peasants' battle (*Les rêveries du promeneur solitaire,* ninth reverie, which served as the starting point for the present study). Baudelaire thus rereads Rousseau in order to refute him with his own images. He readjusts two scenes to make them say the opposite of what Rousseau wished to lead his readers to concede.

In the first part of "Le gâteau," where, no doubt, a personal memory of Baudelaire's intrudes,[170] readers have noted how close the expressions of happiness are to those found in the famous letter by Saint-Preux on Valais.[171] In this case, the fiction uses a mixture of youthful reminiscences and literary formulas: "I stood in the middle of a landscape of irresistible grandeur and nobility." Human activity is announced only by "the bells of the cattle grazing out of sight, far away, on the other side of another mountain." But the description of the harmonious countryside, which forms the first part of the narrative, is

166. Baudelaire, "De quelques préjugés contemporains," 2:54.

167. Baudelaire, "Le poème du haschich" (4), *Les paradis artificiels,* 1:436.

168. Ibid; emphasis in original.

169. See "Texts on the Gift," no. 2, below.

170. This was a trip Baudelaire took to the Pyrenees in 1838 in the company of his father-in-law.

171. See the critical notes by Robert Kopp in his edition of *Petits poèmes en prose* (Paris: José Corti, 1969). See also Starobinski (n. 5 above), "Sur Rousseau et Baudelaire," "Rousseau, Baudelaire, Huysmans," "Don fastueux et don pervers," and Marcel Gutwirth, "A propos du *Gâteau:* Baudelaire, Rousseau et le recours à l'enfance," *Romanic Review* 80, 1 (January 1989): 75–88.

soon marked by the dissonance of irony. It is then no longer possible to doubt that the narrator is making fun of himself: his feelings have steered him wrong. The ecstasy of fusion is devalued almost as soon as it is evoked: "In short, owing to the beauty that surrounded me and filled me with enthusiasm, I felt at perfect peace with myself and with the universe; I even believe that, in my perfect bliss and my total obliviousness to all earthly ills, I had reached the point of no longer finding so ridiculous the newspapers that claim man is born good." The legitimacy of the word "perfect," insistently repeated, is called into doubt by that very insistence, and thus becomes somewhat suspect. Used in that way, the modifier is more appropriate for describing the effects of a toxin—the effect of a euphoria destined to disappear quickly.

"Man is born good."[172] At the end of the sentence, these words of Rousseau himself mark the ironic denial of the ecstatic impulse. Rousseau is not named: his thinking is attacked in the vulgar form it assumes in "the newspapers" that extol the virtues of optimism and progress. Like Joseph de Maistre before him, Baudelaire isolates the extremely famous formulation of Rousseau's doctrine, which, rejecting traditional theology, denies original sin and its propagation from one human generation to the next. Rousseau dared maintain that vice is external in origin and that sin is not part of human nature: therein lies Baudelaire's grievance. We immediately understand that, for the narrator of the prose poem, the journalistic diffusion of the idea of natural goodness disqualifies it: it has lost all philosophical authority and has become part of some impersonal humanitarian chatter.

In *La nouvelle Héloïse,* Rousseau's hero describes the joy and purifying relief he experienced as he climbed the peaks: the traveler was freed from evil in leaving the cities below, where men, captive to appearance and amour-propre, suffer the constraints of poverty and inequality. Saint-Preux becomes once more part of a pastoral world living closer to primitive equity and experiences the joys of "disinterested humanity" and "the zeal of hospitality." In Rousseau's text, the social idyll adds to the aesthetic joy of contemplating vast horizons. "When I arrived in a hamlet in the evening, everyone would eagerly come out to offer me his home, so that I was embarrassed by the choice. . . . Food is abundant and there is no access to the outside world and no excessive consumption within this one. And no mountain farmer, whose labor is a pleasure, becomes less hardworking because of that abundance."[173] The mountain village is the place of the gift.

172. Rousseau repeated this many times: in the *Discours sur l'origine et les fondements de l'inégalité* [Discourse on the origin and foundations of inequality], in the *Profession de foi du vicaire savoyard* [Profession of Faith of the Vicar of Savoy], in the *Lettre à Christophe de Beaumont,* in the third *Dialogue,* etc.

173. Rousseau, *La nouvelle Héloïse,* pt. 1, letter 23, *Oeuvres complètes* (Paris: Gallimard, "Bibliothèque de la Pléiade," 1961), 2:79–80. "After I had taken a walk in the clouds, I reached a more serene place from which, in the proper season, one can see storms and lightning forming below. . . . From there, in the purity of the air in which I found myself, I gradually sorted out the true cause of the change in my mood, and the return of that internal peace that I had so long ago lost. . . . Meditations in that place take on a grand and sublime character, proportionate to the objects striking us, and provide a quiet pleasure that is neither bitter nor sensual. It seems that, in rising above the land of men, one leaves behind all low and earthly feelings, and, as one approaches ethereal regions, the soul acquires something of their unchanging purity. . . . There is something magical or supernatural about this spectacle, which delights the mind and the senses: one forgets everything, one forgets oneself, one no longer knows where one is." Rousseau's text, in which reminiscences of the narrative of Petrarch's ascension of Mount Ventoux can be detected, also contains verses from the *Canzoniere.*

Nothing is asked of the traveler; on the contrary, he is *offered* everything he could desire. Surrounded by the eagerness of his hosts, Saint-Preux tastes the hospitality *received* and becomes the center of a happy world, just as in the ninth reverie, Rousseau becomes the center of a fete where "contented faces" respond to his equitable distribution of a little treat.

In La Chevrette, as we saw, Rousseau did not consider his act true alms, but merely a better "amusement" (compared to that of good society), a little "comedy" whose "denouement" he was happy to provide. In carefully rereading Rousseau's text, we found that the equitable division of the apples was an *aesthetic* choice, even though it was determined by an *ethical* condemnation of the violence provoked by the gingerbread thrown this way and that. And in this aesthetic choice, the narcissistic component, as Rousseau himself admits, was very important.

Baudelaire cannot accept any of all that: not the way Rousseau asks nature to guarantee both the beauty of the world and the goodness of man; not the way a little gift exhibited in front of witnesses permits Rousseau to acquit himself of all the charges he makes against "good society"; not the way Rousseau undertakes to find, in the resources of his own conscience—in his unfailing innocence—the compensation for the evils *they* made him suffer. Above all, Baudelaire does not accept the idealized image of a mountain society where a virtuous autarky assures both frugality and abundance.

Rousseau proposed a little comedy in two acts, where the scene of true joy followed the scene of violence and of "exclusivist tastes engendered by contempt." In constructing his own diptych, Baudelaire reverses the two scenes. The bright scene is the first described, but it is checked by irony since, at the ethical level, this country "nobility" (with its premonitory counterpoint of white and black) is stripped of any convincing value. The dark scene follows. The violence is irrevocable. The curtain falls; the final jot is set in place at the moment when the work of destruction leaves no room for hope. Thus, Baudelaire uses Rousseauian elements to reverse the order that allowed Rousseau to repair the damage done and allowed redemption to triumph over evil. The critique functions by inverting the consoling order of events. In Rousseau, the fete follows the brawl; in Baudelaire, the brawl follows "virtuistic" ecstasy.

78 How does Baudelaire construct the scene of evil after his flight into pseudo unity? The narration hints at recalling to mind everything that contradicts the obliviousness to "earthly things" and the flight toward the false ideal: heaviness, "the imperative of incurable matter," can be felt in the very body of the narrator, who had taken pleasure in his disincarnated "lightness" (of his own thoughts, of the surrounding atmosphere). Artifice and commerce intrude: Where is natural purity when the traveler decides to mix "a certain elixir" sold by "the pharmacists" into the melted snow? He then pulls from his pocket "a big piece of bread":

> I was calmly cutting up my bread when a very soft noise made me look up. Before me stood a ragged creature, black and tousled, whose hollow, fierce, and as it were supplicating eyes were devouring the piece of bread. And I heard him sigh, in a low and raucous voice, the word "cake"! I could not keep myself from laughing upon hearing the name with which he had wished to honor my bread, which was nearly white, and I cut off a nice slice and offered it to him.

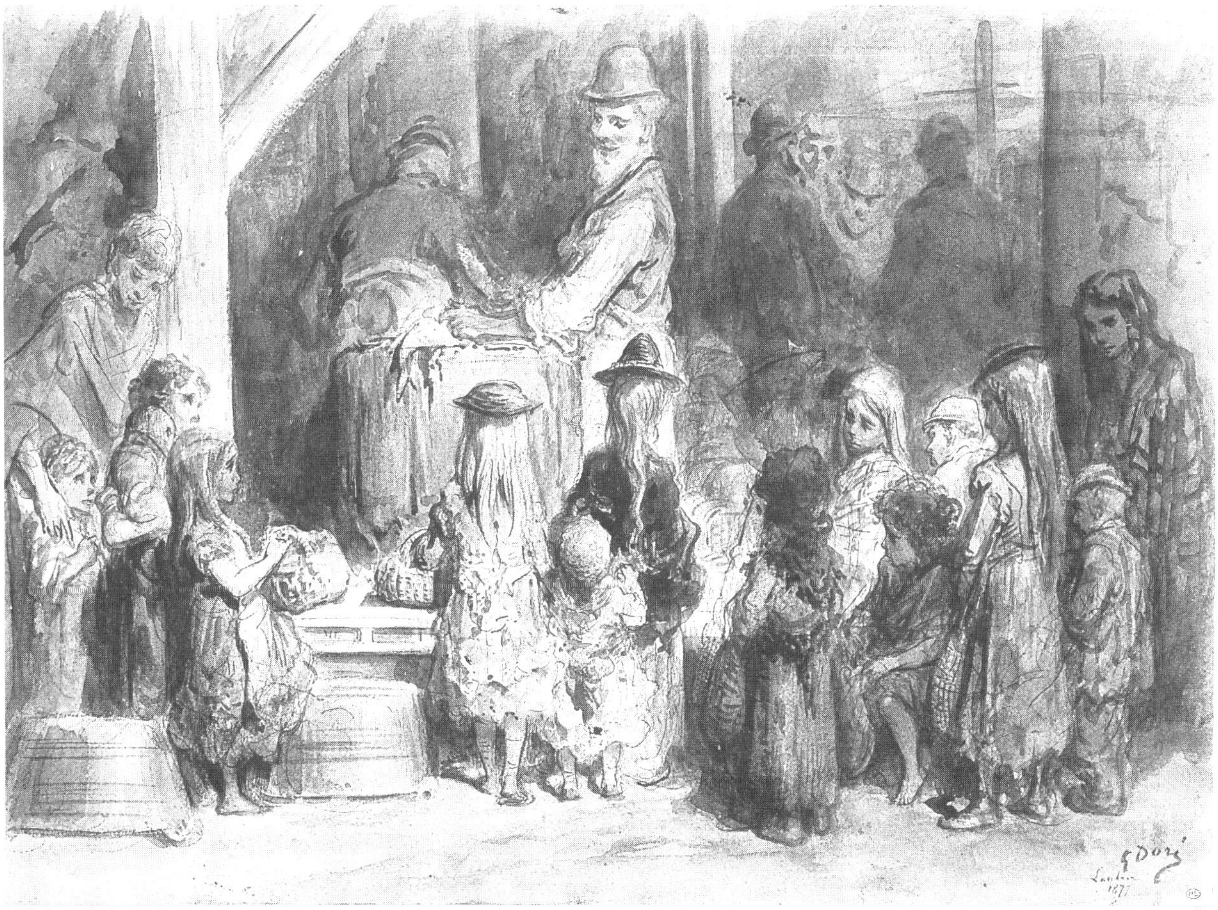

78. Gustave Doré, *The Charity of the Fishmongers,* Louvre Museum, Orsay Museum Collection.

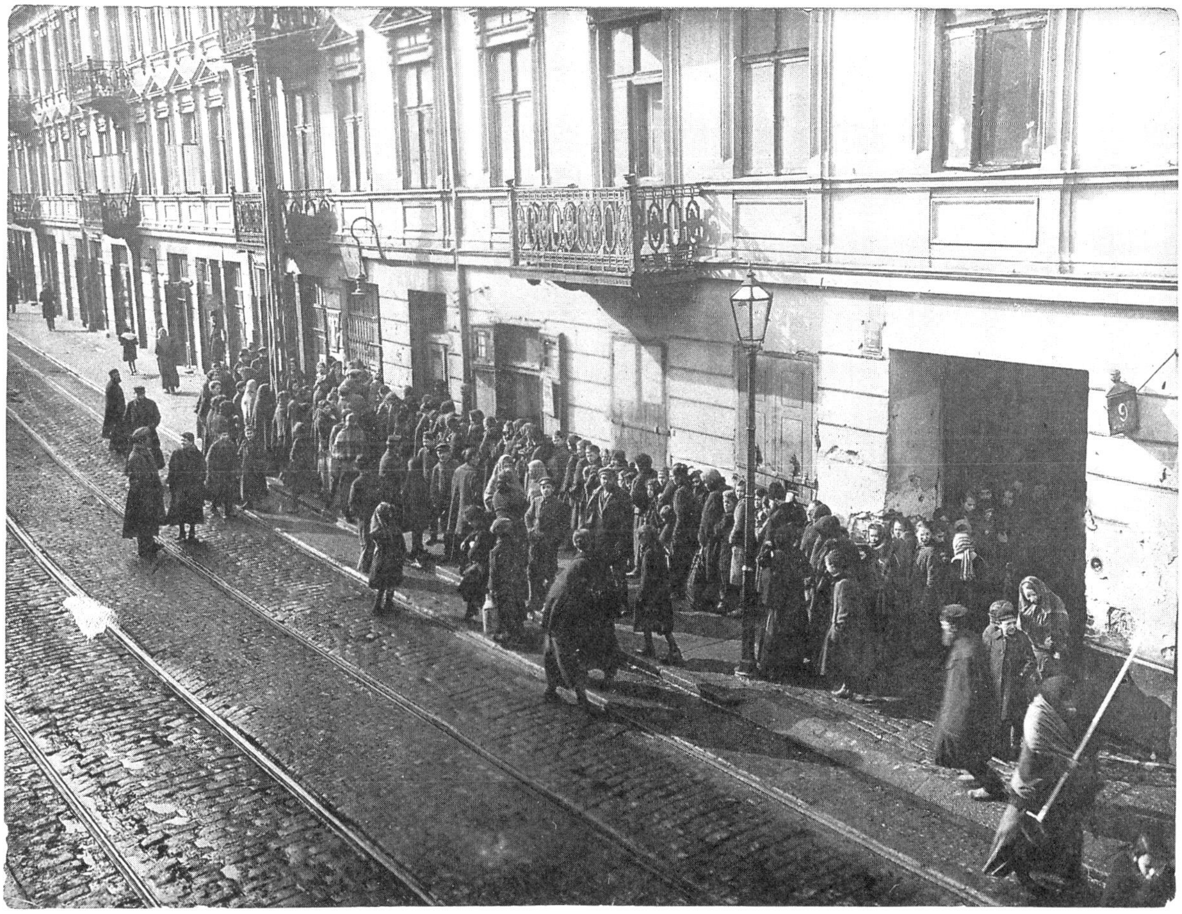

79. Anonymous photographer, *Waiting in Line,* Orsay Museum. The photograph was taken in the Jewish quarter of Warsaw between 1913 and 1922.

The "soft noise" destroys the magic established by the immense and fragile silence
17 of the beginning. The child who has just received the slice of bread is immediately "knocked over by another little savage, come from who knows where, and so perfectly similar to the first that he might have been taken for his twin brother. Together they rolled about on the ground, fighting for the precious prey, neither wishing to sacrifice half to his brother." After a lengthy and atrocious struggle, there is no longer "any object of the battle: the *piece of bread* had disappeared, scattered into crumbs like the *grains of sand* with which it was now mixed" (my emphasis). The annihilation of the "object of the battle" recalls the scene in La Chevrette, where, in the end, the young people maim one another "brutally . . . to grab greedily at a few *pieces of gingerbread* that had been trampled underfoot and covered with *mud*" (my emphasis). In returning to sand or mud, the gift of food is no longer fit for consumption: the effect of the gift is disastrous and may even be attributed to a perverse intention. We also note that, in Rousseau, the debasing hyperbole of "*herds* of men debased by poverty" finds its counterpart in the Baudelairean expression "little *savage*" (Rousseau's writings, in contrast, conferred an idyllic sense on the word "savage").[174] Let us note, in addition, that Baudelaire, as in many other texts, here adopts an allegorical view. The first receiver of the slice of bread necessarily had only one rival, and that rival had to look like him. Not Cain and Abel, but two Cains who are both equally mean.[175] As a result, the combat takes on an emblematic value. It is a lesson concerning human nature under poverty conditions. The narrator is now no more than a dismayed spectator who can no longer return to his initial ecstasy of contemplating the landscape. Rousseau, in contrast, remained a participant in the two scenes (a contributor to them); he set them against each other, tallied up the two events, and, weighing the value *given* and the pleasure *taken,* drew up the balance sheet to his advantage: "I felt with satisfaction the difference between healthy tastes and natural pleasures and those produced by opulence, which are only the pleasures of mockery and the exclusivist tastes engendered by contempt." In the Baudelairian narrative, the narrator does not attribute any merit to himself. Has he performed an act of charity? He saw the first child, met his imploring gaze, registered his envy, and *laughed* at the only word pronounced: "cake." A disproportionate, inappropriate word. Then he cut off and of-

174. A hyperbolic metaphor, in fact. In Baudelaire, the first child pronounces the inappropriate word *cake* to designate the "bread, which was nearly white," which he had as yet never seen or heard named. In doing so, he resorts to what Rousseau calls a metaphor in the *Essai sur l'origine des langues.* Rousseau's example is the frightened man who encounters another man for the first time and calls him *giant.* But Rousseau is using the rhetorical term "metaphor" rather freely. "Cake" and "giant" are passionate aberrations from the norm. This is not the place to comment on Rousseau's conjectural linguistics. On the value of the word "cake" in Baudelaire, see the poem "La voix": "Deux voix me parlaient. L'une insidieuse et ferme, / Disait: 'La Terre est un gâteau plein de douceur; / Je puis (et ton plaisir serait alors sans terme!) / Te faire un appétit d'une égale grosseur!'" [Two voices spoke to me. One, insidious and firm, / Said, 'The Earth is a cake of exceeding sweetness; / I could (and then your pleasure would be without end!) / Make your appetite equal in size.'] (from "Pièces diverses" [17], 1:170; see n. 146 above). In Mallarmé's *La dernière mode,* the gift of cake "to the children of a friend" has become commonplace (Mallarmé, *Oeuvres complètes,* 786; n. 149 above).

175. In the prose poem "Le joujou du pauvre," Baudelaire finally neutralizes the opposition between poor and rich children by making them laugh at each other "with teeth of *equal* whiteness" (1:305). In *Les demoiselles de village,* Gustave Courbet represents giving alms to a little peasant girl, but the element of social criticism discernible in this painting does not have the bitterness of the Baudelairean narrative. In *L'aumône d'un mendiant à Ornans,* we see an old beggar giving alms to a little child in rags. The drawing by Courbet, engraved by Gillot, is reproduced in M. Schapiro, *Modern Art* (n. 11 above). On Courbet, see Michael Fried, *Courbet's Realism* (Chicago: University of Chicago Press, 1990).

fered a slice of bread. No mention of compassion. And, when the second child makes his brutal appearance, the narrator does not attempt to intervene in the struggle. No additional alms, no intercession. The accumulated details lead us to suppose he is fascinated and paralyzed by the spectacle of evil. (*Curiosity* about evil is never absent in Baudelaire, and often—particularly in the narrative "La fausse monnaie"—it appears more excusable to him than hypocritical fraud and the simulation of goodness.) The description is both comic and repugnant. For it records at great length the vicissitudes of a struggle between equals that has no other effect than to destroy the coveted object:

> The first, aggravated, grabbed the second by his hair; then he seized his ear in his teeth, and spit out a bloody bite of it with a superb curse in patois. The legitimate owner of the cake tried to plant his little claws in the eyes of the usurper; in his turn the other applied all his strength toward strangling his adversary with one hand while with the other he tried to slip the prize of the battle into his pocket. But, revived by despair, the vanquished boy got back up and sent the vanquisher rolling onto the ground with a blow from his head to the other's stomach. What is the point of describing a hideous struggle that in truth lasted longer than their childish strength seemed to promise? The cake kept traveling from hand to hand and changed pockets at every moment; but alas, it also changed in volume.

Every part of the body parades by: hair, ears, eyes, teeth, claws, neck, stomach. The narrator has taken pains to vary the aspects of the battle, while using the figure of paraleipsis to suggest he is reporting only a small part of it. "What is the point of describing . . . ?" he writes, having just described an entire series of episodes and provisional triumphs. . . .

In fact, Baudelaire constructed his narrative with an obvious concern for visual effect and with faithfulness to a "dream": his entire aesthetics can be recognized here. The bitten ear and "the bloody bite" spit out by one of the fighters, in increasing the precision of the scene, give an intense splash of color to a text whose chromatic values of bright and dark had until that point been those of a drawing or an engraving.

Let us look even more closely. The description of the ascension into the mountain landscape lays down a vast *background.* The tones of this background are generally bright, and the dark image of the little savages and their battle thus forms a violent contrast to it in the second part of the text. Nonetheless, in anticipation of the major opposition between the two parts of the text, the initial background itself includes the contrast between a general luminosity and the black spot of the "little motionless lake," which also corresponds to "fear" mixed with "joy." In his technique as a sketch artist, which in this case suggests the techniques of Goya or Daumier,[176] Baudelaire distributes the power of black. When the "ragged . . . *black* and tousled" child appears, he has already been anticipated by the lake, "*black* in its immense depth." In the same way, certain repetitions, hardly striking at first glance, contribute toward marking the contrast and at the same time assuring unity. Several terms used in the bright part of the poem and repeated in the dark make the reversal all the more troubling. The word *perfect,* used first as a superlative that modifies the narrator's "peace" and "bliss" when con-

176. For an evocation of the treatment of Daumier's fable, *Les voleurs et l'âne,* see M. Zimmerman, "Trois études sur Baudelaire et Rousseau," in *Etudes Baudelairiennes* 9 (Neuchâtel: Baconnière, 1981), 39. Decamps also represented the scene of the thieves and the ass.

fronted with the beauty of the world, is once more available to the poet as he describes the excess of violence: "a *perfectly* fratricidal war." The "*total* obliviousness to *all* earthly evil" elicits a joy that has "*totally* disappeared" by the end. Not even the *travels* of an (at first) happy consciousness ("I was traveling") is spared an absurd, mechanical, and degraded repetition, when the coveted object *travels* from hand to hand and from pocket to pocket.

Two "little beings" and a disputed slice of bread were all that were needed for everything to be turned upside down, transforming a subjective peace into the most objective of wars. Another symmetry is also striking: just as the first part gave an unwarranted *ethical* meaning to the beauty of the landscape, the second part attributes an unwarranted *aesthetic* value to certain aspects of the "hideous struggle." Note that the "*superb* curse in patois" presupposes an ironic detachment and an attention to "proper usage" that might appear displaced, were we not aware that Baudelaire has become an accomplice (that is, he pretends to be an accomplice) of the well-read reader: the narrative appeared in the periodical *La presse* (24 September 1862). The irony expressed in relation to the newspapers that "claim man is born good" proves that Baudelaire knows the stylistic means to be used to reach a newspaper public (which is always full of scorn for those who subscribe to *another* newspaper). He uses the feature writer's formulas to sarcastically evoke the struggle between the poor children. To be more precise, he adopts resources of style known from the time of Renaissance and seventeenth-century burlesque poems: these consist in using "noble" words or pedant locutions to narrate vulgar incidents. To be sure, the "low" terms are not lacking in the narrative of the fight, but others belong to the "high" register: juridical expressions such as "legitimate owner," "usurper," "prize of the battle," "precious prey," and even "war" solicit a smile because of their pomposity. They must be read from an ironic distance—as recourse to *forced* comedy. In this case, Baudelaire's sketch is caricatural and lends itself to the interpretation he himself gave of caricature. "A curious thing worthy of attention is the introduction of the element of the beautiful which lies beyond our grasp, even in works destined to represent to man his own moral and physical ugliness."[177] The mixture of the beautiful and the ugly does not allow the mind to rest easy. The last paragraph of the prose poem ends with a sentence repeated "endlessly," and thus with the impossibility of resting easy:

> This spectacle had clouded over the landscape for me, and the calm joy my soul had taken pleasure in [*s'ébaudissait*] before seeing these little men had totally disappeared; I remained sad for quite a long time, endlessly repeating: "There is thus a superb country where bread is called cake, and where it is a treat so rare that it is enough to engender a perfectly fratricidal war."

The concluding meditation makes sadness and opacity fall upon the landscape. The "calm joy" of the beginning cannot withstand a reality test. In the retrospective evocation of that joy, the bawdy expression *s'ébaudissait* introduces once more an ironic and diminutive value. Joy has lost its universal dimension. Mystical unity, sensed a moment earlier, has been reduced to a little personal titillation. The transparence so dear to Rousseau is done for. The view of a ruthless struggle of "little men" contradicts in the worst way the

177. Baudelaire, "De l'essence du rire et généralement du comique dans les arts plastiques," 2:526.

idea of childhood innocence and original goodness. An offered slice of bread has become a *casus belli* for its beneficiaries, each of whom is incapable of "sacrific[ing] half for his brother." In the final reflection, the social dimension of evil appears fully, and we are astonished to find in Baudelaire's writing an indictment—with political import—against the "superb country where bread is called cake." But contrary to Rousseau, Baudelaire does not radically distinguish between human nature and social evil. For him, evil is a fundamental "anthropological" given, not the consequence of a defect in the formulation of rules of civil association.

The Folly of Art

On a list of possible projects, Baudelaire noted: "Imagine a poor starving man wishing to take advantage of a public fete and a distribution of foodstuffs to get something to eat. He is knocked down and pummeled by the multitude."[178] Another possible project he jotted down—it is no doubt the same idea—is entitled "Distribution des vivres" (Distribution of foodstuffs).[179] The story outlined brings to mind Melville's "Rich Man's Crumbs." But the outline also resembles "Le gâteau," except that "the multitude" (a singular collective noun) has replaced the twin brother. In any case, it would be a mistake to believe that Baudelaire's intention is simply to imagine a cruel scene under the gaze of a curious witness, who occupies the sadistic role of the tyrant or master of circus games, taking pleasure in the scuffle provoked by a *sparsio*.

In Baudelaire, an obscure drive constantly calls for the violent scene, but the end in view is not the spectacle of destruction: for him, the important thing is to incite to moral revendication, to offer the scene to view as an angel's scourge.[180] In "Le gâteau," the appearance of the two poor children, then their battle, demonstrate the inanity of becoming intoxicated on virtue like Rousseau. The act of giving the slice of bread and its disastrous consequences is the testing of a philosophical thesis through images.

On another occasion, Baudelaire does not hesitate to stage the act of giving to a poor man, in order to contradict another aesthetico-philosophical thesis: namely, "the puerile utopia of the school of *art for art's sake*."[181] Being intoxicated on beauty is no less reprehensible in his eyes than being intoxicated on virtue (Rousseau provides the all too contagious example of the latter). Baudelaire castigates the attitude of "the indefatigable musician or hack artist who has made a satanic pact with his instrument."[182] Their efforts are achieved "outside the law of truth."[183] Baudelaire's attacks against "voluptuosism" (his neologism) are as sharp as his criticism of the presumptuousness of sentiment. According to him, both attitudes fall short of the ethical imperative, which requires that the "true poet" be "an incarnation."[184] When poetry fulfills its "destiny," "it

178. Baudelaire, 1:595.

179. Ibid., 1:368.

180. The prose poem "Assommons les pauvres" [Let's pummel the poor] describes in detail the blows dealt an impoverished man by the narrator. The sadistic complacency is obvious. But the point is to show in fiction how the poor man, as a result of being subjected to unjust violence, finally counterattacks and refuses to be humiliated. The parable, which recalls Swift, entails a practical pedagogy that teaches the feeling of equality. The "slave" achieves recognition if he revolts successfully. The paradox here is that the "master" deliberately pushes the slave to revolt. The master becomes the aggressor working for his own defeat.

181. Baudelaire, "Pierre Dupont [I]," 2:26.

182. Ibid., 27.

183. Ibid.

184. Ibid.

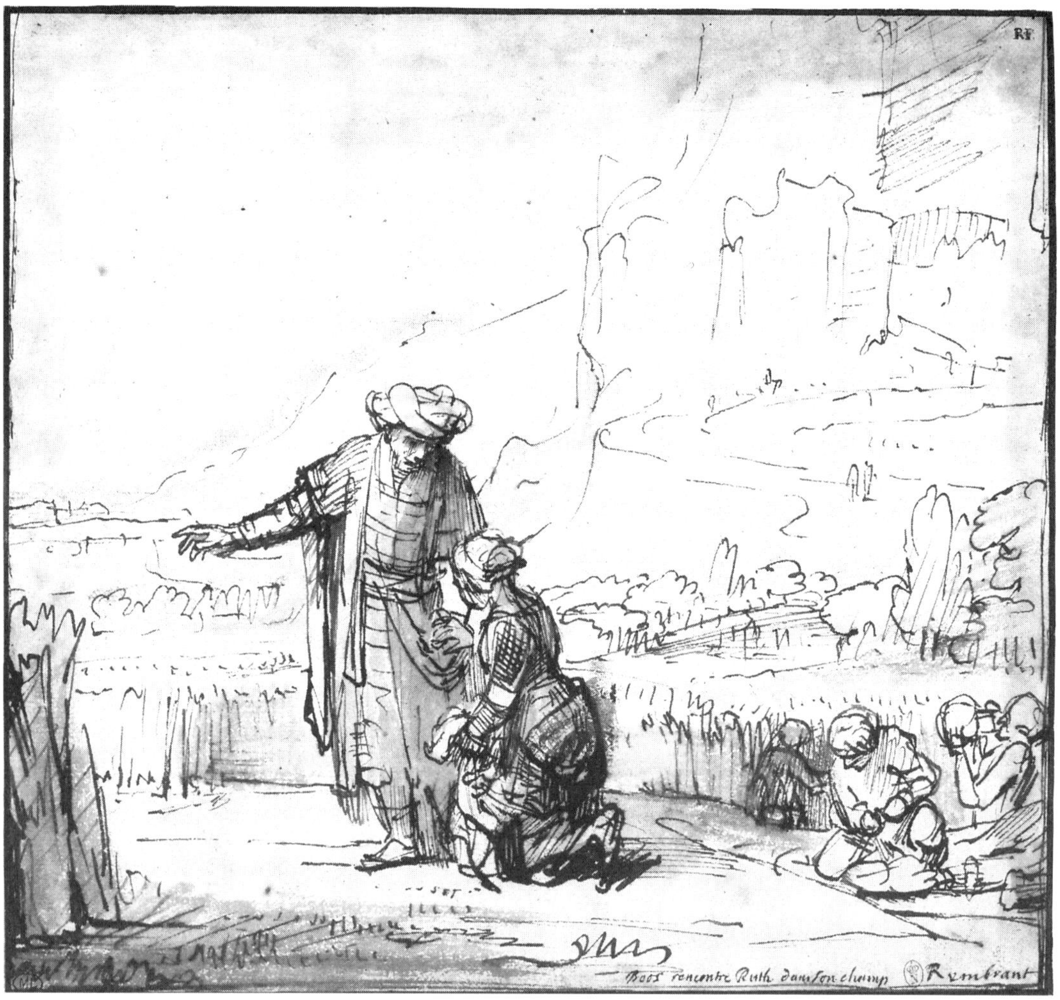

80. Rembrandt, *The Meeting of Ruth and Boaz,* Louvre Museum.

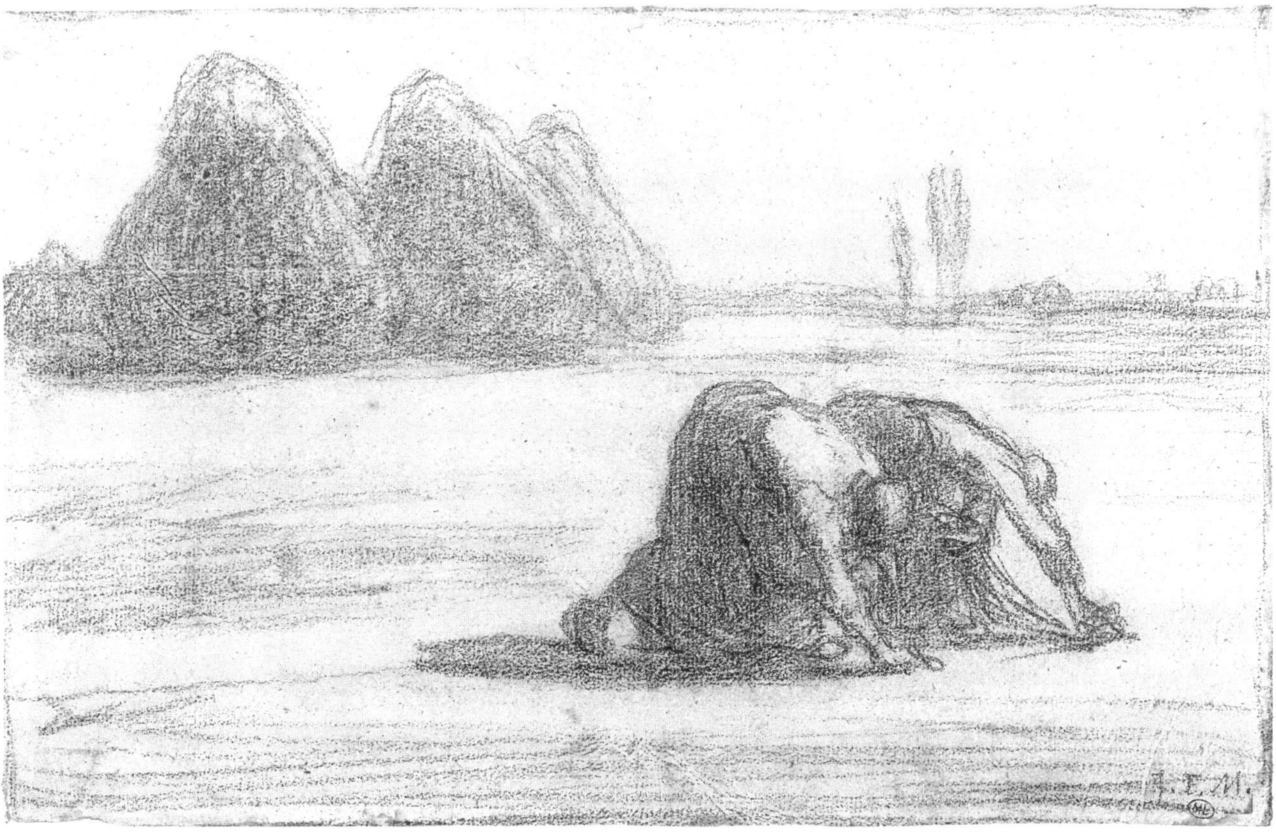

81. Jean-François Millet, *The Gleaners,* Louvre Museum, Orsay Museum Collection.

endlessly contradicts things as they are, at the risk of being no longer."[185] In the article "L'école païenne" [The pagan school], which appeared in 1852, Baudelaire continued his condemnation of aestheticism, and, illustrating his criticism, took as an example the insinuation of falseness into the charitable act, the counterfeit forms of giving, the aberrant pursuit of the picturesque:

> The folly of art is the same as the abuse of the mind. The creation of one of these two supremacies engenders stupidity, a hardness of heart, and an immense pride and egoism. I recall a joker of an artist who, having received a counterfeit coin, said: "I'm keeping it to give to a poor man." The wretched man took an infernal pleasure in stealing from the poor and at the same time enjoying the benefits of a reputation for charity. I heard another one say: "When don't the poor put on gloves to beg? They would make a fortune." And another: "Don't give anything to that one: he is poorly fitted out; his rags do not become him."[186]

"Infernal pleasure," writes Baudelaire. In a later poem, he has Satan himself supply the confirmation:

> Avez-vous donc pu croire, hypocrites surpris,
> Qu'on se moque du maître, et qu'avec lui l'on triche,
> Et qu'il soit naturel de recevoir *deux prix,*
> D'aller au Ciel et d'être riche?[187]

The "joker of an artist" in "L'école païenne" and the "hypocrite" in the poem just cited (1863), are transformed into the "friend" who, in the prose poem "La fausse monnaie" (The counterfeit coin) (1864), gives a poor man a counterfeit coin worth *two francs.* Does the number itself have a symbolic value? Why a coin worth *two* francs? Perhaps because he hopes, like those whom Satan addresses, "to receive *two* prizes" in exchange: "I saw . . . clearly that he had wanted *both* to show charity and to strike a good bargain; to earn forty sous and the heart of God; to capture paradise economically; in short, to secure the certificate of a charitable man at no cost."[188] We should not forget that the perverse gift, the object of an extraordinary narrative representation, is also the parabolic term of comparison, the allegorical image of the artist—musician or hack—who (as we

185. Ibid., 35. Baudelaire continues: "In the prison cell, it revolts; at the window of a hospital, it is the ardent hope of a cure; in the squalid and filthy attic, it adorns itself like a fairy in luxury and elegance; not only does it record, it also repairs. Everywhere it becomes the negation of iniquity."

186. "L'école païenne," 2:49.

187. "L'imprévu," 1:172. "Could you have believed, surprised hypocrites, / That one makes fun of the master, cheats him, / And that it is natural to receive *two prizes,* / That of going to heaven and that of being rich?" (My emphasis.)

188. "La fausse monnaie," *Le spleen de Paris,* 1:232–24. Baudelaire, a reader of Rousseau who tirelessly contradicted him, borrowed two elements of "La fausse monnaie" from the *Rêveries.* This may have been done unconsciously. From the fourth reverie, he borrows a sketch for the sophistic exoneration of the lie, which is compared to counterfeit money: according to Rousseau, if someone "gives counterfeit money to a man to whom he owes nothing, he is no doubt deceiving that man, but he is not stealing from him." (Rousseau may have been recalling his own adolescence. As an apprentice, he engraved medallions with the arms of the Republic: his master accused him of making counterfeit money.) Then, Baudelaire borrows a scene from the ninth reverie, after the account of the fete at La Chevrette. Rousseau mentions an impulse to show charity toward an old invalid: "I was dying to give him a coin worth 24 cents *so he could get some tobacco.*" In the manuscript draft, we read these words, which have been crossed out: "But I saw people looking at me with a . . ." The first sentence of "La fausse monnaie" begins: "As we were leaving the *tobacco* shop . . ." I would like to believe that these points of contact between Rousseau's text and Baudelaire's are not entirely fortuitous, though no other reader has taken note of them. See Jacques Derrida, *Donner le temps,* vol. 1: *La fausse monnaie,* 95–217 (see n. 2 above).

have seen) "made a satanic pact with his instrument." At issue, of course, is the authenticity of the gift; the preliminary (or related) question is that of art for art's sake, the religion of the beautiful.[189] To believe or lead others to believe that you can earn a place in heaven merely through "plastic beauty" is to circulate counterfeit money, thus offending above all those whose distress is greatest and who require real help. (Even the
81 most imaginative and generous artists can find pleasure in seeking plastic beauty in the
72,78 image of the poor: Gustave Doré's little London beggar maids are too dressed up.) To demonstrate that an ethical component must be fully present in art, Baudelaire uses the images of true and false charity; these images show the ethical component in both a literal and a metaphorical sense. The failure of two types of art—virtuous presumptuousness (Rousseau) and the cult of beauty (Gautier, Banville)—to meet their obligation to truth is figured in the images of alms gone awry.[190]

In contrast, the enormous merit of the "charitable and passionate soul" of Marceline Desbordes-Valmore is defined by Baudelaire in one of the very rare verses he cites in the article in praise of her: "As long as one can give, one cannot die."[191]

It is as if the category of the gift—its truth or its perversion—received privileged attention in Baudelaire: some of the most decisive judgments and contributions of his critical thinking occur in that area. This poet, who places such a high price on the conscious mastery of poetic writing, is full of indulgence for what he recognizes as involuntary and "unconscious" in Marceline's self-expression. He pardons her carelessness. In amazement, he discovers that poetry *gives itself* to her, and to express this, Baudelaire rediscovers and revives all the traditional expressions that make inspiration a mysterious gift:

> No author more easily *gathers together* the unique formula of sentiment, of the sublime unaware of itself. Just as the simplest and easiest concerns are an invincible obstacle to that fiery and unconscious writing, what is for anyone else an object of laborious effort comes naturally to *offer itself* to her; it is a perpetual *discovery*.[192]

Could there be a symmetry, a secret correspondence, between the gift to others that Marceline's generosity associates with the very act of living and what Baudelaire sees "offer[ing] itself to her," that is, the gifts of expression that flow spontaneously from her pen? Baudelaire does not say so explicitly, but he does suggest it: the most precious thing one can receive within oneself is the power to give; and the most precious thing one can give to others is that which awakens the capacity to give in them.[193]

189. As Claude Pichois reminds us, examples of this religion of the beautiful were provided by Gautier, Banville, and Leconte de Lisle. See Baudelaire, 2:1099.

190. To be fair, we should add that Baudelaire, who execrated Voltaire, the "antipoet," was willing to celebrate all manners of inebriation, which he refuses to make into an absolute. The prose poem "Enivrez-vous" enjoins its readers: "Get drunk, get drunk all the time! On wine, poetry, virtue, as you like" (*Le spleen de Paris* [33], 1:337). Virtue as well, then, can cause drunkenness! Baudelaire may have been remembering a passage from book 9 of the *Confessions:* "I became virtuous, or at least intoxicated with virtue" (388).

191. Baudelaire, "Marceline Desbordes-Valmore," 2:148.

192. Ibid., 147.

193. "Donner à vivre" [Give to live] was the working title Yves Bonnefoy gave to his contribution (which he never reprinted) to the catalog, *Le surréalisme en 1947* (Paris: Maegt, 1947).

Although Baudelaire condemns "the folly" of an art that forgets its ethical task, he never wishes to separate himself from the memory of childhood, where happiness was closely linked to the dimension of play and to woman's scent. Certain images of gifts are closely associated with this memory. Baudelaire imagines various sorts of gifts that originate in the universe of the fable: gifts of the devil, of fairies, the "moon's benefits." One largesse offered him remained deeply engraved in his memory, to the point of constituting a sort of "primal scene of the gift," linked, in its written reconstruction, to an obviously erotic excitement:[194]

> Many years ago—how many? I have no idea; this goes back to the hazy times of early childhood—I was brought by my mother to visit a lady named Panckoucke. . . . I recall very distinctly that the lady was dressed in velvet and fur. After some time, she said: "Here is a little boy whom I wish to give something so he will remember me." She took me by the hand and we passed through several rooms; then she opened the door to a bedroom where an extraordinary and truly magical spectacle offered itself. The walls were so covered with playthings that they disappeared behind them. The ceiling had vanished under a flowering of playthings that hung like marvelous stalactites. The floor offered barely a narrow pathway for my feet. There was a world of toys of all kinds, from the most expensive to the most modest, from the most simple to the most complicated.
>
> "There," she said, "the children's treasure chest. I have a little budget dedicated to it, and when a nice little boy comes to see me, I take him here so that he can take away a souvenir of me. Choose."[195]

The Rush to Be Photographed

For good reason, Baudelaire was indignant about "the immoderate taste for form" and 73
the "frenetic passion of art," a concern about dress that went so far as to express the wish that the poor man ask for alms in well-fitting rags. His indignation increased when photography was at stake. He explains that to "render the tragic or gracious scenes of ancient history," "odd folk, men and women," are dressed up; photographers "beg these *heroes* to be kind enough to hold their grimace of the moment for the time necessary to the operation." It is obvious Baudelaire is criticizing the pose, where the refinement of "pagan" aestheticism meets the coarseness of photography's early days. We are only too well aware of the unfairness of Baudelaire's anathema; he evokes the *rush* to be photographed as if it were a distribution of food: "Vile society rushed forward like a single Narcissus to contemplate its coarse image on the metal. An extraordinary madness or fanaticism took hold of all these new sun worshippers." But we should not mistake the coherence and concordance of the ideas Baudelaire expresses here for the arguments he had earlier developed against the pagan school. The pose required by the photographic

194. Certain interpreters today might wish to gloss the name Panckoucke (*Pannekoek*) below, which is Flemish for "crêpe," a term that might suggest "cake." This note is for them.

195. Baudelaire, "La morale des joujoux" [The ethics of playthings], 1:581. Regarding parents who "never want to give" playthings, Baudelaire adds a remark that anticipates Mallarmé's poems "Haine du pauvre" [Hatred of the poor] and "Aumône" [Alms]: "[They] do not know and do not allow poetic means for passing time. These are the same people who would willingly give a franc to a poor man, provided he chokes down bread, but would always refuse him 10 cents to quench his thirst at the cabaret."

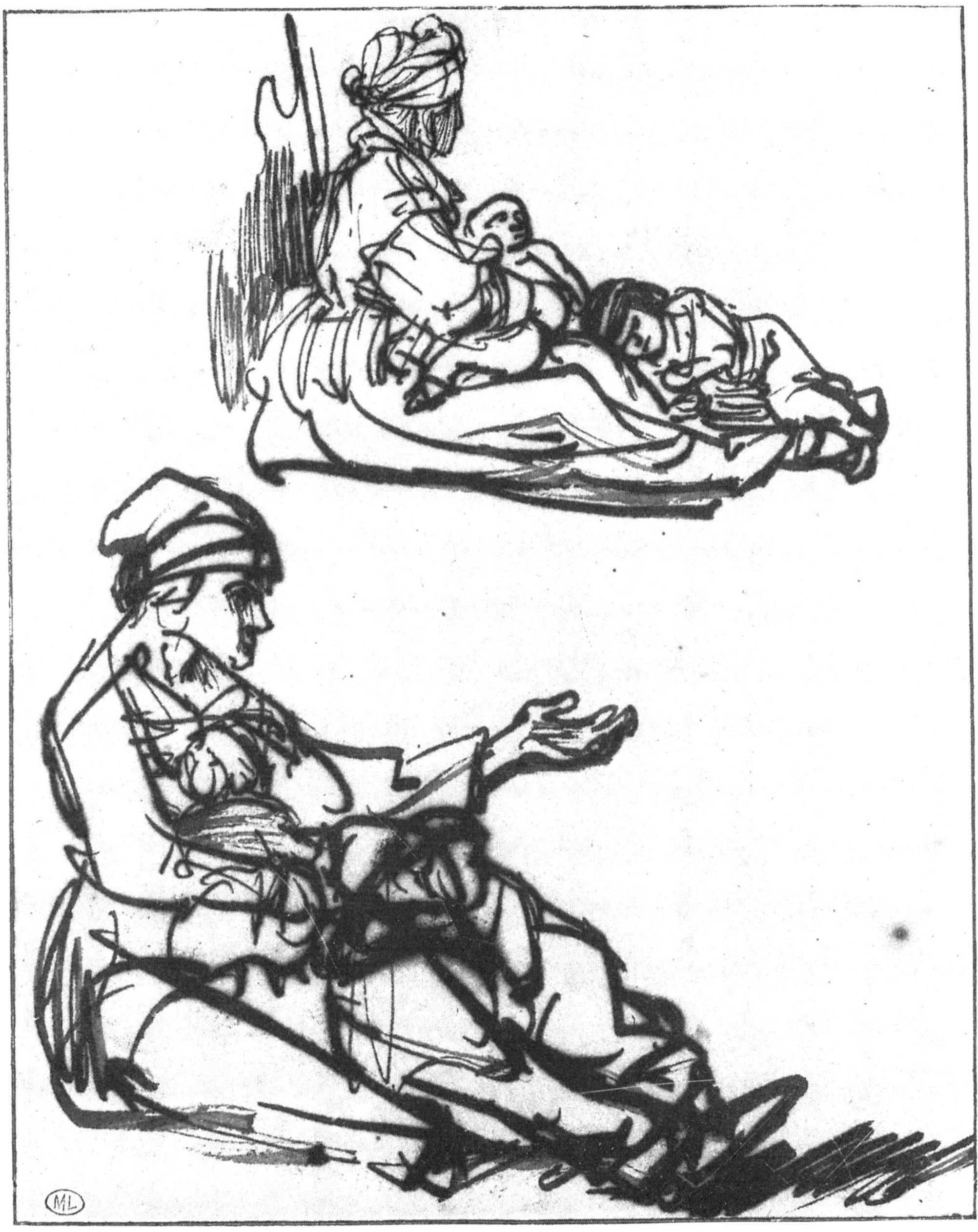

82. Rembrandt, *Two Studies of Beggar Woman.* Louvre Museum.

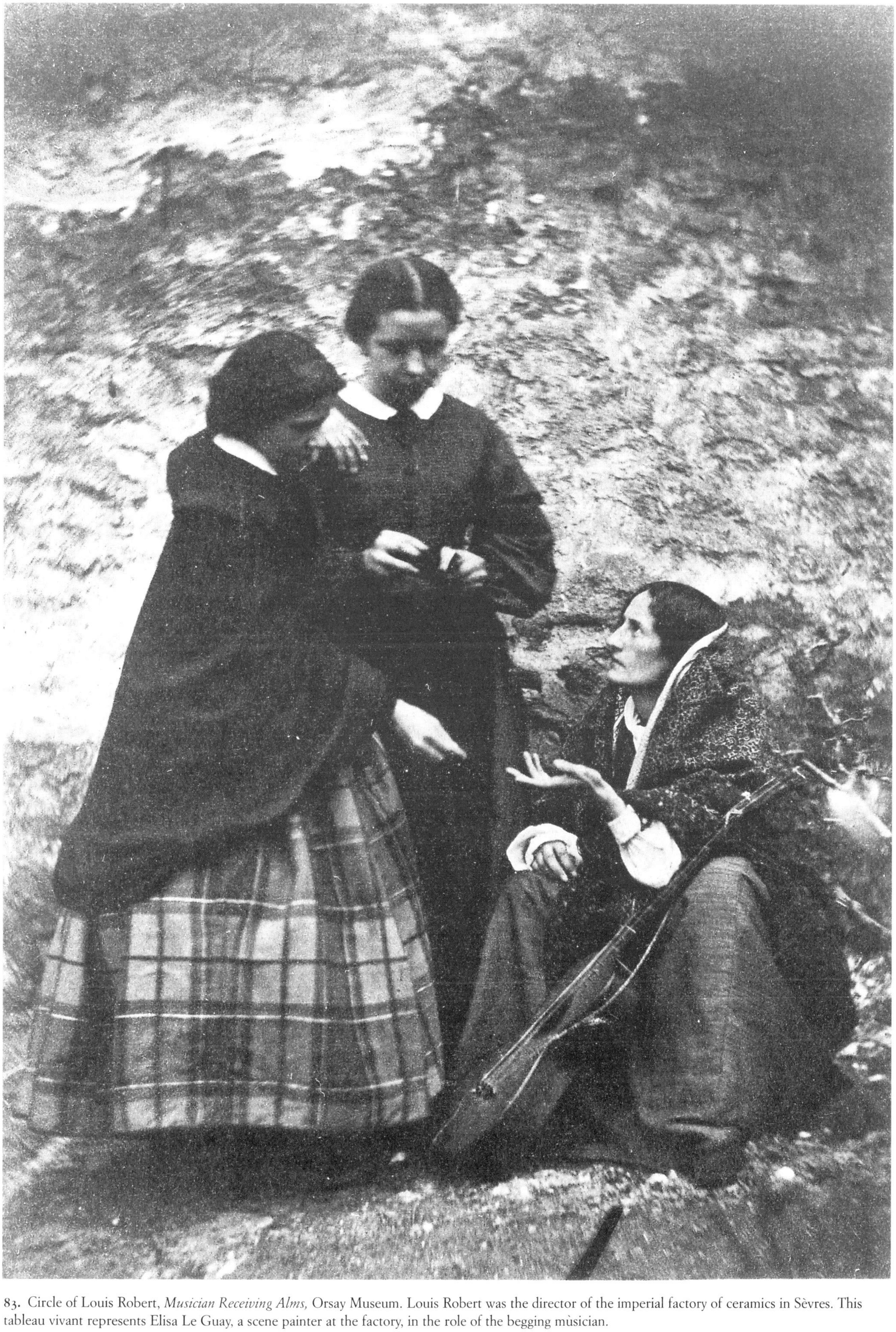

83. Circle of Louis Robert, *Musician Receiving Alms,* Orsay Museum. Louis Robert was the director of the imperial factory of ceramics in Sèvres. This tableau vivant represents Elisa Le Guay, a scene painter at the factory, in the role of the begging musician.

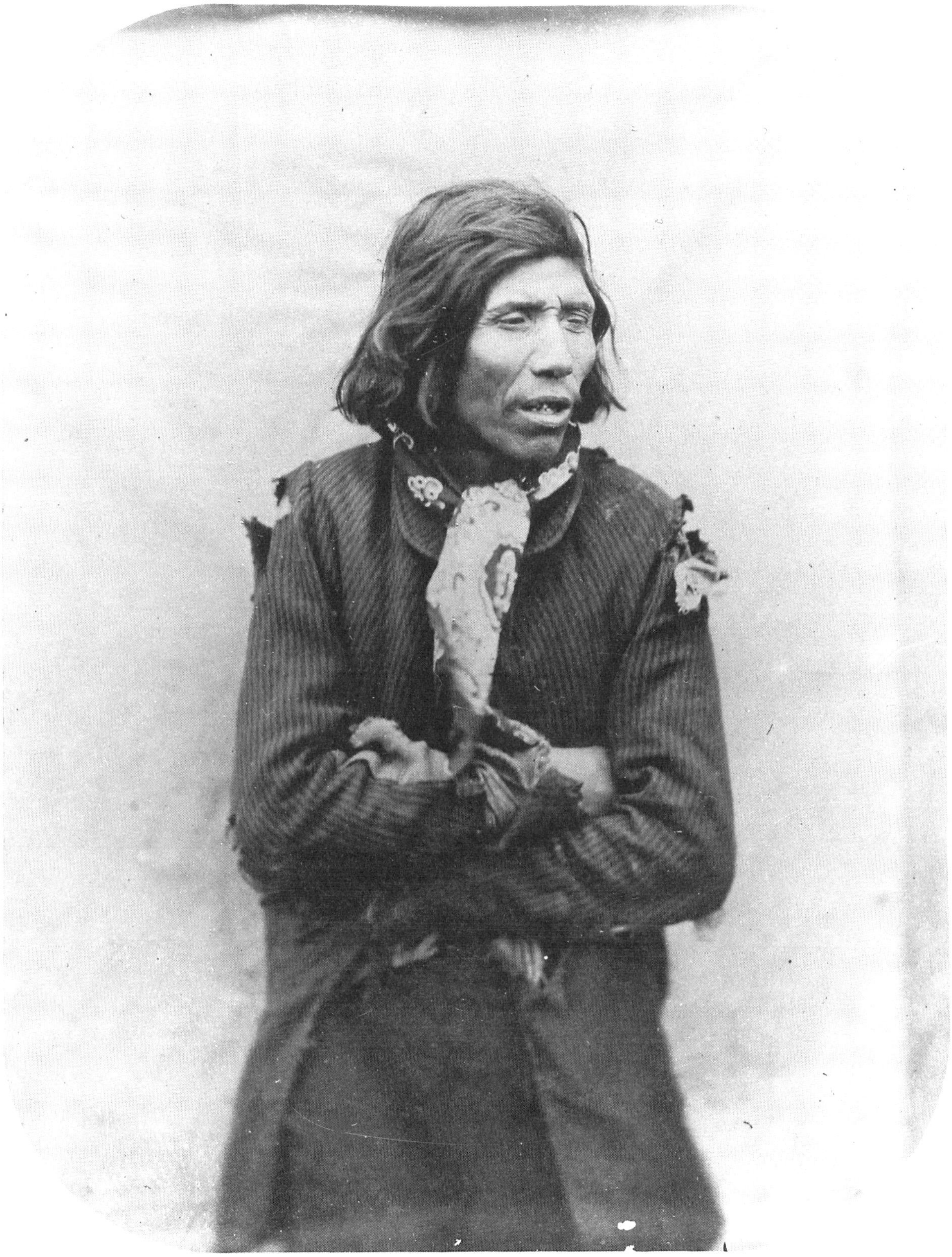

84. Paul-Emile Miot, *Gougou, Prince of the Mic-Macs,* Orsay Museum. The photograph was taken by Miot, a navy photographer, for his report on Newfoundland, in the company of Joseph Arthur de Gobineau. If we are to believe Gobineau, Gougou was the last representative of the ancient royal family of the Mic-Mac Indians: "A few pennies offered him to buy tobacco, which he eagerly accepted, began our acquaintance"

technology of the time brought the beggar's gesture, like the gesture of prayer, closer to 83,97
the tableau vivant and eternalized the element of insistent simulation. The photographed
tableau vivant commits "a double sacrilege" and insults "both divine painting and the
sublime art of the actor."[196] The evocation of the myth of Narcissus is not inappropriate
for designating how the image is closed upon itself, how it fails to meet its obligation to
reveal. With the exception of a few overpowering portraits of fallen Indian chiefs or of 84
sick people, the pose deprived us of any true representation of the poor in the nineteenth
century. The documentation of poverty occurred only when the posing time could be
shortened, that is, when the snapshot was invented, making possible the furtive gaze 79
and anonymity.

The Vile Snack: Huysmans

When Rousseau recounts the peasants' battle in the ninth reverie, he does not claim to
be composing a work of art: he is countering an accusation. Using that text, Baudelaire
wrote "Le gâteau," a prose poem: he constructed a text that defined itself as a work of
art. We have seen how he permuted the narrative sequence, and above all, how he re-
versed the optimistic denouement proposed by Rousseau. As if to respond to Baude-
laire's narrative, another writer was to compose the scene yet again: Joris-Karl Huysmans,
in a chapter of *A rebours* [Against the grain] (1884). Here, a character is dominated to
the point of obsession by the imperative for art. Des Esseintes takes care to exclude from
his universe any trace of ugliness. With the *rich* resources of "artistic writing," Huysmans
too describes the brutal brawl among children over a meager bit of food. The concern 17
for art is further accentuated and the scene grows even more somber.

Tormented by "gastric neurosis," des Esseintes has moved with.great difficulty to the garden of his luxurious villa of Fontenay-aux-Roses, where everything is artifice and novelty. Here is the spectacle played out before him:

> Above the hedge separating the low garden from the raised road leading to the fort, he saw children rolling about in the hot sun, in the light.
>
> He was concentrating his attention on them when another, smaller child appeared, filthy to look at: he had seaweed hair full of sand, two green bubbles beneath his nose, disgusting lips surrounded by the white scum from cream cheese with herbs, which had been smeared onto bread and strewn with crossed strips of green onion. . . . The brats were fighting now. They were tearing off scraps of bread and stuffing them into their cheeks, then sucking on their fingers. Kicks and punches showered down, and the weaker ones, trampled on the ground, kicked and cried, their behinds scraped by the gravel.
>
> This spectacle revived des Esseintes.[197]

The violent play had begun before des Esseintes became a spectator to it. The violence between the children is the initial fact, the original given. Disorder begins "above

196. "Le public moderne et la photographie," *Salon de 1859* (2), 2:617.

197. J.-K. Huysmans, *A rebours,* with a preface by Marc Fumaroli (Paris: Gallimard, Filio, 1977), 291–92. See "Texts on the Gift," no. 3, below. On Huysmans' relation to Baudelaire, see H. Brunner and J.-L. de Coninck, *En marge d'"A rebours'* (Paris, 1929), 116–18.

the hedge," at the property line. It was not necessary to introduce even the slightest gift, charitable or perverse, for the dispute to come about.

In this first moment of the episode, the battle among the children is spontaneous. The aristocratic aesthete, transfixed by pain, is a distant witness to it. He does no more than take an ambivalent interest in it, with disgust predominating. Once more, we find the children's brawl as depicted by Baudelaire, but repeated in a more coruscating style. The word *sand* may function as a lexical signal: the Baudelairean slice of bread ended up mixed with sand, while the little Huysmanian cheese eater has sand in his hair.

The "decadent" dandy does not provoke the popular violence in this case, as the young men of La Chevrette had done. The violence among the "brats" follows naturally, independent of any external cause. It is stirred up with the arrival of the boy possessing a "vile snack," which is immediately fought over. In the relation between the witness and the children, we should note especially the reversal in the desire for food. Contrary to the situation in Rousseau and Baudelaire, it is now the rich man, tormented by his illness, who is hungry. Desire is literally turned backward *(à rebours).* Des Esseintes covets the "children's" snack, just as the impoverished children had coveted the apples in Rousseau, and the "slice of bread, which was nearly white" in Baudelaire:

> Des Esseintes sniffed at the air; a pica, a perversion took hold of him; that vile snack made his mouth water. It seemed to him that his stomach, which had refused all nourishment, would digest that horrid food, and that his palate would take pleasure in it as if it were a delicious treat.
>
> He jumped up, ran to the kitchen, ordered that a round loaf of bread, fromage blanc, and onion be fetched from the village, prescribed that a snack absolutely identical to the one the child had been gnawing on be prepared, and returned to sit under his tree.[198]

Hunger has changed sides: it torments the dilettante worn down by pleasures and elicits in him the mimetic desire to share the children's appetite for the "vile snack."

Huysmans is also recalling another prose poem by Baudelaire, "Le joujou du pauvre" (The poor boy's plaything).[199] In that narrative, the rich child behind the castle gate abandons a "splendid plaything" on the ground in order to watch with envy the live rat that a poor child exhibits before him: "Through the symbolic bars separating two worlds, the main road and the castle, the poor child showed the rich child his own plaything, which the rich child examined greedily as a rare and unknown object." Huysmans, who retains the symbolic borderline separating two worlds, has merely transposed the attraction for the horrible object to his favorite domain—food. This allows him to refer liberally to the register of bodily sensations, of which he was one of the discoverers of the time. And, simultaneously, by heeding the suffering body to an exaggerated degree, he accentuates the egocentric attitude, the prideful revendication, whose presence could already be detected in Rousseau, rendering suspect the apparent disinterest he had shown in relation to the beneficent gift. In des Esseintes, pain, the peak moment of attention to self, is the corollary of the charity refused to others.

While his butler prepares the bread for him, des Esseintes lingers on a misanthropic *rumination.* All his experiences as a collector and aesthete have left him nothing but a

198. Huysmans, *A rebours,* 291–92.

199. Baudelaire, *Le spleen de Paris,* 1:304–5.

confused sadness, which is taken for lucid knowledge: it would have been better if those children had not been born; evil and death await both rich and poor; there is thus no reason to take pity; better to accelerate evil and destruction. Des Esseintes thus rediscovers arguments that justify not only the "good company" of La Chevrette, but also sadistic or Neronian tyrants. If life is not good for anyone, why not take pleasure in seeing peasants fight and maim one another? The fin de siècle aestheticism takes pleasure in both the "refined" and the "barbaric."

When his servant brings him the snack he had prepared, des Esseintes is overcome by "nausea." He cannot swallow it. What to do?

> —Throw that snack, he tells the servant, to those children out on the road who are slaughtering one another; let the weakest of them be maimed, let them get not a bite and, moreover, let them get a major beating from their families when they return home with black eyes and their trousers torn; that will give them a glimpse of the life that awaits them!

Des Esseintes does not seek for one instant to bring pleasure to the children. The sadistic aggressivity is explicit. He has the snack given *so that* the battle will increase in intensity. Moreover, in delegating the mission of the maleficent gift to his servant, he remains off to the side, establishing no contact whatever with the receivers. Even though he looked at them for an instant, he does not wish to be seen in return. In fact, the children have not seen him, have not addressed any request to him. No signs have been exchanged. Huysmans has made the motif of the "supplicating gaze" or "mute eloquence" completely disappear. (This motif played a considerable role in Baudelaire's evocation of the poor; and significantly, one of its first formulations appeared in England at the beginning of the eighteenth century, in the pages of Addison and Steele's *Spectator*).[200] Of all those in our series of texts who gave food—the young men of La Chevrette, Jean-Jacques, the Baudelairean traveler—des Esseintes remains the most apart, the most separated, the most confined within nonreciprocity. His own suffering incites him to practice a perverse pedagogy that consists in accelerating the machinery of violence in order to aggravate the consciousness of evil. This worst-case policy was also that of Russian anarchist groups during the same era.

We can read the scene from Huysmans as an extreme variant of Baudelaire's text—Baudelaire pushed to the limit—but we can discern something more in it, namely, a critical reception of Baudelaire's poem, just as that poem was a critical reception of Rousseau's *Rêveries*. What could Huysmans be suggesting to us through the deforming mirror that makes him a witness for the prosecution against the Baudelairean traveler? Probably this: having given *one* slice of bread to a ravenous child, the traveler remained merely a spectator when the twin brother appeared and the battle began. Did he have a satanic desire to offer himself the spectacle of evil? Horrified by the "hideous struggle" after

200. "The Persons I am speaking of are our common Beggars about this Town; and that what I say is true, I appeal to any Man who has a Heart one Degree softer than a Stone. As for my part, who don't pretend to more Humanity than my Neighbours, I have oftentimes gone from my Chambers with Mony in my Pocket, and returned to them not only Pennyless, but destitute of a Farthing, without bestowing of it any other way than on these seeming Objects of Pity. In short, I have seen more Eloquence in a *Look* from one of these despicable Creatures, than in the Eye of the fairest *She*." *The Spectator,* ed. Donald F. Bond (London: Oxford at the Clarendon Press, 1965), 5:95–96.

feeling a "perfect peace" as he contemplated a sublime landscape, he did not move beyond the responses of *sentiment* (except, belatedly, in writing a poem, a commentary after the fact). Sentimentality and aggressivity often go hand in hand. The Baudelairean traveler has become a sorrowful voyeur: he has not been able to share completely. The poem "Le gâteau" exists only because of that very incomplete charity. The counterfactual hypothesis of a *second* slice of bread would abolish the very possibility of the poem. The opportunity outside literature would have never been *given.*

Could art (which, according to Baudelaire's injunction, claims to be the negation of iniquity) find its nourishment in the inadequacy of charity? That, in any case, is what is revealed in the attitude and feelings Huysmans lends to his character: the luxury that surrounds des Esseintes is for his use exclusively; his prodigality, his largesse, reflect back on him alone. His collections replace the world and make his solitude all the more extreme. Hence the hero's corporeal misery, his ever more agonizing seclusion; the literature and art of every age can offer him no enduring aid. While a number of readers have seen him as an intellectual model (his aesthetic choices are altogether remarkable), others have observed that the physical disaster he faces is only the shadow of an ethical disaster. And the prescription they have proposed to relieve the rich man's gastritis is religious in nature: *panis angelicus,* conversion. Huysmans answered that call, but with a religion that was no less aestheticized.[201]

The Petrified Gift

In des Esseintes's collection, Gustave Moreau occupies a preeminent place; the collector
85 possesses two works—a painting and a watercolor—representing Salome. This is particularly apropos. For at stake in the *capital* scene where the seductress dances is the same type of destructive gift that we saw in the scene of the vile snack: a miserly gift, a mutilating gift, though from a completely different angle, to be sure.

The legend of Salome, a character who appears from time to time in the gospels of Mark and Matthew, lends itself to full symbolic development. In dancing at Herod's banquet, Salome offers only her image. She "pleases" King Herod Antipater. He promises "with an oath to give her whatsoever she would ask" (Matthew 14:7; see also Mark 6:14–29). Bound by his promise, he cannot refuse what she requests, at the instigation
76 of Queen Herodias: the decapitated head of the prophet John the Baptist in a charger. The desire for sexual possession has become bound up and vanquished by the desire for death. Neither the dancer nor the king acts out of free will. Huysmans depicts Salome as blind: she remains withdrawn, surrendering her image like a "sleepwalker," seeing nothing around her. Later, however, "the ghastly head blazes" in the charger and Salome sees "fiery shards" coming out of it that make all "the facets of the jewelry" she is wearing "blaze up." Everywhere, colors become vibrant under the gaze of the dead man. And

201. Des Esseintes's sadism is Neronism in miniature. We know that, for Kierkegaard, Nero was the emblematic melancholic character who pursued "the interesting." He thus characterized the *aesthetic stage.*

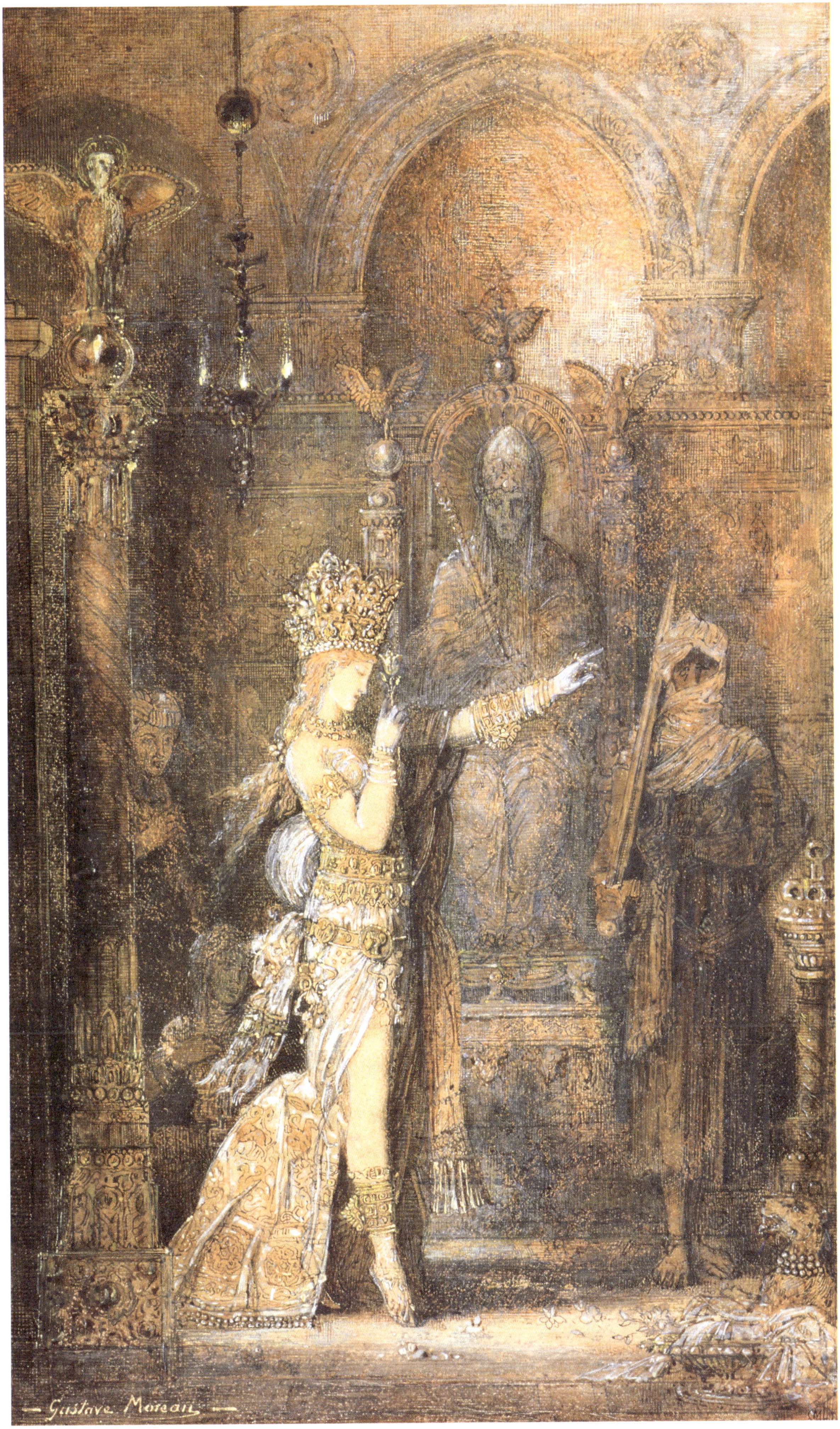

85. Gustave Moreau, *Salome Dancing,* Louvre Museum, Orsay Museum Collection.

these jewels are *stones* that "take on life" "in incandescent shards." These "part-objects," as psychoanalysts call them, amalgamate into a great flash of light.[202]

Gustave Moreau and his contemporaries only revived a theme that had already been developed from ancient times in the cult of John the Baptist.[203] It is a gynophobic myth, and numerous writers and artists at the end of the nineteenth century could project their imaginations onto it, dreaming of the combined figure of Herodias-Salome. To construct this image, they gave themselves the license to combine and measure out powers attributed to the original temptress on one hand and to the Medusa on the other.[204] For them, Salome was a petrifying Eve, a woman-serpent. That image makes a certain fatal aspect of the dancer/acrobat appear, in the many adornments and oriental jewels that surround her. Huysmans warms to his task in describing Salome through the work of Gustave Moreau. And he concludes with a flourish: "Des Esseintes saw that the superhuman and strange Salome he had dreamed of was finally realized. . . . In some sense, she was becoming the symbolic deity of indestructible Lust, the goddess of immortal Hysteria, the cursed Beauty, chosen among all women by the catalepsy that stiffened her flesh and *hardened* her muscles; the monstrous, indifferent, irresponsible, unfeeling Beast, who, like the ancient Helen, *poisoned* everything that came near her, everything that saw her, everything she touched." With the hallucinatory notion of poisoning, the equivocal *Gift/gift* (gift/poison) reappears, and this gift *(dosis),* as we have seen, is also the lethal "dose."

The dancer offers her inaccessible image to the melancholic potentate to obtain in exchange a lifeless head: but the transaction is sterile. It is a vain exchange marked by nothingness. Herod consents to the gift from his high position, exercising his royal prerogative: the gift is "vertical" in nature and it is accomplished through the sharp blade that performs the decapitation.

When des Esseintes contemplates that scene, he himself participates in Herod's confusion: "Like the old king, des Esseintes remained crushed, annihilated, overcome with vertigo."[205] His identification with the monarch, a sad and irritated voyeur, is not accidental. It reveals a cultural and psychological stereotype. In Herod, we are presented with a portrait of the art lover; we would need to show all the implications of this.

In Flaubert's short story "Herodias," the head of Salome, at the end of her dance on her hands, is also petrified: "The colored skirts that enveloped her legs, passing over her shoulders like rainbows, lay beside her face, which was only one cubit from the ground. Her lips were painted, her eyebrows very dark, her eyes almost fierce, and the droplets on her forehead seemed to be vapor on *white marble.*" A head for a head: when the three disciples carry away the decapitated head of John the Baptist to Galilee, it is "*very heavy*" and the three men "take turns" carrying it. The gift requested, obtained, and abandoned by Salome is finally only dead weight. The Medusa's gaze has accomplished its task. The rest is nothing but an illusion.[206]

202. Huysmans, *A rebours,* 85, 89.

203. In the church of Saint-Jean de Mustair (Grisons, Switzerland), a fresco from the twelfth century elaborates the entire story of John the Baptist; Salome dances on the right column.

204. Let us mention merely a few names: Heine's *Atta Troll,* then Flaubert, Mallarmé, Oscar Wilde, etc. In Heine, Herodias is the ghostly companion of Diana "with a face of marble" *(das Antlitz weiss wie Marmor).* And canto 19 of the poem ends with this question: "Why did you look / so tenderly at me, Herodias?" (Warum hast du mich so zärtlich / Angeschen, Herodias?)

205. Huysmans, *A rebours,* 152.

206. On Medusa, see Jean-Pierre Vernant, "Au miroir de Méduse," in *L'individu, la mort, l'amour* (Paris: Gallimard, 1989), 117–29; and Jean Clair, *Méduse* (Paris: Gallimard, 1989).

CHAPTER SIX

Envois

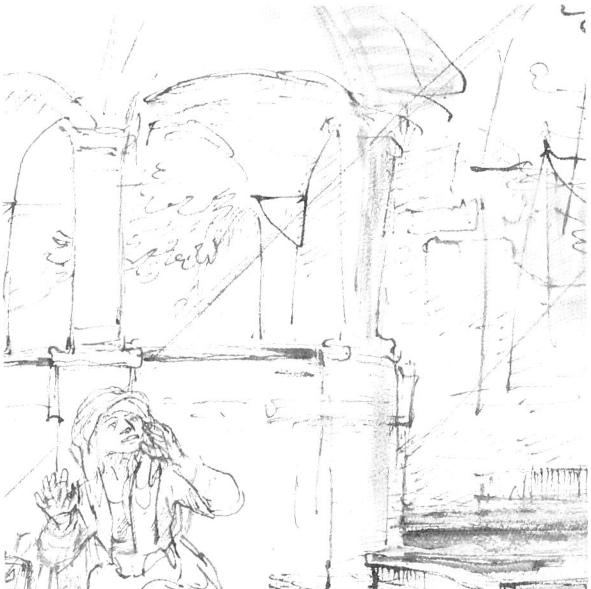

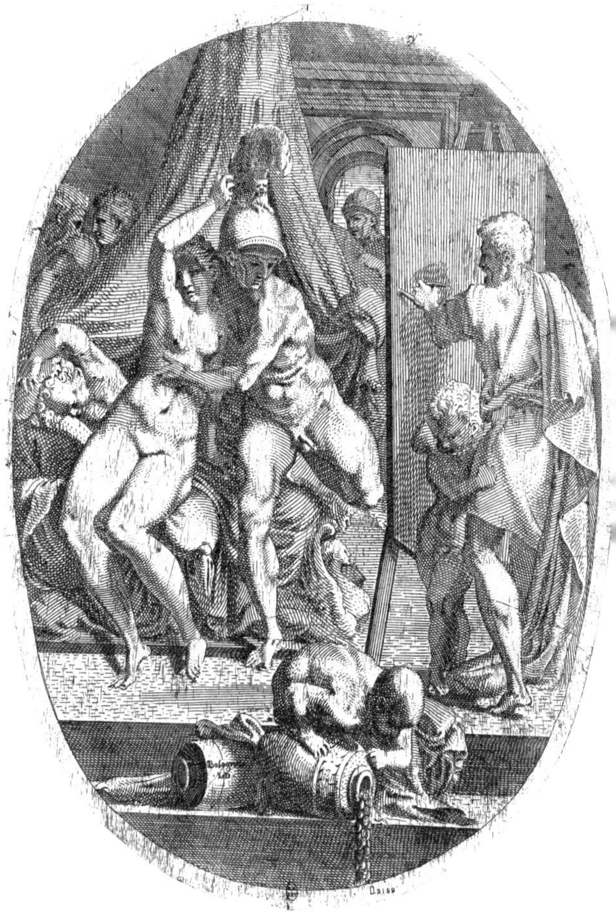

86. Master L. D., *Alexander and Campaspe,* Bibliothèque Nationale.

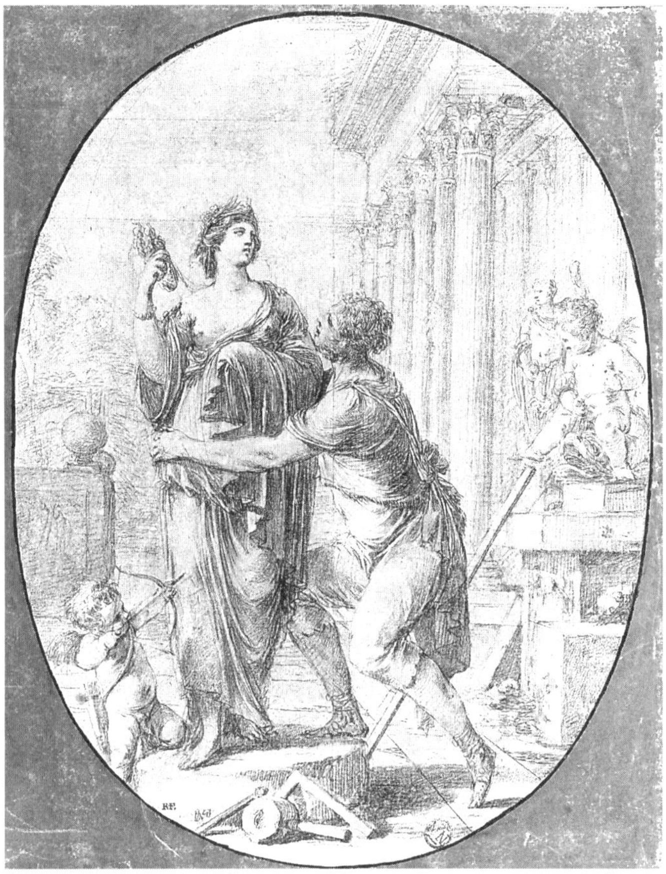

87. Laurent de La Hyre, *Pygmalion,* Louvre Museum.

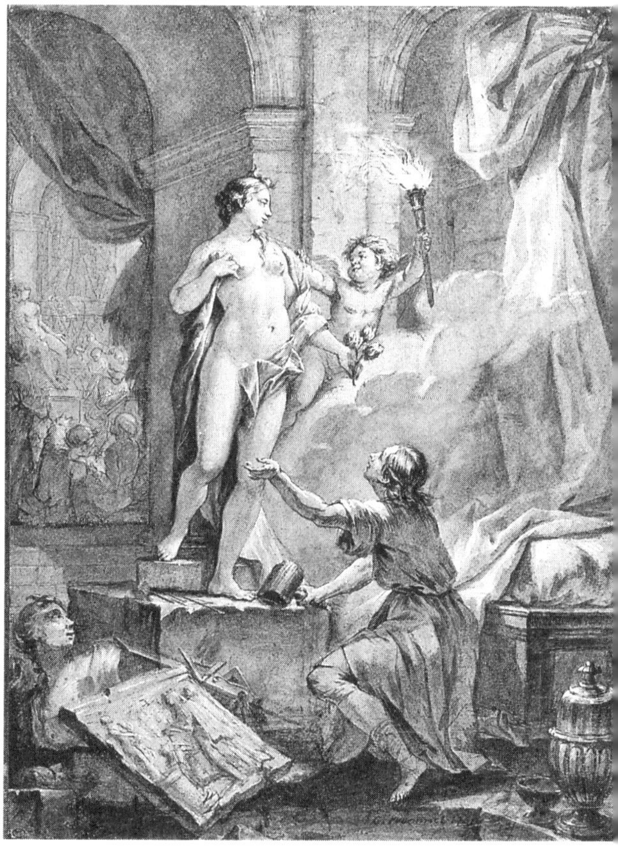

88. Charles Monnet, *Pygmalion,* Louvre Museum, Orsay Museum Collection.

Privileges

Receiving and giving: When the artist seeks an image to represent his powers and privileges, these are once more fundamental gestures.

In European art, there were two scenes of *receiving* that were drawn so often that they became part of the vocabulary of academic emblems. These two legendary examples, *received* examples from the beginning, give narrative form to the artist's wish and its fulfillment. They figure the artist's desire in the form of the demand for property.[207] The enumeration of rival versions of these images, proposed as so many variations on a theme, would never end.

There is, first, the sculptor's wish to possess a woman identical to the statue he has fashioned: *Pygmalion and Galatea.* A threefold gift will result. It is not enough that 87,88
Pygmalion *gives* form to the most beautiful of female images; he also wishes her to become a "sensate" being, endowed with the surplus of life that only the gods can *give,* so that she will *give herself* to him. The sculptor beseeches them—"if it is true you can give everything,"[208] he cries in Ovid's text—and the breath of life is granted by a compassionate Venus. More fortunate than Narcissus, the sculptor receives himself in the figure his desire has inscribed in ivory. The divine gift supplements the gift of form the artist has given; it transforms representation into presence. Blood begins to pulse in what had been simply a large fetish.[209] It remains to be seen whether the miraculous achievement of a conjugal bond with the work of art does not confine the artist to a miser's dream, and whether the apparent triumph of life does not abolish the possibility of true sharing, which is the finality of art. The complete gesture of art goes in search of a gaze, and its condition is that the artist, dispossessing himself, detaching himself from what he has produced, surrenders his work to a receiver beyond himself.

There is, second, the wish that torments the painter, that of no longer being separated from the prince's mistress, whose features he has lovingly traced: *Apelles in His* 86
Studio Receives Campaspe from the Hands of Alexander. This anecdote has become the emblem of the heroic alms kings have granted to artists, those ambitious beggars.

These subjects experienced their greatest success during the eighteenth century, as the rights of genius became the object of a more urgent revendication. The ambiguity in these works of art did not destroy the respect they showed for those who exercised absolute power, but they forced viewers to consider the appearance of new powers. In the story of Campaspe, are we supposed to admire the generosity of the prince surren-

207. These are the desires expressed in the "daydream" *(Tagestraum)* according to Freud's interpretation in the essay "Der Dichter und das Fantasieren" (1907). The daydream, which prolongs child's play, expresses the desire for wealth, erotic satisfaction, and invincibility in an entirely egotistical manner. Art consists in dissimulating the banality of these desires. The artist's formal labor masks them and thus assures "a premium of seduction." In different ways, we can see the gifts granted to Pygmalion and Apelles as the fulfillment of an egocentric wish.

208. *Si Di dare cuncta potestis.* Ovid, *The Metamorphoses* 10.274, English translation by Horace Gregory (New York and Toronto: Viking, 1958), 282 [translation modified].

209. Rousseau composed a "melodrama" (a declaimed monologue combined with music) on this theme. The piece was extremely popular.

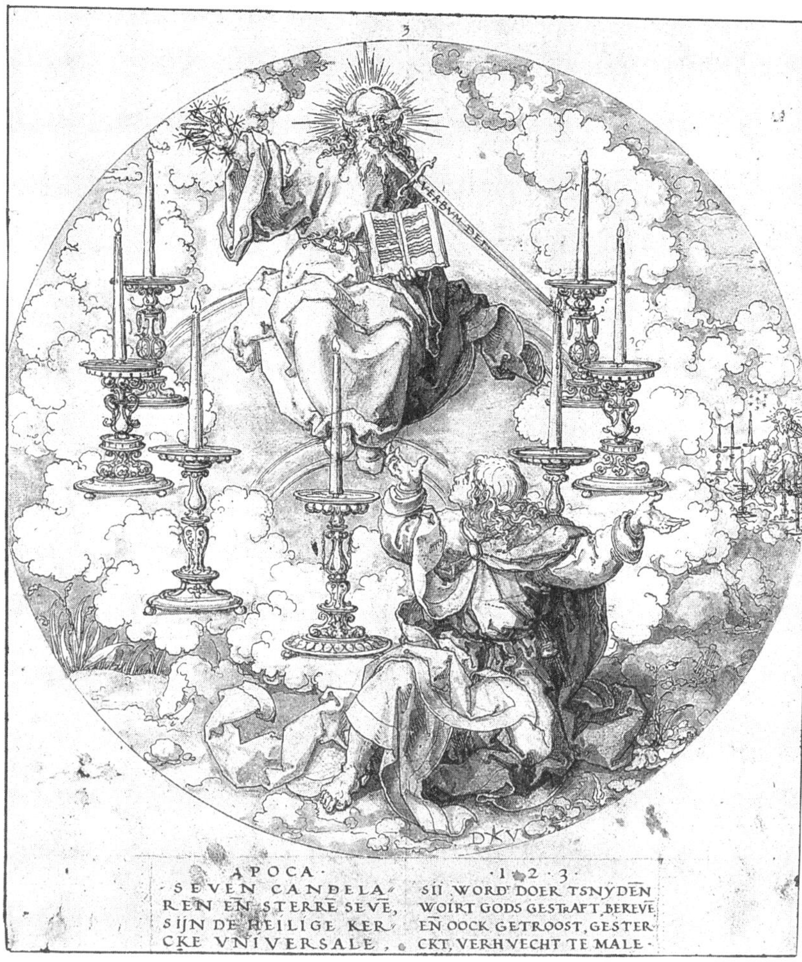

89. Dirk Jacobsz Vellert, *Appearance of the Son of Man amid the Seven Candlesticks,* Louvre Museum, Edmond de Rothschild Collection.

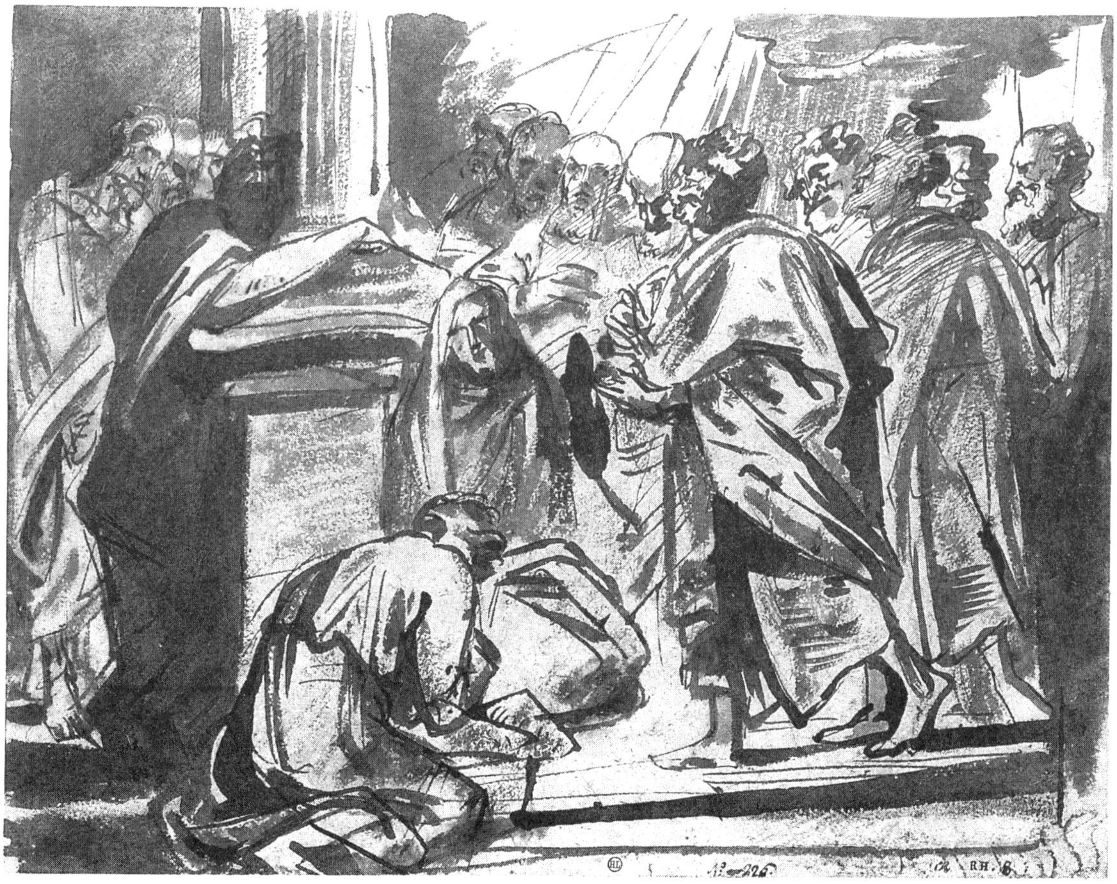

90. Anton Van Dyck, *The Descent of the Holy Spirit,* Louvre Museum.

dering his mistress? Or rather the power of the legendary painter, who forces the conqueror to renounce an unwarranted possession? In that case, charming nudes have the value of manifestos. The public visiting the salons were invited to acknowledge a new order of things: Beauty incarnate belongs by rights to the artist, whether he is the author of that beauty (Pygmalion) or simply the copyist (Apelles). He alone does full justice to it, and the prince's gift is in fact only a restitution. Through such gifts, Venus and Alexander allow the sculptor and painter to participate in their power. It is a sharing of sovereignty.

The artist (according to fables said to be emotionally touching) receives his consecration as a favor from the masters of the world. But beyond that gallant eloquence, a greater gift is claimed: the power to make a gift like that of Venus or Alexander. Artists feel called upon to know and perhaps even to govern the world *alongside* the powers that rule it, commissioned by them, though not with the same authority they have.

Where Does the Poem Come From?

The dictates of the muses, the gifts of Apollo, were still being invoked in the literary and figurative fictions of the classical centuries in Europe, when the imitation of the ancients was cultivated. On the other hand, the invocation of the gift of prophecy, the gift of the spirit, or the gift of tongues, propagated a very ancient religious mantic, even to our own times, in more or less secularized versions. The prophet, the apostle, and at times the priest-king, receive the gift, and the immediate consequence is that they become givers in turn. Poets have dreamed of that legacy.

One of the strongest images of this dream is the gift of the word in the form of nourishment, the thing to be eaten (as so many examples of largesse stubbornly pointed toward). "Open thy mouth, and eat what I give thee. And when I looked, behold, an hand *was* sent unto me; and, lo, a roll of a book *was* therein. . . . Then did I eat *it;* and it was in my mouth as honey for sweetness" (Ezekiel 2:8–9, 3:3).[210] This passage antici-
pates a text from Revelation: both speak of incorporation. What will be given in pro- 89
phetic utterances has already been given to the prophet in the food of written truth.
Even when the visual Pentecostal image of tongues of fire takes the place of the book that 90
is consumed, it is still a question of the *innate* gift, issued from the sovereign Authority, descended into the innermost substance of the elect, and manifested in their power of speech.

There is, of course, a considerable difference between prophecy—uttering a *prior* 92
"ingurgitated" text—and the production of an *original* work of art, which results from a "gift of nature," a faculty "possessed" by the human subject because he himself "belongs" to the natural order. Kant writes that "*genius* is the innate disposition of the mind [*ingenium*] through which nature *gives* its rules to art."[211] What does it matter if the

210. The act of eating the book recurs in Revelation 10:8–11, after the announcement of the abolition of time.

211. Immanuel Kant, *Critique of Judgment,* section 46: "Genie est die angeborene Gemüthsanlage [*ingenium*], durch welche die Natur der Kunst die Regel giebt." I retain this use of the verb "give" even though it has moved away from the *liberal* gesture to which I wanted to confine myself in this book.

rules *given* in that way are above all an obligation that must remain inconspicuous. Through this extended conception of genius, the artist can consider himself the source of gifts, the inventor of writing and language, dependent only on himself. Submission to these rules of nature is replicated in a revolt in the name of nature against any authority imposed from the outside, with the exception of the precious strangeness the artist perceives in himself. There are, then, no favors to expect and no favors to return, except from self to self. The—exalting or agonizing—alternative persists between authority and impotence, beginning with that first "given" that every human existence is to itself: a given that art exalts, for example in dance steps, to the point of making the dancer, according to Mallarmé, the "inexhaustible fount of herself."[212] The image of running water that, as we have seen, is associated etymologically with the word largesse *(largitio)* is thus renewed in a superb image of waves and abundance.

Mallarmé also writes that "*the gift is produced* in the writer, by piling up radiant clarity with the words he utters, Truth and Beauty for example."[213] Mallarmé opposes the light (of the uttered words) to the absence of luster, the smoke, of large numbers representing sums of money. The abstract power of gold is dull and drab; Mallarmé calls this the "defect money has of shining abstractly." Where does the writer's gift for "piling up clarity" come from? The question of the gift's source refers back to the gift itself: the gift produces itself, as if it were born of itself from within. The reflexive verb "to produce oneself" expresses the advent of the gift as if it were absolute, as if it were grounded in its own "mystery."

For all that, the writer is not freed from the responsibility of "uttering" words, setting them in place, "piling up" the luminous elements of the poem. In *producing itself,* the gift is only a preliminary: it makes the production of a thought possible. Beginning with that first gift, there is a task to be accomplished. In an illustrious text by Mallarmé [*Un coup de dés*], this task takes shape as "a throw of the dice." We are met once more
93 with the throw, the *sparsio!* "Every thought emits a Throw of the Dice." Here the task of piling up comes to resemble the gesture of dispersion: dice falling from the horn of Fortune, so to speak. *Fortuna sive Natura.*

Diderot imagined nature playing dice with the atoms of matter, creating the world and producing intelligent beings from the probabilities of a "multitude of throws." Mallarmé in turn makes thought and chance an indissoluble couple, so indissoluble that he gives the poem on the page, its shape, its open syntax, its vast spaces, the look of scattered *missilia,* cast forth in an almost regular movement, from the top to the bottom of the double page, from the heights to the "abyss." The throw is like a milky way, with in abeyance—on the last page—"a constellation." The gift given is a "total reckoning in formation," that is, a world, and at the same time an infinitely vacant space: "Nothing will have taken place but the place." Mallarmé situates his effort "beside the personal

212. Mallarmé, "Crayonné au théâtre," *Oeuvres complètes,* 311. The dancer is "la Loïe Fuller."

213. Mallarmé, "Variations sur un sujet. Grands faits divers, Or," *Oeuvres complètes,* 398–99. The text was written on the occasion of the Panama scandal. In an earlier version, Mallarmé spoke of the "tarnished effacement of gold" and added: "This gift of piling up radiant clarities falls to the writer, through the mere words he utters, like the well-placed words of Truth and Beauty" (1578). On gold in Mallarmé, see Bertrand Marchal, *La religion de Mallarmé* (Paris: José Corti, 1988), 403–44.

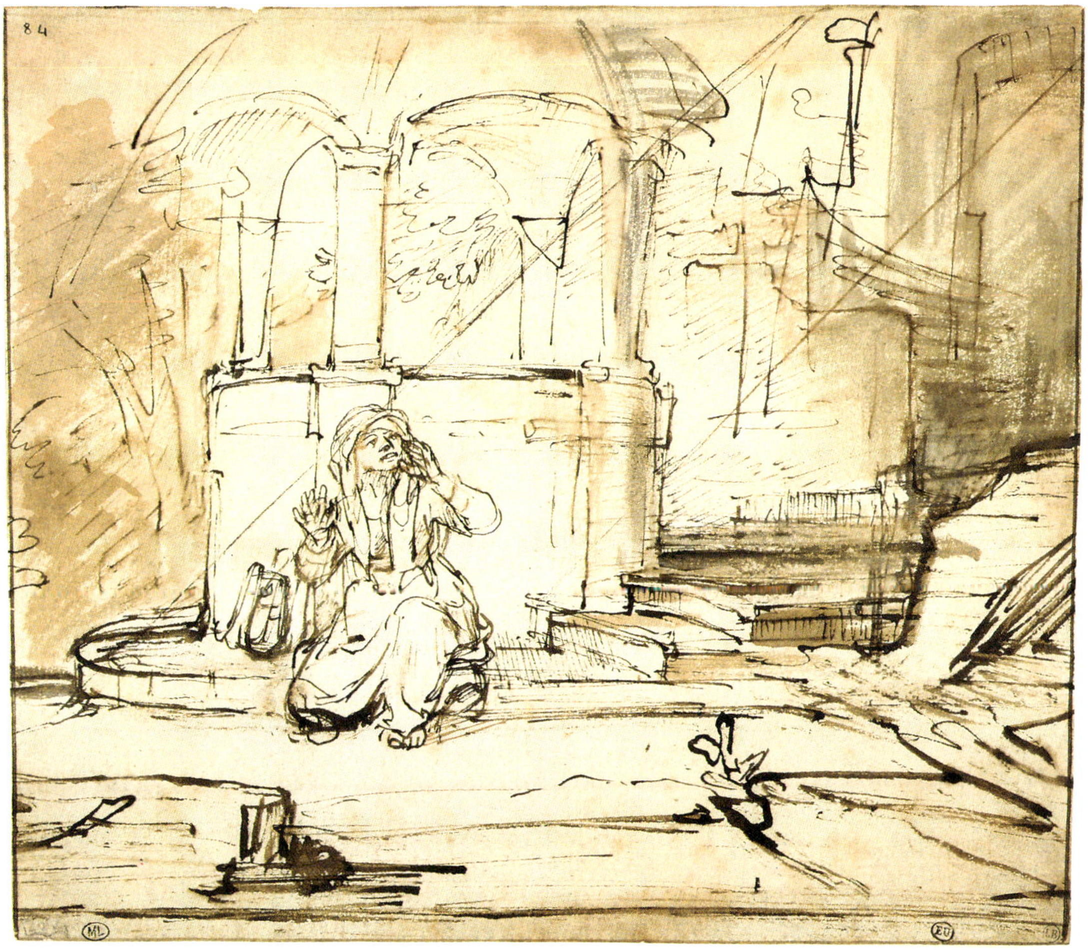

91. Rembrandt, *Hagar at the Fountain,* Louvre Museum.

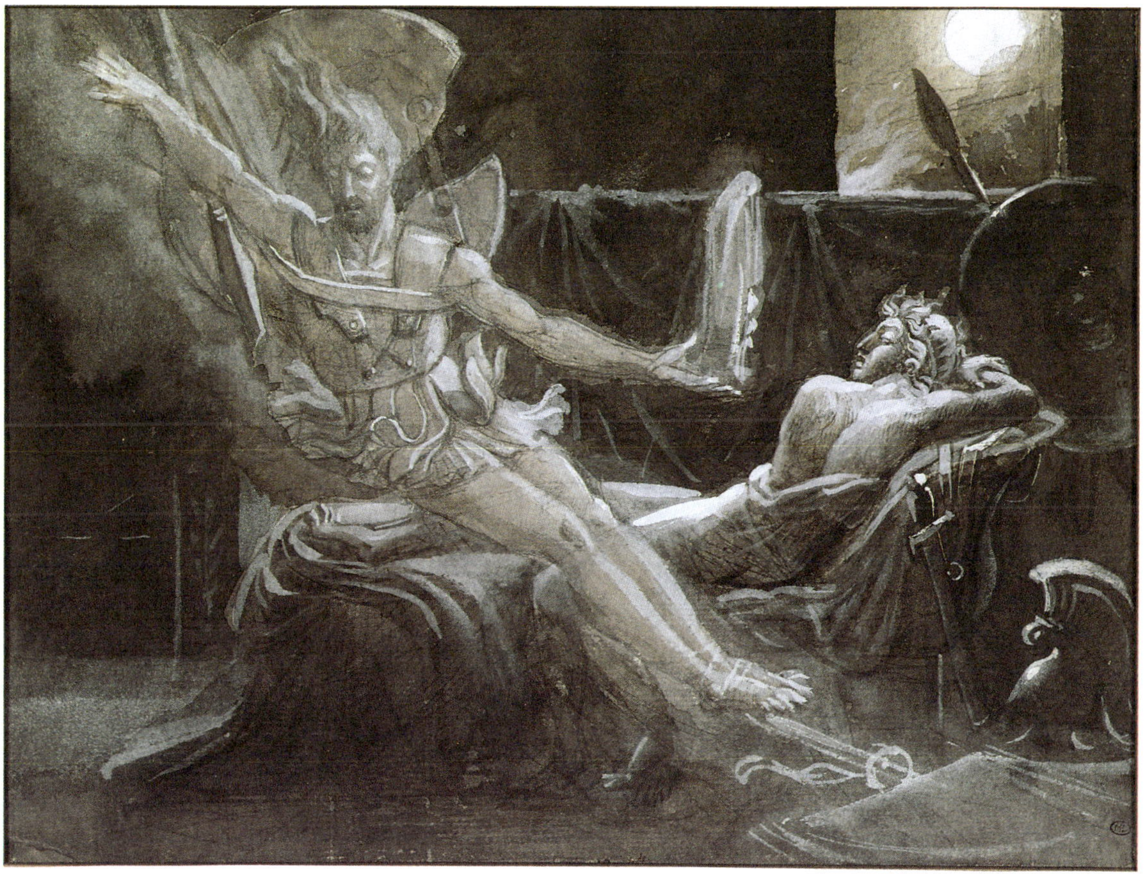

92. Girodet, *The Dream of Aeneas,* Louvre Museum. The drawing is inspired by Virgil (*Aeneid* 2.268–98). On the night preceding the fall of Troy, the ghost of Hector appears to Aeneas while he is asleep, and gives him the order to flee, handing him the tutelary gods—*di Penates*—of the city. These gods, transported by Aeneas, will become the gods of Rome, that is, of the second Troy rebuilt on Latin soil.

song."[214] Yet it is not impersonal chance speaking here, but a "pure and complex imagination."[215] As a last resort, Mallarmé persists in keeping alive the image of the throw and the spurt: at the end of his preface to *Un coup de dés,* he calls poetry the "unique spring of water."[216]

And to Whom Is Poetry Destined?

And he hopes the water in that spring will not be totally wasted and dispersed. He dreams it will respond to "a call" made by those who, for the moment, are paying little attention: the crowd, which must be brought together around a new religion. The ceremony he imagines, in the modern figure of fireworks, again takes the form of *sparsio* (the technology of gunpowder has made it possible to propel gifts skyward): "A multitude under the evening sky does not constitute the spectacle, but ahead of them the multiple and illuminating spray surges up, in the middle of the sky, representing in a considerable emblem its gold, its annual riches, and the harvest of its grains, and leads to the explosion of gazes at the normal heights."[217]

The burst of light is destined for the gazes that encounter it. In other words, poetry and art invoke the spring not only in the *figure* of the gift, but also in its destination. Since antiquity, all votive poems have begun with the words "I offer," "I give," or "I bring." These words consecrate bread, adornments, weapons, perfumes. They recall an oath and a promise that has been kept. Sometimes they make explicit the loving intention behind a gift. Most often, however, the gift itself is fictive.[218] Then the poem alone is the gift, or pretends to be, since its destiny is only the paper itself, though it elicits an imagined addressee. We read these texts today as if poetry were speaking of itself as it named the objects offered. "Je vous envoie un bouquet, que ma main / Vient de trier de ces fleurs épanies" (I send you a bouquet, which my hand / Has just picked out from these flowers in full bloom), sings Ronsard. The romantics liked to end their poetic cycles with an envoi. Hence the author of *To the Beloved Far Away,*[219] immortalized by Beethoven: "Nimm sie hin denn, diese Lieder" (Take them far away, these songs I have sung for you). Beethoven must have liked the envoi: we know the part it played in the composition of the poem (by Christoph Kuffner, one of his friends) for Fantasia for Piano, Choir, and Orchestra, op. 80. The final stanza is an envoi to the "beautiful souls"; in almost the same terms as in the lieder cycle, it expressly mentions the gift: "Nehmt den hin, ihr schönen Seelen, froh die Gaben schöner Kunst" (Beautiful souls, accept, take joyously away the marvelous gifts of art).

In an admirable poem from *West-östlicher Diwan,* Goethe evokes the spiny green fruit on the branch, which ripens, seeks the light, and then falls to the ground. And
2 Suleika becomes a Danaë: "So fallen meine Lieder / Gehäuft in deinen Schoss" (Thus

214. Mallarmé, *Un coup de dés* (Paris: Bibliothèque littéraire Jacques Doucet), preface. See fig. 93 above.

215. Ibid.

216. [In the original, *unique source,* which can also be "unique" or "sole source."—*Trans.*]

217. Mallarmé, "Villiers de l'Isle-Adam," in *Médaillons et portraits, Oeuvres complètes,* 499.

218. The candied fruit accompanied by a quatrain from Mallarmé on New Year's Day was probably not fictive: "Sous un hiver qui neige, neige, / Rêvant d'Edens quand vous passez! / Pourquoi Madame Madier, n'ai-je / A donner que des fruits glacés?" [Under a winter that snows, snows, / Dreaming of Edens when you pass by! / Why, Madame Madier, Have I / Only candied fruit to give?] Mallarmé, *Oeuvres complètes,* 118.

219. Aloys Jeitteles (1798–1854).

my songs fall, piling up in your bosom).[220] And in a different register, Baudelaire writes "Je te donne ces vers" (I give you these lines), while Mallarmé, in a poem of dawn that expresses the "horrible birth" of the nocturnal poem, writes: "Je t'apporte l'enfant d'une nuit d'Idumée" (I bring you the child of a night of Idumea).

The votive work integrates its dedication, or the appearance of a dedication, into itself. Between the work of art that *represents* the gift of a work of art, and the one that simply *is* itself a gift, the forms of giving are countless. At one extreme (for example), there are the "mises en abyme," illuminations that show, at the head of a solemn book, the author kneeling, handing that same illuminated book to the prince. At the other, there is the painting or sketch that the painter signs and offers to the student, the friend, naming the dedicatee on it. But sometimes as well, much more secretly, the artist adds something to the student's work with the stroke of a pencil or a touch of paint, and the gift of technique combines with the disciple's effort. The gift is then no longer represented; we discover it only when we have learned enough from the documents gathered together by historians. Michelangelo supported Sebastiano del Piombo in that way: to help him execute the figure of the dead Christ on an altarpiece, he sent him a superb **94**
drawing after an ancient sleeping Cupid. The gift, in this case, attests to a generous superiority, and at the same time to a desire to communicate the power of giving.

Testaments

At the moment of birth, the child receives not only life but the gifts that accompany it: these gifts are announced and distributed by the Fates and fairies.[221] At the brink of death, a man loses his life and his riches. But he still expresses the will to have command over his present wealth in the future. At the moment of death, possession is interrupted. Everything is up for grabs, available to others, to anyone at all perhaps, unless a prior act—authenticated, acknowledged, and protected by the institution of law—has attested to the desire animating the gift, which is destined for precisely designated heirs. **96**
Their coming into possession compensates for the dispossession of the dying man.

From the (supposedly *fateful*) whispers of fairies to the last will and testament—from the magical word that *bestows gifts* on newborns to the document that makes a bequest and allows the dying man to "vest the living"—language manifests its power to bring about what it utters.[222] The fabulous omnipotence of the oath is given narrative form in the short story; the effective omnipotence of the last will and testament takes the form of a legal document. Great texts express the importance of the ultimate act of giving. *King Lear* is its tragic exposition: the last decree of a will can be a blind decision

220. Goethe, *West-östlicher Diwan,* 8.31.

221. See the beginning of Perrault's "Sleeping Beauty": "It was a lovely baptism; the little Princess was given all the Fairies who could be found in the land as her godmothers (there were seven of them), so that, as each one gave her a gift (this was the custom of the Fairies at that time), the Princess would have every form of perfection imaginable." The maleficent gift is bestowed by the old fairy who was not invited.

222. Philosophers and linguists speak of *performative utterances.* See J. L. Austin, *How to Do Things with Words* (New York: Oxford University Press, 1962).

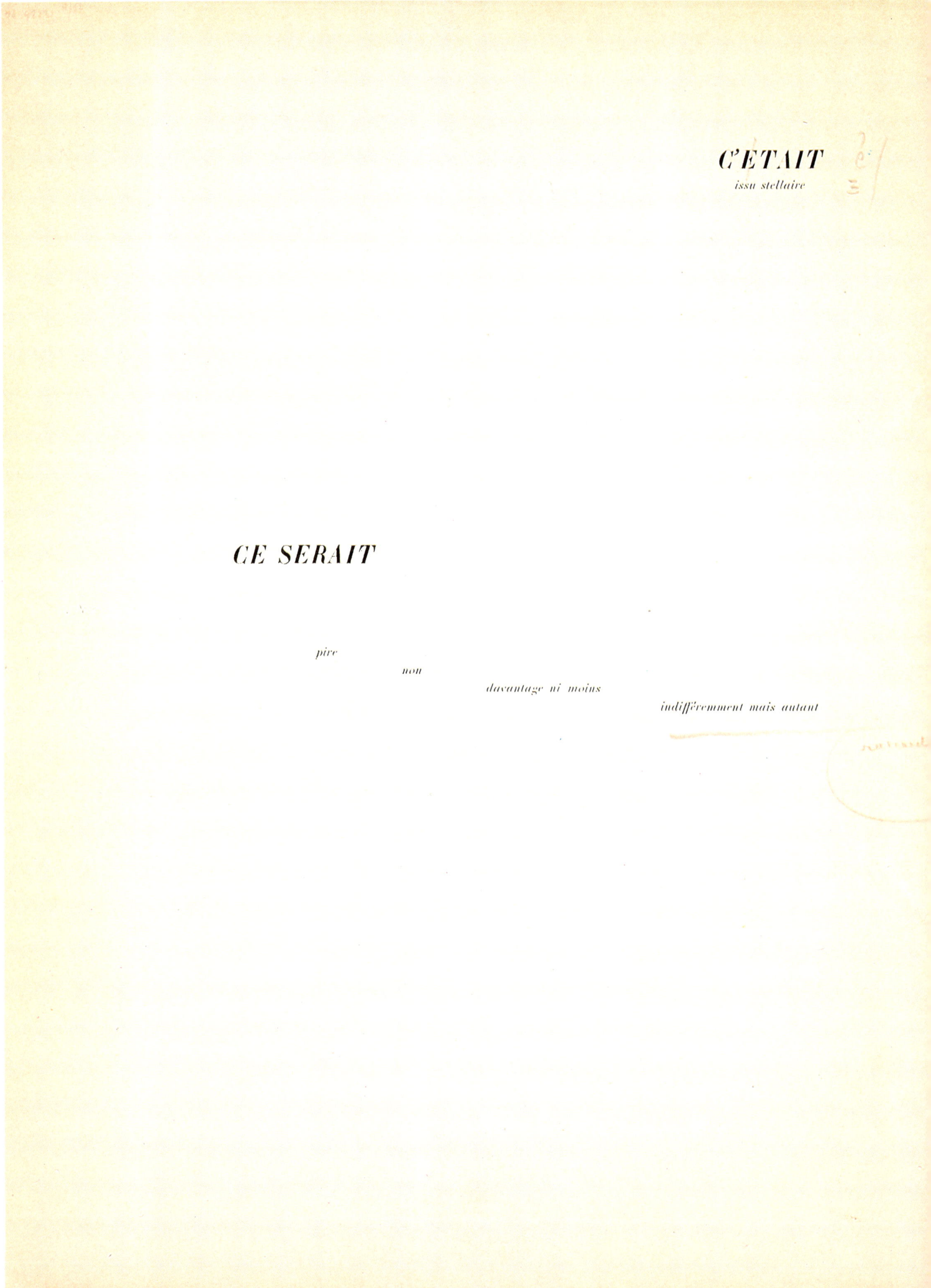

C'ETAIT

issu stellaire

CE SERAIT

pire

non

davantage ni moins

indifféremment mais autant

93. Stéphane Mallarmé, *Un coup de dés jamais n'abolira le hasard* (A throw of the dice will never abolish chance), Paris, Bibliothèque littéraire Jacques Doucet.

LE NOMBRE

EXISTÂT-IL
autrement qu'hallucination éparse d'agonie

COMMENÇÂT-IL ET CESSÂT-IL
sourdant que nié et clos quand apparu
enfin
par quelque profusion répandue en rareté
SE CHIFFRÂT-IL

évidence de la somme pour peu qu'une
ILLUMINÂT-IL

LE HASARD

Choit
la plume
rythmique suspens du sinistre
s'ensevelir
aux écumes originelles
naguères d'où sursauta son délire jusqu'à une cime
flétrie
par la neutralité identique du gouffre

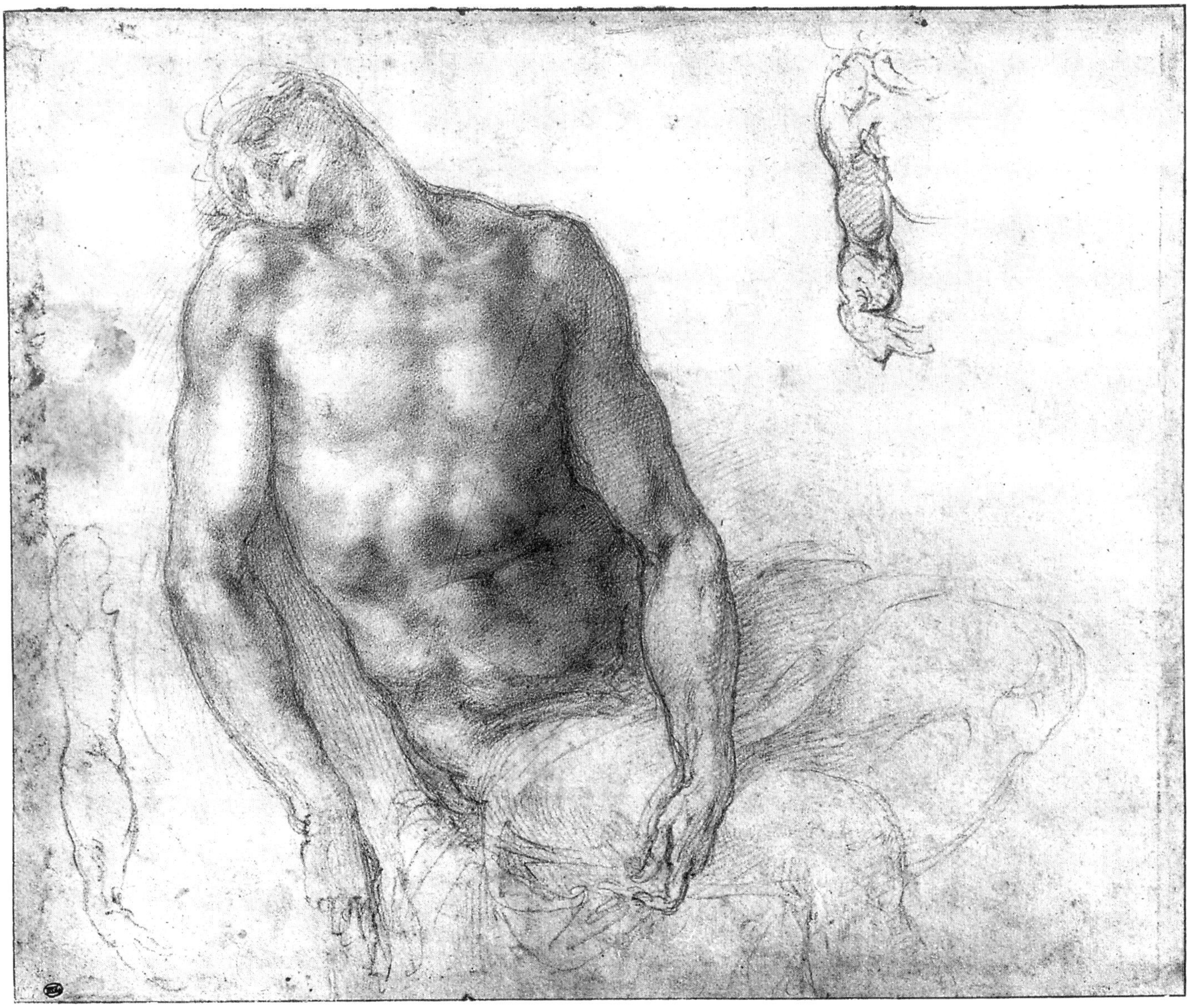

94. Michelangelo, *Study for a Pietà,* Louvre Museum. This is one of the drawings sent—*given*—by Michelangelo to Sebastiano del Piombo, to help him in his work on a Pietà that had been ordered from him. Michelangelo drew inspiration from a classical *Sleeping Cupid,* which he himself had earlier copied.

from a man unable to discern love, a man who favors greedy heirs and precipitates destruction. In Dante, those who fraudulently act against the words of a will are criminals.[223]

But another poet—François Villon, in both his *Lais* and his *Testament*—pretends to be a dying man and adopts the language of the testator, amusingly declaring his game. "I leave . . . I give and leave." The game is both comic and serious. It makes a spectacle of the gesture of giving. "He gave everything" but possessed nothing, "not even a sprig of parsley."[224] "When he died he had only rags."[225] Destitute, he gives the little or the nothing he has: the wind, imaginary retribution, songs, wagtails, ballads. He also gives the lash of a whip; he distributes words of ridicule, shame, supplication. In doing so, he takes inventory of his life and his world—his friends and enemies, his loves and hates. He "leaves" to others what they already have, by throwing their stupidity and vices back in their faces. And precisely because the pleasure of the language game is insubstantial, without material content, it enjoys absolute freedom, even as it designates real places, addressing beings who are not fictive and whom he touches with the ray of poetry. As a result, his poetic discourse does not convey anything other than the name of his heirs and the simulacrum of his bequests, forcing the reader's ears and eyes to lend themselves to the game. And what a sight that can be! We need only recall how the make-believe gift of the poet's "great eyeglasses" to the blind men of Quinze-Vingt leads us to look toward the cemetery of the Saints-Innocents, toward real death: "When I consider those skulls, / Piled up in those charnels."[226] The volley of cruel words Villon spews includes as much aggressivity, as much affirmation of power (but for a desperate cause), as the swarms of gifts thrown to the people by the emperors during saturnalia.

The Eclipse of Largesse?

As I said at the beginning of this book, during the century that is now coming to an end, the gift or donation has been a matter of reflection for philosophers, theologians, sociologists, and psychologists. Is this the nocturnal flight of Minerva's bird at day's end? Some great literary and artistic works of all kinds, though disconcerting, still have the value of a gift. Others deliberately want to be a riposte, a provocation, a challenge: the opposite of a gift, its furious denial. Of course, rarely have works made the gift their explicit theme (a theme all too figurative for the plastic arts) or represented the condition of art through any of the varieties of gifts or alms. Still, the wish to share, the desire for the "sharable" (*partageable;* Yves Bonnefoy), has remained fresh in the consciousness of poets. The desire to safeguard the living substance at the heart of the gift has to be asserted, first, against the desertification that endlessly threatens human relations, and second, against the forms of the gift—largesse by invitation, for instance—that dissimulate a strategy of subjugation.[227]

223. Dante places Gianni Schicchi in his Inferno: this forger secretly took the place of a dead man in order to name himself in the will (canto 30).

224. François Villon, *Le Testament,* 177, epitaph and rondeau.

225. Ibid., 185, another ballad.

226. Ibid., 160–65.

227. Today, the critique of the "paternalist" gift in its many aspects is implicitly understood. The canonical references for this ethical matter lie in a few illustrious literary passages. For example, in Dostoevsky's *Idiot,* there is the astonishing chapter (1.26) where Nastasia Philippovna throws the package of 100,000 rubles brought by Rogozhin into the fire.

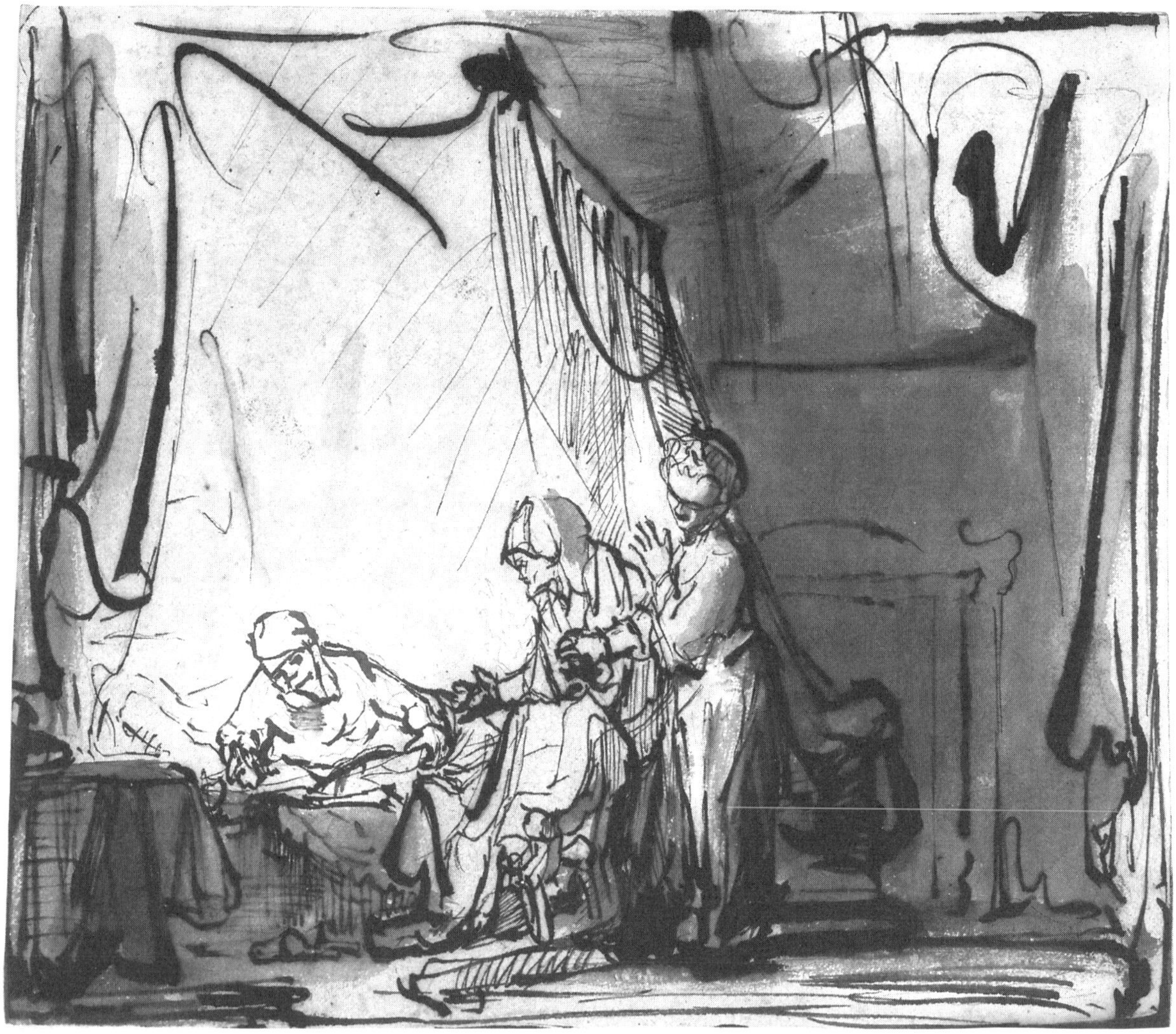

95. Rembrandt (school of), *Sarah Presenting Hagar to Abraham,* Louvre Museum, Edmond de Rothschild Collection.

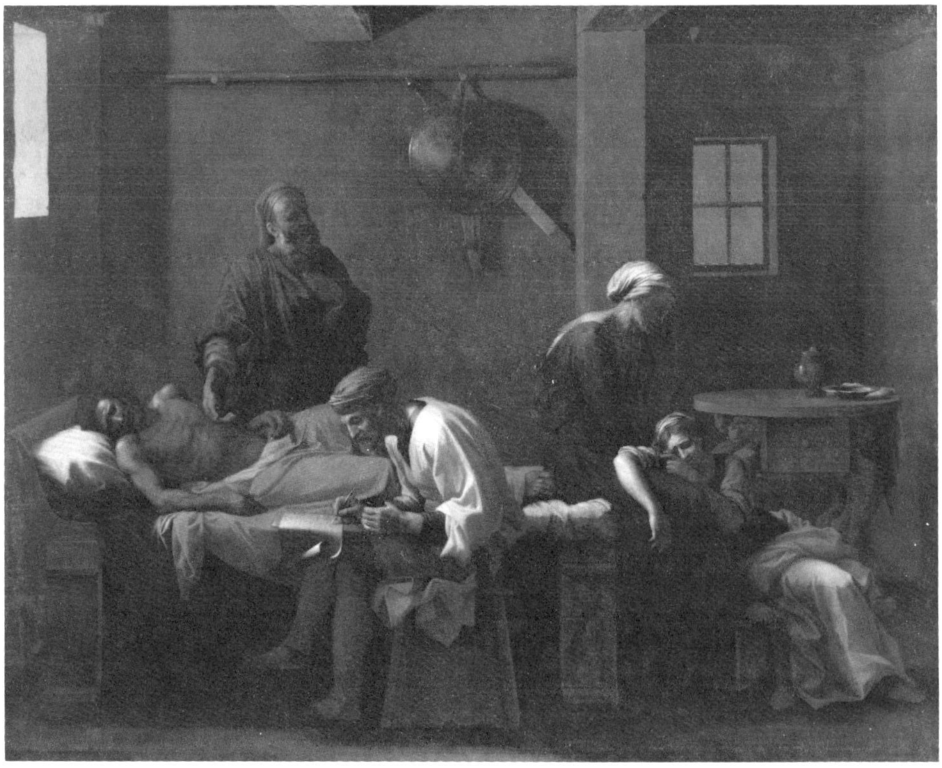

96. Nicolas Poussin, *The Testament of Eudamidas,* Copenhagen, Statens Museum for Kunst.

The word "liberality" has disappeared from the modern vocabulary of theologians. They prefer to return to its "principle": love, charity.[228] And in literature? It is not uncommon in recent texts to see talk of the gift or of alms, but at the distance of a dream or even of oblivion, as if from a space of fiction. In Borges's *El Aleph,* the Immortal, who believes his end is near, adds this reflection to all the books he has written or transcribed: "When the end approaches, images of memory no longer remain, only words remain." And Borges comments by way of conclusion: "Words, displaced and mutilated words, words borrowed from others, such were *the poor alms* that the hours and centuries left him" (my emphasis).[229] All literature since Homer is no more than those tenuous remains, confined within the limits of absolute destitution. . . . Another example: a brief narrative (unfolding like a dream) by Georges Henein, presents "a haughty and hard beggar woman. . . . At her feet, a heavy sign, a light coat of arms, these words: I BEG FOR NO REASON." This beggar woman offers love to a man she declares lost.[230] Begging and giving seem linked by a peculiar reversibility.

There is at least one text in the literature of the twentieth century that could be considered a great desperate parable on the gift and the artist: "Babette's Feast," by Karen Blixen.[231] Babette, a great Parisian cook exiled to Norway after the Commune and now a modest servant, wins 10,000 francs in the lottery. Hence the reader encounters Fortune once more. We also encounter largesse and the gift of food: Babette, instead of returning to Paris, spends her entire new fortune to offer a feast, amid a community of puritans, to the austere women she works for. Almost unbeknownst to them, the guests experience a moment of intense happiness, but the extraordinary gift is not truly acknowledged. The giver is never thanked. The only one who has guessed what was offered him, a melancholic old general, remains confined within his sorrow. "You ought not to have given away all you had for our sake," someone tells Babette the next day. "I am a great artist," she responds. The irony of the story is that the deceased pastor whose birthday the feast celebrated was in the habit of telling his flock: "The only things which we may take with us from our life on earth are those which we have given away." The parable concerns not only puritan repression but also the incapacity to receive what is most substantial and generous.

For several great poets of our age, it is because the gift does not go without saying that it takes on a new urgency. In fact, André Frénaud borrows voices from his earlier writings (sometimes attributed to a female figure) in his "Quelques approches pour un 'Je suis'" [Some approaches toward an "I am"]—that is, toward a self-definition—in order to speak of the gift with force and simplicity. In opposition to pride of any kind, he formulates a cogito of the gift of self:

228. See André de Bovis's article "Liberalité" in the *Dictionnaire de spiritualité* (vol. 9).

229. "Palabras, palabras desplazadas y mutiladas, palabras de otros, fué la pobre limosna que le dejaron las horas y los siglos." Jorge Luis Borges, *El Aleph,* in *Obras completas* (Buenos Aires: Emecé Editores, 1974), 544.

230. Georges Henein, *Notes sur un pays inutile* (Paris: Le Tout sur le Tout, 1982), 37–39.

231. Isak Dinesen (Karen Blixen), "Babette's Feast," *Anecdotes of Destiny* (New York: Random House, 1958), 21–68. In order for Babette to have something to give, a small fortune had to be given to her by chance. Aleksandr Solzhenitsyn's Matryona *(Matryona's House)* has no desire to possess: she helps her neighbors without asking for anything from them, and lets herself be deprived of the little she has. The gift of her life is, so to speak, invisible. She is nonetheless "the righteous woman without whom the world could not continue."

Je me donne donc je suis, un instant
Je me rends libre, j'existe désespérée
Je donne et je reçois, je donne, ainsi je suis.[232]

Let us also recall the words of a beautiful poem by Frénaud, "La fiancée juive" [The Jewish fiancée]. The words are attributed to Rembrandt, who addresses the fiancée and announces the gift he is making of her, through his painting, to the viewer's eyes:

—Je te donne, non pas pour me plaire,
ni pour satisfaire un songe impérieux
—qu'il m'arrive d'approcher seulement
lorsque ma main à force d'imaginer
    et de rompre, d'être mue
m'en fait reconnaître une vibration
quand une clarté va sourdre de la ténèbre.

Je te donne, pour me pardonner d'être en ce monde
    et d'y poursuivre.
Je te donne, pour m'assurer de faire émaner
    quelquefois pour nous tous
je ne sais quelle miséricordieuse lumière.
Je te donne. . . . Et pour cela, femme, je te bénis.[233]

The Present in All Its Strangeness

It should not be too difficult, I hope, to now decipher the modern versions of a few of the gestures whose history I have sketched. The ancient throwing of gifts? Today, in prosperous countries, this corresponds to the inexhaustible diffusion of images, the commodity disguised as a gift, the scattering of throwaway objects: free samples, sales, premiums, coupons. Saturnalia now take place all year long. Organized plunder? Today, there is the world smorgasbord, the rush toward all the well-stocked tables, toward all the amusement parks. Charity? Today, it is humanitarianism as spectacle, benefactors filmed against a background of food cargo, alms as performance. This was recently illustrated by the "artistic" distribution of dollars to illegal aliens crossing the border between Mex-

232. André Frénaud, *Haeres* (Paris: Gallimard, 1982), 239–40. "I give myself therefore I am, for an instant / I render myself free, I exist desperate. / I give and I receive, I give, hence I am."

233. Ibid., pp. 265–68.

—I give you, not to please myself,
nor to satisfy an imperious dream
—which I manage to approach only
when my hand by dint of imagining
and of breaking, and of being moved,
leads me to recognize a vibration of it
when a brightness springs up from the darkness.

I give you, to be pardoned for being in this world
and for proceeding here.
I give you, to make sure that
sometime for all of us
Some unknown and merciful light will emanate.
I give you. . . . And for that, woman, I bless you.

See the explanations of the motif of the Magi (*Rois mages* is the title of Frénaud's first collection) given by the author in *Entretiens avec Bernard Pingaud* (Paris: Gallimard, 1966). See also *Notre inhabileté fatale* (Paris: Gallimard, 1979), 53–56, 147–49. The giving king offers his tribute to a divinity who is the creation of his hope and pity: "Who wishes to give to whom? And who can receive?"

ico and the United States.[234] And today in addition, through a peculiar extension of the word, there is the "gift of life," the donation of organs, blood, sperm. Gifts hardly imaginable in the past, eclipsing the old miracles, returning the power of life to the mortally ill, but gifts that rarely depend on a voluntary donor and a conscious sacrifice: gifts of one's intimate substance, but cold, aseptic gifts—they are usually frozen—gifts called such for lack of another term.[235]

But is all this radically new? Have people not always divined and denounced the countless simulacra that accompany the gift like its own shadow, thus eliciting doubt about the generosity of intentions, the legitimacy of dispersed riches, the quality of the metal in the coins distributed? Have we not seen, in every era, charlatans who made people believe that overabundance sprang directly from them as they threw out handfuls of inferior products? Today, illusionism has at its disposal an extraordinary arsenal of deception.

But who could deny that, in the face of enormous distress, the need to give is still very much alive or that institutions do devote themselves to giving with true compassion? It is the serpent who sometimes whispers in our ear that the gifts we are witnessing are not true gifts, but only the guise of egoism.

And what are we to think of the transformations that affect our vocabulary? We are reluctant today to use the old words, "liberality" and "charity": they continue to designate great virtues, however, whose actual disappearance would be disastrous. But they seem to imply a separation between rich and poor. We prefer to speak of solidarity (or of humanitarian action). The word "solidarity" is of modern use: in the sense given it today, it appeared in the French language only in 1795, that is, within the context of revolutionary thought. It is now preferred because it appears to bear within it an imperative for equality and equity without condescension; it appears to designate the horizontal dimension alone. It has taken hold to such a point that solidarity is often the discreet name that persistent charity hides behind. But convincing figurations of solidarity are rare. Solidarity hands out cans, blankets, and plates of food or invites its beneficiaries to discreet distribution facilities. It sends out ambulances and emergency vehicles, sometimes through the worst sorts of danger. There are sincere people with true vocations, ready to give their time, their resources, and even their lives without the slightest ostentation, in all simplicity and goodness. They make themselves invisible. I speak of them now, unable to show pictures of them. Solidarity, which makes a virtue of discretion, does not take the form of a memorable ceremony. Why is that?

234. I am referring to an article signed "Seth Mydans" on the front page of the *New York Times,* 12 August 1993. It was entitled "Endowment of the Arts and by the Artists: Handouts by Artists as an Art": "Encinitas, Calif., Aug. 10—In the scrub-covered hills north of the Mexican border, a group of three experimental artists supported by a federal arts grant is handing out crisp $10 bills to illegal immigrants. To David Avalos, one of the artists, the act of giving money is a work of art and a political statement about 'the interaction of physical space with intellectual space and civic space.'" The final work of art is made up of the receipts signed by the immigrants. A photo illustrates the scene with the caption: "Eager for $10 bills, illegal aliens form a line next to David Avalos, second from right, and Louis Hock, who calls it art, not largess."

235. This form of gift, among others, is the object of Lewis Hyde's *The Gift: Imagination and the Erotic Life of Property* (New York: Vintage Books, 1979). See, more generally, *La revue du Mauss* 11 ("Donner, recevoir et rendre: L'autre paradigme") and 12 ("Le don perdu et retrouvé") (Paris: La Découverte, 1991).

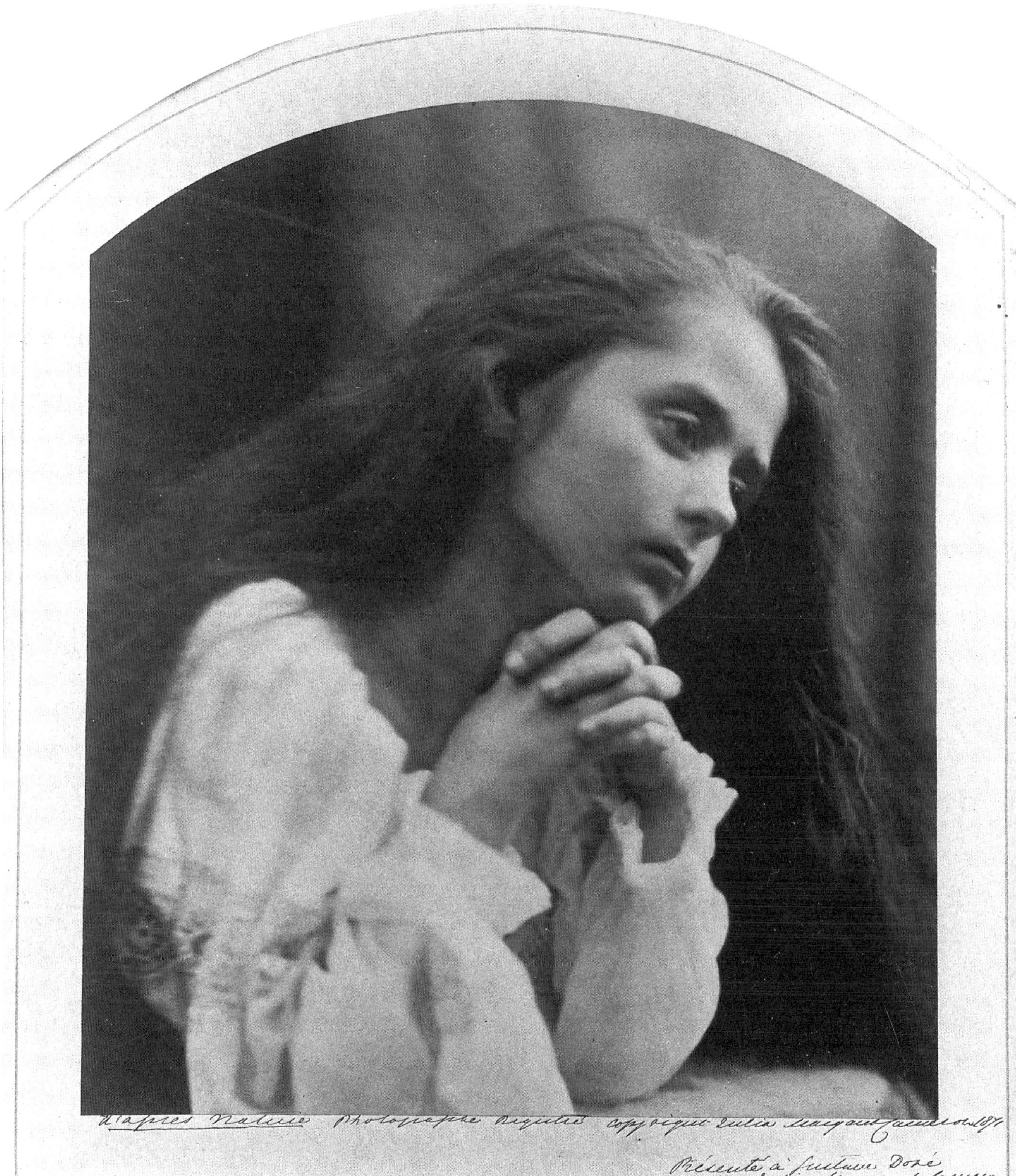

97. Julia Margaret Cameron, *Little Girl in Prayer* (1871), Orsay Museum. The photograph is dedicated, a gift from one artist to another. We read lower right: *Présenté à Gustave Doré par Julia Margaret Cameron* (Presented to Gustave Doré by Julia Margaret Cameron).

The scenes of beneficence, the hands held out, the supplicating gazes, have often been painted and drawn, to be immortalized in their glory. Today the image is captured on the spot and transmitted throughout the world; using the speed of video, every effort is made to improve on the tableau vivant fixed by the earliest photographers. The television viewer does not have to look far to find new children's battles, and often, the assaults of a crowd rushing toward those who, by their own will or by force, are placed in the situation of donors. But between the great misery of a far-off continent—or the appeal launched on behalf of it—and the gift given (generally in a collective manner), the distance is so great and the disproportion such that the gesture of largesse has become *unrepresentable.* There is no longer a consecrated place to serve as framework for the act of giving. One hundred thousand benefactors sign a check in absentia. The "picturesque" places that, in the past, served as the theater of largesse and charity—the public square, the steps of a cathedral, the country road—no longer have that function in today's civilization. There remain, it is true, the entrances to museums, the exits of department stores, subway platforms. To my knowledge, art has not captured the posture of someone asking or giving in such places. What painter would dare that kind of kitsch? Contemporary art does not see destitution as an anecdote. For the best artists, lack is everywhere and plenitude is everywhere.

The ancient forms of largesse—distribution in public—are now perceived as an archaic ritual. I still retain the image of tyranny in Central America (the regime in question has since fallen), which appeared on my television screen: a black limousine moving through the streets of an impoverished city, bank notes escaping from the window opened just a crack, showering down like dead leaves on a disorderly crowd, which rushed toward them. What a sinister carnival! . . . Let us compare this to Cornelisz van Haarlem's *Public Festivities.* The crowd presses forward in the same way. There has **24,17**
merely been a change in the material support, we would like to believe: in the fleeting images of our television screens we find again the scenes that draftsmen recorded on paper or that painters fixed on wood or canvas. But this is not the case. With the change in material support, with instantaneity and the movement of the image, everything has changed. The new scenes we are tempted to declare similar to the old may resemble them, but to no avail; they repeat ancient displays and ancient perversions, but they have nothing in common with them. The image is now fixed neither by the pencil nor by ink. It passes, it provokes, it jostles; but, even if it were to stop, it would not address us, it would not teach us anything, it would merely leave us troubled. We must resign ourselves to losing it. Even during its brief reality, it was already out of reach. It says only one thing: "It was thus." If there was a plea, it can no longer be satisfied. If there was a gift, it was not ours. What troubles us may be the fact that we cannot participate in any way. What remains within our hands? Must we believe we inhabit an arid world, where nothing that gives itself can last, not even the image or fable of an event?

But should there occur spontaneously an instant of happiness, an oblique beam of light on the prairie, a downpour on the dried-out earth, the swaying of a branch that bears a ripe apple, then thoughts of the gift reawaken within us, all the more alive. We sometimes feel the irresistible desire to write, to find the right words, to use pencil or paintbrush, a stroke or a daub of color, to give thanks.

Thus, we cannot end here: this is the point where the inquiry should broaden and branch out in every direction, in the present in all its strangeness.

Appendix: Texts on the Gift

The Peasants' Battle

1.
Jean-Jacques Rousseau
Les rêveries du promeneur solitaire
"Neuvième promenade"*

I was in La Chevrette for the saint's day of the master of the house. His entire family had come together to celebrate it, and all the splendor of noisy pleasures was set in place to that effect. Games, spectacles, feasts, fireworks—no expense was spared. You had no time to catch your breath; everyone went about in a daze instead of having a good time. After supper everyone went to get some air along the avenue; a kind of fair was going on. People were dancing. Gentlemen deigned to dance with peasant girls but ladies maintained their dignity. There was gingerbread for sale. A young man from the company decided to buy some of it and to throw pieces one after the other into the crowd. All the onlookers took such pleasure in seeing all those peasants rush forward, fight, and knock one another down to get some gingerbread that they all wanted to give themselves the same pleasure. Gingerbread was flying left and right, while girls and boys ran in, piled up, maimed one another. Everyone found it charming. Out of bashfulness, I did the same as everyone else, but inside I was not having as much fun as they were. Soon bored with emptying my purse to see people get crushed, I left the good company and went walking about the fair by myself. The variety of objects amused me a great deal. Among other things, I saw five or six Savoyards around a little girl, who still had about a dozen sorry-looking apples on her tray, which she would very much have liked to be rid of. For their part, the Savoyards would have liked to get rid of them for her, but they had only two or three pennies among them, and that was not enough to make much of a dent in the apples. For them, this tray was the garden of Hesperides, and the little girl was the dragon guarding it. This comedy amused me for a long time; I finally provided the denouement by buying the apples from the little girl and distributing them to the little boys. I then was witness to one of the sweetest spectacles that can flatter a man's heart, that of seeing joy and the innocence of youth spreading around me. For when the spectators saw it, they too shared it, and I, who shared that joy at so little expense, had the additional joy of feeling it was my doing.

*Standard punctuation has been inserted.

In comparing that amusement with those I had just left, I felt with satisfaction the difference between healthy tastes and natural pleasures and those produced by opulence, which are only the pleasures of mockery and the exclusivist tastes engendered by contempt. For what sort of pleasure could one take in seeing herds of men, debased by poverty, piled up, suffocated, and brutally maiming one another to grab greedily at a few pieces of gingerbread that had been trampled underfoot and covered with mud?

When I reflected back on the sort of pleasure I had experienced, I found that it consisted less in a feeling of beneficence than in the enjoyment of seeing contented faces. That aspect has a charm for me which, even though it penetrates my heart, seems to be solely a matter of sensation. If I did not see the satisfaction I caused, even if I were sure of it, my pleasure would be cut in half. In fact, it is a disinterested pleasure for me, which does not depend on the part I might play in it. For at fetes for the common people, the pleasure of seeing happy faces has always greatly attracted me.

Oeuvres complètes, ed. Marcel Raymond and Bernard Gagnebin (Paris: Gallimard, "Bibliothèque de la Pléaide," 1959), 1:1092–93.

2.
Charles Baudelaire
Le spleen de Paris
Poem 15, "Le gâteau"

I was traveling. I stood in the middle of a landscape of irresistible grandeur and nobility. No doubt at that moment something happened within my soul. My thoughts were fluttering about with a lightness equal to that of the atmosphere; vulgar passions such as hate and profane love now appeared as distant as the clouds that paraded at the bottom of the abysses under my feet. My soul seemed as vast and pure as the cupola of the heavens that enveloped me. The memory of earthly things reached my heart only weakened and diminished, like the bells of the cattle grazing out of sight, far away, on the other side of another mountain. Over the motionless little lake, black in its immense depth, there sometimes passed the shadow of a cloud, like the reflection of the mantle of an airborne giant flying across the sky. And I remember that this solemn and rare sensation, caused by a great and perfectly silent movement, filled me with a joy mixed with fear. In short, owing to the beauty that surrounded me and filled me with enthusiasm, I felt at perfect peace with myself and with the universe; I even believe that, in my perfect bliss and my total obliviousness to all earthly ills, I had reached the point of no longer finding so ridiculous the newspapers that claim man is born good.—Then, the imperative of incurable matter again made its wishes known, and I decided to treat my fatigue and satisfy my appetite caused by my long ascension. I took from my pocket a big piece of bread, a leather cup, and a flask of a certain elixir that pharmacists were selling to tourists at that time, so that they could combine it with melted snow when the occasion arose.

I was calmly cutting up my bread when a very soft noise made me look up. Before me stood a ragged creature, black and tousled, whose hollow, fierce, and as it were supplicating eyes were devouring the piece of bread. And I heard him sigh, in a low and raucous voice, the word "cake"! I could not keep myself from laughing upon hearing the name with which he had wished to honor my bread, which was nearly white, and I cut off a nice slice and offered it to him. Slowly he approached, not letting his eyes leave the coveted object; then, snatching away the piece of bread, he quickly retreated, as if he feared my offer was not sincere or that I was already thinking better of it.

But at that instant, he was knocked over by another little savage, come from who knows where, and so perfectly similar to the first that he might have been taken for his twin brother. Together they rolled about on the ground, fighting for the precious prey, neither wishing to sacrifice half to his brother. The first, aggravated, grabbed the second by his hair; then he seized his ear in his teeth, and spit out a bloody bite of it with a superb curse in patois. The legitimate owner of the cake tried to plant his little claws in the eyes of the usurper; in his turn the other applied all his strength toward strangling his adversary with one hand while with the other he tried to slip the prize of the battle into his pocket. But, revived by despair, the vanquished boy got back up and sent the vanquisher rolling onto the ground with a blow from his head to the other's stomach. What is the point of describing a hideous struggle that in truth lasted longer than their childish strength seemed to promise? The cake kept traveling from hand to hand and changed pockets at every moment; but alas, it also changed in volume. And when, finally worn out, panting and bleeding, they stopped because they found it impossible to continue, there was, in truth, no longer any object of the battle: the piece of bread had disappeared, scattered into crumbs like the grains of sand with which it was now mixed.

This spectacle had clouded over the landscape for me, and the calm joy in which my soul had taken pleasure before seeing these little men had totally disappeared; I remained sad for quite a long time, endlessly repeating: "There is thus a superb country where bread is called cake, and where it is a treat so rare that it is enough to engender a perfectly fratricidal war!"

Oeuvres complètes, ed. Claude Pichois (Paris: Gallimard, "Bibliothèque de la Pléiade," 1975), 1:297–99.

3.
Joris-Karl Huysmans
A rebours

[Des Esseintes] took refuge in his garden and found shelter under a tree that provided a circle of shade. Seated on the lawn, he looked in a daze at the plots of vegetables the servants had planted. He looked at them, but it was an hour before he perceived them, for a greenish fog was floating before his eyes, letting him see only blurred images whose aspect and hue kept changing, as if he were under water.

. . . Above the hedge separating the low garden from the raised road leading to the fort, he saw children rolling about in the hot sun, in the light.

He was concentrating his attention on them when another, smaller child appeared, filthy to look at: he had seaweed hair full of sand, two green bubbles beneath his nose, disgusting lips surrounded by the white scum from cream cheese with herbs, which had been smeared onto bread and strewn with crossed strips of green onion.

Des Esseintes sniffed at the air; a pica, a perversion took hold of him; that vile snack made his mouth water. It seemed to him that his stomach, which had refused all nourishment, would digest that horrid food, and that his palate would take pleasure in it as if it were a delicious treat.

He jumped up, ran to the kitchen, ordered that a round loaf of bread, fromage blanc, and onion be fetched from the village, prescribed that a snack absolutely identical to the one the child had been gnawing on be prepared, and returned to sit under his tree.

The brats were fighting now. They were tearing off scraps of bread and stuffing them into their cheeks, then sucking on their fingers. Kicks and punches showered down, and the weaker ones, trampled on the ground, kicked and cried, their behinds scraped by the gravel.

This spectacle revived des Esseintes; the interest he took in that battle turned his thoughts away from his ills. Confronted with the relentlessness of those nasty kids, he thought of the cruel and abominable law of the struggle for existence, and even though these children were ignoble, he could not avoid taking an interest in their fate, believing it would have been better for them if their mothers had never whelped.

. . . The servant interrupted these charitable ruminations by des Esseintes, bringing him the snack he had wished for on a plate of gilded silver. Nausea churned up inside him; he was not up to biting into that bread, for the unhealthy excitation of his stomach had ended. A sensation of horrible disrepair returned; he had to get up; the sun was moving and taking over his place little by little; the heat was becoming more oppressive and more intense.

—Throw that snack, he said to the servant, to those children out on the road who are slaughtering one another; let the weakest of them be maimed, let them get not a bite and, moreover, let them get a major beating from their families when they return home with black eyes and their trousers torn; that will give them a glimpse of the life that awaits them! And he returned to his house and collapsed in a weakened state into an arm chair.

Ed. Marc Fumaroli (Paris: Gallimard, "Folio," 1977), chap. 13, 290–96.

Other Battles

4.
Seneca
Ad Lucilium epistulae morales
Letter 74

Whoever has largely surrendered himself to the power of Fortune has made for himself a huge web of disquietude, from which he cannot get free; if one would win a way to safety, there is but one road,—to despise externals and to be contented with that which is honourable. For those who regard anything as better than virtue are spreading their arms to gather that which Fortune tosses abroad, and are anxiously awaiting her favours [*ad haec quae a fortune sparguntur sinum expandit, et sollicitus missilia ejus exspectat*]. Picture now to yourself that Fortune is holding a festival, and is showering down honours, riches, and influence upon this mob of mortals: some of these gifts have already been torn to pieces in the hands of those who try to snatch them, others have been divided up by treacherous partnerships, and still others have been seized to the great detriment of those into whose possession they have come. Certain of these favours have fallen to men while they were absent-minded, others have been lost to their seekers because they were snatching too eagerly for them, and, just because they are greedily seized upon, have been knocked from their hands. There is not a man among them all, however,—even he who has been lucky in the booty which has fallen to him,—whose joy in his spoil has lasted until the morrow.

The most sensible man, therefore, as soon as he sees the dole being brought in, runs from the theatre; for he knows that one pays a high price for small favours. No one will grapple with him on the way out, or strike him as he departs; the quarrelling takes place where the prizes are. Similarly with the gifts which Fortune tosses down to us; wretches that we are, we become excited, we are torn asunder, we wish that we had many hands, we look back now in this direction and now in that. All too slowly, as it seems, are the gifts thrown in our direction; they merely excite our cravings, since they can reach but few and are awaited by all. We are keen to intercept them as they fall down. We rejoice if we have laid hold of anything; and some have been mocked by the idle hope of laying hold; we have either paid a high price for worthless plunder with some disadvantage to ourselves, or else have been defrauded and left in the lurch. Let us therefore withdraw from a game like this, and give way to the greedy rabble; let them gaze after such "goods," which hang suspended above them and be themselves still more in suspension.

The Epistles of Seneca, English trans. Richard M. Gummere (Cambridge and London: Harvard University Press and William Heinemann, 1962), 2.117–19.

5.
D. A. F. de Sade
Histoires de Juliette ou les Prospérités du vice
Part 6

The king had proposed that we come watch one of the oddest fetes in his kingdom, from a balcony of his palace. This was to be a *cocagne.* I had often heard of this extravagance, but what I saw was very different from the idea I had formed of it. . . .

"If you are not familiar with this spectacle," the king told us, as soon as we had had our chocolate, "you will find it quite barbaric."

"That's how we like it, sire," I responded; and I confess I have long wished for such games in France, or for gladiators. The energy of a nation is maintained only through blood spectacles: a nation that does not adopt them grows soft. When an imbecilic emperor, raising that idiotic Christianity to the throne of the Caesars, closed down the Roman circus, who became the masters of the world? . . . Abbots, monks, and dukes.

"Should the life of all those rogues count for anything when our pleasures are at stake?" said Charlotte. "If we have the right to slaughter them for our self-interest, we should also have the right to do so for our pleasures."

"Well, then, lovely ladies," said Ferdinand, "give your orders. Depending on the amount of rigor and the level of law and order I establish for the celebration of these orgies, I can have six hundred more, or six hundred fewer, killed. So tell me what you desire in that respect."

"The worst, the worst!" responded Clairwil. "The more rascals get slaughtered, the more fun we'll have."

"Go on then," said the king, handing down his order to one of his officers.

Then, at the sound of a cannon shot, we moved onto the balcony. There were an excessive number of people on the square; then we caught sight of the whole view.

On a great platform adorned with rustic ornaments stood a prodigious quantity of food, set out so as to compose a part of the decoration. There were inhumanely crucified geese, chickens, and turkey which, suspended while still alive and attached solely by a nail, amused the people with their convulsive movements; bread, dried cod, quarters of beef; sheep grazing in a part of the decorations that represented a field guarded by well-dressed cardboard men; pieces of canvas arranged to form waves around a ship laden with food and furniture for the common people. This was the bait, arranged with great art and taste, which had been prepared for that savage nation, to perpetuate its voracity and its excessive love of thieving. For once you have seen that spectacle, it is difficult not to agree that it was much more a school for plunder than a true celebration.

We had hardly had time to take in the stage when a second cannon shot rang out. At that signal, the chain that restrained the people opened quickly. The people leapt forward, and instantaneously, everything was taken away, snatched up, and plundered, with a speed . . . a frenzy, that is impossible to represent. This frightening scene, which reminded me of a pack of hounds going in for the kill, always ended more or less tragically, because everyone fought over the booty, wanting to get at it and to keep his neighbor from taking any. In Naples, such discussions are settled only by knife fights. But this time, in accordance with our desires, through the cruel attentions of Ferdinand, when the stage was full and there were perhaps seven or eight hundred people on it, all of a sudden, it collapsed and more than four hundred people were crushed.

Oeuvres complètes, ed. J.-J. Pauvert (Paris: Au cercle du livre précieux, 1966), 9:399–401.

6.
Comtesse de Ségur, née Rostopchine
Les mémoires d'un âne
"Un baptême"

The basket of Jordan almonds was ready. Someone took it to Camille, while Pierre was given the basket of pennies. Camille took a handful and let them shower down on the children. A real battle began; it was like a pack of hungry dogs. The children fought over the almonds and pennies, and everyone rushed for the same spot. They tore out one another's hair, hit one another, rolled on the ground, fought over every almond and every penny. Half were lost, trampled underfoot, disappearing into the grass. Pierre was not laughing. Camille, who had laughed at the first handfuls, was laughing no longer: she saw that these were serious battles, that several children were crying, and that others had scratches on their faces.

(Paris: Bibliothèque Rose, 1860), chap. 18, 166–67.

7.
Charles Fourier
Le nouveau monde amoureux

Enormous preparations had been made during the night and, at three o'clock in the morning, the great bell of Babylon witnessed three rows of tanks proceeding by torchlight out of every gate in Babylon, bringing dishes and convoys of food, cases of wine and liquor, provisions for more than 100,000 guests. From another gate there came legions of porters carrying poles charged with chance objects, masterpieces from the kitchens, candy, chests of fruit, and cold meats prepared the night before. . . . The camps were working with the same flurry of activity. Before four o'clock the table was set for 300,000 persons: everywhere there were pyramids of poultry, fish, salty treats and pastries, altars covered with assorted wines, altars covered with sweets and ice cream in various flavors. In one corner, legions were cranking ice cream makers by the thousands, in another, more legions were making punch and garlands of liqueurs and other drinks. Loads of flowers decorated hams and baskets of fruit.

The cooking staff made haste with the soups and hot substances. At four-thirty, there appeared on the high Euphrates the fleet of pious crusading shoemakers, and soon the center of the river was covered from afar with rows of lanterns placed atop the masts. They landed at the spacious piers, and the tower of Babylon gave the signal with three cones of fire, followed by a magnificent fireworks display, which ended with a flaming shoe and the legend spelled out underneath: "Long live the pious shoemakers." The battle ovens were preparing to spew forth torrents of pies, and everything suggested that the combat was to be entered into with unprecedented fervor all along the line.

Ed. S. Debout-Oleszkiewicz (Paris: Anthropos, 1967), 366–67.

8.
Alfred Jarry
Ubu Rex
Act 2

Scene 6. *The King's Palace*
PA UBU, MA UBU, CAPTAIN MACNURE

PA UBU. No! Nothing doing, I say! Do you want to ruin me just for those buffoons?
CAPTAIN MACNURE. But look here, Old Ubu, don't you see that your people are expecting gifts to celebrate your glorious coronation?
MA UBU. If you don't give them a great feast and plenty of gold, you'll be overthrown in a couple of hours.
PA UBU. A feast, yes, but money, never! Slaughter three old nags, that's quite good enough for such scum.

MA UBU. Scum yourself! How did such a crummy creature as you ever get slapped together?
PA UBU. Do I have to repeat myself? I intend to get rich, I won't fork out a penny.
MA UBU. Don't forget you hold in your hands all the treasure of Poland!
CAPTAIN MACNURE. Yes, I know where there's a vast hoard hidden in the chapel; let's distribute that.
PA UBU. Just you try that on, you wretch.
CAPTAIN MACNURE. Listen, Old Ubu, if you don't distribute some money, no one will want to pay taxes.
PA UBU. Is that really true?
MA UBU. Yes, yes!
PA UBU. Oh, in that case, I agree to everything. Bring up two or three million gold pieces, roast a hundred and fifty oxen and the same number of sheep, and see that there's plenty left over for me.

They go out.

Scene 7. *The Courtyard of the palace, full of people*
PA UBU, *crowned;* MA UBU, CAPTAIN MACNURE, LACKEYS, *loaded with dishes of roasted meat.*

PEOPLE. There's the King! Long live the King! Hurrah!
PA UBU (*throwing gold*). Here, you catch. Don't thank me. All this throwing gold away is no pleasure to me at all, but my old woman insisted. At least, promise you'll pay your taxes now.
ALL. Yes, yes!
CAPTAIN MACNURE. Just look, Madam Ubu, how they are fighting over the gold. What a battle!
MA UBU. Perfectly dreadful! Ugh! There's one who's had his skull bashed in.
PA UBU. What a beautiful sight! Bring up more chests of gold.
CAPTAIN MACNURE. How about organizing a race?
PA UBU. Yes, that's an idea. (*To the* PEOPLE.) My friends, you see this chest of gold? It contains three hundred thousand rose-nobles in gold, all genuine Polish coin of the realm. Those who want to run in the race, go to the end of the courtyard. You start running when I wave my handkerchief, and the winner gets the chest. And for the losers, there's this second chest of gold to share out as a booby prize.
ALL. Yes! Long live Old Ubu! What a decent king! We never had fun like this during the reign of Wenceslas.

In *The Ubu Plays,* trans. Cyril Connolly and Simon Watson Taylor (London: Methuen, 1968), 35–36.

Fortune

9.
Pliny the Elder
Natural History

Throughout the whole world, in every place, at all times and in all men's mouths, Fortune alone is sought unto and called upon: she only is named and in request; she alone is blamed, accused, and indicted. None but she is thought upon; she only is praised, she alone is reproved and rebuked: yea, and worshipped is she, with railing and reproachful terms: and namely when she is taken to be wavering and mutable: and of the most sort supposed also blind: roving at random, inconstant, uncertain, variable, and favouring the unworthy: whatsoever is laid forth, spent and lost, whatsoever is received, won and gotten: all that comes in, all that goes out, is imputed to Fortune: and in all men's reckoning and accounts, she makes up the book and sets all straight. So abject we are, so servile also and enthralled to Lots, that even the very chance of Lots is taken for a god, than which nothing maketh us more doubtful and ignorant of God.

English trans. Paul Turner (Carbondale: Southern Illinois University Press, 1962).

Roman Charity

10.
Valerius Maximus
Factorum dictorumque memorabilium libri novem

Fortune has no punishment and poverty no tatters that can debase and degrade filial tenderness; in fact, the proof of such piety is all the more certain when it occurs in the most difficult of circumstances. A free gentlewoman, sentenced for a capital crime at the praetor's court, was handed over by that court to the triumvir, to be executed in prison. The jailer who received her was moved by pity and did not immediately strangle her; he even gave the daughter of his prisoner free access to her, though he always searched her carefully, for fear she would bring her mother some food. He thought the unfortunate woman would soon die of want. But, after several days, seeing that the woman was still alive, he sought out the reason, and his curiosity led him to catch the daughter with her breast revealed, nursing her mother to alleviate the horrors of hunger. The news of such an admirable event was transmitted from the jailer to the triumvir, from the triumvir to the praetor, and from the praetor to the council of judges. It earned the condemned woman full remission of her punishment. Where does filial piety not lead, what does it not suggest, when it finds such a novel means to save a mother in prison? What is more extraordinary, more unheard of, than to see a mother nursed by her own daughter? It would seem to be against nature, if the first law of nature were not to love the author of our days.

The filial piety of Pera deserves the same praise. Her father, Cimon, worn down by age and the object of a similar sentence, was also thrown into a dungeon; she nursed him like her own child, with milk from her own breast. We are captivated by the depiction of that sign of love, and the admiration caused by the spectacle of this ancient scene gives it all the more reality for us; in these mute and insensate figures, we believe we can see moving, breathing bodies. The literary account makes the same impression on our minds; its scenes, even more than other representations, have the power to give to ancient events the attraction of novelty. [Haerent ac stupent hominum oculi, quum hujus facti pictam imaginem vident, casusque antiqui conditionem praesentis spectaculi admiratione renovant, in illis mutis membrorum lineamentis viva ac spirantia corpora intueri credentes: quod necesse est animo quoque evenire, aliquanto efficaciore pictura literarum, vetera pro recentibus admonito recordari.]

Ed. C. Kemp (Leipzig, 1889), 5.4 (p. 247).

Largesse and Foolish Largesse

11.
Guillaume de Lorris
The Romaunt of the Rose

[In the Garden of Mirth, Largesse dances the carol with Beauty, Riches, and Courtesy (ll. 1127–90):]

And after on the daunce wente
Largesse, that sette al hir entente
For to be honourable and free.
Of Alexandres kyn was she;
Hir most joye was, ywys,
Whan that she yaf, and seide, "Have this."
Not Avarice, the foule caytyf,
Was half to gripe so ententyf,
As Largesse is to yeve and spende;
And God ynough alwey hir sende,
So that the more she yaf awey
The more, ysys, she hadde alwey.
Gret loos hath Largesse and gret pris;
For bothe wys folk and unwys
Were hooly to hir baundon brought,
So wel with yiftes hath she wrought.
And if she hadde an enemy,
I trowe that she coulde craftely
Make hym full soone hir freend to be,
So large of yift and free was she.
Therfore she stod in love and grace
Of riche and power in every place.
. . . .
Largesse haddle on a robe fresh
Of riche purpur Sarsynesh.
Wel fourmed was hir face and cleer,
And opened hadde she hir coler;
For she right there hadde in present
Unto a lady maad present
Of a gold broche, ful wel wrought.
And certys, it myssat hir nought;
For thorough hir smokke, wrought with silk,
The flesh was seen as whit as mylk.

[Ami describes the path of Give-Too-Much and the castle of Foolish Largesse. At the end of this road, among the ruins, lives Poverty as well. It is better to give small gifts of fruit and flowers. But one should know that there is no love in the lady who surrenders to the conquering man as a result of these methods (ll. 7896–8278)].

Trans. Geoffrey Chaucer, ll. 1149–70, 1187–96. Reprinted in *Le roman de la rose,* ed. Stephen G. Nichols (New York: Appleton Century Crofts, 1967), 183–84.

12.
François Rabelais
Gargantua and Pantagruel
Chapter 50, "Gargantua's Speech to the Vanquished"

Alpharbal, king of Canarre . . . was . . . in a set fight justly taken and vanquished by my father, whom God preserve and protect. But what? Whereas other kings and emperors, yea, those who entitle themselves Catholics, would have dealt roughly with him, kept him a close prisoner and put him to an extreme high ransom; he entreated him very courteously, lodged him kindly with himself in his own palace, and out of his incredible mildness and gentle disposition, sent him back with a safe conduct, laden with gifts, laden with favours, laden with all offices of friendship. What fell out upon it? Being returned into his country, he called a parliament, where all the princes and states of his kingdom being assembled, he showed them the humanity which he had found in us, and therefore wished them to take such course by way of compensation therein, as that the whole world might be edified by the example, as well of their honest graciousness to us, as of our gracious honesty towards them. The result hereof was that it was voted and decreed by a unanimous consent that they should offer up entirely their lands, dominions and kingdoms, to be disposed of by us according to our pleasure.

Alpharbal, in his own person, presently returned with nine thousand and thirty-eight great ships of burden, bringing with him the treasures, not only of his house and royal lineage, but almost of all the country beside. For he embarking himself to set sail with a west-north-east wind, every one, in heaps, did cast into the ship gold, silver, rings, jewels, spices, drugs and aromatical perfumes, parrots, pelicans, monkeys, civet-cats, black-spotted weasels, porcupines, etc. He was accounted no good mother's son that did not cast in all the rare and precious things he had.

Being safely arrived, he came to my said father, and would have kissed his feet. That action was found too submissively low, and therefore was not permitted, but in exchange he was most cordially embraced. He offered his presents. They were not received, because they were too excessive. He yielded himself voluntarily a servant and vassal, and was content his whole posterity should be liable to the same bondage. This was not accepted of, because it seemed not equitable. He surrendered, by virtue of the decree of his great parliamentary council, his whole countries and kingdoms to him, offering the deed and conveyance, signed, sealed and ratified by all those that were concerned in it. This was altogether refused, and the parchments cast into the fire. In the end, this free good will and simple meaning of the Canarrians wrought such tenderness in my father's heart that he could not abstain from shedding tears, and wept most profusely; then by choice words, very congruously adapted, strove in what he could to diminish the estimation of the good offices which he had done them, saying that any courtesy he had conferred upon them was not worth a rush, and what favour soever he had showed them, he was bound to do it. But so much the more did Alpharbal augment the repeat thereof.

What was the issue? Whereas for his ransom, in the greatest extremity of rigour and most tyrannical dealing, could not have been exacted above twenty times a hundred thousand crowns, and his eldest sons detained as hostages till that sum had been paid, they made themselves perpetual tributaries, and obliged to give us every year two millions of gold, at four-and-twenty carats fine. The first year we received the whole sum of two millions; the second year, of their own accord they paid freely to us three-and-twenty hundred thousand crowns; the third year, six-and-twenty hundred thousand; the fourth year, three millions; and do so increase it always out of their own good will, that we shall be constrained to forbid them to bring us any more. This is the nature of gratitude and true thankfulness; for time, which gnaws and diminisheth all things else, augments and increaseth benefits, because a noble action of liberality done to a man of reason, doth grow continually by his generous thinking of it and remembering it.

In *The Urquhart-Le Motteux Translation of the Works of Francis Rabelais,* ed. Albert Jay Nock and Catherine Rose Wilson (New York: Harcourt Brace, 1931), 1:306–8.

13.
William Shakespeare
Sonnet 4

Unthrifty loveliness, why dost thou spend
Upon thyself thy beauty's legacy?
Nature's bequest gives nothing but doth lend,
And being frank she lends to those are free,
Then, beauteous niggard, why dost thou abuse
The bounteous largess given thee to give?
Profitless usurer, why dost thou use
So great a sum of sums, yet canst not live?
For having traffic with thyself alone,
Thou of thyself thy sweet self dost deceive.
Then how, when nature calls thee to be gone
What acceptable audit canst thou leave?
    Thy unus'd beauty must be tomb'd with thee,
    Which, used, lives th'executor to be.

In *The Complete Works of Shakespeare,* ed. Hardin Craig and David Bevington (Glenview, Ill., and Brighton, England: Scott, Foresman, and Co., 1973), 472.

14.
William Shakespeare
Antony and Cleopatra
Act 5, Scene 2

DOLABELLA, CLEOPATRA

DOL. I understand not, madam.
CLEO. I dream'd there was an Emperor Antony:
O, such another sleep, that I might see
But such another man!
DOL. If it might please ye,—
CLEO. His face was as the heav'ns; and therein stuck
A sun and moon, which kept their course, and lighted
The little O, the earth.
DOL. Most sovereign creature,—
CLEO. His legs bestrid the ocean: his rear'd arm
Crested the world: his voice was propertied
As all the tuned spheres, and that to friends;
But when he meant to quail and shake the orb,
He was as rattling thunder. For his bounty,
There was no winter in 't; an autumn 'twas
That grew the more by reaping: his delights
Were dolphin-like; they show'd his back above
The element they liv'd in: in his livery
Walk'd crowns and crownets; realms and islands were
As plates dropp'd from his pocket.
DOL. Cleopatra!
CLEO. Think you where was, or might be, such a man
As this I dream'd of?
DOL. Gentle madam, no.
CLEO. You lie, up to the hearing of the gods.
But, if there be nor ever were one such,

It's past the size of dreaming: nature wants stuff
To vie strange forms with fancy; yet, t' imagine
An Antony, were nature' piece 'gainst fancy,
Condemning shadows quite.

In *The Complete Works of Shakespeare,* ed. Hardin Craig and David Bevington (Glenview, Ill., and Brighton, England: Scott, Foresman, and Co., 1973), ll. 76–100 (p. 1105).

15.
Etienne de La Boétie
The Politics of Obedience: The Discourse of Voluntary Servitude
(1574)

Plays, farces, spectacles, gladiators, strange beasts, medals, pictures, and other such opiates, these were for ancient peoples the bait toward slavery, the price of their liberty, the instruments of tyranny. By these practices and enticements the ancient dictators so successfully lulled their subjects under the yoke, that the stupefied peoples, fascinated by the pastimes and vain pleasures flashed before their eyes, learned subservience as naively, but not so creditably, as little children learn to read by looking at bright picture books. Roman tyrants invented a further refinement. They often provided the city wards with feasts to cajole the rabble, always more readily tempted by the pleasure of eating than by anything else. The most intelligent and understanding amongst them would not have quit his soup bowl to recover the liberty of the Republic of Plato. Tyrants would distribute largess, a bushel of wheat, a gallon of wine, and a sesterce: and then everybody would shamelessly cry, "Long live the King!" The fools did not realize that they were merely recovering a portion of their own property, and that their ruler could not have given them what they were receiving without having first taken it from them. A man might one day be presented with a sesterce and gorge himself at the public feast, lauding Tiberius and Nero for handsome liberality, who on the morrow, would be forced to abandon his property to their avarice, his children to their lust, his very blood to the cruelty of the magnificent emperors, without offering any more resistance than a stone or a tree stump.

Trans. Harry Kurz (Montreal: Black Rose, 1975), 70.

16.
Journal de Barbier
"Le mariage du dauphin, février 1745"

On Tuesday the twenty-third, the day of the wedding, the seven public halls in Paris were lit up at seven o'clock at night. . . . These halls cost a great deal because they were great in size and solidly built. The buffets, arranged on tiers, were adorned with large tin platters, which were nailed down. In these halls, there were quarters of cut mutton, turkeys, tongue, saveloy, bread, and wine.

But despite the expense, these halls did not fit the bill. The goal of M. le prévôt of merchants was to provide the public, that is, the Paris bourgeoisie, with entertainment, a place to come to dance and amuse themselves. But that was not to the bourgeoisie's taste. Since people entered from all sides, as if into covered halls, there was a horrible confusion. The place was filled only with riff-raff of the worst sort, who threw all sorts of things off the buffets: tongue, saveloy, bread, turkey legs. And catch as catch can! This caused quite a stir. The large symphony, which was quite good, played quadrilles; but no one danced, except once in awhile a gang of urchins in a circle. A shoemaker's wife or a seamstress would have felt dishonored to have danced there. The police were there in great force, patroling on horseback and on foot in each hall; so that no disorder occurred despite the wine, which many people got drunk on. At ten o'clock in the evening, the Place de Vendôme, the Carrousel, and the Pont-Neuf were filled with coaches coming to watch these fetes, despite the world concourse that was at Versailles. Men of every condition came down for a moment to get a closer look at the halls.

In general, this made for a fine sight and a peculiar spectacle, but for terrible confusion. M. de Bernage, prévôt of merchants, was unhappy. The great expense was to no one's taste and did him no honor. It is difficult to satisfy the public. One must follow the times and customs. Today, when there is great luxury and when money can do anything, everything in Paris is in a state of confusion. Well-off artisans and rich merchants no longer know their place. They do not count themselves among the common people; and, in fact, in such a great city, there is a distinction to be made between the countless common people and the bourgeoisie.

Chronique de la régence de Louis XV, ou Journal de Barbier, 8 vols. (Paris: Charpentier, 1857), 4:18–20.

17.
Journal de Barbier
"Fête pour la naissance du duc de Bourgogne, cortège du roi, septembre 1751"

Along his route, two officers of the guard, who stood at the door of his coach, threw money to the people, in coins of six francs, three francs, one and a half francs, and half a franc. Sometimes they even threw ten-franc gold pieces mixed with silver. As usual, that caused quite a stir as people collected the money; but in addition, no one shouted "Long live the king!" The officers themselves had to tell the people to shout; and the officers were heard. In general, the people are not happy because taxes have not been reduced, and the price of bread has gone up recently.

Chronique de la régence de Louis XV, ou Journal de Barbier, 8 vols. (Paris: Charpentier, 1857), 5:102–8.

For the price of the fetes not given, the king decides to

marry off six hundred girls in Paris (*Journal de Barbier,* 5:104–5).

18.
Giacomo Casanova, *History of My Life*

On the next day, which was the last day of the Carnival, I went to the Corso on horseback, dressed as Pulcinella, throwing sweetmeats into all the landaus in which I saw children and finally emptying my basket on Momolo's daughters.

Trans. Willard R. Trask (New York: Harcourt, Brace and World, 1969), 253–54.

Charity

19.
Pierre Corneille
L'imitation de Jésus-Christ, book 1, 23

Give to the holy duties of a Christian
All that God gives you to live.

Oeuvres complètes, ed. Georges Couton (Paris: "Bibliothèque de la Pléiade," 1984), 2:870, ll. 2201–2.

20.
Jacques-Bénigne Bossuet
"Carême du Louvre: Sermon du mauvais riche, 5 mars 1662"

All the holy Fathers are agreed in saying that the inhumane rich man of our gospel stripped poor Lazarus because he did not clothe him, and cruelly slaughtered him because he did not feed him: *Quia non pavisti, occidisti.* And that murderous callousness was born of the abundance he enjoyed and of his pleasures.

O merciful and just God! That is not why you gave the great men of this earth a ray of your powerful light. You made them great to serve as fathers to your poor; in your providence, you took care to divert ills away from their heads so that they might think of those of their neighbor; you made them wealthy and free so that they would work toward bringing relief to your children. And yet, their greatness makes them scornful, their abundance makes them cold, and their happiness, unfeeling. And yet every day they see, not multitudes of poor and destitute souls, but rather misery and poverty in person, crying and moaning at their door.

I am not surprised, dear Christians; for there are other poor, hungrier and more persistent, who have found access to the rich man's home, who have discovered a secret passage and have used up his liberality. Let me explain myself clearly: I am speaking of the poor within his heart, who never cease to complain, no matter how much care is taken to satisfy them, who are always greedy, always hungry, even amid bounty and excess. I mean passions and desires. O poor Lazarus, you moan at the door to no avail, for they are already inside the house; they do not present themselves at the door, but take the place by siege; they do not ask, but grab. O Lord! What violence! Imagine for yourselves, Christians, the sedition of riff-raff in fury, arrogant in their demands, ready to seize whatever they are refused. That is what is happening in the soul of that evil rich man. And let us not go seeking him in the parable, for many will find him in their own conscience. Thus, in the soul of this evil rich man and his cruel imitators, where reason has lost dominion and the laws have no more force, there ambition, greed, refinement, and all the other passions form a mutinous and irascible herd. Their seditious shouts echo everywhere: "Bring, bring," is all they cry. *Dicentes: Affer, affer* (Proverbs 30:15). Bring food for my greed; bring ever more refined sumptuousness to this rare and delicate luxury; bring more exquisite pleasures for this appetite disgusted by abundance. Among the furious cries of those impudent and insatiable poor, how could you hear the listless voice of the poor who tremble before you, who are ashamed of their poverty, accustomed as they are to overcome it through relentless work. That is why they are starving to death. Yes, gentlemen, they are starving to death on our lands, in our castles, in the cities, in the country, at your doors, and around your mansions. No one runs to help them. Alas! They ask only for the superfluous, a few crumbs from your table, a few remains from your grand meal. But these poor whom you nourish so well within you are using up all your resources. They need bounty; not only the superfluous, but excess is necessary to them. And there is no longer any hope for the poor of Jesus Christ, if you do not calm that internal tumult and sedition. And yet *they* would manage to survive if only you gave something of the prodigality spread about you, something of what your greed controls.

Oeuvres oratoires de Bossuet, ed. Abbot J. Lebarq (Paris: Desclée de Brouwer, 1892), 4:108–10.

21.
Jean-Baptiste Massillon
Sermons pour le Carême (1699)
"The Bad Rich Man"

First of all, Lazarus was a public beggar, *mendicus;* and one is naturally less attentive to the suffering of these declared indigents, who have an entire city as their witness and as resources for their indigence: one can always persuade oneself that their eternal importunities are mere artifice, and that idleness more than need is the cause of their complaints and poverty. In a word, the same pretexts you use every day to rebuff those poor wanderers, the rich man could have used toward Lazarus. Perhaps secret needs or public works of mercy that better flattered his vanity might have found him more merciful and feeling.

Second, Lazarus was completely covered with sores, and he lay in front of the rich man's door: *Ulceribus plenus, jacebat ante juanuam divitis.* An object so worthy of pity ought to have touched the rich man no doubt; but at least, there is something in the fact that he tolerated a spectacle as horrible as Lazarus must have been without sending him away from his door; and in the fact that no bitter or hard word ever came out of that rich man's mouth, even though he was offended by the sight that was always before his eyes; and in the fact that he had allowed that unfortunate man to make the entrance to his house his usual shelter. You, my dear listener, might have hastened to give some largesse, but the eagerness to distance such a disgusting object from your sight would have played more of a role than the desire to bring relief to someone who is one with Jesus Christ. And perhaps, to spare your delicacy a single instant of disgust, you might even have believed your afflicted brother unworthy to receive the offering from your own hands, and might have called upon a servant to distribute it on your behalf. You might not have recognized, in the flesh covered with sores, the image of the shameful sores that your soul displays to the eyes of God, might not have expiated all your crimes, by letting your eyes rest on a disagreeable object. . . .

Thus, when Abraham, from his home on high, tells him the reason for his condemnation, he does not say, as Jesus Christ said publicly to the reprobates: Lazarus was naked, and you did not clothe him; he was hungry, and you did not feed him; he was sick and you did not offer him relief. He says simply: My son, remember that you received wealth during your life: *Fili, recordare quia recepisti bona in vita tua.* Remember that you suffered nothing on earth. That is not the way to attain the rest promised my posterity. Your fathers were always wanderers, fugitives, strangers in the world; they possessed nothing. They now enjoy the promised inheritance they yearned after for so long. You, however, sought your consolation on earth; you no longer belong to the people of God. You are no longer a child of the promise. You have not been blessed in me, and your fate is with the infidels. You have made of the place of your pilgrimage the place of your pleasures. Such unjust happiness could not last. Everything changes its aspect here: the tears of Lazarus are wiped away and his affliction consoled; but your laughter and joy have changed into the gnashing of teeth and your pleasures of an instant have become torments that will never end.

Oeuvres de Massillon, 2 vols. (Paris: Didot), 1:273–74.

22.
Molière
Dom Juan
Act 3, scene 2

THE POOR MAN: I am a poor man, sir, retired all alone to this wood ten years now, and I would be sure to pray Heaven to give you every sort of wealth.

D. JUAN: Well, pray for a suit of your own, and don't get mixed up in the affairs of others. . . .

What is your occupation among these trees?

POOR MAN: I pray Heaven all day long for the prosperity of gentlemen who give me something.

D. JUAN: Then I take it you're quite well off out here?

POOR MAN: Alas, sir, I am in the greatest of need.

D. JUAN: You've got to be kidding! A man who prays to heaven all day long has to be successful in his affairs.

POOR MAN: I assure you, sir, often I do not have a piece of bread to chew on.

D. JUAN: That's strange. You are poorly compensated for your trouble. Here now, I'll give you a gold coin right now if you agree to curse.

POOR MAN: Oh, sir, would you want me to commit such a sin?

D. JUAN: Just make up your mind whether you want to earn a gold coin or not. Here's one: I'll give it to you if you curse, but now, you have to curse.

POOR MAN: Sir.

D. JUAN: Unless you don't want it.

SGANARELLE: Go on, curse a little, there's no harm in it.

D. JUAN: Take it, there, take it I say, but now curse.

POOR MAN: No, sir, I prefer to starve to death.

D. JUAN: Go on then, I'll give it to you for the love of humanity.

Oeuvres complètes de Molière, "Théâtre, 1664–1665," ed. René Bray (Paris: Belles Lettres, 1951), 169–71.

Poetry

23.
Goethe, *Wilhelm Meister's Apprenticeship*

When Wilhelm had cleaned his brow with a little powder-knife, [Philina] said to him, "Put it in your pocket, and think of me when you see it." It was a pretty knife: the haft, of inlaid steel, had these friendly words wrought on it, "Think of me." Wilhelm put it up, and thanked her, begging permission at the same time to make her a little present in return.

At last they were in readiness. Laertes had brought round the coach, and they commanded a very gay excursion. To every beggar, Philina threw out money from the window, giving along with it a merry and friendly word. Scarcely had they reached the Mill, and ordered dinner, when a strain of music struck up before the house. . . .

So, with a few lively songs, which she could sing very beautifully, Philina cut short their conversation, and urged them to a quick return homewards, that they might arrive in time for seeing the performance of the rope-dancers in the evening. On the road back she continued her lavish generosity, in a style of gaiety reaching to extravagance; for at last, every coin belonging to herself or her companions being spent, she threw her straw hat from the window to a girl, and her neckerchief to an old woman.

English trans. Thomas Carlyle, *Goethe's Works* (New York: International Publishing, 1901), 3:113–15.

24.
William Wordsworth
"The Old Cumberland Beggar"

I saw an aged Beggar in my walk;
And he was seated, by the highway side,
On a low structure of rude masonry
Built at the foot of a huge hill, that they
Who lead their horses down the steep rough road
May thence remount at ease. The aged Man
Had placed his staff across the broad smooth stone
That overlays the pile; and, from a bag
All white with flour, the dole of village dames,
He drew his scraps and fragments, one by one;
And scanned them with a fixed and serious look
Of idle computation. In the sun,
Upon the second step of that small pile,
Surrounded by those wild unpeopled hills,
He sat, and ate his food in solitude:
And ever, scattered from his palsied hand,
That, still attempting to prevent the waste,
Was baffled still, the crumbs in little showers
Fell on the ground; and the small mountain birds,
Not venturing yet to peck their destined meal,
Approached within the length of half his staff.

Him from my childhood have I known; and then
He was so old, he seems not older now;
He travels on, a solitary Man,
So helpless in appearance, that for him
The sauntering Horseman throws not with a slack
And careless hand his alms upon the ground,
But stops,—that he may safely lodge the coin
Within the old Man's hat; nor quits him so,
But still, when he has given his horse the rein,
Watches the aged Beggar with a look
Sidelong, and half-reverted. She who tends
The toll-gate, when in summer at her door
She turns her wheel, if on the road she sees
The aged Beggar coming, quits her work,
And lifts the latch for him that he may pass.
The post-boy, when his rattling wheels o'ertake
The aged Beggar in the woody lane,
Shouts to him from behind; and, if thus warned
The old man does not change his course, the boy
Turns with less noisy wheels to the roadside,
And passes gently by, without a curse
Upon his lips, or anger at his heart.

He travels on, a solitary Man;
His age has no companion. On the ground
His eyes are turned, and, as he moves along,
They move along the ground; and, evermore,
Instead of common and habitual sight
Of fields with rural works, of hill and dale,
And the blue sky, one little span of earth
Is all his prospect. Thus, from day to day,
Bow-bent, his eyes for ever on the ground,
He plies his weary journey; seeing still,
And seldom knowing that he sees, some straw,
Some scattered leaf, or marks which, in one track,
The nails of cart or chariot-wheel have left
Impressed on the white road,—in the same line
At distance still the same. Poor Traveller!
His staff trails with him; scarcely do his feet
Disturb the summer dust; he is so still
In look and motion, that the cottage curs,
Ere he had passed the door, will turn away,
Weary of barking at him. Boys and girls,
The vacant and the busy, maids and youths,
And urchins newly breeched—all pass him by;
Him even the slow-paced waggon leaves behind.

But deem not this Man useless.—Statesmen! ye
Who are so restless in your wisdom, ye
Who have a broom still ready in your hands
To rid the world of nuisances; ye proud,
Heart-swoln, while in your pride ye contemplate
Your talents, power, or wisdom, deem him not
A burthen of the earth! 'Tis Nature's law
That none, the meanest of created things,
Of forms created the most vile and brute,
The dullest or most noxious, should exist
Divorced from good—a spirit and pulse of good,
A life and soul, to every mode of being
Inseparably linked. Then be assured
That least of all can aught—that ever owned
The heaven-regarding eye and front sublime
Which man is born to—sink, howe'er depressed,
So low as to be scorned without a sin;
Without offence to God cast out of view;
Like the dry remnant of a garden-flower
Whose seeds are shed, or as an implement
Worn out and worthless. While from door to door,
This old Man creeps, the villagers in him
Behold a record which together binds
Past deeds and offices of charity,
Else unremembered, and so keeps alive
The kindly mood in hearts which lapse of years,
And that half-wisdom half-experience gives,
Make slow to feel, and by sure steps resign

To selfishness and cold oblivious cares.
Among the farms and solitary huts,
Hamlets and thinly-scattered villages,
Where'er the aged Beggar takes his rounds,
The mild necessity of use complies
To acts of love; and habit does the work
Of reason; yet prepares that after-joy
Which reason cherishes. And thus the soul,
By that sweet taste of pleasure unpursued,
Doth find herself insensible disposed
To virtue and true goodness.

Some there are,
By their good works exalted, loft minds,
And meditative, authors of delight
And happiness, which to the end of time
Will live, and spread, and kindle: even such minds
In childhood, from this solitary Being,
Or from like wanderer, haply have received
(A thing more precious far than all that books
Or the solicitudes of love can do!)
That first mild touch of sympathy and thought,
In which they found their kindred with a world
Where want and sorrow were. The easy man
Who sits at his own door,—and, like the pear
That overhangs his head from the green wall,
Feeds in the sunshine; the robust and young,
The prosperous and unthinking, they who live
Sheltered, and flourish in a little grove
Of their own kindred;—all behold in him
A silent monitor, which on their minds
Must needs impress a transitory thought
Of self-congratulation, to the heart
Of each recalling his peculiar boons,
His charters and exemptions; and, perchance,
Though he to no one give the fortitude
And circumspection needful to preserve
His present blessings, and to husband up
The respite of the season, he, at least,
And 'tis no vulgar service, makes them felt.

Yet further,——Many, I believe, there are
Who live a life of virtuous decency,
Men who can hear the Decalogue and feel
No self-reproach; who of the moral law
Established in the land where they abide
Are strict observers; and not negligent
In acts of love to those with whom they dwell,
Their kindred, and the children of their blood.
Praise be to such, and to their slumbers peace!
—But of the poor man ask, the abject poor;
Go, and demand of him, if there be here
In this cold abstinence from evil deeds,
And these inevitable charities,
Wherewith to satisfy the human soul?
No—man is dear to man; the poorest poor
Long for some moments in a weary life
When they can know and feel that they have been,
Themselves, the fathers and the dealers-out
Of some small blessings; have been kind to such
As needed kindness, for this single cause,
That we have all of us one human heart.
—Such pleasure is to one kind Being known,
My neighbour, when with punctual care, each week
Duly as Friday comes, though pressed herself
By her own wants, she from her store of meal
Takes one unsparing handful for the scrip
Of this old Mendicant, and, from her door
Returning with exhilarated heart,
Sits by her fire, and builds her hope in heaven.

Then let him pass, a blessing on his head!
And while in that vast solitude to which
The tide of things has borne him, he appears
To breathe and live but for himself alone,
Unblamed, uninjured, let him bear about
The good which the benignant law of Heaven
Has hung around him; and, while life is his,
Still let him prompt the unlettered villagers
To tender offices and pensive thoughts.
—Then let him pass, a blessing on his head!
And, long as he can wander, let him breathe
The freshness of the valleys; let his blood
Struggle with frosty air and winter snows;
And let the chartered wind that sweeps the heath
Beat his grey locks against his withered face.
Reverence the hope whose vital anxiousness
Gives the last human interest to his heart.
May never HOUSE, misnamed of INDUSTRY,
Make him a captive!—for that pent-up din,
Those life-consuming sounds that clog the air,
Be his the natural silence of old age!
Let him be free of mountain solitudes;
And have around him, whether heard or not,
The pleasant melody of woodland birds.
Few are his pleasures: if his eyes have now
Been doomed so long to settle upon earth
That not without some effort they behold
The countenance of the horizontal sun,
Rising or setting, let the light at least
Find a free entrance to their languid orbs.
And let him, *where* and *when* he will, sit down
Beneath the trees, or on a grassy bank
Of highway side, and when the little birds
Share his chance-gathered meal; and finally,
As in the eye of Nature he has lived,
So in the eye of Nature let him die!

In *Poems,* ed. John O. Hayden (Penguin Books, 1977), 1:262–68.

24.
Alfred Lord Tennyson
"The Beggar Maid"

Her arms across her breast she laid;
She was more fair than words can say;
Barefooted came the beggar maid
Before the king Cophetua.
In robe and crown the king stept down,
To meet and greet her on her way;
"It is no wonder," said the lords,
"She is more beautiful than day."

As shines the moon in clouded skies,
She in her poor attire was seen;
One praised her ankles, one her eyes,
One her dark hair and lovesome mien.
So sweet a face, such angel grace,
In all that land had never been.
Cophetua sware a royal oath:
"This beggar maid shall be my queen."

In *The Poetic and Dramatic Works of Alfred Lord Tennyson* (Boston and New York: Houghton Mifflin, 1899), 147.

Illustrations

Drawings and Engravings
by Régine Bonnefoit

Unless otherwise indicated, exhibited works belong to the collections of the Louvre Museum, Department of Graphic Arts. Dimensions are given in centimeters.

The author wishes to express her profound gratitude to Régis Michel for his consistently keen advice.

Antonio Allegri (Correggio)
(about 1489–1534)
Eve Offering the Apple
1

Eve tendant la pomme. Red chalk heightened with white (11.6 × 10.4). Inscribed on back in pen: *Coregio.*
BIBLIOGRAPHY: Tauzia 1881, no. 8; Popham 1957, pp. 72, 160, no. 53, repr. pl. 60b; Bacou 1968, no. 38; Tassi 1968, p. 159n. 41; Giampaolo and Muzzi 1990, no. 66 (with complete bibliography).

Study of the figure of Eve for the ornamentation of the cupola in the cathedral at Parma, which Correggio executed at the height of his career, in 1526–28 (repr. Popham, 1954, pl. 59). In a fresco of the Assumption, Eve appears among angels and biblical figures, who seem to be drawn upward, as if in a whirlwind. The audacity of the foreshortening and the effects of light and illusion serve as a prelude to baroque conceptions in the seventeenth century. Eve is depicted at the moment when she offers the forbidden fruit from the Tree of Knowledge to the Virgin; it is a fatal gift, which Satan's seductive words made her accept (Genesis 3:1–8). According to the canonical exegesis, Mary is the new Eve, who will redeem the sin of the first.

Antonin Artaud (see "Two Drawings by Antonin Artaud" by Agnès de la Beaumelle, below 200–201).

Federico Barocci
(1535?–1612)
The Madonna of the Rosary
6

La Madone du rosaire. Pen and brown ink, brown wash (17.5 × 14.5).
BIBLIOGRAPHY: Anselmi 1905, pp. 140–45; Schmarsow 1911, p. 90; Krommes 1912, p. 102; Olsen 1962, p. 188; Emiliani 1985, pp. 267, 448, fig. 562.

This is one on the many preparatory drawings for the painting of the *Madonna of the Rosary,* executed between 1589 and 1593 for the Brotherhood of the Assumption and the Rosary of Senigallia (twenty-six preparatory drawings are recorded by Olsen 1962, 187–88). The painting, which is today in the episcopal palace of Senigallia, was ordered in a rivalry with the competing Brotherhood of the Cross and Sacrament, for which Barocci painted a *Deposition of Christ* in 1582 (Santa Croce, Senigallia). True to the pious program of the brotherhood that commissioned the painting, Barocci conceived of an unprecedented symbiosis between the Assumption and the appearance of the Virgin of the Rosary to Saint Dominic. According to the legend, dating back to the fifteenth century, the Virgin appeared to him in Albi and gave him a rosary.

Jacques Bellange
(before 1575–1616)
Beggars' Brawl
16

Rixe des mendiants. Etching (31.0 × 21.1). Inscription lower right: *J. Bellange fecit.* First state. Paris, Bibliothèque Nationale, Print Room
BIBLIOGRAPHY: Robert-Dumesnil 1841, vol. 5, no. 46; Weigert 1939, vol. 1, no. 51; Pariset 1948, p. 291, pl. 48.4; Oberhuber 1967–68, no. 273, pl. 56; Walch 1971, no. 18; Thuillier 1992, p. 266, repr. no. 83.

This engraving and *Le mendiant à la vielle* (The Hurdy-Gurdy Man) (Robert-Dumesnil, 1841, vol. 5, no. 45) are the only realist pieces by Bellange; they were widely diffused. This etching attests to the fact that the painter of the Lorrainian court did not neglect popular subjects, though, as Thuillier notes, he took nothing from them but a certain aggravated picturesque quality. But the style escapes realism: the modeled draperies and the antique sandals are features belonging to an artist Pariset calls the "champion of the most quintessential mannerism" (Pariset 1948, 2). The engraver Matthaeus Merian (1593–1650) made a copy of this print, adding the moral in Latin: *Mendicus mendico invidet* (The beggar is envious of the beggar). We should not neglect the importance of this engraving, which leads directly to Callot's *Gueux* (Tramp) (Lieure, 479–503) and to Georges de La Tour's *Rixe des musiciens* (Musicians' Brawl) (Malibu, Getty Museum).

Giulio Benso
(about 1601–68)
Saint Leonard of Limoges Refusing Presents
61

Saint Léonard de Limoges refusant des présents. Pen and brown ink, brown wash, on sketch in black chalk (15.3 × 21.2).

Tradition has it that Saint Leonard, a hermit in Limoges during the sixteenth century, founded the Noblac monastery near that city. It is said he was the godson of Clovis I and prayed for the felicitous childbirth of Queen Clotilde. This earned him the king's promise that every prisoner Leonard visited would be freed. *The Golden Legend* recounts that the saint "shone with such great miracles that if anyone invoked his name in prison, his chains were broken at once, and he took his freedom without hindrance, and brought his bonds or his shackles to the saint. Several such, in fact, remained with Leonard, and served the Lord there" (Voragine 1941, p. 659). In this sketch, we see the ascetic among his disciples. The old man on the right, wearing a turban, displays his chains, which his servant is holding on a tray. He offers them to Leonard to thank him for his liberation. Turčić has linked the scene to Benso's painting, in the church of S. Gerolamo di Quarto in Genoa, representing the liberation of Bohemond through the intercession of Leonard of Limoges (Newcome-Schleier 1985, p. 58, no. 37). According to Abbot Arbellot's *Vie de saint Léonard* (1863), the saint appeared to Bohemond, the prince of Antioch during the twelfth century, while he was being held by the satrap of the Saracens. Once liberated, Bohemond made a pilgrimage to Noblac to hang his chains in the saint's tomb (1863, pp. 146ff.). The drawing shows him offering precious vases and silver as well, which the saint refuses with an impetuous gesture. The cult of Saint Leonard, which began at the end of the Middle Ages, was no less popular in Italy than in its country of origin, as the representation of the subject in a Genoa church attests. After his training in the studio of G. B. Paggi in Genoa, the painter acquired an international reputation. He executed numerous paintings for the Benedictines of Weingarten (southern Germany), an abbey where he spent some time in 1628 (Newcome 1979, p. 28). A drawing by the artist, conserved in Stuttgart, signed and dated *Benso opera fatta in Francia 1648,* is a sketch for an ornamental detail in the *Myth of Phaethon,* which he painted on the ceiling of the Grimaldi castle in Cagnes-sur-Mer (Lorgues 1987, pp. 403–13).

Ferdinand Bol
(1616–80)
Woman Nursing a Child
48

Femme allaitant un enfant. Pen and brown ink, brown wash, red chalk, heightened with white (14.6 × 11.2). Inscribed in pen and brown ink lower left: *Rembrandt.*
BIBLIOGRAPHY: Hofstede de Groot 1906, no. 813; Kruse 1920, p. 43; Benesch 1973, vol. 2, no. 359, pl. 433; Sumowski 1979, vol. 2, repr. no. 96; Blankert 1982, p. 165; Brugerolles 1984, p. 13; Starcky 1988, p. 152, no. 211 (with complete bibliography).

Kruse was the first to recognize this drawing as the work of Ferdinand Bol, one of Rembrandt's most gifted students, who entered the master's studio in about 1635. Modern-day criticism is agreed in considering it one of Bol's most beautiful drawings, although Benesch vigorously defended the attribution to Rembrandt, considering it an autograph work of 1636–37. The woman with child resembles the figure of Mary in the *Repos pendant la fuite en Egypte* (Rest on the flight into Egypt) of Dresden, which is signed and dated *F. Bol fecit 1644* (Blankert 1982, no. 16, pl. 5). The same date (about 1644) is also valid for the present sketch, where the artist's desire to approximate Rembrandt is obvious. It was during the 1640s that the student was closest stylistically to the master. He moved away from him after the mid-century mark, when, in accordance with the pompous baroque taste, he painted large and grandiloquent decors for public buildings, notably the city hall of Amsterdam.

Abraham Bosse
(1602–76)
The Works of Mercy

Les oeuvres de miséricorde (Louvre Museum, Edmond de Rothschild Collection).

Feed the Hungry
51

Nourrir ceux qui ont faim. Etching retouched with burin and drypoint (25.5 × 32.3), with squaring. First state. Signed lower right of composition: *ABosse inu. et fe.* Inscription engraved below in four columns: "Toy que les richesses friuoles / Entretiennent de vains esbas; / Et qui des choses d'icy bas / En fais tes Dieux et tes Idoles; / Ne doute point que tes remors, / Si tu ne fais de bonnes oeuvres; / Ne soient comme autant de Couleuures, / Qui te causeront mille morts. / Si tu vois la Fain accable / Celuy que tu peux soulager; / Presente luy dequoy manger, / Avec une main secourable, / Tu peux rachetter ton peché / Par cette Aumosne salutaire, / Ton Esprit estant destaché / D'une Avarice volontaire" [You whom frivolous riches / Maintain in vain pursuits; / And who make things here below / Into your gods and idols; / Do not doubt that, / If you do not do good works, / Your remorse will be like so many snakes, / Causing you a thousand deaths. / If you see that Hunger is striking / Someone you can re-

lieve; / Present him with something to eat, / With a helping hand, / You can redeem your sin / Through such salutary alms, / Because your spirit will separate itself / From willful greed]. With the name of the publisher: *Le Blond excud auec Priuilege du Roy.*
BIBLIOGRAPHY: Duplessis 1859, p. 20, no. 50; Blum 1924, p. 49, no. 1021; Weigert 1939, p. 479, no. 50; Villa 1967, pl. 20; ex. cat. Tours 1982, no. 17a.

Give Drink to the Thirsty
52

Abreuver ceux qui ont soif. Etching, with a few retouches in burin (25.5 × 32.4), with squaring. First state. Signed at bottom left of composition: *ABosse inu. et fe:* Inscription engraved below in four columns: "Tu scais qu'en un Desert aride / Le sacré Prince des Hébreux, / Abreuua ce Peuple nombreux, / A qui luy seul seruoit de Guide. / Cela t'apprend à secourir / Ceux qui dans l'ardeur violante / Dont l'auide soif les tourmante, / Sont presque reduits à mourir. / Leur peine n'estant pas petite, / Tu dois tesmoigner un grand soin / De les soulager au besoin, / Pour en accrestre ton merite. / Le salaire en sera si beau, / Que sans augmenter ta despence, / Il te viendra d'un verre d'eau / Une Eternelle recompence" [You know that in an arid desert / The sacred prince of the Hebrews, / Who alone served as their guide, / Gave his numerous people to drink. / That teaches you to aid / Those who in the violent heat / Are tormented by avid thirst, / And are about to die. / Their pain is no small thing, / And you must show great care / To relieve them as need be, / To increase your own merit. / The wages will be so great, / That without increasing your expense, / There will come from a glass of water / An eternal reward]. With the name of the publisher: *Le Blond excud. auec Priuilege du Roy.*
BIBLIOGRAPHY: Duplessis 1859, pp. 20ff., no. 51; Blum 1924, p. 49, no. 1022; Weigert 1939, p. 479, no. 51; Villa 1967, pl. 21.

Give Lodging to Pilgrims
53

Loger les pélerins. Etching, retouched with burin (25.6 × 31.0, including text), with squaring. Inscription engraved at bottom in four columns: "Doit-on pas admirer ce Vieillard et ces Dames, / Qui sans apprehender n'y perte, ny dangers, / Usent des biens qu'ils ont, pour le bien de leurs Ames, / Et recoivent chez eux ces pauvres Estrangers? / Sçachant que cette Vie est un Pelerinage, / Ils s'ouurent le chemin, qui mene droit aux Cieux; / Et pour gagner un jour l'éternel Héritage, / Ils rendent au Prochain des soings officieux. / De quelque Nation que soient les Misérables, / Qu'un mauvais sort cōduit ē des lieux incog'; Parmy les gens de bien, au besoin secourables, / Ils trouvent le couuert, et sont les biens venus. / Habitans de la Terre, il faut qu'il vous souuienne / Au milieu des grandeurs, où le Ciel vous a mis; / Que pour l'amour de Dieu, la charité chrestiene, / Vous oblige à loger vos propres Ennemis" [Must one not admire this old man and these ladies, / Who without apprehension for loss or dangers, / Use the wealth they have for the good of their souls, / And receive in their homes these poor strangers? / Knowing that this life is a pilgrimage, / They open the path for themselves that leads straight to heaven / And one day to the eternal inheritance, / They give voluntary care to their neighbor. / From whatever nation the impoverished, / Whom an ill fate leads to unknown places; / Among the gentle people aiding in times of need, / They find a meal and are welcomed. / Citizens of the Earth, you must remember / Amid the greatness that heaven bestowed on you; / That for the love of God, Christian charity, / Obliges you to lodge your own enemies]. With name of the publisher: *Le Blond exc. Auec Priuil. du Roy.*
BIBLIOGRAPHY: Duplessis 1859, p. 21, no. 52; Blum 1924, p. 49, no. 1023; Weigert 1939, p. 479, no. 52; Villa 1967, pl. 22; ex. cat. Tours 1982, no. 17b.

Visit Prisoners
54

Visiter les prisonniers. Etching, retouched with burin (25.4 × 32.2), with squaring. Signed at bottom of composition, toward the center: *ABosse inv et fe.* Inscription engraved at bottom in four columns: "L'homme dans son inquietude / Qui ne fat que le tourmanter / Ne scauroit iamais s'exempter / De frison, ny de seruitude. / Par un contraire mouuement / L'Amour, la Haine, La Contreinte, / Le Soing, l'Esperance et la Creinte / Le captiuent incessament. / Estant vray que son Ame mesme / Est prisonierre de son Corps, / Soit par dedans, soit par dehors, / Il est gesné d'un mal extreme. / Ce n'est doncques pas sans raison, / Qu'il cherche a tirer de misere / Ceux que la Fortune contraire / A reduits dans une prison" [Man in his distress / Which does nothing but tourment him / Could never escape prison or servitude. / By a contrary movement / Love, hatred, constraint, care, hope, and fear / Endlessly hold him captive. / Since it is true that his soul itself / Is prisoner to his body, / Either from within or without, / He is troubled by extreme ills. / It is thus not without reason, / That he seeks to relieve from misery / Those whom a contrary fortune / Has landed in prison]. With the name of the publisher: *Le Blond excud auec Priuilege du Roy.*
BIBLIOGRAPHY: Duplessis 1859, p. 22, no. 53; Blum 1924, p. 49, no. 1024; Weigert 1939, p. 479, no. 53; Villa 1967, pl. 23; ex. cat. Tours 1982, no. 17c.

Visit the Sick
55

Visiter les malades. Etching retouched with burin (21.5 ×

31.6), with squaring. First state. Inscription engraved at bottom in four columns: "Est-il quelque Barbare à qui ne persuade / D'auoir pour son Prochain une sainte amitié / Ce Pauvre, dans son lict languissant, et malade, / Qui les coeurs les plus durs peut fléchir de pitié? / Tandis qu'apesanty des foiblesses humaines, / Il cede à tant de maux, on luy voit endurer, / Sa femme, et ses Enfans, au millieu de ses peines, / Ne cessent de gemir, de pleindre, et de pleurer. / Le Ciel inspire alors aux Ames equitables / Un genereux desir de s'employer pour luy; / Et fait qu'en l'assistant de leurs soins charitables, / Ils tâchent de guerir son mal et son ennuy. / Chrestien, cela t'apprend que si d'un franc courage / Tu secours ton Prochain, de biens abandonné; / Tu receuras le double, et cent fois dauantage, / De la main de Celuy par qui tout est donné" [Is there a barbarian who is not persuaded / To have as his neighbor in holy friendship / This poor man, languishing in his bed and ill, / Whom the hardest hearts can move to pity? / Weighed down by human weakness, / He gives in to so many ills, which we see him endure, / While his wife and his children, amidst his pains, / Endlessly moan, and lament, and cry / . Heaven then inspires equitable souls / With a generous desire to do good works for him; / And contrives that in assisting him with their charitable cares, / They attempt to cure his ills and his distress. / Christian, that teaches you that if with such frank courage / You aid your neighbor who is stripped of his wealth / You will receive the double, and a hundred times more / From the hand of Him from whom all is given]. With the name of the publisher: *Le Blond excud. auec Priuilege du Roy.*
BIBLIOGRAPHY: Duplessis 1859, pp. 22ff., n. 54; Blum 1924, p. 49, no. 1025; Weigert 1939, p. 479, no. 54; Villa 1967, pl. 24.

Clothe the Naked
56

Vêtir ceux qui sont nus. Etching retouched with burin (22.5 × 32.4), with squaring. Signed at bottom of composition, toward the center: *ABosse inv. et fe.* Inscription engraved at bottom in four columns: "Par un effet assez connu, / L'Homme, vray sujet de misere; / Sortant du ventre de sa Mere, / Entre dans le Monde tout nu. / Pour s'exempter de la froidure, / Il se couure contre ses maux / De la laine des Animaux, / Et s'eschaufe auec leur fourrure. / Mais comme par la Pauvreté / Toutes choses luy sont contraires; / Il peut manquer des necessaires, / Et le voir dans la nudité. / Alors par un soing véritable, / Il faut que charitablement, / Tu l'assistes de vestemens, / Prenant pitié de son semblable" [By a well-known cause / Man, true subject of misery, / Coming out of his mother's belly, / Enters the world naked. / To escape the cold, / He covers himself against his ills / With the wool of animals, / And warms himself with their fur. / But since through poverty / Everything works against him; / He can lack the necessities, / And find himself naked. / Then, with true care, / You must charitably assist him with clothing, / Taking pity on your neighbor]. With the name of the publisher: *Le Blond excud. auec Priuilege du Roy.*
BIBLIOGRAPHY: Duplessis 1859, p. 23, no. 55; Blum 1924, p. 50, no. 1026; Weigert 1939, p. 479, no. 55; Villa 1967, pl. 25; ex. cat. Tours 1982, no. 17d.

Bury the Dead
57

Ensevelir les morts. Etching retouched with burin (22.1 × 30.6), with squaring. Signed bottom left of composition: *ABosse inu. et fec.* Inscription at bottom in four columns: "Si respirant cet air, qui passe comme un vent, / Soubs les traits de la mort, l'homme à la fin succombe, / Ne vous estonnés point, quand il n'est plus viuant, / De voir que des mortels le portent dans la Tombe. / Tous vos pleurs, et vos crys, ne ranimeront pas. / Le vaisseau de ce Corps, plus fragile que verre; / Il fut formé de terre, en naissant icy bas. / Et c'est auec raison qu'on le rend à la Terre. / Voulez vous donc que Dieu benisse vos desseins? / Assistez le Prochain en ce dernier office; / Et vous adiousterez, comme les plus grands saincts, / A la misericorde, en acte de Justice. / Ainsi, pour tous les soings que prit d'enseuelir, / Sans craindre aucun danger, les corps priuez de vie; / Merueilleux fut le fruict, que l'on vid receuillir, / A tous les descendans du bon Vieillard Tobie" [If breathing the air that comes out like a gust, / From the face of death, man in the end succumbs, / Do not be astonished that, when he is no longer living / Mortals carry him to the grave. / All your tears, all your cries, will not bring him back. / The vessel of this body, more fragile than glass; / Was formed of earth, in its birth here below. / And it is right that it should be returned to the Earth. / Do you then wish for God to bless your plans? / Assist your neighbor in this last office / And you will add, like the greatest saints, / To mercy, an act of justice. / Hence, for all the cares he took to bury / Without fearing any danger, the bodies deprived of life; / Marvelous was the fruit gathered / By all the descendants of the good old Man Tobit]. With the name of the publisher: *Le Blond excud. auec Priuil. du Roy.*
BIBLIOGRAPHY: Duplessis 1859, p. 24, no. 56; Blum 1924, p. 50, no. 1027; Weigert 1939, p. 480, no. 56; Villa 1967, pl. 26.

These prints form a series illustrating the works of mercy: feed the hungry; give drink to the thirsty; lodge the stranger; clothe the naked; care for the sick; visit prisoners; bury the dead. The first six follow the gospel parable of the wise and foolish virgins (Matthew 25:35–37). Depending upon whether they carried out the works of mercy, they are saved or damned. The seventh work was added only in the twelfth century. Abraham Bosse, who was no doubt the most illustrious French engraver under Louis XIII, treats this religious theme in a manner that flattered the elites of his time, who were acquitting themselves of their charitable duties. The cycle attests to the moral intentions of the Calvinist Bosse and to the active spirituality of the first half of the seventeenth century. Blum fixes its date as 1635, but not without reservations.

Michelangelo Buonarroti (Michelangelo)
(1475–1564)
Study for a Pietà
94

Etude pour une Pietà. Black chalk (25.4 × 31.8).
BIBLIOGRAPHY: Thode 1913, vol. 3, no. 475; Panofsky 1927, p. 150ff.; Berenson 1970, vol. 2, no. 1586; Wilde 1953, pp. 95 and 104; Dussler 1958, no. 664; Tolnay 1960, p. 180; Hartt 1971, no. 454; Bacou and Viatte 1975, no. 23; Tolnay 1975, vol. 1, no. 92 recto; Wilde 1978, pp. 177–79; Hirst 1981, pp. 129ff.; Hirst 1988, pp. 39, 61, repr. 68ff.; Deswarte 1988–89, p. 393; Perrig 1991, p. 141, no. 60.

Justi was the first to link this study to the small altar painting by Sebastiano del Piombo, which shows the dead Christ with the Virgin holding the instruments of the Passion (Ubeda, Andalusia, Church of San Salvador). The Pietà was painted between 1533 and 1539, on the order of Don Ferrante Gonzaga, for the funeral chapel belonging to Francisco de los Cobos, secretary to Charles V, in San Salvador of Ubeda. The obvious relation between the drawing and the painting led E. Panofsky and Dussler to attribute this study to the Venetian. The correspondence exchanged between the two artists at the beginning of the 1530s shows clearly that Michelangelo sent drawings to his friend Sebastiano (*Il carteggio di Michelangelo,* ed. P. Barocchi and R. Ristori [Florence, 1973], 3:419). The Casa Buonarroti of Florence possesses a second study (Inv. 96 F recto), prior to that of the Louvre, for Christ's pose. It is derived from a classical sleeping Cupid, which Michelangelo had already copied onto a Windsor sheet (Inv. 12763). On the verso of the drawing at the Casa Buonarroti, there are studies for the *Last Judgment* of the Sistine Chapel, which led Hirst to fix the date of both sheets during Michelangelo's stay in Rome, which began in autumn 1533. During that time, he could have discussed the project for the altarpiece with Sebastiano in person. Sebastiano must have returned this drawing, since it was acquired from the Buonarroti family at the end of the eighteenth century, by the painter Jean-Baptiste Wicar.

Giulio Clovio
(1498–1578)
Christ Handing Over the Keys to Saint Peter
9

Le Christ remettant les clefs à saint Pierre. Illumination on vellum (38.4 × 29.2).

"And I will give unto thee the keys of the kingdom of heaven: and whatsoever thou shalt bind on earth shall be bound in heaven: and whatsoever thou shalt loose on earth shall be loosed in heaven" (Matthew 16:19). These are Christ's words to Peter. The apostle, who already holds one key in his left hand, is receiving a second. According to tradition, one is the key to heaven; the other, the key to earth. Their duality symbolizes the power to bind and to loose. The episode is situated in a landscape of ancient monuments, among which we recognize the temple of Minerva at the Forum of Nerva and Trajan's column. The power of the figures attests to Clovio's emulation of Michelangelo, whom he copied on several occasions. Hence, one is hardly surprised that Vasari, who considered Clovio the greatest miniaturist of his lifetime, called him "little Michelangelo" (ed. 1984, 10:154). The Royal Library of Windsor conserves another version of this theme by the same artist.

Correggio (see Allegri)

Jacques-Louis David
(1748–1825)
Homer Reciting His Poems
70

Homère disant ses poèmes. Paintbrush and gray wash, with strokes in black crayon and red chalk (27.2 × 34.5).

This drawing and its companion piece, *Homère endormi* (Homer sleeping) (Louvre, Inv. 26079), were conceived by the artist in prison at the palace of Luxembourg (September–December 1794), during the Thermidor Revolution. A letter from David to M. de Mainbourg (8 November 1794) proves that the artist planned to devote a painting to Homer. It was never executed, however. Fashion made Homer the favorite poet of neoclassicism at the end of the eighteenth century: the David sales catalog (17 April 1826, no. 30) still calls Homer "the father of poetry."

Gustave Doré
(1832–83)
Whiterfiors Bridge
72

Sans-abri de Londres endormis sur un banc. Graphite and stumping with retouches in pen and black ink. Verso: quick sketches in graphite (23.5 × 21.5). Title, date, and signature bottom right: *Whiterfiors Bridge / London 1870 / Gv Doré.* Louvre Museum, Orsay Museum Collection.
BIBLIOGRAPHY: Leblanc 1931, pp. 506–7.

Like the etching *A la belle étoile sur le pont de Londres* (By starlight on London Bridge) (1872; J. Valmy-Baysse, *Gustave Doré* [Paris, 1930], repr. p. 297), this sheet depicts with implacable realism the atrocious poverty in the poorer districts of London, where the artist went regularly beginning in 1868. The next year, Doré prepared illustrations for

London: A Pilgrimage (1872), a book written by his English friend Blanchard Jerrold (1826–84), who was a journalist for the *Daily News,* then for the *Illustrated London News.* In view of this collective work, the two friends made pilgrimages to different sections of London where luxury rubbed shoulders with the darkest poverty. Jerrold recounts an anecdote linked to the drawing: "We went, once, at midnight to London Bridge, and remained there an hour, while [Doré] meditated over the two wonderful views—that above, and that below, the bridge. His heart was touched by some forlorn creatures huddled together, asleep, on the stone-seats." (Jerrold 1891, 153). The book, a response to the new aesthetics of social realism, was immensely successful; it remains one of the great masterpieces of Gustave Doré.

The Charity of the Fishmongers
78

La charité des poissoniers. Watercolor, retouched in pen and black ink, on graphite (33.3 × 48.2). Signed and dated lower right: *G. Doré London 1877.* Louvre Museum, Orsay Museum Collection.
BIBLIOGRAPHY: Leblanc 1931, pp. 468, 472.

The watercolor, which figured in the first exhibit of the Sociéte des Aquarellistes Français (Society of French watercolorists) in 1878, shows that, five years after the publication of *London: A Pilgrimage* (see the preceding entry), Doré had not grown tired of describing the lower depths of the city. A group of children in hieratic poses, standing in front of the fishmonger's stall, are gravely awaiting his chance charity. Géricault had already treated the subject in one of his London prints a half-century earlier.

Albrecht Dürer
(1471–1528)
Large Fortune (Nemesis)
31

La Grande Fortune (Nemésis). Burin (33.3 × 23.0), with squaring. Second state, impression *a.* Signed with monogram on a tablet, at bottom toward the right. Louvre Museum, Edmond de Rothschild Collection.
BIBLIOGRAPHY: Bartsch 1808, vol. 7, p. 62, no. 44; Meder 1932, p. 98, no. 72; Panofsky 1987, pp. 129–32, fig. 109; Hollstein c. 1962, vol. 7, p. 66, repr. no. 72; Bartsch, illus. 1980–81, vol. 10, p. 69, repr. no. 77; *Commentaire* 10, pp. 172–74, no. 77; Böhme 1990, p. 9, fig. 2.

Entitled *Large Fortune* by Bartsch to distinguish it from the *Small Fortune* (Hollstein 6:65, repr. no. 71), the engraving, executed between 1501 and 1503, is mentioned by Dürer in his Netherlands travel journal under the name *Nemesis,* that is, divine vengeance. Curiously, the artist shows the goddess on the sphere of instability, after a Latin poem by Politian *(Manto),* which the erudite circle of Lawrence the Magnificent valued highly. In this poem, *Nemesis* is identified with capricious Fortune: "Clad in a white mantle, she hovers in the void, tearing the air with strident wings, driven hither and thither by the gales, and always wielding the goblet and the bridle—symbols of favor and castigation—with a contemptuous smile" (Panofsky 1954, 81). True to the proportions vaunted by Vitruvius, whose theoretical work Dürer discovered in 1500, the figure appears to have been taken directly from a treatise on anthropometry. E. Panofsky has underlined the conflict between this didactic (and in fact naturalist) treatment and the fantastical character of the divinity. The landscape replicates a lost study of Chiuso (Klausen), near Innsbruck, which Dürer made on his return to Italy in 1495 (Strauss 1974, vol. 2, 1495/43; Panofsky 1987, p. 132). The British Museum conserves two preparatory drawings for the engraving on copper.

Paolo Farinati
(1524–1606)
Mercury and Fortune
19

Mercure et la Fortune. Pen and brown ink, brown wash, heightened with white on a sketch in black chalk, on blue paper (35.8 × 27.7).
BIBLIOGRAPHY: Varanini 1987, p. 80, fig. p. 80; Sueur 1991, vol. 2, p. 135, no. 91; vol. 3, fig. 91.

Preparatory study for the *Allegory of Fortune* painted in the Red Room on the ground floor of Fabio Nichesola's villa in Ponton S. Ambrogio near Verona. Most of the numerous folios relating to this decoration have been regrouped by G. M. Varanini (1987, pp. 65–82). A late date is generally proposed for the decor (1590–1606; Sueur 2:132). The study is signed at bottom right with the famous coquille, the emblematic signature that was also used by Farinati's son Orazio. Fortune (*Tychè* for the Greeks, *Fortuna* for the Romans) sails through the water, her element of predilection, sails swollen by the wind, an attribute inherited from Isis-Pelagia, the protective goddess of navigators. The helm marks her role as helmswoman *(Fortuna gubernans),* while the globe symbolizes both her power over the world and her fundamental instability (Panofsky 1966, 308ff.). The long lock of hair and her bare neck are the attributes of Opportunity *(Occasio),* the goddess of the opportune moment: the lock of hair allows persons to seize her when they cross her path, and the smooth neck forbids it once she has passed. The Farinati figure extols temerity: one must tempt fortune. It is Mercury, a god of keen intelligence, who seizes the lock of Fortune-Opportunity (D. Miller 1986, 446–49). Panofsky has underscored the role of Mercury in classical literature, where he serves as an antithesis to Fortune (1966, p. 313).

Paolo Farinati (after)
(copy from the seventeenth century?)
Epimetheus Opening Pandora's Box
34

Epiméthée ouvrant la boîte de Pandore. Pen and brown ink, brown wash heightened with white, sketch in black chalk, on beige paper (36.1 × 24.7). Inscribed at top: SERO NIMIRUM SAPERE CAEPIT.
BIBLIOGRAPHY: Sueur 1991, vol. 2, pp. 166ff., no. 121; vol. 3, fig. 121.

The source for this theme is found in the *Adagiorum chiliades tres* (Three thousand proverbs) (1508) by Erasmus of Rotterdam: "Jupiter, angry at Prometheus because of the stolen fire he had abstracted from heaven and handed over to the mortals, and wishing to take revenge by a similar fraud, commanded Vulcan to form out of clay, as skillfully as he could, the image of a maiden. This done, he asked all the gods and goddesses each to bestow a gift upon this image; hence, it appears, the maiden was named Pandora. This maiden, then, showered with all the gifts of beauty, grooming, intelligence, and eloquence, was sent to Prometheus with a box, it, too, most beautiful in shape but concealing within every kind of calamity. Prometheus refused this present and admonished his brother not to accept any present delivered in his absence. Pandora returns, captivating Epimetheus and presenting the box to him. As soon as he [or she] had opened it, so that the evils flew out, and as soon as he had realized that Jupiter's gifts were 'no-gifts,' he surely became a wise man too late" (quoted in Panofsky and Panofsky 1962, 16–17). Erasmus gave a "modern" version of the myth, in contrast to Hesiod, where Pandora herself opened the fatal box (*Opera et dies,* 57–101). But a grammatical ambiguity suggests that it was Epimetheus and not Pandora who committed the error, as the drawing attests: *Eam simul ac aperuisset . . . sero nimirum sapere coepit* (As soon as he [or she] had opened it . . . he became a wise man, assuredly too late). The last four words appear on the banderole held by Prometheus, whose brother had ignored his advice. The eagle refers to the punishment of the hero, whom Zeus chained with iron bands to the Caucasus Mountains, sending an eagle every day to devour his liver, which always grew back. It is difficult to say whether this copy is a studio work or a later pastiche. The hypothesis that copies were executed stroke for stroke after the originals, which belonged to Jabach at the time, cannot be ruled out. We know that certain artists were hired as copyists in the service of the Paris collector. The Kunsthalle of Hamburg conserves the original model for *Pandora and Epimetheus* (Inv. 21196), dated 1594 (or 1584). The Louvre possesses other copies after Farinati in the same hand, relating to the myth of Prometheus and Pandora (Inv. 4907, 4904, 4908). They were to constitute a logical sequence, and refer to a single pictorial set, of which they are the sole survivors (Sueur 1991, vol. 2, pp. 162, 166–67).

Frans I De Vriendt (Floris) (manner of?)
(1516–70)
Moses Smiting the Rock
41

Moïse frappant le rocher. Pen and indigo wash (38.7 in diameter). Louvre Museum, Edmond de Rothschild Collection.

Moses's smiting of the rock to make water flow and thereby save the Hebrews in the desert, a biblical miracle described in Exodus 17:6, is the central motif of this graphic *tondo.* The taste in fifteenth- and sixteenth-century Netherlands for the circular format can be seen in numerous projects for stained glass windows (see the entry on Vellert), in engravings on wood, and in the famous series of twelve paintings by Pieter Bruegel the Elder (1559), *Flemish Proverbs* (Antwerp, Museum Mayer van den Berg). The style of the figures attests to Floris's long stay in Rome beginning in 1541, the year the *Last Judgment* was begun in the Sistine Chapel. Floris cited its motifs on several occasions in his own work. In contrast, the landscape is entirely Flemish. Lugt and Benesch have contested the autography of the drawing, which they attribute to the manner rather than the hand of Floris. Benesch has even considered an artist of the German school (oral communication).

Hubert Gerhard
(1550–1622/23)
Naiad Holding a Horn of Plenty (fountain project)
27

Naïade tenant une corne d'abondance. Oil on paper prepared with red violet ochre (23.0 × 22.1).
BIBLIOGRAPHY: Adhémar 1954, p. 127, pl. 29; Starcky 1988, no. 35.

Behrmann was the first to take this grisaille, attributed in the past to the Fontainebleau school (ex. cat. Louvre 1965, p. 165), for a work by Hubert Gerhard, a Netherlands artist who was one of the principal sculptors in Bavaria at the end of the sixteenth century. After working for the Fuggers, he entered the service of William V of Bavaria, then of the archduke Maximilian III in Innsbruck. The female figure corresponds to one of the sculptures decorating the famous Augustus Fountain on Perlach Square in Augsburg, which was ordered in 1589 by the notables of that city, and installed in 1594. The four sculptures that include this naiad stand at each corner of the basin and symbolize the rivers of the city. The fountain is dominated by the statue of Augustus, founder of the city of Augsburg *(Augusta Vindelicorum).* The Louvre conserves a second study of the same model seen from the back.

Théodore Géricault
(1791–1824)
The Old Beggar
74

Le vieux mendiant. Lithograph (31.7 × 37.6). First state with additional marks: three sketches in the right margin, *Homme assis auprès de deux chevaux* [Man seated next to two horses], *Balayeur* [Sweeper], and *Cheval harnaché* [Harnessed horse]. Bibliothèque Nationale, Print Room
BIBLIOGRAPHY: Clément 1879, no. 27; Delteil 1924, no. 31; ex. cat. Rome, 1979–80, no. 94; Eitner 1983, pp. 213, 229, 351n. 77; ex. cat. Japan 1987 and 1988n, no. E-27; Michel 1992, repr. p. 104.

Enamored with Germany, where he exhibited the *Radeau de la Méduse* (Raft of the Medusa) (Louvre) in 1820, Géricault returned there in early 1821 and stayed nearly a year. He actively practiced a new art then in vogue: the lithograph. When he arrived in London, he got in touch with Hullmandel, a printer and lithographer, and with the publishers Rodwell and Martin. Through them, between February and May 1821, he published the series of thirteen lithographs entitled *Various Subjects Drawn from Life and on Stone by J. Gericault.* It is known as "the great English series" and includes the present print. This is the only sheet from the first state known to exist. The second state bears the legend: "Pity the sorrows of a poor old Man! / Whose trembling limbs have borne him to your door." Clément adds that the print draws its title from a nursery rhyme (1974, p. 385). A beggar in rags, but wearing a dignified hat, officiates on the pavement in front of a bakery, asking for bread. Poverty is expressed in the play of contrasts between the baker woman's full hands and the poor man's empty hand, and between the prosperous client and the hobo. Curiously, these last two figures have the same features and are wearing the same hat—this doubly reinforces the contrast in social condition (Michel 1992, p. 104). Géricault was one of the first to track down the poverty-stricken margins of London streets, criticizing through his images the human cost of the industrial revolution.

Anne-Louis de Girodet-Trioson (Girodet)
(1764–1824)
The Trojan Horse
38

Le cheval de Troie. Pen and brown ink (36.9 × 32.0). Inscribed in pen on the horse: ATENAIOS and EPEOS.
BIBLIOGRAPHY: Boucher 1930, pp. 309–10, pl. 306–7; Bernier 1975, p. 178, pl. p. 177.

In a letter of 17 February 1811 (cited in Lambert 1974, p. 73), Girodet confides to his student P.-A. Coupin that he is working assiduously on the illustrations for the first book of the *Aeneid.* The large number of drawings—Baron Boutard, art critic for the *Journal des Débats,* mentions two hundred—proves that Girodet was preparing this project well before 1811. A selective collection of lithographs, edited by Antoine Pannetier, appeared posthumously in 1827. This drawing was the only one to be published by Henri Boucher, of a series of eighteen compositions illustrating the second book of the poem (see R. Michel, ex. cat. Louvre 1989, pp. 67–69). Virgil describes how the wooden horse constructed by Epeos entered Troy. The name "Epeos" appears on the horse's leg; the Greeks are hidden inside. "Into the darkened city, buried deep / In sleep and wine, they made their way" (2.264–65). In the foreground, two sleepy guards are leaning against columns that suggest the palace of Priam, which a Greek is invading with the help of a ladder. The last warriors are leaping from the horse's neck, which bears the Athenian owl, illustrating the origin of the assailants.

The Dream of Aeneas
92

Le rêve d'Enée. Brown and gray wash, heightened with white, on crayon strokes (23.9 × 32.1). Inscribed bottom center: *10 pds.*
BIBLIOGRAPHY: Coupin 1829, vol. 1, p. 71.

The episode of the Trojan horse follows the dream of Aeneas, which Virgil makes a portent of the disaster, before his account of the sacking of Troy (2.268–98). The ghost of Hector advises the dozing Aeneas of the final fall and orders him to escape with the *palladium,* the divine statue, protector of the city, which Hector himself hands over to the sleeper. To underscore the contrast between this scene and the assault by the Greek warriors, Girodet chose the wash, propitious for a nocturne. In the embrasure, a fire in the city sets the night ablaze.

Giulio Romano (see Pippi)

Hendrick Goltzius
(1558–1617)
Allegory of Plenty (fountain project)
26

Allégorie de l'Abondance. Pen and brown ink, heightened with white and watercolor (32.7 × 19.5). Signed and dated on pedestal: *A° H.G. 98.* Louvre Museum, Edmond de Rothschild Collection
BIBLIOGRAPHY: Lugt 1929, vol. 1, no. 293, repr. pl. 52; Reznicek 1961, pp. 114–15, no. 158, pp. 300–301, repr. pl. 316; Bacou 1968, no. 73; Arquié-Bruley, Labbé, and Bicart-Sée 1987, vol. 1, repr. p. 146, no. 26; Nichols 1992, p. 27, fig. 25.

The woman is holding a horn of flowers and fruit, the canonical attribute of plenty. She presses her breast and water spurts out, as it spurts from her tiara, in many fine sprays. According to Reznicek, this was a drawing for a sculpted monument, apparently a fountain, which has not been identified. In the engraved work of Wendel Dietterlin (1550/51–99) and Hans Vredeman de Vries (1527–1606), many fountain projects attest to the popularity of the motif among mannerists at the end of the sixteenth century. Such drawings often served merely as a pretext for extremely free inventions, with no desire on the artist's part to realize them. The stretched-out proportions of the figure and the perceptible forward movement, repeated in the study sketch on the same sheet, denote the influence of Bartholomaeus Spranger (1546–1611). Carel van Mander, a theorist of mannerism, introduced Goltzius to Spranger's work; Goltzius gave these inventions a broad diffusion.

Old Woman in Love
29

La vieille amoureuse. Pen and brown ink, brown wash heightened with white and watercolor (20.3 × 28.1). Signed toward center with monogram and dated at bottom left: *HG A° 1600.* Louvre Museum, Edmond de Rothschild Collection.
BIBLIOGRAPHY: Judson 1959, p. 76; Reznicek 1961, no. 194, pl. 352.

Old Man in Love
30

Le vieillard amoureux. Pen and brown ink, brown wash, heightened with white and watercolor (20.3 × 28.1). Signed with monogram toward the center. Louvre Museum, Edmond de Rothschild Collection.
BIBLIOGRAPHY: Reznicek 1961, no. 193, pl. 353.

An old woman offers a gallant a handful of coins to buy his favors. But a troubled-looking young woman holds her lover by the hand, away from the seductress. The man, between the two women, cannot help glancing over at the tempting offer. In the companion piece, Goltzius reverses the roles. The seducer is an old man coveting a young woman who, disdainful of the riches offered, turns toward her lover. Jan Saenredam engraved the drawings reversed (Thieme-Becker, vol. 24, s.v. "Jacob Matham"), and the two subjects are already part of the engraved oeuvre of Crispin de Passe or his studio, with variants (Hollstein, vol. 15, nos. 859, 29 and 850, 30). We may conclude that Goltzius drew inspiration from these engravings if, with Rezniecek, we accept the date on one of the sheets as authentic (1600).

Jean-Baptiste Greuze
(1725–1805)
Roman Charity
47

La charité romaine. Pen and black ink, gray wash on sketch in black chalk (32.6 × 41.6).
BIBLIOGRAPHY: Mathey 1933, pp. 183–84; Munhall 1965, p. 27, fig. 5.

Illustration of the classical theme of Roman charity, a popular subject among such eighteenth-century painters as J. J. Bachelier and Lagrenée the Elder, who borrowed it from Valerius Maximus (*De pietate in parentes* 5.4). Pera breastfed her father, Cimon, who was condemned to starve to death in his jail cell. According to Mathey (1933, pp. 183–84), the drawing is a study made in 1767 as the admission piece that the Academy required of Greuze, who had been accepted ten years earlier. The artist opted for another subject, *Septime Sévère reprochant à Caracalla, son fils, d'avoir voulu l'assassiner* (Septimius Severus reproaching his son, Caracalla, for attempting to assassinate him) (1769, Louvre), a painting that caused a scandal, as we know from Diderot's *Salon de 1769.* The Fogg Art Museum conserves the drawing of a nude woman pressing her breast (Harvard University, Cambridge, Mass.). It could be a preliminary study for the figure of Pera. The obvious kinship between *Roman Charity* and the Rubens painting on the same subject, conserved at the Hermitage (Oldenburg, n.d., repr. p. 43) suggests that Greuze had the opportunity to see the painted work at the sale held by Marquis J. de Julienne in Paris (30 March–22 May 1767, no. 97).

The Lady of Charity
68

La dame de bienfaisance. Paintbrush and gray wash (23.0 × 30.0). Signed at bottom right: *J. B. Greuze.* Agen, Museum of Fine Art.
BIBLIOGRAPHY: Recours 1933, p. 31; Vilain 1974–75, p. 151; Munhall 1976–77, p. 170, no. 76ter; ex. cat. Caen 1980, no. 26.

Preparatory sketch for the painting in the Lyon museum. The first known image after the painting, engraved by Massard, dates from 1772. F. de Laharpe, who saw the work exhibited in Greuze's studio in 1775, describes the scene in his *Correspondance littéraire:* "The lady is visiting a sick man whom one supposes to be of noble condition, given the sword hanging above his bed. He is in a poor and miserable bed with his wife, who is also ill. The lady of charity has a child of five or six present him with a purse. This is her daughter, whom she wishes to accustom to charity" (Paris, 1804, 1:268–69). In the specific genre of preaching through images, *The Lady of Charity* serves as a striking prelude to the famous diptych *Malédiction paternelle: Le fils ingrat* (Paternal curse: The ungrateful son) and *Le fils puni* (The son punished) (1767–68, Louvre). It illustrates in a remarkable way what Diderot called "moral painting," of which he was a convinced advocate: "What then! Hasn't the paintbrush been dedicated to debauchery and vice long enough, too long in fact?" (*Salon de 1763,* ed. 1975, p. 233). The composition draws inspiration from Poussin's *Testament d'Eudamidas* (Testament of Eudamidas) (Copenhagen, Statens Museum for Kunst), which Greuze could have seen in Paris before 1759 or may have known from the engraving by Jean Pesne (1623–1700).

Maerten van Heemskerck (1498–1574) *The Parable of the Rich Man* 63

La parabole de l'homme riche. Pen and brown ink (16.0 × 22.6). Traces of perforations. Signed bottom right in pen and brown ink: *Martinus van / Heemskerck / inventor,* and dated, toward the center: *1560.* Louvre Museum, Edmond de Rothschild Collection.

A literal illustration of the famous gospel parable: "It is easier for a camel to go through the eye of a needle, than for a rich man to enter into the kingdom of God" (Matthew 19:25). On the left, a man burdened with bags of money is held captive by the narrow walls. On the right, three men are undertaking to have a camel pass through the eye of a needle, which is held by a heavenly hand. The perforation of the sheet and the technique of the drawing (regular cross-hatching) suggest this is a preparatory sketch for an engraving. Van Heemskerck, primarily involved with prints, first borrowed his subjects from the Bible and hagiography, but theological and moral allegories took on increasing importance in his engravings under the influence of the humanists, especially the moralist Dirck Volkertsz. The power of the figures suggests a late date, after the stay in Rome (1532–35), where he was able to study the works of Raphael and his school.

Sebastián de Herrera Barnuevo (1619–71) *Elijah and the Widow of Zarephath* 45

Elie et la veuve de Sarepta. Pen and brown ink, brown wash, sketch in black chalk on cream paper (21.2 × 27.1).
BIBLIOGRAPHY: Brown 1983, p. 404, no. 8, pl. 29a; Boubli 1991, pp. 149–52.

Preparatory study for one of the sixty-eight panels on the high altar of the chapel of Our Lady of Guadalupe in the cloister of the monastery of Descalzas Reales. The monastery was dedicated in 1653 by the Infanta Anna Dorotea, marchioness of Austria and the illegitimate daughter of Emperor Rudolph II. The central statue of the Virgin of Guadalupe is surrounded by forty-six scenes relating to the life of the Virgin and Christ. Twenty-one panels of larger dimensions frame the altar and are devoted to the illustrious women of the Old Testament, who all prefigured Mary by their merits and virtues. The literary source of the iconographical program was identified by H. D. Wethey and A. Sunderland Wethey (1966) as a book by Don Martín Carillo, abbot of Monte Aragón, entitled *Elogios de mugeres insignes del Viejo Testamento* (Praise of the illustrious women of the Old Testament) (1627). The drawing shows the prophet Elijah being given food and drink by the widow of the city of Zarephath, near Zidon, where he had gone on the order of Jehovah (1 Kings 17:7–16). Elijah had asked her to draw water and prepare a meal cake, predicting that her provisions would not be used up as long as the drought lasted. According to Carrillo, the episode prefigures the Incarnation of the Trinity, which the resurrection of the widow's son by Elijah symbolizes (1 Kings 17:7–24). For medieval theologians, Elijah prefigures Christ, and the widow, the church of the gentiles, which welcomes the Savior, whom the synagogue did not wish to recognize. The water symbolizes the sacrament of baptism, which reminds us that Elijah is also the precursor of John the Baptist (Réau 1956, 2:349–52). In the cycle decorating the altar, the scene is paired with the resurrection by Elisha of the son of the Shunammite, which anticipates the resurrection of Lazarus.

Hans Holbein the Younger (1497–1543) *The Triumph of Wealth* 77

Le triomphe de la richesse. Pen and brown ink, brown wash heightened with white. Squared with black chalk (25.1 × 56.9). Inscribed in pen and brown ink to identify the allegories from left to right: "BONA FIDES / LIBERALITAS / AEOVALITAS / NOTITIA / VOLVNTAS / SIMONIDES / CONTRACTVS / SICHEVS / PITHIVS / CRISFLNS / BASSA / RATIO / VIVIDIVS / LEO BIZANTIVS / FORTVNA / THEMISTOCLES / VENTIDIVS / GADAREVS / NARCISSVS / PLVTVS / TATALVS / MYDAS / CRESVS / CLEOPATRA / NEMESIS."
BIBLIOGRAPHY: Koegler 1933, p. 90; Ganz 1939, repr. no. 120; Christoffel 1950, p. 94, fig. 252; Bacou 1968, repr. no. 27; Rowlands 1985, p. 224; Monbeig Goguel 1988, p. 24, fig. 16.

The only autograph vestige of one of the two great allegorical compositions, *Triumph of Wealth* and *Triumph of Poverty,* painted by Holbein during his second stay in London (about 1532) for the banquet room of the merchants of La Hanse in their Steelyard House on Thames Street. These two grisailles, heightened with gold and watercolor, disappeared in 1752 in the fire of the Kremsier castle, where they had ended up after many adventures (Rowlands 1985, p. 223). The differences between the Louvre drawing and the numerous copies after the disappeared panels (L. Vostermann, J. de Bischop, F. Zuccaro, etc.) show that the present study is still far from the final work. Although faithful to the humanist motif of Petrarch's *Triumphs,* established in the middle of the fifteenth century (yoked cart, allegorical frieze) and replicated by Dürer in the *Triumph of Maximilian* (B. 139), Holbein gives a very personal version of the motif. Under the canopy of charity, Plutus, god of wealth, sits enthroned, flanked by a horn of plenty, which evokes his mother Ceres, goddess of fertility. Before him appears blindfolded Fortune on a sailing ship, distributing gold pieces to the famous "plutocrats" of antiquity who flank the chariot: Sicheus, Tantalus, Midas, Croesus, Cleopatra, and so on. Hovering over the procession on the right is Nemesis, vengeful deity, guardian of measure, whose classic attributes are the bit and the square. The chariot is driven by Reason *(Ratio),* who holds the reins of Knowledge *(Notitia)* and Will *(Voluntas).* The four horses, which, according to the copies, symbolize the perversions of money (Avarice, Usury, Simony, and Contract) are under the domination of the four virtues of the Christian Vulgate: Liberality, Equity, Justice, and Good Faith. The moral apologue of this ambitious allegory figures in Latin on the dial cases that provide captions for the copies of the painting: "Gold is the father of seduction and the son of pain: whoever is lacking it suffers, whoever has it fears."

Grégoire Huret (attributed to)
(1606–70)
The Wheel of Fortune
21

La roue de Fortune. Black chalk (30.1 × 41.5).

In the spirit of the Renaissance, Farinati's *Fortune* extols the initiative of man, master of his own destiny (see entry on Farinati); Huret's Fortune resembles the ancient Nemesis, which punishes pride, excess, and worldly ambition. The medieval motif of the wheel, symbol of instability, becomes an infernal machine, an instrument of torture. Fortune gleefully turns the crank to lift up human beings, only to better let them fall. Her long lock of hair and her bare neck make her a kind of Fortune-Opportunity, the tutelary figure of the propitious moment (see entry on Farinati). In Boethius's *Consolation of Philosophy* (38), Fortune declares: "I turn the wheel that spins. I delight to see the high come down and the low ascend. Mount up, if thou wilt, but only on condition that thou wilt not think it a hardship to come down when the rules of my game require it." In the midst of the classical age, the artist is faithful to that medieval conception: in the four parts of the sheet, he describes in turn expectation, prosperity, the fall, and despair. But, in addition to Fortune, other elements intervene in the destiny of men: the Demon, who propels the wheel with his breath alone; Justice, which strikes down the powerful; and Plenty, which scatters the fruit from its horn to the poor. Drawings by Huret, who was admitted to the Royal Academy as an engraver in 1663, are very rare. The Biblioteca Nacional de Madrid conserves thirty-two preparatory studies for *The Passion of Christ* (1664). But there are no fewer than five hundred items in his oeuvre of engravings.

Jacob Jordaens
(1593–1678)
Philemon and Baucis
62

Philémon et Baucis. Black chalk, brown wash, heightened with white (16.3 × 21.3). Enlarged, perhaps by Jordaens himself, on all four sides.

BIBLIOGRAPHY: Tauzia 1881, no. 191; Bouchet-Saupique 1930–31, p. 90; Lugt 1949, no. 730, pl. 87; Puyvelde 1953, p. 198; d'Hulst 1956, pp. 260, 380, nos. 145, 419; d'Hulst 1957–58, pp. 147, 150; d'Hulst 1974, vol. 2, no. A264, and vol. 4, fig. 280.

With the deaths of Rubens (1640) and Van Dyck (1641), Jordaens became the most renowned artist of Antwerp. Between 1645 and 1650, he often treated this notorious episode from Ovid's *Metamorphoses* (8.611–724). Jupiter and Mercury, disguised as simple travelers, knock at the doors of the citizens of Phrygia in search of a place to stay. No one wants to receive them, with the exception of an old couple of poor peasants, Philemon and Baucis, who extend their hospitality. In their anger, the gods let loose a flood on the entire country, sparing only the old couple's cottage, which they make a temple. This moral apologue, which rewards the charity of the poor and punishes the avarice of the rich, was discussed by Carel van Mander at the beginning of the century (*Wtlegghingh op den Metamorphosis* [Haarlem, 1604], fol. 72, verso). Jordaens, famous for his genre scenes, which are realist in style and moral in spirit, can no doubt be linked to the tradition of van Mander.

Laurent de La Hyre
(1606–56)
The Community of the First Christians
44

La communauté des premiers chrétiens. Black chalk (37.0 × 62.7).

Laying Hands on the Seven Deacons
13

L'imposition des mains aux sept diacres. Black chalk (36.5 × 55.0).

BIBLIOGRAPHY: Augarde and Thuillier 1962, p. 19, repr.

In 1646 (at the latest), La Hyre was asked to execute a series of drawings after the life of Saint Stephen, for tapestries that were to decorate the Paris church of Saint-Etienne-du-Mont. Only five hangings were woven, and no fragment has yet been found of them. The series of nineteen drawings, duly framed, remained in the office of the churchwarden at the parish, until they were moved to the Louvre during the Revolution. These projects belong to the artist's late period, which Rosenberg and Thuillier call the "atticism of the Regency" (1645–56), when the classical taste was expressed in the rigor of lines and the austerity of architecture (ex. cat. Grenoble, Rennes, Bordeaux, 1989–90). The distribution of bread and money characterized the life of the first Christians, related in Acts: "And they continued stedfastly in the apostles' doctrine and fellowship, and in the breaking of bread, and in prayers. . . . And all that believed were together, and had all things common; and sold their possessions and goods, and parted them to all *men,* as every man had need" (2:42–46). The account continues with the laying on of hands of the seven deacons: "And they chose Stephen, a man full of faith and of the Holy Ghost, and Philip, and Prochorus, and Nicanor, and Timon, and Parmenas, and Nicolas a proselyte of Antioch: Whom they set before the apostles: and when they had prayed, they laid *their* hands on them" (Acts 6:5–6).

Pygmalion
87

Pygmalion. Black chalk and wash, heightened with white (28.3 × 21.3). Oval format.
BIBLIOGRAPHY: Rosenberg and Thuillier 1985, repr. no. 32.

La Hyre seems to be the first great artist of French classicism to illustrate the story of Pygmalion, a sculptor from Cyprus who was so in love with his statue that Venus made the work come to life (Ovid, *Metamorphoses* 10.243–98). The drawing, whose oval format led some to believe that it was a study for a decor, is considered a mature work, dated about 1640 (ex. cat. Grenoble, etc., 1989–90, no. 190).

Jean-Jacques Lagrenée the Younger
(1739–1821)
God Giving Moses the Ten Commandments
42

Dieu donne à Moïse les Tables de la Loi. Pen and brown ink, brown wash, heightened with white, on gray paper (33.0 × 26.5). Oval format.
BIBLIOGRAPHY: Arquié-Bruley, Labbé, and Bicart-Sée 1987, repr. no. 150.

In contrast to traditional iconography, where God remains invisible, hidden in the clouds, four angel musicians evoking the Last Judgment are drawing the curtain of heaven, where God the Father appears, pointing out the Ten Commandments to Moses. He must transmit them to the people of Israel. The oval format and the upward-looking perspective suggest a plan for a ceiling. We know that the artist liked decors in the air and was one of the most sought-after masters of them. His piece for admission to the Academy, exhibited at the Salon of 1775, was an allegory of winter, painted for the ceiling of the Apollo gallery at the Louvre. In 1779, he also did the ceiling for Marie Antoinette's theater in Trianon park. As Sandoz has noted, Lagrenée was first concerned with the baroque tradition of chiaroscuro and was not exempt from Bolognese influences, which he studied in Rome during his stay in the Médicis villa from 1763 to 1768. It is therefore logical to link this sheet, where the plays of light introduce fantastic accents, to his early period, still very far from neoclassicism (Sandoz 1962, 131).

Jacopo Ligozzi
(1547–1626)
Death Exterminating the Human Race
32

La Mort exterminant le genre humain. Pen, brown ink, brown wash heightened with gold on paper washed brown (27.9 × 20.9). Signed with monogram bottom left and dated *1625.*
BIBLIOGRAPHY: Voss 1920, p. 422; Viatte 1977, repr. pp. 347 and 353; Viatte 1988, p. 148, no. 259.

Woman at Her Toilette Surprised by Death
33

Femme à sa toilette surprise par la Mort. Pen, brown ink, brown wash heightened with gold on paper washed yellow brown (24.2 × 19.1). Inscription bottom left: *Jac. Ligozio.*
BIBLIOGRAPHY: Voss 1920, p. 422; Viatte 1988, p. 148, no. 261.

These two sheets are part of a series of allegories of Death. The Louvre (Inv. 5033 and 5035), the Pierpont Morgan Library of New York, and the Accademia in Venice conserve the other copies. The set can be dated 1625. Of all the Italian artists at the end of the sixteenth century, Ligozzi, a painter at the Médici court in Florence beginning in 1577, was the one with the most affinities for Nordic art. A drawing in the Pierpont Morgan Library, *Amants surpris de la mort* (Lovers surprised by death), was inspired by a tint drawing by Hans Burgkimair. In 1538, Hans Holbein the Younger illustrated the *Danse macabre,* which depicts the triumph of equality in the face of universal Death, who makes a mockery of different social conditions. Ligozzi implacably renders this medieval idea by showing Death exterminating the human race. The cadavers are piled up every which way, and the grimacing skeleton, brandishing his sword, tramples the baubles of power under his feet: the crown, the tiara, the episcopal miter, and the cardinal's hat. A skull is blowing its lethal breath over the earth. The woman at her toilette surprised by Death was a popular subject among painters of the German Renaissance. Ligozzi places the heroine at her toilette, in front of her mirror and among jewels and precious vases, as a classical allegory of the vanity of earthly wealth (beauty, riches). The sarcastic skeleton approaching her is brandishing an hourglass, symbol of the "eternal fall of time," in Lamartine's expression. Vanity has become funereal.

Tobias and the Angel
39

Tobie et l'ange. Pen, brown ink, brown wash, heightened with gold; squared in black chalk (20.7 × 23.0). Signed bottom left with monogram and dated: *1605*.
BIBLIOGRAPHY: Viatte 1988, p. 142, no. 249.

The book of Tobit in the Old Testament gives an account of an episode where the hero Tobias, on the advice of the archangel Raphael, gathers together the liver and gall of a fish, which allows him to exorcise his wife Sara and to restore sight to his blind father (Tobit 6:4–6). The naturalist style of the fish cannot fail to evoke the Vienna collection (Bibliothèque Nationale) recently published by Conigliello), which contains miniatures of fish of many species, observed from life out of scientific interest, or taken from ichthyological treatises that had been circulating in Europe since the middle of the fifteenth century (1991, pp. 23–27, fig. 23–39). Conigliello set the date of the collection, then in the library of the Austrian emperor Rudolph II, as 1577, before Ligozzi settled in Florence. There he continued to paint plants and animals in the service of the grand duke of Tuscany.

Master L. D.
(active in Fontainebleau between 1540 and 1565)
Alexander and Campaspe
86

Alexandre et Campaspe. Burin (34.1 × 24.0). Oval format. Monogram *LD* bottom right with the inscription: *Bologna.* Bibliothèque Nationale, Print Room.
BIBLIOGRAPHY: Herbet 1896, vol. 1, p. 24, no. 13; Zerner 1969, no. 51.

The most prolific engraver of the Fontainebleau school signed his plates with the initials *L. D.* He interpreted the works of Primaticcio in particular, and that collaboration has been compared to the one between Marcantonio Raimondi and Raphael (Zerner 1969, xxi). His personality and his name remain an enigma, and the monogram *L. D.* has elicited diverse interpretations (Herbet 1896, 7). The oldest and most probable hypothesis is to read it as *Léon Daven* or *Davent,* in accordance with the inscription accompanying the monogram on an engraving after Giulio Romano (Zerner 1969, nos. 53–56). The rare prints that are dated by the master tell us that he engraved between 1540 and 1565. The inscription *Bologna* on the upturned urn refers to the author of the composition, Primaticcio, called "Bologna," after the name of his native city. According to Pliny (*Natural History* 35.36), Alexander the Great ordered an effigy of his mistress Campaspe from Apelles, the most famous portraitist of antiquity. The artist fell in love with the model during the execution of the work, and the prince, pleased with the painting, gave him Campaspe as a reward. The Cupid slipping between Apelles and his canvas alludes to the artist's love for the favorite, whom Alexander, wearing his helmet, still holds in his embrace.

Danaë
2

Danaé. Burin (21.5 × 29.0). Oval format. Monogram *LD* on the right (almost imperceptible, beneath the foot of Danaë). Bibliothèque Nationale, Print Room.
BIBLIOGRAPHY: Bartsch 1818, vol. 16, p. 321, no. 40; Herbet 1896, p. 20, no. 4; Zerner 1969, no. 8.

Engraving after a composition by Primaticcio, painted in 1537 in the Francis I Gallery of Fontainebleau. The original drawing is in the Condé Museum in Chantilly (Barocchi 1951, fig. 256). Acrisius, sovereign of Argos, confined his daughter Danaë to a bronze chamber to prevent the fulfillment of the oracle, which threatened that Acrisius would be killed by his grandson. Zeus, in love with the princess, managed to enter the chamber through a gap in the roof, in the form of a shower of gold. He impregnated her and she gave birth to Perseus (Ovid, *Metamorphoses* 4.611). At the foot of the bed, a Cupid is undertaking to distance the nurse, while the divine cloud scatters its fertile shower on Danaë's bosom.

Michelangelo (see Buonarroti)

Pierre Mignard (after)
(seventeenth century)
Spring
10

Le printemps. Black chalk, brown wash, heightened with white on prepared beige paper.
BIBLIOGRAPHY: Fenaille 1903, vol. 2, no. 116; Langlade 1968, p. 118, no. 47.

Studio copy after a lost drawing by Mignard for the allegorical cycle of the four seasons, ordered from the artist in 1677 by the duke of Orléans, brother of Louis XIV, for the decor of the Apollo gallery in the castle of Saint-Cloud (oral communication from J.-F. Méjanès). As an allegory of spring, Mignard chose the marriage of Zephyrus and Flora, a lush image of the ostentatious gifts of prodigal nature. In *Fasti* (5.193–214), Ovid writes that Zephyrus, the gentle west wind that makes flowers grow, fell in love with Chloris and abducted her. At the moment he kissed her, she turned into Flora, the reigning goddess of flowers. Flowers immediately began to bloom on her lips, as we already see in Botticelli's famous *Spring* (Uffizi, Florence). The copy shows Zephyrus scattering flowers over his wife, flowers that nymphs and cupids gather for him, and which Fortune brings him in her horn of plenty. The Louvre conserves the drawings of the other three seasons in the same cycle, figured by Ceres (summer), Bacchus (autumn), and Cybele (winter), by the same copyist's hand. If we except the engravings by J.-B. Poilly and the tapestries by the Gobelins (woven in 1686 after Mignard's cartoons), these very finished drawings are all that remains of the decor, which was destroyed in 1870 in the castle fire started by the Commune.

Jean-François Millet
(1814–75)
The Gleaners
81

Les glaneuses. Black crayon on beige paper (16.5 × 26.7). Signed bottom right with the initials: *JFM.* Louvre Museum, Orsay Museum Collection.

One of the numerous studies for the *Gleaners,* a famous painting exhibited at the Salon of 1857, along with Courbet's *Demoiselles des bords de Seine* (Young ladies on the banks of the Seine) (Orsay Museum).

The composition is grounded in the contrast between the silhouettes of the laboring women, who are gathering ears of corn left behind by the reapers, and the massive silhouettes of the ample haystacks. After he settled in Barbizon in 1849, Millet left behind the portrait genre, which he had practiced intensively, to devote himself entirely to rustic themes. *The Gleaners* was poorly received by criticism on the right because of the social image of the peasant, which was judged revolutionary. The artist sensed very well the virtual political meaning of his paintings, without, however, laying claim to it or seeking it out as such. The scene attests to the interest in peasant subjects proper to the mid-century. This interest was manifested in art and literature throughout Europe (e.g., Charles Dickens, George Eliot, Honoré de Balzac, George Sand). The aesthetic phenomenon was linked to the 1848 revolution and the subsequent triumph of social realism, whose masters in France, in addition to Millet, were Courbet and Daumier.

Charles Monnet
(1732–1808)
Pygmalion
88

Pygmalion. Pen and brown ink, brown wash, sketch in black chalk, heightened with white, on bluish paper (37.4 × 27.7). Signed and dated bottom right: *C. Monnet 1762.* Louvre Museum, Orsay Museum Collection.

During the age of neoclassicism, the myth of Pygmalion, a sculptor in love with his own statue, which was endowed with life by Venus (see the entry on La Hyre above), became a popular subject among artists (Falconet, Lemoine, Girodet). Monnet, who studied at the Academy under the direction of Jean Restout, was inspired by a painting by his master, which appeared at the Salon of 1745 (left side of the dismembered painting; deposited by the Louvre at the Mobilier national, Inv. 7452, preparatory drawing at the Museum of Fine Arts in Orléans). From Restout, the artist borrowed the idea of the *putto* holding the torch, symbol of the fires of love and the powers of Venus, who is animating the ivory becoming flesh.

Gustave Moreau
(1826–98)
Salome Dancing
85

Salomé dansant. Watercolor on strokes of graphite, heightened with gold gouache (33.6 × 21.3). Signed bottom left in gold: *Gustave Moreau.*
BIBLIOGRAPHY: Leprieur 1889, p. 34, no. 1; Bouyer 1900, p. 596; Rouchès and Huyghe 1938, vol. 11, repr. no. 11756; Mathieu 1976, p. 128, repr. no. 341.

The Gospel of Matthew (14:6) tells the story of Salome, who consented to dance before Herod to have as her reward the head of John the Baptist. In Moreau's watercolor, which is a replica of the famous painting of long gestation that appeared at the Salon of 1876 (Los Angeles County Museum), the dancer holds a lotus flower, symbol of sexual desire. The subject fascinated all the artists and writers of the fin du siècle: Puvis de Chavannes and Henri Regnault (1870), Mallarmé (*Hérodiade,* 1871), Théodore de Banville (*Sonnet d'Hérodias,* 1874), and especially Flaubert, whose *Hérodias* is the jewel of the *Trois contes* (1877). The painting by Moreau was celebrated by J.-K. Huysmans in *A rebours* (1884).

Jan Harmensz Muller (after Cornelis Cornelisz van Haarlem)
(1571–1628)
Blind Fortune Distributing Her Wealth
25

La Fortune aveugle distribuant ses biens. Bibliothèque Nationale, Print Room. Burin (50.3 × 91.0) (in two parts). Signed at bottom: *Cornelis Corneliades Harlemeñ / inuenit et pinxit.—Johannes Mullerus Amsterad: Sculpsit.* Inscription in the margin: "Me rerum Dominam celebrant, Divamqz potentem / Mortales faciunt, super astra locant /

Munifica dicor nunc hos extollere dextra, / Nunc illos varijs exagitare malis. / Praecipit videor, rapidaeqz insistere sphaerae, / Quod mihi non constem lubrica, simqz vaga. / Praevelant, oculos, rectum discernere bruta, / Quod nequeam justis dura benigna malis. / Occiput est calvum, propendent fronte capilli, / Obvia quod possim, non fugitiva capi. / At cum provideat divina potentia rebus, / Nomen inane mihi, non mihi numen adest" [The mortals celebrate me as the queen of the world, / powerful divinity whom they place above the stars. / They claim that I cover some with gifts / and that I torment others with various ills. / They represent me pressed and perched on a rapid sphere. / They have blindfolded me so that I cannot see, / Hard toward the just, favorable toward the bad. / My neck is bare, from my forehead hangs a lock of hair / So that one can grasp me from the front before I run away. / But since divine providence provides all things, / My name is nothingness and my oracles have ceased to act]. Inscription at top left, in cartouche: *Prudentissimis Reip. Harlemensis Moderatibus, / Adriano Berckenrodio Guilielmo Dei—manno, Thomae Thomae f., & Gerardo Guilielmp, Dominis suis plurimum observandis. Cornelius Corneliades Pictor, gratus civis dedicabat. An.∞D.XC.*
BIBLIOGRAPHY: Bartsch 1803, vol. 3, no. 33; Hollstein, vol. 14, p. 109, no. 71; ex. cat. Lausanne 1981–82, p. 71, no. 84; Mirimonde 1982, p. 83.

Engraved in 1590 after the painting by Cornelis Cornelisz van Haarlem (1562–1638) at the Museum of Art and History in Geneva. According to Brulhart and van Thiel, the painter executed his painting with the idea of engraving the composition, a procedure contrary to the usual and more economical practice of engraving after a drawing. Van Thiel has, in fact, located two other cases where Cornelis made a model in oil and then placed it at the disposition of the engraver (ex. cat. Lausanne, 1981–82, no. 84). Hence the oddity of the iconography, where Fortune is distributing her favors with her left hand. In inverting the scene, Muller, who was probably an apprentice of Cornelisz van Haarlem and Goltzius, reestablishes the natural gesture. Fortune's pose (leaning backward and seemingly losing her balance) makes her a symbol of instability. She blindly lavishes or refuses her gifts, defying logic and morality. Fortune throws her boons to the crowd, which is greedily fighting to collect the riches, and those she disdains remain in poverty. In contrast to the drawing by Huret (see that entry), where Justice corrects the arbitrariness of Fortune, human destiny is here completely dependent upon her. "Divine providence," invoked by a moral caption, is noteworthy for its absence.

Giulio Pippi (Giulio Romano) (1499–1546)
Psyche Receiving the Vase of Proserpine
36

Psyché recevant le vase de Proserpine. Pen and brown ink, brown wash, sketch in black chalk on beige paper in the shape of a lunette (19.8 × 37.0). Outlines partially incised with a stylus. Inscribed in pen and brown ink, bottom right: *Jul. Ro.*
BIBLIOGRAPHY: Hartt 1958, no. 171, fig. 270; Pouncey and Gere 1962, p. 60 under no. 74; sales cat. Ellesmere 1972, p. 67, under no. 31; Verheyen 1977, p. 118.

A model for the eleventh of twelve lunettes for the Hall of Psyche, the principal room of the north wing of the Palazzo del Te, painted in 1528 with the assistance of Benedetto Pagni and Rinaldo. Giulio takes up the story of Psyche recounted by Apuleius in *The Golden Ass,* which was in vogue in the humanist environment of the time. Raphael had treated it ten years earlier on the vault of the Farnesina, and Perino del Vaga took it as the subject for the Saint-Ange castle. The scene shows one of the expiatory labors imposed by Venus on her daughter-in-law Psyche, whom she forces to descend into Hades to obtain the vase of beauty from Proserpine. Psyche is kneeling before the throne of Proserpine and Pluto, who are surrounded by Cerberus and the three infernal deities: Alecot, Maegera, and Tisiphone. A preliminary sketch from this model can be found in the British Museum (Pouncey and Gere 1962, no. 74, pl. 67). The Ellesmere collection had a second drawing, which belongs to Ian Woodner (New York), and which P. A. Tomory considers a copy after the fresco (Verheyen 1977, p. 118, fig. 48, pl. 92).

Giulio Pippi (Giulio Romano) (school of) (sixteenth century)
Salome Carrying the Head of John the Baptist
76

Salomé portant la tête de Jean Baptiste. Pen and brown ink, brown wash, heightened with white, on bluish paper (21.0 × 37.1).
BIBLIOGRAPHY: Rouchès n.d., p. 27, no. 35 (G. Romano); Parker 1956, vol. 2, p. 121.

A triumphant Salome carries the head of John the Baptist in a charger to offer to her mother Herodias (Matthew 14:10–12). The scene takes place in the dark, and the only light source is a torch. The funeral procession is moving toward a door, no doubt the entrance to the banquet hall. On the right, two characters express their horror with lively gestures. The Ashmolean Museum of Oxford conserves a study of the same composition, but of inferior quality. Pouncey attributes it to Giulio Campi (about 1500–72), a painter from Cremona who was influenced by Giulio Romano (Parker 1956, 2:121, no. 252).

Francesco Primaticcio (1504–70)
Eliezer and Rebekah
40

Eliézer et Rébecca. Red chalk, heightened with white, on paper washed with red chalk (26.4 × 32.6). Inscribed top left: *Bologne fecit;* and at bottom right: *Primatice* and 95 (?).
BIBLIOGRAPHY: Dimier 1900, p. 424, no. 3; Adhémar 1954, p. 128, pl. 35; Béguin 1967, no. 117; Cordellier 1983–84, no. 212; Arquié-Bruley, Labbé, and Bicart-Sée 1987, vol. 1, repr. no. 82.

Eliezer, sent to Mesopotamia to find a wife for Abraham's son Isaac, meets Rebekah near a well. She gives him and his camels to drink. At this sign, Eliezer recognizes the woman destined for Isaac (Genesis 24:18–20). Through its technique, format, style, and even its historical account, this drawing is the companion piece to *Isaac bénissant Jacob* (Isaac blessing Jacob) (Louvre, Inv. 8512). Dimier catalogued them as original works by Primaticcio, without indicating the date or the destination. According to Adhémar, they are studio models for an unknown patron who "refused them for being too ornate" (1954, p. 128). He situates them in about 1550, when Primaticcio, at the apogee of his career, was decorating the gallery of Ulysses at the castle of Fontainebleau, where he worked from 1541 almost until his death. Mariette mentions copies of two drawings in pen from the Louvre, which he attributes to Luca Penni or "one of the disciples of Primaticcio" (*Abécédario* 4:219). The scene seems to be viewed through a lens that deforms the proportions of the figures.

Marcantonio Raimondi
(about 1470–80 until before 1534)
The Judgment of Paris
37

Le jugement de Pâris. Burin (29.4 × 43.8), with squaring. Signed bottom center: RAPH.VRBI / INVEN / MAF. Inscription on a tablet bottom left: SORDENT PRAE FORMA / INGENIVM. VIRTVS. / REGNA. AVRVM. Louvre Museum, Edmond de Rothschild Collection.

Bartsch 1813, vol. 14, p. 197, no. 245; Passavant 1864, vol. 6, p. 25, no. 137; De Witt 1968, pl. 40; Bianchi 1968, repr. p. 660, fig. 24 and p. 661, fig. 25; Ferrara and Bertelà 1975, repr. no. 401; Gardey, Lambert, and Oberthür 1978, p. 24, repr. no. 114; Bartsch 1978, vol. 26, p. 242, repr. no. 245-I; Müller Hofstede 1989, repr. p. 172ff; Damisch 1992, pp. 61–68, 160ff.

In 1662 Roland Fréart de Chantelou wrote in his *Idée de la perfection de la peinture:* "The first sheet that bore the name Raphael outside Italy, and which let all the painters of his century know that he was their Coriphée, was the noble and famous print of the Judgment of Paris" (Fréart 1662, ed. 1973, p. 23). The composition, which was inspired by two Roman sarcophagi (today in the Médici villa and the Pamphili villa in Rome), found tenacious echoes over the centuries, up to the famous *Déjeuner sur l'herbe* by Manet, which took the group composed of the nymph and the river gods as a model (1863, Paris, Orsay Museum). Raimondi engraved it in about 1517–20, after a drawing by Raphael, which is described by Vasari (ed. 1984, 7:68). That drawing has since vanished. When the gods assembled for the wedding of Thetis and Peleus, Eris (Discord) threw in a golden apple, which was to go to the most beautiful of the three goddesses: Venus, Juno, or Minerva. Mercury took them to Mount Ida, where the shepherd Paris—the son of Priam, sovereign of Troy—was entrusted with the role of judge. According to Apollodorus, Juno promised Paris that, for the price of his vote, he would reign over all men; Minerva promised victory in war; and Venus promised the hand of Helen of Troy (*Bibliothèque,* 2:12, 5ff.). Paris gave the apple to Venus, while Nike, goddess of victory, placed a laurel wreath on the head of the winner. The inscription justifies the judgment: SORDENT PRAE FORMA INGENIVM VIRTVS REGNA AVRVM (Reason, virtue, and the power of gold seem insignificant next to beauty.) All the Olympian gods got together in heaven to attend the event, which would lead to the Trojan war: Apollo in his chariot, the Dioscuri, and Castor and Pollux, the twin sons of Helen, whom Venus had promised to Paris. On the right appears Jupiter, accompanied by Diana. If we are to believe the tradition, this engraving was the first made by Raimondi, Raphael's student, for the public.

Rembrandt Harmensz van Rijn (Rembrandt)
(school of)
(seventeenth century)
Sarah Presenting Hagar to Abraham
95

Sarah présentant Agar à Abraham. Pen and brown ink, brown wash, india ink on sketch in black chalk (25.3 × 18.2). Louvre Museum, Edmond de Rothschild Collection.
BIBLIOGRAPHY: Blum 1939, no. 3, pl. 6–3 (Rembrandt).

Rembrandt Harmensz van Rijn (Rembrandt)
(1606–69)
Hagar at the Fountain
91

Agar à la source. Pen and brown ink, brown and gray wash (19.1 × 22.6).
BIBLIOGRAPHY: Hofstede de Groot 1906, no. 666; Valentiner 1925–34, no. 16; Lugt 1933, no. 1109, p. 2; Benesch 1973, vol. 3, no. 560, pl. 690; Van de Waal 1974, pp. 92, 93, 98; Schatborn 1981, p. 22; Starcky 1988–89, no. 38 (with complete bibliography).

These two sheets illustrate two successive episodes in the story of Hagar, which Rembrandt and his students often treated in their drawings, engravings, and paintings. The aged Abraham had remained childless in the land of Canaan for ten years; his wife, Sarah (or Sarai), in despair about being barren, presents him with her Egyptian slave, Hagar, so that he may make her his concubine: "Behold now, the Lord hath restrained me from bearing: I pray thee, go in unto my maid: it may be that I may obtain children by her" (Genesis 16:2). The first drawing shows Abraham on his bed as Sarah presents him with her slave. Hagar became pregnant, and "when she saw that she had conceived, her mistress was despised in her eyes. . . . And when Sarai dealt hardly with her, she fled from her face. And the angel of the Lord found her by a fountain of water in the wilderness, by the fountain in the way to Shur." He advised her to return to her mistress, saying, "Behold, thou *art* with child, and shalt bear a son, and shalt call his name Ishmael; because the Lord hath heard thy affliction" (Genesis 16:4–11). The angel does not appear in Rembrandt's drawing, which suggests the messenger of God through rays of light falling on Hagar, who is kneeling near the well. There exist two other drawings for the scene of the presentation (Benesch 1973, vol. 4, A35, A 51), which Lugt attributes to Ferdinand Bol (1616–80), as he does the drawing in the Edmond de Rothschild collection. Bol joined Rembrandt's studio soon after 1635 (1933, no. 1205; M. Sérullaz proposes Govaert Flinck as an alternative [handwritten notes]). The authenticity of *Hagar at the Fountain* was also contested as a result of numerous later additions in pen and brush (infrared photography shows inks with different carbon contents), which altered the original character of Rembrandt's drawing. Benesch dates the drawing as 1644–45.

Two Studies of Beggar Woman
82

Deux études de mendiante. Pen and brown ink on paper washed brown (17.5 × 14.0).
BIBLIOGRAPHY: Hofstede de Groot 1906, no. 647; Lugt 1933, no. 1186, pl. 50 (1635–40); Benesch 1973, vol. 2, no. 197, pl. 213 (1632–33); Vogel-Köhn 1981, pp. 52, 54, 59, no. 48; Starcky 1985, pp. 259, 260, 264, fig. 12; Starcky 1988–89, no. 23 (1638–40, with complete bibliography).

Family of Beggars Receiving Alms
67

Famille de mendiants recevant l'aumône. Etching, retouched with drypoint and burin (16.5 × 13.0) on plate. First state. Signed and dated: *Rembrant f. 1648.* Louvre Museum, Edmond de Rothschild Collection.
BIBLIOGRAPHY: Bartsch 1797, p. 157, no. 176; Dutuit 1882, vol. 2, p. 431, no. 172; Hind 1912, p. 137, repr. no. 233; Biörklund and Barnard 1955, p. 95, repr. no. 48-C; Hollstein 1969, vol. 18, no. B176, repr. vol. 19, p. 142; White 1969, vol. 1, pp. 167ff.; vol. 2, p. 258, fig. 249; Hellerstedt 1981, pp. 16ff.; Bevers 1991–92, no. 26.

The theme of beggars occupies an important place in Rembrandt's oeuvre. In Leiden in 1630, he undertook a series of prints of the destitute and of lepers and cripples, which revealed his familiarity with Jacques Callot's tramp cycle, published in Nancy about 1620. But Rembrandt's marginals are never ridiculed or reduced to archetypes, as are Callot's. It is true that the seventeenth century was marked by a growing awareness of pauperism. The studies of the beggar woman asking for alms bears witness to this contemporary character. But, in this image of a family begging, the artist repeats an iconographical tradition characteristic of the beginning of the century: the blind hurdy-gurdy man, already treated by Bellange and Georges de La Tour. The old man in the background holds a hurdy-gurdy (barely visible) and turns its handle. His empty gaze suggests he is blind. As K. J. Hellerstedt has shown, Rembrandt was inspired by the *Vielleur aveugle* (Blind hurdy-gurdy man) painted by Vinckboons (Amsterdam, Rijksmuseum), which he saw in Amsterdam in about 1632 (1981, p. 18, fig. 3). The gesture of the young woman holding out her hand, and her props (the basket and baguette), also characterized the female companion of the blind man in Vinckboons. Benesch links the engraving to another Rembrandt drawing, *Le mendiant aveugle, avec femme et enfants* (The blind beggar with wife and children) (no. 749 recto). In any case, the scene appears to serve as an apologia for Christian charity: one must help indigents to assure one's own salvation through works of mercy (see the engravings by Bosse).

The Naming of John the Baptist
12

L'imposition du nom de saint Jean Baptiste. Pen and brown ink, brown and gray wash (19.9 × 31.4). Inscribed bottom right: *Rembrandt,* in a later hand.
BIBLIOGRAPHY: Hofstede de Groot 1906, no. 601 (1650–55); Valentiner 1925–34, no. 272 (1655); Lugt 1933, no. 1125 (1650–55); Sumowski 1961, p. 18; Bacou 1968, no. 84; Benesch 1973, no. 1007, pl. 1219 (1656).

The image focuses on the old Zacharias, who was struck dumb because he refused to believe he would have a son, despite the prophecy of the angel Gabriel. His wife Elizabeth is holding the child in the chamber. When the prophecy was fulfilled, Zacharias was asked through signs what he wished to call his son, and he wrote on a tablet: "His name is John." According to the Gospel of Luke, "His mouth was opened immediately, and his tongue *loosed,* and he spake, and praised God" (Luke 1:64). At first skeptical about the authenticity of the heightening wash, Benesch came to agree with Lugt's opinion, which holds that the

Rembrandt drawing is a major work in the grand style of his mature years (after 1650).

The Meeting of Ruth and Boaz
80

La rencontre de Ruth et de Booz. Pen and brown ink, brown wash (18.3 × 20.3). Inscribed in pen at bottom right: *Booz rencontre Ruth dans son champ* (Boaz meets Ruth in his field); and: *Rembrandt.*
BIBLIOGRAPHY: Lugt 1933, pl. 6 (1640); Benesch 1973, vol. 3, no. 610, pl. 741 (1648–49).

Ruth the Moabite, widowed and reduced to poverty, goes gleaning behind the harvesters in Boaz's fields, with her mother-in-law, Naomi. Out of charity, Boaz grants her his protection: "Go not to glean in another field, neither go from hence, but abide here fast by my maidens: *Let* thine eyes *be* on the field that they do reap, and go after them" (Ruth 2:8–9). According to the canonical exegesis, the meeting of Ruth and Boaz evokes the union between Jesus and the Church. The drawing was classified as "Rembrandt school" because of the slightly hard style of its figures. But Lugt recognized the hand of the master, which is manifested in the sketch of the summer landscape and in the group of harvesters at rest. Benesch dates the sheet as about 1648–49.

The Good Samaritan
65

Le bon samaritain. Etching, retouched with burin (24.4 × 20.4), with squaring. First state with marks in right margin. Louvre Museum, Edmond de Rothschild Collection.
BIBLIOGRAPHY: Bartsch 1797, p. 93, no. 90; Dutuit 1882, vol. 2, p. 361, no. 75; Hind 1912, p. 104, no. 101; Biörklund and Barnard 1955, p. 50, no. 33A; Hollstein 1969, vol. 18, no. B90 and vol. 19, p. 87; White 1969, vol. 1, p. 192 and vol. 2, p. 260, repr. no. 285; Clark 1976, pp. 806–9, fig. 3.

An engraving after the small painting in the Wallace collection (London) that Rembrandt painted in Leiden in 1630. The painting was certainly inspired by an etching on the same subject by Jan van de Velde (Münz 1952, repr. 2:94). The inscription *Rembrandt inuentor et fecit 1633* on the fourth state of the plate attests to the fact that the artist made an engraving of it after he settled in Amsterdam in 1631. The print adds the realist motif of the dog in a vulgar pose that is hardly biblical. Goethe could not refrain from commenting on it in his study on the artist (*Rembrandt als Denker*). The inn where the good Samaritan takes the waylaid traveler (Luke 10:30–35) is again found in a drawing conserved in the Kunsthalle of Hamburg (Benesch 1954, 2:107, no. 462, pl. 520).

Cristoforo di Michele (Robetta)
(1462–1522)
Plenty
15

L'Abondance. Burin (25.0 × 18.5), with squaring. First state. Louvre Museum, Edmond de Rothschild Collection.
BIBLIOGRAPHY: Bartsch 1811, p. 403, no. 18; Passavant 1864, vol. 5, p. 59, no. 18; Hind 1910, D.2, 13; ex. cat. Cambridge, Mass., 1915, p. 92, repr. no. 28; Hind 1923, repr. no. 29; Hind 1938, vol. 3, D.2.28, p. 291; Levenson 1973, no. 121.

This naked woman burdened with children has elicited many interpretations. Bartsch makes her out to be a Venus surrounded by cupids, which squares poorly with the vegetal symbols. Passavant prefers to see her as a figure of charity with her two children to feed, a canonical attribute of *caritas,* love of one's neighbor. But the tiara of flames, a symbol of divine love, which we find in another of Robetta's engravings devoted to Charity, is missing here (Hind 1938, vol. 3, D.2.25, 1; pl. 288). Hind takes the figure for an allegory of plenty, because of the vase full of flowers that she holds up like a horn. Levenson sees her as the goddess Tellus, or Mother Earth, the nurturing idol, whose symbolism also includes the idea of plenty. The double presence of the ears of corn, in the vase and in the hand of a *putto,* argues for this identification: Tellus sometimes plays the role of Ceres in mythology. The landscape attests to the goldsmith Robetta's admiration for Albrecht Dürer, whose landscape backgrounds he slavishly copied, incorporating them into his own prints. In contrast, the canon of figures is completely Italian. The dead tree, which contrasts with plenty, and whose tablet suggests the name of the artist, was inspired by the Saint Eustachius that Dürer engraved in about 1500 (B. 57). It is commonly inferred from this manifest influence that Robetta's print is subsequent to that date.

Romano (see Pippi)

Félicien Rops
(1833–98)
Satan Sowing the Chaff
18

Satan semant l'ivraie. Engraving with soft varnish (27.8 × 21.0). Bibliothèque Nationale, Print Room.
BIBLIOGRAPHY: Ramiro 1887, vol. 2, pp. 174ff., no. 223; Exsteens 1928, no. 783; Bory 1977, pp. 23ff., no. 520; ex. cat. New York 1983, no. 128.

The first print for the *Sataniques,* a series of five plates that Rops engraved in 1883, during his stay in Bièvres (Essonne). He treated them with soft varnish—not a widespread practice—which he used for most of his engravings. J.-K. Huysmans described the plate, whose subject was inspired by the parable of the grain and the chaff (Matthew 13:24–30): "At night, above sleeping Paris, an immense sower fills the sky; his feet, weighed down by heavy sandals, is resting on the roofs of the right bank and on the summit of the towers of Notre Dame. . . . With one hand Satan is lifting his apron in which larvae of women are swarming and, with the other, he cuts across the firmament with a gesture that throws these seeds of evil haphazardly over the silent city. . . . In examining the horrible face closely, we can discern the cold, decided jubilation of the Devil, who knows the foul virtues of the larvae he is spreading. He also knows that the harvest is sure, and his hideous lips murmur Rogations backward, mockingly inviting his silent Rival to bless these evils of the earth, to consecrate the formidable harvest of crimes that this seed is preparing" (*Certains* [Paris, 1908], cited by Bory 1977, p. 23). In the series of engravings, woman plays the role of the devil's accomplice and victim, in accordance with the age-old tradition: "Through women, Satan attracts men to his line" (Bodin, *De la démonomanie des sorcières* [Rouen, 1604]). One year before the execution of the *Sataniques,* Rops illustrated *Les Diaboliques* by Barbey d'Aurevilly, whom Rops had known in Belgium (1865), and who, with Baudelaire, was his master in "the path of Satanism," to use Huysmans' words.

Francesco de' Rossi (Salviati)
(1510–63)
Prudence Seizing Opportunity
20

La Prudence saisissant l'Occasion. Pen and brown ink, brown wash, heightened with white on blue paper (43.2 × 24.0). At bottom right, inscription in pen, cut off: *Frances*[co] *Salviat*[ti].
BIBLIOGRAPHY: Monbeig Goguel 1971, p. 141, repr. no. 176; Nova 1980, p. 60, n. 59.

This copy can be linked to the allegorical group decorating the Sala dell'Udenza (audience room) at the Palazzo Vecchio in Florence, which Salviati painted between 1543 and 1545 for Cosimo I de Médicis (Allegri and Cecchi 1980, p. 41, no. 2). Prudence, one of the four cardinal virtues (with Strength, Justice, and Temperance), like Janus, possesses two faces looking in opposite directions, which attest to her lucidity. The serpent surrounding her waist illustrates an iconographical tradition going back to the Gospel of Matthew: "Be ye therefore wise as serpents" (10:16). The attributes of Opportunity (*Kairos* for the Greeks, *Occasio* for the Romans) are the lock of hair and the globe, symbol of inconstancy, which is also expressed in her unstable pose. In contrast to Muller, Farinati, and Huret (see related entries), Salviati shows her with a helmet. In about 1554, at the Sacchetti palace in Rome, the artist painted an allegory of Fortune, also wearing a helmet, and who, according to C. Dumont, borrowed the features of Minerva (Nova 1980, p. 34). Prudence occupies the role Mercury plays in the drawing by Farinati. The moral seems to be the same: whoever is prudent will receive the favors of fortune. Soon afterward, the motif of Prudence seizing Opportunity became the emblem *(impresa)* of Pope Julius III (1550–55). A drawing by Salviati, recently exhibited at Colnaghi's, represents the same subject under the sign of Capricorn, the emblem of Cosimo I (New York and London 1991, no. 4).

Martin Schongauer
(about 1450–91)
Saint Martin
3

Saint Martin. Burin (15.2 × 10.4), with squaring. Monogrammed *M* with oblique downstrokes, bottom center. First state. Louvre Museum, Edmond de Rothschild Collection.
BIBLIOGRAPHY: Bartsch 1818, vol. 6, p. 145, no. 57; Lehrs 1925, vol. 5, p. 271, no. 62; Minott 1971, p. 47, repr. 106, no. 62; Bartsch 1980, vol. 8, p. 265, repr. no. 57; Hébert 1982, p. 78, repr. no. 252.

The Golden Legend tells the story of Martin, a Roman soldier who shared his coat with a beggar on a winter day in Amiens. The saint's pose was directly inspired by the famous sculpture on the memorial portal of the cathedral of Mayence, which was dedicated to Saint Martin. The sculpted effect is rendered in the print through the use of cuts and countercuts, which model the draperies. According to the chronology proposed by A. Châtelet (ex. cat. Colmar 1991, p. 244), this is a work of the artist's central period, between 1473 and 1480, characterized by small format productions. The print of Saint Martin belongs to a series of four saints (Lehrs 1925, vol. 5, nos. 59, 67, 70). In his early works (1470–72), Schongauer signed using a monogram *M* with straight downstrokes, but here he uses the *M* with oblique downstrokes. The cross that separates the two letters is decorated with an arc on one side, which no doubt evokes the crescent moon belonging to the coat of arms of the Schongauer family.

Ottavio Semino
(1520?–1604)
Sophonisba Receiving the Hemlock
35

Sophonisbe recevant la ciguë. Pen and brown ink, brown wash on black chalk. Squared with red chalk (21.1 × 29.3).

The scene, taken from Livy's *Ab Urbe condita libri*

30.15) shows Sophonisba, queen of Numidia, receiving the hemlock that her second husband Masinissa sent to her. Fearing that Sophonisba would incite her husband to join the Carthaginian alliance, Scipio asked for her extradition to Rome. Masinissa preferred to poison the queen, to spare her such a fate without opposing the orders of the Roman general. Sophonisba accepts the messenger's lethal gift, to the laments of her servants. The theme enjoyed great success in baroque paintings, with Rembrandt in the lead (Madrid, Prado), and also inspired numerous tragedies (Mairet 1634; P. Corneille 1663; Voltaire 1770). We do not know the date and destination of the drawing by Semino, a history painter who joined Luca Cambiaso to found a school of painting and drawing. He is known for, among other things, the decor of the Doria palace, one of his best Genoese works.

Jan van der Straet (Stradanus)
(1523–1605)
Saint John Gualbert Distributing Grain to the People
43

Saint Jean Gualbert fait distribuer du grain au peuple. Pen and brown ink, brown wash, heightened with white (22.5 × 16.6).

BIBLIOGRAPHY: Lugt 1968, p. 118, repr. no. 559; Van Sasse van Ysselt 1987, p. 154, fig. 11.

This drawing is part of a series of illustrations of the life of Saint John Gualbert (985–1073), who was a Bendictine monk in San Miniato of Florence, before founding a new order in the valley of Vallombrosa. D. van Sasse van Ysselt discovered eleven drawings and two engravings from the same series. The Cooper-Hewitt Museum and the Pierpont Morgan Library in New York possess thirteen preliminary studies in pen. Owing to their autograph inscriptions, these studies allowed Van Sasse van Ysselt to identify the subject (1987, pp. 148–70, pl. 1–19). The source is a saint's biography, published in Florence in 1583 by the monk Eudosio Loccatelli. The drawing shows the miracle of the multiplication of grain, which the saint, visible on the left in front of the convent of Vallombrosa, has distributed to the people during a famine. An inscription by Baldinucci on the old mounting identifies the monk as Peter Ignus, confrère of John Gualbert, a name that Lugt accepts only with reservations (1986, 117ff.). When Stradanus executed these works in Florence toward the end of the sixteenth century, the city was experiencing a true cult of the saint, whose relics are conserved in the Santa Trinità church.

Philip II Receiving the Tribute of Malta
8

Philippe II recevant l'hommage de Malte. Pen and brown ink, brown wash, heightened with white, on sketch in black chalk on ochre paper (32.0 × 48.3). Signed bottom center: *prassia / 156[5] della Strada fiamingho invento.* Inscribed left: *figurata p[er] vise / Re di / sisila.*

BIBLIOGRAPHY: Lugt 1968, p. 120, repr. no. 569; Pillsbury and Caldwell 1974, no. 22; Van Sasse van Ysselt 1990, pp. 154ff., fig. 5.

The model for a painting decorating the triumphal arch erected near the Strozzi palace for Joanna of Austria's arrival in Florence on 16 December 1565. She was the wife of Francesco I de Médicis and sister of Emperor Maximilian II. This short-lived decor was executed by the members of the Accademia del Disegno under the direction of Vasari, following the iconographical program of Vincenzo Borghini. Stradanus, who collaborated with Vasari on various projects between 1550 and 1570, was assigned to execute several paintings on the arch, to glorify the Habsburgs. The drawing corresponds to the one that decorated the central arcade, on the rear face of the triumphal arch, as G. B. Cini mentions in his description of Joanna's entrance into the city. Vasari published the description in the second edition of his *Vite* (ed. 1906, 8:543ff.). The woman who sports the Maltese cross on her breastplate is an allegorical figure for the island: she holds the *corona obsidionalis* (crown of siege) or *corona graminea* (crown of Gramineae), which cities in Roman antiquity offered the general who delivered them from siege. Thus the allegorical figure of Malta, surrounded by knights, offers the crown to Philip II, king of Spain. It was through his support that, in 1565, Don Garcia of Toledo, viceroy of Sicily, was able to liberate the island besieged by the Turks. The liberator is to the left of the monarch, as the coat of arms on his seat and the mention of his title attest: *vise Re di sisila* (viceroy of Sicily).

Anton Van Dyck
(1599–1641)
The Descent of the Holy Spirit
90

La descente du Saint-Esprit. Pen and brown ink, brown wash. Inscribed in pen toward center with the number *226* and, at bottom toward right, the number *8*. On verso, sketch in black chalk of a reclining nude, and, in pen, of drapery (20.7 × 28.0).

BIBLIOGRAPHY: Tauzia 1881, no. 177; Guiffrey 1882, repr. p. 33; Lugt 1949, no. 588, pl. 54; Vey 1958, p. 98; Vey 1962, vol. 1, no. 69; vol. 2, figs. 90, 93; Roy 1980, p. 118.

One of the first efforts in view of the painting of the Pentecost ordered from the painter by the Bridgetines of Hoboken (near Antwerp), which is today the castle of Sans Souci in Potsdam. Van Dyck evokes the famous episode from Acts 2:1–41 through powerful effects of light and a vehemence of gestures on the part of the disciples who surround the Virgin. The scene takes place in the dark and is marked by two columns. There exist several preparatory studies for the painting (Brunswick, Herzog Anton-Ulrich Museum; Weimar, Schlossmuseum; Vienna, Albertina), all of which have in common the angular style and violent lighting of his earliest drawings. They were executed over two years at the beginning of the artist's career, between the time he obtained his master's degree (February 1618) and his departure for England (1620).

Dirk Jacobsz Vellert
(active in Antwerp from 1511 to 1544)
Appearance of the Son of Man amid the Seven Candlesticks
89

Apparition du Fils de l'Homme entre les sept candélabres. Louvre Museum, Edmond de Rothschild Collection. Pen and black ink, gray wash, on strokes in black chalk (32.4 × 27.7). Signed at bottom in pen and black ink with the artist's monogram. Inscribed at bottom in pen and brown ink, probably by another hand: APOCA / SEVEN CANDELA / REN EN STERRE SEVE, / SIJN DE HEILIGE KER / CKE VNIVERSALE, / I 2 3 / SII WORDT DOER TSNYDEN / WOIRT GODS GESTRAFT BEREVE / EN OOCK GETROOST, GESTER / CKT, VERHVECHT TE MALE [Seven candelabra and seven stars are the holy universal church, etc.]. Inscribed on the blade: VERBUM DEI (Word of God). Numbered above the circular composition: 3.
BIBLIOGRAPHY: Beets 1906–8 and 1912, vol. 6, pp. 133ff; vol. 7, pp. 105ff.; vol. 10, pp. 89ff.; vol. 18, pp. 129ff.

The Edmond de Rothschild collection conserves a series of seventeen circular compositions by Vellert, illustrating the Revelation of Saint John (Inv. 589 to 605 D.R.). The present drawing shows the vision of the saint, who is in the foreground, as Revelation described it: "And being turned, I saw seven golden candlesticks; and in the midst of the seven candlesticks *one* like unto the Son of man. . . . His head and *his* hairs *were* white like wool, as white as snow; and his eyes *were* as a flame of fire. . . . And he had in his right hand seven stars: and out of his mouth went a sharp twoedged sword" (Revelation 1:12–16). A voice then revealed the mystery of the seven candlesticks, which represent the seven churches of Asia or the universal church; the seven stars are "the angels of the seven churches" (1:20). Vellert figures the scene in a smaller format, with variants, to the right of the composition. The caption spells out in condensed form the most striking passages. According to Beets, this series of drawings was executed in 1521 under the influence of Dürer's *Apocalypse* (B. 60 to 75), which Vellert, an engraver, draftsman, and artist in stained glass from Antwerp, met during Dürer's brief stays in that city, in January and May 1521. The Son of Man's pose is an almost literal quotation of Dürer's wood engraving on the same subject (B. 62).

Tommaso Vincidor
(d. about 1536)
The Wedding of Alexander and Roxane
7

Les noces d'Alexandre et Roxane. Pen and brown ink, brown wash, heightened with white, on two sheets of brown paper joined at the middle. Squared in black chalk. Later heightening with white by Michel II Corneille (28.5 × 35.4).
BIBLIOGRAPHY: Popham and Wilde 1949, p. 316; Oberhuber 1967, no. 123, p. 94 (Vincidor); Golahny 1983, no. 8, p. 673 (after Raphael); Lossky 1983, p. 23 (Raphael studio); Mitsch 1983, under no. 42, p. 126; Massari 1985, under no. 10/1, p. 160 (Vincidor); Bernini Pezzini 1985, under no. 10/3, p. 161; Monbeig Goguel 1988, p. 823 (Vincidor); Sérullaz 1988, no. 42 (Vincidor).

This illustration of a famous episode in the life of Alexander the Great, related by Lucian in *Herodotus* (4–6), shows the moment when the hero gives his crown to Roxane, daughter of the Bactrian baron, Oxyartes. Roxane was captured by the Greeks with her father and became the wife of the conqueror. The nude ephebe who points to the future queen is Hymen, god of marriage. He is accompanied by Hephaestion, the companion of Alexander, who holds the torch, a classical symbol for the fires of love. A group of *putti* frolic around the newlyweds, not without attempting to adorn Roxane. The sheet is a copy after a lost drawing by Raphael for the fresco decor of the Alexander and Roxanne Room at the casino of Farnesina, which Giovanni Antonio Bazzi, called Il Sodoma, painted in 1512, in place of the master and in a different spirit. The *putto* flying over Alexander is directly inspired by a winged child in the loggia of Psyche (1517) at the Farnesina. Oberhuber was the first to attribute the drawing to the Bolognese Vincidor, who was a student of Raphael.

David Vinckboons
(1576–1632)
The Ungrateful Children
64

Les enfants ingrats. Pen and brown ink, brown wash, passed over with tip (32.0 × 47.0). Inscribed at bottom left, in pen and brown ink, in ancient handwriting: *D. Vinkabon;* and, on verso, in the same hand: *Kinderen ryk gevond in syn do. [?] willen haar onder niet kennen* (children richly lodged in their [?] do not want to recognize their parents).
BIBLIOGRAPHY: Benesch 1976, pp. 166–69, pl. 40; Klessmann 1978, no. 13; Wegner and Pée 1980, p. 92, no. 44.

Illustrations of the popular theme of ungrateful children who reject their poor parents who have come begging at their door. From the end of the sixteenth century, this moral episode enjoyed a great vogue in Amsterdam, where the family of Vinckboons settled in 1591, after emigrating to northern Netherlands in 1586. Bartholomaeus Dolendo had engraved a plate on the same subject in 1590. According to Bernoulli, it was the inspiration for the present composition, which Wegner and Pée situate in about 1608–9. At the same time (1609), Claes Jansz. Visscher executed an engraving in Amsterdam of *Ungrateful Children,* with a moral caption that gives it a contemporary interpretation. It warns parents that their excessive selflessness will not be rewarded when they are old and poor. An inscription on the verso of the drawing paraphrases this admonishing commentary. Benesch underscores Vinckboons's activity as draftsman for the print (1957, pp. 285ff.). The two principal engravers for his drawings were Claes Jansz. Visscher and Joannes van Londerseel. The tip marks attest to the fact that this drawing was engraved. There exists, in fact, a reversed print by Hessel Gerrits, an engraver from Amsterdam who was a contemporary of Vinckboons (Hollstein, 7:107, no. 16). The Albertina in Vienna conserves a copy after that drawing (Benesch 1976, fig. 2).

Photographs

by Philippe Néagu and Françoise Heilbrun

Circle of Louis Robert
(second half of the nineteenth century)
Musician Receiving Alms (1865–70)
83

Musicienne recevant l'aumône. Print on albumen paper from a glass negative, coated with collodion, mounted on cardboard (14.6 × 10.3). Orsay Museum.

The imperial factory of ceramics in Sèvres was a key site for French photography, with Victor Regnault (1810–78) and Louis Robert (1811–82), two great "primitives" of the 1850s, directing the establishment. In addition to landscapes of the Saint-Cloud forest and the banks of the Seine, they each made an admirable series of portraits on paper negatives of artists, scientists, and technicians at the factory. The acquisition of five albums (about four hundred images) by the Orsay Museum in 1984 on the private lives of the Sèvres staff in the early 1870s attests to the survival of a studio over which Louis Robert still exercised artistic and technical authority. The central character of this living report was Elisa Le Guay, a scene painter at the factory, who may have collected the images and who was the owner of the albums. In addition to individual portraits, group portraits, and motif studies (patches of nature, rustic objects), these albums include a few tableaux vivants, in which Elisa Le Guay, no doubt the scriptwriter if not the director, often participated. Here, we see a woman and adolescent girl about to give alms to a street musician, an elegant Bohemian woman portrayed by Elisa Le Guay, who had a delicate profile and grave face. While these playlets still belong to the tradition of the romantic print, certain group portraits suggest analogies to Claude Monet's *Femmes au jardin* (Women in the garden) (1867, Orsay Museum), especially in the free arrangement of the figures. These images, intended for private use, possess a freshness of inspiration and technical composition of figures that is lacking in productions of this type by professional photographers. As a result, they are an important witness to nineteenth-century French photography.—P. N.

Anonymous photographer
(active in Poland in the early twentieth century)

Waiting in Line (1914–19?)
79

La file d'attente. Silver print (11.8 × 16.3). Pho 1991–23 (58).

Little Girl against a Wall (1914–19?)
75

Fillette adossée à un mur. Silver print (13.9 × 87.0). Pho 1991–23 (20). Orsay Museum.

Parallel to the Photo-Secessionist movement, which began in the last decade of the nineteenth century, social reportage developed in America and Europe. With *photojournalism,* it acquired a new dimension during the interwar period. Through the violence of its subjects and the situations it denounced, this unsparing photographic school appears today as a visually rich field in the history of photography, whether one thinks of Lewis Hine's images of child labor in the United States or the arrival of emigrants to Ellis Island, of Hermann Drawe's photographs of the lives of the homeless in Vienna, or of Heinrich Zille's images of the poor neighborhoods of Berlin.

The two anonymous images presented here belong to a set of seventy-six photographs retracing the conditions of existence among members of a Jewish community in Poland. These people might be immigrants who fled the Ukraine following the 1919 pogroms and received aid from the Jewish Distribution Comity, a charity organization created in the United States in 1914 (oral communication from Laurence Cigale). In addition to the group scenes—crowds in the streets, children in Talmud classes, families in their homes—this collection includes isolated figures. We do not know whether all the images are related to the same historical event. The collection also includes images of even more pathos (Néagu 1992, 98–99), though not foreign to the spirit that characterizes the genre scene.

This collection belonged to the archives of the Polish painter of Jewish extraction Henryk Berlewi (1894–1967), a precursor of the cinematic arts who spent most of his artistic career in Paris but who lived in his native country from 1913 to 1922.—P. N.

Julia Margaret Cameron
(1815–79)
King Cophetua and the Beggar Maid
73

Proof on albumen paper from a glass negative, coated with wet collodion, glued onto blue cardboard, and surrounded by gold string. Signed at bottom right on the print; titled at bottom middle. Inscription handwritten by the artist at bottom left: *From Life Registered Photograph Copyright.* To the left of the mounting is affixed a facsimile of the autograph manuscript of the Tennyson poem "The Beggar Maid" (32.0 × 26.3). Orsay Museum.
BIBLIOGRAPHY: Cameron 1875, vol. 2, pl. 8; Millard 1973.

The Idylls of the King by Tennyson (1809–1892), inspired by the medieval legends of the fifteenth-century poet Thomas Malory, was a major iconographical source for pre-Raphaelite painters such as Rossetti, Burne-Jones, and Aubrey Beardsley. In fact, the poem was as important an influence as the work of Malory himself. The "poet laureate" Tennyson, a close friend of J. M. Cameron, asked the photographer to illustrate his Arthurian collection, composed between 1842 and 1859, and other poems for which he had a fondness (e.g., *Maud*). Of the some two hundred photographs by Cameron, twenty-six were chosen as illustrations for a limited number of copies. Only five of these survive today. The only copy in France, conserved in the Orsay Museum, was dedicated to Maria Jackson, J. M. Cameron's cousin and the mother of Julia Jackson (one of the photographer's favorite models). Julia Jackson was the mother of Virginia Woolf, who was interested enough in photography to publish a book on the Victorian portrait in 1926, and a charming play, *Freshwater* (from the name of the house where Cameron practiced her art on the island of Wight), in which Cameron is a central character, beside Tennyson and Watts. This photograph shows the moment when King Cophetua meets the beggar maid, barefoot and in rags. He decides to make her his queen because she is more beautiful than day and possesses the grace of an angel. The photograph has the merit of faithfully illustrating Tennyson's poem and demonstrates the artist's psychological acuity; Cameron artfully arranges the characters not as a portrait but as a fiction.—P. N.

Little Girl in Prayer (1871)
97

Fillette en prière. Proof on albumen paper from a glass negative, coated with collodion, glued onto blue cardboard. Inscription under the print: *d'après nature Photographe registré. Copyright Julia Margaret Cameron. 1871;* and at bottom right: *Présenté à Gustave Doré par Julia Margaret Cameron* [Presented to Gustave Doré by Julia Margaret Cameron]. Orsay Museum.
BIBLIOGRAPHY: Weaver 1984, p. 29; Rosenberg 1990–91, p. 246.

J. M. Cameron discovered her vocation as a photographer late in life and, as a result, produced one of the most innovative oeuvres in the history of the medium. In challenging the commonly acknowledged documentary function of photography, she resolutely set it off on a path that had seemed prohibited to it, that of fiction and the fable. She revolutionized the art of the portrait. Her powerfully lyrical art is purely a product of the Victorian sensibility and owes a great deal to pre-Raphaelite painting (she was linked to certain painters in the movement and left behind admirable effigies of them), but she distinguished herself from it through her aesthetics of the soft focus and her use of close-ups, which anticipate developments in the language of cinematography.

Woman and child, those two oppressed beings of Victorian society, are favorite characters in her idealized universe. Whether the figure is treated in isolation or in a group, it often serves as an allegorical expression that is classical or (especially) Christian in nature. The themes of the Madonna and Child, of the Annunciation, of prayer, and the figures of prophets and sibyls attest to the artist's eye for Italian painting from the end of the fifteenth and the beginning of the sixteenth centuries. Above all, they bear witness to the ideal of innocence and purity that she sought to translate into the medium of photography. In another image of the little girl in prayer (Néagu 1992, p. 65), the softness of the face, the decorative yet abstract treatment of the fabrics, and the violence of the lighting bear witness to a more experimental approach. In contrast, this photograph, which was given to Gustave Doré, focuses primarily on the linearity of the features.—P. N.

Gertrude Käsebier
(1852–1934)
The Manger
46

Photograph on Japanese vellum, developed from the original negative (21.3 × 15.0). Sheet (29.2 × 20.2). Orsay Museum.
BIBLIOGRAPHY: *Camera Work* 1903, ill. 2, part 1; *Camera Work* (Kraus Reprint) 1969; Margolis 1978, p. 1; Keller 1991, p. 263.

Following the appearance, in the last decade of the nineteenth century, of secessionist movements intending to revalorize photographic art and secure its recognition, lush magazines appeared in Europe and the United States to defend this "pictorialist" aesthetics. *Camera Work,* created by Alfred Stieglitz (1864–1946), himself a great photographer, was the most remarkable of these publications, as much for the care taken in the illustrations (photogravures that had the value of the original image, as far as the artists were concerned), as for the importance of the photographers worldwide who contributed to it. The militant magazine was of an exceptional longevity, active from 1903 to 1917. Although dedicated to photography, it was also the first in America to publish paintings, sculptures, and drawings by the French avant-garde (Rodin, Matisse, Picasso, etc.), since it conceived of photography in its relations to the other arts.

Gertrude Käsebier was one of the most prolific artists of the "pictorialist" movement in the Americas, though she was uneven in her inspiration. She made numerous intimist portraits, which secured her a great reputation. Among other things, she photographed scenes of motherhood conceived as moments of everyday life, even while making clear reference to the motif of the Virgin and Child. Mary, dressed in a virginal robe and seated in an authentic stable, is contemplating Jesus. The representation of the stable is the only element that may give the conventional image a suggestion of modernity.—P. N.

Paul-Emile Miot
(1827–1900)
Gougou, Prince of the Mic-Macs
84

Gougou prince des Mic-Macs (Prince Gougou, last representative of the Mic-Mac Indian tribe), Orsay Museum. Print, cut and bent at all four corners, on albumen paper from a glass negative, coated with collodion (16.0 × 12.1). BIBLIOGRAPHY: Gobineau 1861, pp. 60–62; Gobineau 1863, pp. 415–16.

Miot had a brilliant career in the navy, which he joined in 1846, creating a photographic laboratory in 1857. In March 1859, he reported on Newfoundland, no doubt at the request of the count de Gobineau, then charged with a diplomatic mission to assign fishing rights to Newfoundland. The report included, among other things, some portraits of Indians, taken on Miot's sloop. Gobineau had several of them reproduced as wood engravings to illustrate the article he devoted to the expedition in the magazine *Le Tour du Monde.* In his narrative *Le voyage à Terre-Neuve* (Voyage to Newfoundland), Gobineau relates his encounter with the descendants of ancient Acadia, at the port of Sidney in Nova Scotia: "While I had encountered their kin in the past, namely, the still victorious descendants of the ancient Mongols and Tartars, conquerors of Turkestan, India, and Persia . . . the first specimens of that ancient race whom I met certainly did not present a heroic aspect. . . . In comparing these poor people's past to their present, I went away rather moved by the sadness in their eyes, their fading smiles, their expression of resignation." In *Le Tour du Monde,* Gobineau describes Prince Gougou in particular: "The savages had come down from the interior [of Sidney], in greater number than we had ever seen them, and their wigwams extended into the neighboring woods. Groups of these good folk moved about in the streets, selling their baskets and sometimes asking for alms. This allowed us to meet an important personage named Gougou, who was nothing less than the last representative of the ancient royal family of the Mic-Macs. We were assured that he enjoyed great consideration among his compatriots. He knew what was due him in deference to the bloodline from which he stemmed; but he was particularly plagued by worries about his very meager means. . . . A few pennies offered him to buy tobacco, which he eagerly accepted, began our acquaintance. Of the whole band, this prince was indisputably the most neglectful of his appearance. At all times, in fact, he wore a very frayed black suit, open in more than one place, with only a single button remaining on it. His pants were in complete disarray."—F. H.

Georges Henry Seeley
(1880–1955)
The Tribute (about 1907)
28

Print on tinted silver paper (42.0 × 34.5). Orsay Museum.

Georges Seeley, a still-life painter and amateur photographer, became a member of the Photo-Secessionist group led by Alfred Stieglitz, and published numerous photographs in *Camera Work* in 1907–8. His oeuvre includes some admirable landscapes where the aesthetics of the soft focus, pushed to its paroxysm, and the choice of point of view open an original path for abstract photography. His art belongs entirely to Symbolism, especially in the treatment of the figure and the dreamlike feeling that emanates from his best images. *The Tribute* participates in this "pictorialist" lyricism with its timeless feminine figure moving through a shimmering landscape, owing to its use of a subtle focusing technique.—P. N.

Mallarmé's "Coup de dés"
by Bertrand Marchal

Stéphane Mallarmé
(1842–98)
Un coup de dés jamais n'abolira le hasard (A throw of the dice will never abolish chance)
93

Corrected proofs in a folder and mosaic case belonging to Monique Mathieu (38.2 × 29.5; 12 p.).

By 1897, poetry had been experiencing a "crise de vers" for ten years, leading to the revendication of free verse. In that year, an unprecedented poem appeared in the May issue of *Cosmopolis,* a "work of an entirely new character," in the words of the magazine itself. The magazine was trying to fend off the foreseeable protests by its readers, first, by preceding "Un coup de dés jamais n'abolira le hasard" with an author's note in the form of "operating instructions," and second, by publishing an "Apologia from the Editor." Yet this first state of "Coup de dés" did not give a true picture of the innovation involved. Although the text itself was already nearly definitive, its distribution in space remained confined to a single page, due to the constraints of the magazine. An essential part of the poem's originality was thus sacrificed, and only its publication in book form could guarantee a realization true to the poet's wishes—provided, at least, that a publisher and printer capable of giving form to this new poetic object could be found. At the end of 1896, the art dealer Ambroise Vollard let Mallarmé know of his desire to publish something he had written, with illustrations by the painter Redon. He wanted to make it "the most beautiful edition in the world." As soon as "Coup de dés" appeared in *Cosmopolis,* the preparations began for what was supposed to be the genuine edition. Vollard turned to the services of the printer Didot with that purpose in mind.

For the occasion, Mallarmé produced a life-size manuscript, with very precise indications concerning the fonts to be used, and received the first proofs in the beginning of July. But the unprecedented problems posed by the composition of the text as a two-page spread, which required rigorous alignment, increased the number of proofs. Although he declared he was unsatisfied with these proofs, Mallarmé generously distributed sets to his friends. It was by this means that the set of proofs exhibited here, no doubt one of the last, fell into the hands of a privileged reader, Paul Valéry. In May 1898, the edition was still being discussed in a letter to Vollard, but at that date Mallarmé set to work once more on *Hérodiade.* When he died in September 1898, "Coup de dés" had still not appeared. It was finally published only in 1914, not by Vollard but by Gallimard—in Elzévir type rather than Didot—and without Redon's lithographs.

Much has been written about "Coup de dés," and there has been much debate about its relation to the "Grand Oeuvre," "an orphic explanation of the Earth" that is discussed in an autobiographical letter to Verlaine. What is certain is that Mallarmé was experimenting with a new form that established poetry in *space* and that took its cue from music. In the all-too-rare commentaries he left behind (the preface to the *Cosmopolis* and two letters to Gide and Camille Mauclair), the poet particularly insisted on the novelty of the pagination and the typographical composition, which makes the poem a true score, as well as a generalized ideogram, or what he calls a print: "I believe," he wrote to Mauclair, "that every sentence or thought, if it has a rhythm, must model it on the object it aims at, and reproduce, thrown bare, immediately, as if spurting into the mind, a bit of the attitude of that object in relation to the all. Literature thus makes *its proof:* there is no other reason to write on paper."

At once poem, score, and painting in motion, "Coup de dés," according to Valéry's expression,[1] was able "to elevate . . . a page to the power of the starry sky." It finally realized, with the resources of poetry alone and exclusively within the—mental—space of vellum, the "Fable, virgin of everything, place, time, and person over and above, . . . the Fable written on the page of Heaven." In 1885, Mallarmé had opposed that notion of fable to Wagner's mythology, with its theatrical and musical synthesis of the arts.

1. Valéry was no doubt one of the first, if not the first, to contemplate this "act of insanity," but the account he gave of his last visit to Mallarmé on 14 July 1898 (where he speaks of the "great edition put together at Lahure," when it was in fact Didot) is unreliable.

Two Drawings by Antonin Artaud
by Agnès de la Beaumelle

Antonin Artaud
(1896–1948)
The Theater of Cruelty
(about March 1946)
5

Le théâtre de la cruauté. Crayon and colored chalks (62.0 × 46.0). Signed at bottom right. The title is inscribed at the top and bottom of the drawing. At top left, the given name *Catherine.* Private collection.

The Inca
(about March 1946)
4

L'Inca. Colored chalks (62.0 × 46.0). Signed lower right. Top left, the given name *Elah.* Private collection.
BIBLIOGRAPHY: Thévenin and Derrida 1986, p. 262, no. 63.

"Ce qui est vraiment le théâtre, / c'est faire trisser le son / jusqu'à ce que la fibre de la vie grince" [What is truly theater, / is to sound thrice / until the fiber of life creaks].[1]

For the author of *The Theater of Cruelty,* an impossible project that remained at the state of theoretical writing—still dazzling today—the time had come to live in the very site of his psychic body, the true "theater of cruel treatment."[2] These were years of bodily collapse and mental disaster, of psychiatric internment in the hospital in Rodez (from February 1943 to May 1946), where he underwent the ordeal of electroshock treatments. To sound thrice: the work of breath and voice impresses meaning-making vibrations, rhythms, modulations, and intonations on this veritable flood of words and signs that fill the schoolboy notebooks one after the other. Like the written text (which is also a fully oral text, with its balanced undulations, its cries of aggravation, its glossolalia), drawings ("written" drawings, adds Artaud) are a true *ex-pression* (in the first and second meanings of the term), expulsed with all the force of breath and gesture, which set off and fill up the pencil. They are emissions of pictograms: at times, they are perfectly sharp and precise formal elocutions, at other times exorbitant exhortations, projections of coarse and brutal signs. "There is a kind of moral music in my drawings, which I made by experiencing my strokes not only in my hand, but also in the breath rattling my windpipe, and in my masticating teeth."[3] That graphic expression is altogether *acted out (actée)* (perhaps even more on loose pages than in the margins of a notebook) and pushed to the point where "the fiber of life creaks." Like the act of writing, the practice and mastery of that form of expression are, for Antonin Artaud, so many acts—imprecations, exorcisms—necessary in the struggle against corporeal and mental disintegration, the struggle against death, so many "forced" efforts to pillory the residue of his splintered being, to reorganize a lost or destroyed integrity and identity.

This practice consists in "frenzying the subjectile" (forcener le subjectile), as Jacques Derrida magnificently wrote.[4] This does not only mean mistreating or "spoiling" this "subjectile" denounced by Antonin Artaud—that is, quality paper, acquired language, accepted forms, the inert substance of past and future layers that swathe the mind—and imposing upon it the soundings of this "projectile," the writing or drawing pencil (the mallet against the block). It also means eliciting the cry from that other—even more hateful—subjectile, the vile thingness of man, extracting the truth of his "innate" being, his "beingness" *(êtreté).* "And this agile-clumsy act of force is destined to give birth to the innate, with forceps if necessary":[5] This is an act of second birth, a "revendication" of birth.

To consider the set of drawings executed in Rodez: the first, originally titled *Les canines cercueil* (The canines coffin)[6] ("four coffins in the form of a wine cork, with the heads of the four beings I love most in the world, but where are they today? Tell me where, in what country, is Flora the beautiful Roman")[7] and later titled, precisely, *The Theater of Cruelty,* constitutes one of the most significant "documents" ("clumsily drawn so that the gaze that looks upon them will fall") of his frenzied efforts. The stumbling pencil and the lamentation make what he calls "totems of being" appear on the paper: stretched-out architectures of bones, dismembered stakes or piles of hieroglyphic signs (like the totemic trees of the Tarahumaras), faces of tutelary women, with each shape inserted into a coffin with sharp points, coffins that are so many canines screeching from "the jaws of his brain," from which "the dramatic larva of his thought" has escaped, or so many "revelations" of this new

1. Antonin Artaud, *Oeuvres complètes* (Gallimard), 25:117.
2. Excerpted from a text that appeared in *Le Disque Vert* 4 (November–December 1953): 40–41.
3. Artaud, *Oeuvres complètes,* 21:265.
4. Paule Thévenin and Jacques Derrida, *Antonin Artaud: Dessins et portraits* (NRF-Gallimard, 1986), 55.
5. Ibid., 99.
6. The drawing entitled "Les canines cercueil" appears on the seventh list of the Rodez drawings established by Antonin Artaud in the notebook for the second half of April 1946 (*Oeuvres complètes,* 21:707). It appears under the title *Le théâtre de la cruauté* on his list of drawings to be exhibited at the Galerie Pierre Loeb in July 1947.
7. Letter from Antonin Artaud to Dr. Deqreker, 22 March 1946 (*Oeuvres complètes,* 11:206).

theater of revendication lived by the man who was to write *Le retour d'Artaud le Mômo* (The return of Artaud the mummy).

"And theater is the gangling puppet that musics with trunks by metal barbed barbs keeps us in a state of war against the man who corseted us" (Et le théâtre est ce pantin dégingandé qui musique de troncs par barbes métalliques de barbelés nous maintient en état de guerre contre l'homme qui nous corsetait).[8] In the drawing entitled *The Inca,* Antonin Artaud represents himself, this time at the very site of the subjectile, within the heart or rather the head of the king of the Incas, who, in a savage burst of blue and blood red ochre lines, of night and sun, seems to act out his insurrectional power as an innate being, half-dog, half-bird, master of the instruments of torture, of members divided up into sections or stumps, of smashed coffins, of all the playthings of crime: a cruel and clownish puppet in ridiculous armor. The drawing, it too "voluntarily slapdash, thrown onto the page in contempt for shapes and strokes, to show contempt for the idea behind it and thus to make it fall,"[9] seems here to fulfill the function of a barbarously theatrical pictogram. It is a tattoo on paper that claims to be the self-presentation, merely sketched out but still operative, of a body both grotesque and glorious, whose splendor may reside in the very ruin of its exhibition.

8. Ibid., 22:277.

9. Ibid., 20:170–73, commentary on the drawing *La maladresse sexuelle de Dieu* (Rodez, February 1946).

Eisenstein and the Faces of Ivan

by Pierre Coural

Sergey Mikhaylovich Eisenstein (1898–1948) *Ivan the Terrible: The Shower of Gold* 11

Ivan le Terrible: La pluie d'or. Still photograph from the film *Ivan the Terrible,* 35 mm black and white and color, music by Sergey Prokofiev, cinematography by Eduard Tisse and Andrei Moskvin, with Nikolai Cherkassov as Ivan IV.

S. M. Eisenstein was stage designer at the Meyerhold theater before working with Lupu-Pick, the great master of German expressionism, in films such as *The Rail* (1921) and *The Night of the Feast of Saint Sylvester.* There he learned the predominant role a set could play; he also learned of the possibility of elevating props to the dignity of performers. His career as a producer truly began with *Strike* (1924), a film without actors, which followed the theories of Lev Kuleshov. The next year he produced *Battleship Potemkin,* which was banned, particularly in France (until 1952), because of its revolutionary ideals. During an era dominated by the rise of Stalinism, Eisenstein pursued his work in *October* and *General Line,* a film described as the "philosophy of the tractor" defending "the pathos of the separator," because of its excessive propaganda. The 1930s were a difficult period for the director. He left his native land for Paris, where he made *Romance sentimental,* then for Mexico, where he produced an unfinished and probably unfinishable film, *Que viva Mexico!* (1932). It consisted of more than sixty kilometers of film, a portion of which was shown by Mary Seaton in 1934, under the title *Time in the Sun.* This film represents a major break—both ideological and aesthetic—in the master's evolution. When he returned to the Soviet Union, he was condemned "for having allotted the foremost place to the passion for destruction." Aesthetically, Eisenstein abandoned materialist mysticism in favor of formal mysticism, a true messianism of the image. He worked for two years on *Bezhin Meadow,* which he eventually abandoned because of the difficulties he encountered. Developments in Europe—the formation of the Axis powers, then the German invasion of 1941—returned him to the forefront of Soviet cinema, with two war masterpieces, *Alexander Nevsky* (1938) and *Ivan the Terrible* (1944).

Nevsky and Ivan were both Russian heroes who defended the nation against Teutonic knights. The root ideology of the films is clear, but the visual result is more ambiguous. The script of *Ivan the Terrible* eliminated everything that could be troublesome in the title character, a brutal and bloody tyrant who murdered his own son. These historical truths no longer had any importance. The film presented a legend in progress, not an epic to be relived. Eisenstein became totally invested in the character of Ivan, through a certain number of autobiographical transferences: the conflict with the mother, and even homosexuality. In this case, propaganda fell into its own trap: out of concern for keeping its hands clean, it ended up having no hands at all. The film was to be composed of three parts, gradually evolving from black and white to color. The producer made only two parts, and the second elicited such debates within the central committee of the Communist Party that Eisenstein preferred to abandon it. The censors, having no control over the filmmaker, preferred to prohibit him from shooting. Eisenstein died two years later, on 11 February 1948. He was barely fifty years old.

The first part of *Ivan the Terrible* is articulated around four monarchical rites: the anointing of the tsar, his wedding, the tsarina's extreme unction, and her funeral. The film begins with the crowning of the Grand Duke of Moscovy, the young Ivan IV. It is the first anointing for a tsar who will become master of all Russia. The Moscow cathedral is filled with a crowd of courtiers, prelates, diplomats, and boyars dressed in brilliant colors. Songs ring out. The metropolite advances, accompanied by the prince, whose face is hidden from us. He blesses the crown; then Ivan, seen from the back, puts it on himself with a gesture of power rife with symbolism. Ivan's hand takes the scepter and globe from the hands of the metropolite. His face is still hidden, for the gift of royalty is a divine gift, which does not reveal itself to the world: the crown serves as a metaphorical substitute for this gift. When the ritual words are uttered, Ivan turns around. He is now the tsar. The scene of the shower of gold begins, to startling effect. The monarch's face remains impassive under the torrent of coins that rain down upon his head. We have returned to the earthly world, where a new network of exchanges and gifts, of the pleasure in submission and the pleasure in power, is instituted. In editing the scene, Eisenstein uses his favorite procedure, overlapping planes, where each shot repeats the action just before the instant where the preceding shot leaves off. The result is a dilation of time, which manifests the solemnity of the rite. And by again and again cutting from the shower of gold to the female faces in the audience, the scene becomes a metaphor for sexual pleasure: Jupiter and Danaë.

Eisenstein thus reestablished his ties to the great lesson of expressionism. The entire balance of the scene is grounded in a tension in the setting: between the cathedral, a microcosm of power, and a prop, the crown, a little sun, which governs the complex cosmography of the edifice. It is this space between that summons forth Ivan's face. It is a hidden face, relayed by the crown that, with the shower of gold, changes into the face of the tsar, in the name of political alchemy, where absolute power is articulated. In the end, the film is nothing more than an exploration of these facial metamorphoses. For the tsar's face in *Ivan the Terrible* is the equivalent of the crowd in *Potemkin*.

Bibliography

Adhémar, J. *Le dessin français au XVIe siècle.* Lausanne, 1954.

Allegri, E., and A. Cecchi. *Palazzo Vecchio e i Medici, guida storica.* Florence, 1980.

Anselmi, A. "Un secondo quadro del Barocci a Senigallia." *Rassegna Bibliografica dell'Arte Italiana* 8, nos. 8–10 (1905): 140–45.

Arbellot, F. *Vie de saint Léonard, solitaire en Limousin, ses miracles et son culte.* Paris, 1863.

Arquié-Bruley, F., J. Labbé, and L. Bicart-Sée. *La collection Saint-Morys au Cabinet des Dessins du musée du Louvre.* 2 vols. Paris, 1987.

Augarde, T., and J. Thuillier. "La Hyre." *L'Oeil* 88 (April 1962): 16–25, 74–75.

Bacou, R. *Dessins du Louvre, écoles allemande, flamande, hollandaise.* Paris, 1968.

———. *Dessins du Louvre, école italienne.* Paris, 1968.

Bacou, R., and F. Viatte. *Michel-Ange au Louvre, les dessins.* Paris, 1975.

Barocchi, P. "Preciazioni sul Primaticcio." *Commentari* 2, nos. 3–4 (July–December 1951): 203–23.

Bartsch, A. *Catalogue raisonné de toutes les estampes qui forment l'oeuvre de Rembrandt . . .* Vienna, 1797.

———. *Le peintre-graveur.* 21 vols. Vienna, 1803–21.

———. *The Illustrated Bartsch, 26 et 27.* Formerly vol. 14 (pts. 1 and 2): *The Works of Marcantonio Raimondi and of His School.* Ed. K. Oberhuber. New York, 1979.

———. *The Illustrated Bartsch,* 8. Formerly vol. 6 (pt. 1). *Early German Artists.* Ed. J. C. Hutchison. New York, 1980.

———. *The Illustrated Bartsch,* 10. Formerly vol. 7 (pt. 1). *Sixteenth Century German Artists: Albrecht Dürer.* Ed. Walter L. Strauss. 2 vols. New York, 1980–81.

Bean, J., and F. Stampfle. *Drawings from New York Collections.* Vol. 1: *The Italian Renaissance.* Catalog of the exhibit, Metropolitan Museum of Art. New York, 1965.

Beets, N. "Dirick Jacobsz Vellert peintre d'Anvers." Excerpts from *La Revue de l'Art Flamand et Hollandais* 6 (December 1906); 7 (March 1907); 10 (1908); and 18 (1912).

Béguin, S. *Le cabinet d'un grand amateur, P.-J. Mariette.* In catalog of the exhibit, Louvre Museum. Paris, 1967.

Benesch, E. "'The Parents at the Door of Their Rich Children' by David Vinckeboons." *Master Drawings* 14, 2 (1976): 166–69.

Benesch, O. Review of *David Vinckboons,* by Korneel Goossens. *Kunstchronik* 10, 1 (1957): 285–92.

———. *The Drawings of Rembrandt: Complete Edition in Six Volumes.* London, 1954–57. Rev. ed. by E. Benesch. London, 1973.

Berenson, B. *The Drawings of the Florentine Painters.* 3 vols. 1938; reprint Chicago and London, 1970.

Bernier, G. *Anne-Louis Girodet, 1767–1824, Prix de Rome 1789.* Paris and Brussels, 1975.

Bernini Pezzini, G. In *Raphael Invenit—Stampe da Raffaello nelle collezioni dell'Istituto Nazionale per la grafica.* Catalog of the exhibit. Ed. G. Bernini Pezzini, S. Massari, S. Prosperi Valenti Rodinò. Rome, 1985.

Bernoulli, R. "Matthäus Merian und seine Bedeutung für die Wanderung von Bildmotiven." *Zeitschrift für Schweizerische Archäologie und Kunstgeschichte* 10, 1–2 (1948): 169–75.

Bevers, H. *Rembrandt: The Master and His Workshop. Drawings and Etchings.* Catalog of the exhibit. Berlin, Kupferstichkabinett (SMPK); Amsterdam, Rijksmuseum; London, the National Gallery, 1991–92.

Bianchi, L. *La fortuna di Raffaello nell'incisione.* Vol. 2. In M. Salmi. *Raffaello, l'Opera, le Fonti, la Fortuna.* 2 vols. Novare, 1968, 647–90.

Biörklund, G., and O. H. Barnard. *Rembrandt's Etchings True and False.* London, 1955.

Blankert, A. *Ferdinand Bol, 1616–1680, Rembrandt's Pupil.* Doorsnpijk, 1982.

Blum, A. *Oeuvre gravée de Abraham Bosse.* Paris, 1924.

———. *Rembrandt, 1606–1669: Quartorze dessins du Louvre publiés par A. Blum.* Paris, 1939.

Bodin, J. *La démonomanie des sorcières.* Rouen, 1604.

Boethius, *The Consolation of Philosophy.* Trans. H. R. James. London and New York, n.d.

Böhme, H. *Albrecht Dürer, Melancolia I.* Frankfurt-am-Main, 1989.

Bory, J.-F. *Félicien Rops: L'oeuvre graphique complète, avec un texte contemporain de l'artiste par J. K. Huysmans.* Paris, 1977.

Boubli, L. *Dessins espagnols: Maîtres des XVIe et XVIIe siècles.* Catalog of the exhibit, Louvre Museum. Paris, 1991.

Boucher, H. "Girodet illustrateur: A propos des dessins inédits de l'Enéide." *Gazette des Beaux-Arts* (November 1930): 304–19.

Bouchet-Saupique, J. "Quelques dessins flamands du fonds du musée du Louvre." *De Kunst der Nederlanden* 1 (1930–31): 90–91.

Bouyer, R. "Le Don Hayem au musée du Luxembourg." *Gazette des Beaux-Arts* (December 1900): 592–98.

Brookner, A. *Jacques-Louis David.* London, 1980.

Brown, J. "Selected Drawings by Spanish Baroque Masters." *Master Drawings* 21, 4 (1983): 401–7.
Brugerolles, E. *Les dessins de la collection Armand-Valton.* Paris, 1984.
Camera Work (January 1903).
Camera Work. Kraus reprint. Liechtenstein, 1969.
Camera Work. Introduction by F. Heilburn. Paris, 1983.
Cameron, J. M. *Illustrations to Tennyson's Idylls of the King and Other Poems.* London, 1875.
Cantinelli, R. *Jacques-Louis David, 1748–1825.* Paris and Brussels, 1930.
Catalogue of the Ellesmere Collection. Part 2: *Drawings by Giulio Romano and Other Sixteenth-Century Masters.* Sotheby Sales Catalog. London, 1972.
Christoffel, U. *Hans Holbein d. J.* Berlin, 1950.
Clark, K. "Rembrandt's 'Good Samaritan' in the Wallace Collection." *Burlington Magazine* 118, 885 (1976): 806–9.
Clément, C. *Géricault: Etude biographique et critique, avec le catalogue raisonné de l'oeuvre du maître.* Paris, 1879; new edition, 1974.
Conigliello, L. "Pesci, crostacei e un'iguana per l'imperatore Rodolfo II." *Paragone* 493–95 (1991): 22–29.
Cordellier, D. In *Hommage à Raphaël: Raphaël et l'art français.* Catalog of the exhibit, Galeries nationales du Grand Palais. Paris, 1983–84.
Cordellier, D., and B. Py. *Inventaire général des dessins italiens, V. Raphaël, son atelier, ses copistes.* Paris, 1992.
Coupin, P.-A. *Oeuvres posthumes de Girodet-Trioson, peintre d'Histoire, suivies de sa correspondance, précédées d'une notice historique et mises en ordre par P.-A. Coupin.* 2 vols. Paris, 1829.
Damisch, H. *Le jugement de Pâris: Iconologie analytique 1.* Paris, 1992.
Delaborde, H. *Marc-Antoine Raimondi, étude historique et critique suivie d'un catalogue raisonné des oeuvres du maître.* Paris, 1888.
Delteil, L. *Le peintre-graveur illustré (XIXe et XXe siècle). XVIII, Théodore Géricault.* Paris, 1924.
Deswarte, S. "'Opus Micaelis Angeli': Le dessin de Michel-Ange de la collection de Francisco de Holanda." *Prospettiva* 53–56 (April 1988–January 1989): 388–98.
De Witt, A. *Marcantonio Raimondi: Incisioni scelte e annotate.* Florence, 1968.
Dimier, L. *Le Primatice, peintre, sculpteur et architecte des rois de France.* Paris, 1900.
Duplessis, G. *Catalogue de l'oeuvre de Abraham Bosse.* Paris, 1859.
Dussler, L. *Die Zeichnungen des Michelangelo.* Berlin, 1958.
Dutuit, E. *Manuel de l'amateur d'estampes.* Tome 5: *Ecoles flamande et hollandaise.* Vol. 2. Paris and London, 1882.
Eitner, L. E. A. *Géricault: His Life and Work.* London, 1983.
Emiliani, A. *Federico Barocci.* Bologna, 1985.
Exsteens, M. *L'oeuvre gravé et lithographié de Félicien Rops.* Paris, 1928.
Fenaille, M. *Etat général des tapisseries de la Manufacture des Gobelins depuis son origine jusqu'à nos jours, 1600–1900.* Vol. 2. Paris, 1903.
Ferrara, S., and G. Gaeta Bertelà. *Catalogo Generale della raccolta di stampe antiche della Pinacoteca Nazionale di Bologna, Gabinetto della Stampe. III. Incisori Bolognesi ed Emiliani del sec. XVI. Appendice ai volumi Incisori Bolognesi ed Emiliani del'600 e del'700.* Bologna, 1975.
Fréart, R. *L'idée de la perfection de la peinture.* Le Mans: Minkoff, 1662; repr. Geneva, 1973.
Fried, M. *Absorption and Theatricality: Painter and Beholder in the Age of Diderot.* Berkeley, Los Angeles, and London, 1980.
Galerie de Bayser. *Dessins de Maîtres anciens.* Paris, 1981.
Ganz, P. *Les dessins de Hans Holbein le Jeune.* Geneva, 1939.
Gardey, F., G. Lambert, and M. Oberthür. "Marc-Antoine Raimondi, illustration du catalogue de son oeuvre gravé, par Henri Delaborde, publié en 1888." *Gazette des Beaux-Arts* (July–August 1987): 2–52.
Giampaolo, M. di, and A. Muzzi. *Le Corrège: Les dessins.* Umberto, 1990.
Gionini-Visani, X. *Giulio Clovio: Miniaturist of the Renaissance.* New York, 1980.
Gobineau, Comte de. *Voyage à Terre-Neuve.* Paris, 1861; new edition, 1989.
———. *Le tour du monde.* Paris, 1863.
Golahny, A. "Rembrandt's Early Bathsheba: The Raphael Connection." *Art Bulletin* 65, 4 (December 1983): 671–75.
Guiffrey, J. *Antoine van Dyck, sa vie et son oeuvre.* Paris, 1882.
Hartt, F. *Giulio Romano.* 2 vols. New Haven, 1958.
———. *The Drawings of Michelangelo.* London, 1971.
Hautecoeur, L. *Louis David.* Paris, 1954.
Hébert, M. *Inventaire des gravures des écoles du Nord, Bibliothèque nationale, département des Estampes.* 2 vols. Paris, 1982–83.
Hellerstedt, K. J. "A Traditional Motif in Rembrandt's Etchings: The Hurdy-Gurdy Player." *Oud Holland* 95, 1 (1981): 16–30.
Herbet, F. *Les graveurs de l'école de Fontainebleau.* 5 fasc. in 1 vol. Paris, 1896–1900.
Hind, A. M. *Catalogue of Early Italian Engravings Preserved in the British Museum.* Ed. S. Colvin. 2 vols. London, 1920 (illustrations, 1909).
———. *Rembrandt's Etchings, an Essay and a Catalogue. . . .* 2 vols. London, 1912.
———. "Cristofano Robetta." *Print-Collector's Quarterly* (December 1923): 368–402.
———. *Early Italian Engravings: A Critical Catalogue with Complete Reproduction of All the Prints Described.* 7

vols. London, 1938 (vols. 1–4); London, 1948 (vols. 5–7).
Hirst, M. *Sebastiano del Piombo.* Oxford, 1981.
———. *Michelangelo and His Drawings.* New Haven and London, 1988.
Hofstede de Groot, C. *Die Handzeichnungen Rembrandts.* Haarlem, 1906.
Hollstein, F. W. H. *Dutch and Flemish Etchings, Engravings and Woodcuts, ca. 1450–1700.* Amsterdam, 1949–1990. 36 vols.
———. *German Engravings, Etching and Woodcuts, ca. 1400–1700.* 37 vols. Amsterdam, 1954–90.
Holma, K. *David, son évolution et son style.* Paris, 1940.
Hulst, R. A. d'. *De Tekeningen van Jacob Jordaens.* Brussels, 1956.
———. "Nieuwe gegevens omtrent enkele tekeningen van Jacob Jordaens." *Gentse Bijdragen tot de Kunstgeschiedenis en de Oudheidkunde* 17 (1957–58): 135–55.
———. *Jordaens Drawings.* 4 vols. Brussels, 1974.
Humbert, A. *Louis David, peintre et conventionnel: Essai de critique marxiste.* Paris, 1936.
Jerrold, B. *Life of Gustave Doré.* London, 1891.
Judson, J. R. *Gerrit van Honsthorst: A Discussion of His Position in Dutch Art.* The Hague, 1959.
Keller, J. *History of Photography.* Department of Photographs at the Getty Museum, Malibu, 15, 4 (1991).
Klessmann, R. In *Die Sprache der Bilder, Realität und Bedeutung in der niederländischen Malerei des 17. Jahrhunderts.* Catalog of the exhibit, Herzog Anton Ulrich-Museum. Brunswick, 1978.
Koegler, H. "Holbeins Triumphzüge des Reichthums und der Armut." *Jahresberichte der öffentlichen Kunstsammlungen* N.F. 38–89 (1933): 50–95.
Krommes, H. R. *Studien zu Federigo Barrocci.* Leipzig, 1912.
Kruse, J. *Die Zeichnungen Rembrandts und seiner Schule im National Museum zu Stockholm.* The Hague, 1920.
Lacambre, J. *Le néo-classicisme français: Dessins des musées de province.* Catalog of the exhibit, Grand Palais. Paris, 1974.
Langlade, S. de. *Catalogue des dessins de Pierre Mignard au Cabinet des Dessins du musée du Louvre.* Manuscript essay from l'Ecole du Louvre. Paris, 1968.
Leblanc, H. *Catalogue de l'oeuvre de Gustave Doré: Illustrations, peintures, dessins, sculptures, eaux-fortes, lithographies.* Paris, 1931.
Lehrs, M. *Geschichte und kritischer Katalog des Deutschen, Niederländischen und Französischen Kupferstichs im XV. Jahrhundert.* 9 vols. 1908–34.
Leprieur, P. *Gustave Moreau et son oeuvre.* Paris, 1889.
Levenson, J. A. In *Early Italian Engravings from the National Gallery of Art, Washington.* By J. A. Levenson, K. Oberhuber, and J. L. Sheehan. Catalog of the exhibit, National Gallery. Washington, D.C., 1973.
Lieure, J. *Jacques Callot.* 5 vols. Paris, 1924–27; new edition in 8 vols. New York, 1969.
———. *Catalogue raisonné de l'oeuvre gravé.* 2 vols. Vol. 1: *Texte.* Vol. 2: *Planches.* San Francisco, 1989.
Loccatelli, E. *Vita del Glorioso Padre San Giovangualberto Fondatore dell'Ordine di Vallombrosa: Insieme con le Vite di tutti Generali, Beati et Beate, che ha di tempo in tempo havuto la sua Religione.* Florence, 1583.
Lorgues, C. "Décorateurs génois du Seicento en Provence orientale, Giovan Battista Carlone et Giulio Benso au château des Grimaldi de Cagnes et au palais Lascaris à Nice." *"Il se rendit en Italie": Etudes offertes à André Chastel.* Rome and Paris, 1987, pp. 403–13.
Lossky, B. "Sources d'inspiration d'une fresque bellifontaine: L'*Alexandre et Roxane* de Primatice." *Bulletin de la Société de l'Histoire de l'Art Français* (1981; 1983), 21–25.
Lugt, F. *Musée du Louvre, Inventaire général des dessins des écoles du Nord.* Vols. 1–2: *Ecole hollandaise;* vol. 3: *Rembrandt.* Paris, 1929–33.
———. *Musée du Louvre, Inventaire général des dessins des écoles du Nord. Ecole flamande;* 2 vols. Paris, 1949.
———. *Musée du Louvre, Inventaire général des dessins des écoles du nord. Maîtres des anciens Pays-Bas nés avant 1550.* Paris, 1968.
Margolis, M. F. *Alfred Stieglitz, Camera Work, a Pictorial Guide.* New York, 1978.
Mariette, P.-J. *Abecedario de Mariette et autres notes inédites de cet amateur sur les arts et les artistes.* In P. de Chennevières et A. de Montaiglon. *Archives de l'Art Français.* 6 vols. 1851–60.
Massari, S. In *Raphael invenit—Stampe da Raffaello nelle collezioni dell'Istituto Nazionale per la grafica.* By G. Bernini Pezzini, S. Massari, and S. Prosperi Valenti Rodinò. Catalog of the exhibit. Rome, 1985.
Mathey, J. "Greuze et Fragonard copistes de Rubens." *Bulletin de la Société de l'Histoire de l'Art Français* 2 (1933): 183–84.
Mathieu, P.-L. *Gustave Moreau, sa vie, son oeuvre: Catalogue raisonné de l'oeuvre achevé.* Paris, 1976.
Meder, J. *Dürer-Katalog.* Vienna, 1932.
Michel, R. *Géricault: L'invention du réel.* Paris, 1992.
Michel, R., and M. C. Sahut. *David, l'art et la politique.* Paris, 1988.
Millard, C. D. "Julia Margaret Cameron and Tennyson's Idylls of the King." *Harvard Library Bulletin* (April 1973).
Miller, D. "Allegory of Fortune." *Art Bulletin* 68, 3 (1986): 446–49.
Minott, C. I. *Martin Schongauer.* New York, 1971.
Mirimonde, A. P. de. "Les allégories de la destinée humaine et 'La roue de fortune' d'Edward Burne-Jones." *Gazette des Beaux-Arts* (February 1982): 78–86.
Mitsch, E. *Raphael in der Albertina aus Anlass der 500.*

Geburtstages des Künstlers. Catalog of the exhibit, Graphische Sammlung Albertina. Vienna, 1983.

Monbeig Goguel, C. *Inventaire général des dessins italiens.* Vol. 1: *Maîtres toscans nés après 1500, morts avant 1600: Vasari et son temps.* Paris, 1972.

———. "Taste and Trade: The Retouched Drawings in the Everard Jabach Collection at the Louvre." *Burlington Magazine* 130, 1028 (November 1988): 821–35.

Müller Hofstede, Justus von. "'Stolidi Iudicium Paridis': Zur Ikonologie des Parisurteils bei Peter Paul Rubens." *Wallraf-Richartz-Jahrbuch* 50 (1989): 163–87.

Munhall, E. "Les dessins de Greuze pour Septime Sévère." *L'Oeil* (April 1965).

———. *Jean-Baptiste Greuze.* Catalog of the exhibit. Hartford, Wadsworth Atheneum; San Francisco, the California Palace of the Legion of Honor; Dijon, Musée des Beaux-Arts, 1976–77.

Münz, L. *The Etchings of Rembrandt, Complete Edition.* 2 vols. London, 1952.

Nanteuil, L. de. *Jean-Louis David.* New York, 1985; Paris, 1987.

Néagu, P. *Photographie—Dix ans d'enrichissement des collections publiques.* Paris, 1992.

Newcome, M. "Giulio Benso." *Paragone* 355 (September 1979): 27–40.

Newcome-Schleier, M. *Le dessin à Gênes du XVIe au XVIIe siècle.* Catalog of the exhibit, Louvre Museum. Paris, 1985.

Nichols, L. W. "The 'Pen Works' of Hendrick Goltzius." *Philadelphia Museum of Art Bulletin* 88, 373–74 (winter 1992).

Nova, A. "Occasio pars Virtutis, Considerazioni sugli affreschi di Francesco Salviati per il Cardinale Ricci." *Paragone* 365 (July 1980).

Oberhuber, I. In *Le cabinet d'un grand amateur, P. J. Mariette, 1694–1774.* Catalog of the exhibit, Louvre Museum. Paris, 1967.

———. *Zwischen Renaissance und Barock: Das Zeitalter von Brueghel und Bellange.* Catalog of the exhibit, Graphische Sammlung Albertina. Vienna, 1967–68.

Oldenburg, R. *Peter Paul Rubens.* Berlin and Leipzig, n.d.

Olsen, H. *Federico Barocci.* Copenhagen, 1962.

Ovid. *The Metamorphoses.* Trans. Horace Gregory. New York and Toronto: Viking, 1958.

Panofsky, E. "Die Pietà von Ubeda: Ein kleiner Beitrag zur Lösung der Sebastiano-Frage." *Festschrift für Julius Schlosser zum 60. Geburtstag.* Ed. A. Weixlgärtner and L. Plarescig. Vienna, 1927.

———. *The Life and Art of Albrecht Dürer.* Princeton, 1954.

———. "Good Government of Fortune? The Iconography of a Newly Discovered Composition by Rubens." *Gazette des Beaux-Arts* (December 1966): 305–26.

Panofsky, D., and E. Panofsky. *Pandora's Box: The Changing Aspects of a Mythological Symbol.* Princeton, 1962.

Pariset, F.-G. "Brentel et l'Argenis de Barcaly." In *Trois siècles d'art alsacien 1648–1948.* Strasbourg and Paris, 1948, 1–21.

Parker, K. *Catalogue of the Collection of Drawings of the Ashmolean Museum.* 2 vols. Oxford, 1956.

Passavant, J. D. *Le peintre-graveur.* 6 vols. Leipzig, 1860–64.

Perrig, A. *Michelangelo's Drawings: The Science of Attribution.* New Haven and London, 1991.

Pillsbury, E., and J. Caldell. *Sixteenth Century Italian Drawings, Form and Function.* Catalog of the exhibit, Yale University Art Gallery. New Haven, 1974.

Pittaluga, M. *L'Incisione Italiana del Cinquecento.* Milan, 1928.

Popham, A. E. *Corregio's Drawings.* London, 1957.

Popham, A. E., and J. Wilde. *The Italian Drawings of the XV and XVI Centuries at Windsor Castle.* London, 1949.

Pouncy, P., and J. A. Gere. *Italian Drawings in the Department of Prints and Drawings in the British Museum, Raphael and His Circle.* London, 1962.

Puyvelde, L. van. *Jordaens.* Paris and Brussels, 1953.

Ramiro, E. *Oeuvre gravé de Félicien Rops.* 2 vols. Paris, 1887.

Réau, L. *Iconographie de l'art chrétien.* 6 vols. Paris, 1955–58.

Reznicek, E. K. J. *Die Zeichnungen von Hendrick Goltzius.* Utrecht, 1961.

Robert-Dumesnil, A. P. F. *Le peintre-graveur français ou Catalogue raisonné des estampes gravées par les peintres et les dessinateurs de l'école française, ouvrage faisant suite au peintre-graveur de M. Bartsch.* 11 vols. Paris, 1835–71.

Rosenberg, P. *De main de Maître: Trois siècles de dessin français dans la collection Prat.* Catalog of the exhibit, New York, Fort Worth, Pittsburgh, Ottawa. 1990–91.

Rosenberg, P., and J. Thuillier. "Laurent de La Hyre 1606–1656." *Cahiers du Dessin Français* 1 (1985).

Rouchès, G., and R. Huyghe. *Cabinet des dessins du musée du Louvre, catalogue raisonné. Ecole française.* Paris, 1938.

Rowlands, J. K. *The Paintings of Hans Holbein the Younger.* Oxford, 1985.

Roy, A. *Les envois de l'Etat au musée de Dijon, 1803–1815.* Paris, 1980.

Sandoz, M. "Jean-Jacques Lagrénée, peintre d'histoire, 1739–1821," *Bulletin de la Société de l'Histoire de l'Art Français* (1962). Paris, 1963, pp. 121–33.

Schatborn, P. "Van Rembrandt tot Crozat: Vroege verzamelingen met tekeningen van Rembrandt." *Nederlands Kunsthistorisch Jaarboek* 32 (1981): 1–54.

Schmarsow, A. "Federico Baroccis Zeichnungen, III. Die Zeichnungen in den Sammlungen ausserhalb Italiens." *Abhandlung der k. S. Gesellschaft der Wissenschaften, phil.-hist. Kl.* 39, 11 (1911).

Schnapper, A. *David témoin de son temps.* Freiburg, 1980.

Sérullaz, A. In *L'an V. Dessins des grands maîtres.* Catalog of the exhibit, Louvre Museum. Paris, 1988.

Starcky, E. "Quelques dessins de Rembrandt dans les collections du Louvre: Problèmes de chronologie." *Revue du Louvre et des musées de France* 35, 4 (1985): 255–65.

———. *Musée du Louvre, Inventaire général des dessins des écoles du Nord. Supplément à l'inventaire F. Lugt.* Paris, 1988.

———. *Rembrandt et son école, dessins du musée du Louvre.* Catalog of the exhibit, Louvre Museum. Paris, 1988–89.

Sueur, H. *Le dessin à Vérone de 1530 à la peste en 1630. Paolo Farinati (1524–1606) et son entourage. Catalogue raisonné des collections du Louvre.* Paris, 1991 (unpublished doctoral thesis).

Sumowski, W. *Drawings of the Rembrandt School.* 8 vols. New York, 1979–84.

Tassi, R. *La cupola del Correggio nel Duomo di Parma.* Milan, 1968.

Tauzia, L. Both de. *Notice des dessins de la collection His de la Salle exposés au Louvre, par le vicomte Both de Tauzia.* Paris, 1881.

Thévenin, P., and J. Derrida. *Artonin Artaud, dessins et portraits.* Paris, 1986.

Thode, H. *Michelangelo, Kritische Untersuchungen über seine Werke.* 3 vols. Berlin, 1913.

Thuillier, J. In *L'art en Lorraine au temps de Jacques Callot.* Catalog of the exhibit, Musée des Beaux-Arts. Nancy, 1992.

Tolnay, C. de. *Michelangelo: The Final Period.* Princeton, 1960.

———. *Corpus dei Disegni de Michelangelo.* 4 vols. Novara, 1975.

Valentiner, W. R. *Rembrandt: Des Meisters Handzeichnungen.* 2 vols. Stuttgart, Berlin, and Leipzig, 1925–34.

Van de Waal, H. "Hagar in the Wilderness by Rembrandt and His School." In *Steps towards Rembrandt: Collected Articles, 1937–1972.* Amsterdam and London, 1974, 90–112.

Van Sasse van Ysselt, D. "Een serie tekeningen van Johannes Stradanus met scènes uit het leven van de Heilige Giovanni Gualberto." *Oud Holland* 10, 3 (1987): 148–70.

———. "Johannes Stradanus: De decoraties voor intochten en uitvaarten aan het hof van de Medici te Florence." *Oud Holland* 104, 3/4 (1990): 149–79.

Varanini, G. M. *La Valpolicella nella prima età moderna.* Verona, 1987.

Vasari, G. *Le vite de' più eccellenti pittori, scultori ed architettori, con nuove annotazioni e commenti di Gaetano Milansei.* Vol. 8. Florence, 1878–85; new edition 1906.

Verheyen, E. *The Palazzo del Te in Mantua: Images of Love and Politics.* Baltimore and London, 1977.

Vey, H. *Van Dyck-Studien.* Cologne, 1958.

———. *Die Zeichnungen Anton van Dycks.* 2 vols. Brussels, 1962.

Viatte, F. "Allegorical and Burlesque Subjects by Stefano della Bella." *Master Drawings* 15, 3 (1977): 347–65.

———. *Musée du Louvre, Inventaire général des dessins italiens.* Vol. 3: *Dessins toscans XVI*e*–XVIII*e* siècle.* Paris, 1988.

Villa, N. *Le XVII*e* siècle vu par Abraham Bosse, graveur du Roy.* Paris, 1967.

Virgil. *The Aeneid.* Trans. Robert Fitzgerald. New York, 1983.

Vogel-Köhn, D. *Rembrandts Kinderzeichnungen.* Cologne, 1981.

Voragine, J. de. *The Golden Legend.* Trans. Granger Ryan and Helmut Ripperger. New York, London, and Toronto, 1941.

Voss, H. *Die Malerei der Spätrenaissance in Rom und Florenz.* Berlin, 1920.

Walch, N. *Die Radierungen des Jacques Bellange.* Munich, 1971.

Weaver, M. In *Julia Margaret Cameron.* Catalog of the exhibit, British Council. London, 1984.

Wegner, W., and H. Pée. "Die Zeichnungen des David Vinckboons." *Münchner Jahrbuch der Bildenden Kunst* 31 (1980): 35–128.

Weigert, R. A., continued by M. Préaud. *Bibliothèque nationale: Cabinet des Estampes, Inventaires du Fonds français. Graveurs du XVII*e* siècle.* 9 vols. Paris, 1939–80.

Wethey, H. E., and A. Sunderland Wethey. "Herrera Barnuevo and His Chapel in the Descalzas Reales." *Art Bulletin* 48 (1966): 15–34.

White, C. *Rembrandt as an Etcher, A Study of the Artist at Work.* 2 vols. London, 1969.

Whiteley, J. "Homer Abandoned: A French Neoclassical Theme." In *The Artist and the Writer in France: Essays in Honour of Jean Seznec.* Oxford, 1974, 40–51.

Wilde, J. *Italian Drawings in the Department of Prints and Drawings in the British Museum, Michelangelo and His Studio.* London, 1953.

———. *Michelangelo, Six Lectures.* Oxford, 1978.

Wildenstein, D., and G. Wildenstein. *Documents complémentaires au catalogue de l'oeuvre de Louis David.* Paris, 1973.

Zerner, H. *Ecole de Fontainebleau. Gravures.* Paris, 1969.

Exhibits

Aarau, 1963. *Handzeichnungen und Aquarelle aus den Museen Frankreichs,* Aarau, Aarauer Kunsthaus, 1963.

Baden-Baden, 1964. *Gustave Moreau,* Baden-Baden, Staatliche Kunsthalle, 1964.

Bologna, 1975. *Mostra di Federico Barocci: Catalogo critico a cura di A. Emiliani con un repertorio dei disegni di G. Gaeta Bertelà,* Bologna, Museo Civico, 1975.

Bourg-en-Bresse, 1963. *L'oeuvre de Doré,* Bourge-en-Bresse, Musée de l'Ain, 1963.

Brussels, 1975. *De Watteau à David: Peintures et dessins des musées de province français,* Brussels, Palais des Beaux-Arts, 1980.

Caen, 1980. *Dix ans d'enrichissement du musée des Beaux-Arts et de la collection Mancel.* Caen, Musée des Beaux-Arts, 1980.

Caen, 1986. *L'allégoire dans la peinture: La représentation de la charité au XVIIe siècle,* Caen, Musée des Beaux-Arts, 1986.

Cambridge, Mass., 1915. *A Loan Exhibition of Early Italian Engravings,* Cambridge, Harvard University, Fogg Art Museum, 1915.

Colmar, 1991. *Le Beau Martin: Gravures et dessins de Martin Schongauer,* Colmar, Musée d'Unterlinden, 1991.

Darmstadt, 1972. *Von Ingres bis Renoir,* Darmstadt, Hessisches Landesmuseum, 1927.

Grenoble, Rennes, Bordeaux, 1989–90. *Laurent de La Hyre, 1606–1656, l'homme et l'oeuvre,* Grenoble, Rennes, Bordeaux, 1989–90.

Hamburg, 1980–81. *Goya und das Zeitalter der Revolutionen,* Hamburg, Kunsthalle, 1980–81.

Hartford, San Francisco, and Dijon, 1976–77. *Jean-Baptiste Greuze,* Hartford, Wadsworth Atheneum; San Francisco, California Palace of the Legion of Honor; Dijon, Musée des Beaux-Arts, 1976–77.

Japan, 1987–88. *Géricault,* Kamakura, Museum of Modern Art; Kyoto, National Museum of Art; Fukuoka, Museum of the Fine Arts of the City, 1978–88.

Lausanne, 1981–82. *Fortune,* Lausanne, Musée de l'Elysée, 1981–82.

Lawrence, Chapel Hill, and Wellesley, 1981–82. *The Engravings of Marcantonio Raimondi,* Spencer Museum of Art, University of Kansas, Lawrence, 1981–82; Auckland Art Museum, University of North Carolina, Chapel Hill, 1982; Wellesley College Art Museum, Wellesley, Massachusetts, 1932.

Lille, 1968. *Au temps du Roi Soleil, les peintres de Louis XIV (1660–1715),* Lille, Musée des Beaux-Arts, 1968.

Maisons-Laffitte, 1931. *Dessins de Mignard et Lebrun,* Maisons-Laffitte, Château de Maisons-Laffitte, 1931.

New York and Paris, 1974–75. *Italian Renaissance Drawings from the Musée du Louvre,* New York, Metropolitan Museum of Art; Paris, Louvre Museum, 1974–75.

New York, 1983. *Audacious Eroticism: The Unconventional Art of Félicien Rops (1833–1898),* Theodore B. Donson, New York, 1983.

New York and London, 1991. *An Exhibition of Master Drawings Presented by Jean-Luc Baroni,* Colnaghi, New York and London, 1991.

Ottawa, 1980. *Le jeune Van Dyck,* The National Gallery of Canada, Ottawa, 1980.

Paris, Bibliothèque nationale, 1908. *Oeuvres de Rembrandt: Dessins et gravures,* Paris, Bibliothèque nationale, 1908.

Paris, Bibliothèque nationale, 1974. *Gustave Doré,* Paris, Bibliothèque nationale, 1974.

Paris, Carnavalet, 1939. *La Révolution française dans l'histoire—dans la littérature—dans l'art.* Paris, Musée Carnavalet, 1939.

Paris, Galerie Claude Aubry, 1974. *Dessins des écoles du Nord dans les collections privées françaises,* Paris, Galerie Claude Aubry, 1974.

Paris, Galerie Georges Petit, 1906. *Gustave Moreau,* Paris, Galerie Georges Petit, 1906.

Paris, Grand Palais, 1975–76. *Jean-François Millet,* Paris, Galeries nationales du Grand Palais, 1975–76.

Paris, Grand Palais, 1983–84. *Raphaël dans les collections françaises,* Paris, Galeries nationales du Grand Palais, 1983–84.

Paris, Grand Palais, 1991–92. *Géricault: Catalogue de l'exposition du bicentenaire,* Paris, Galeries nationales du Grand Palais, 1991–92.

Paris, Louvre, 1952. *Dessins des écoles allemandes du XVe au XVIIe siècle de Stephan Lochner au liminisme d'Adam Elsheimer,* Paris, Louvre Museum, 1952.

Paris, Louvre, 1960. *Dessins de Jean-François Millet,* Paris, Louvre Museum, 1960.

Paris, Louvre, 1964. *Dessins de l'école de Parme,* Paris, Louvre Museum, 1964.

Paris, Louvre, 1965. *Le XVIe siècle européen,* Paris, Louvre Museum, 1965.

Paris, Louvre, "Gravure italienne," 1965. *La gravure italienne au Quattrocento et au début du Cinquecento: II, Florence et le nord de l'Italie,* Cabinet E. de Rothschild, Paris, Louvre Museum, 1965.

Paris, Louvre, 1965–66. *Le XVIe siècle européen, gravures et dessins du cabinet Edmond de Rothschild,* Paris, Louvre Museum, Collection E. de Rothschild, 1965–66.

Paris, Louvre, 1967. *Le cabinet d'un grand amateur, P. J. Mariette 1694–1774,* Paris, Louvre Museum, 1967.

Paris, Louvre, 1969–70. *Les plus belles eaux-fortes de Rembrandt choisies dans les quatre principales collections de Paris,* Paris, Louvre Museum, 1969–70.

Paris, Louvre, 1970. *Rembrandt et son temps, dessins des*

collections publiques et privées en France, Paris, Louvre Museum, 1970.
Paris, Louvre, 1972. *Dessins français de 1750 à 1825: Le néo-classicisme,* Paris, Louvre Museum, 1972.
Paris, Louvre, 1978. *Rubens, ses maîtres, ses élèves,* Paris, Louvre Museum, 1978.
Paris, Louvre, 1980. *Maîtres de l'eau-forte des XVIe et XVIIe siècles,* Cabinet E. de Rothschild, Paris, Louvre Museum, 1980.
Paris, Louvre, 1983. *L'aquarelle en France au XIXe siècle,* Paris, Louvre Museum, 1983.
Paris, Louvre, 1983–84. *Autour de Raphaël, Dessins et peintures du musée du Louvre,* Paris, Louvre Museum, 1983–84.
Paris, Louvre, 1984–85. *Dessins français du XVIIe siècle,* Louvre Museum, 1984–85.
Paris, Louvre, 1985. *Le dessin à Gênes du XVIe au XVIIIe siècle,* Paris, Louvre Museum, 1985.
Paris, Louvre, 1986. *Les mots dans le dessin,* Paris, Louvre Museum, 1986.
Paris, Louvre, 1988. *L'an V, dessins des grands Maîtres,* Paris, Louvre Museum, 1988.
Paris, Louvre, 1988–89. *Rembrandt et son école, dessins du musée du Louvre,* Paris, Louvre Museum, 1988–89.
Paris, Louvre, 1989. *Le beau idéal ou l'art du concept,* Paris, Louvre Museum, 1989.
Paris, Louvre, "Michel-Ange," 1989. *Michel-Ange dessinateur,* Paris, Louvre Museum, 1989.
Paris, Louvre, 1989–90. *David,* Paris, Louvre Museum and Versailles, Musée National du Château, 1988–90.
Paris, Louvre, 1990. *Acquisitions 1984–1989,* Paris, Louvre Museum, 1990.
Paris, Louvre, 1990–91. *Jacques Derrida, Mémoires d'aveugle, l'autoportrait et autres ruines,* Paris, Louvre Museum, 1990–91.
Paris, Louvre, 1991. *Dessins espagnols: Maîtres des XVIe et XVIIe siècles,* Paris, Louvre Museum, 1991.
Paris, Louvre, 1991–92. *Dessins de Dürer et de la Renaissance germanique,* Paris, Louvre Museum, 1991–92.
Paris, Louvre, "Graveurs allemands," 1991–92. *Graveurs allemands du XVe siècle dans la collection Edmond de Rothschild,* Paris, Louvre Museum, 1991–92.
Paris, Orangerie, 1937. *Rembrandt, dessins et eaux-fortes,* Paris, Collection Edmond de Rothschild, Orangerie des Tuileries, 1937.
Paris, Orangerie, 1947. *Rembrandt (1606–1669), tableaux, eaux-fortes et dessins,* Paris, Orangerie des Tuileries, 1947.
Paris, Orangerie, 1957. *Les incunables sur bois et sur métal de la collection Edmond de Rothschild,* Paris, Orangerie des Tuileries, 1957.
Paris, Orangerie, 1967–68. *Vingt ans d'acquisitions au musée du Louvre, 1947–1967,* Paris, Orangerie des Tuileries, 1967–68.
Paris, Orangerie, 1977–78. *Collection de Louis XIV, dessins, albums, manuscrits,* Orangerie des Tuileries, 1977–78.
Paris, Orangerie et Versailles, 1948. *David: Exposition en l'honneur du deuxième centenaire de sa naissance,* Paris, Orangerie des Tuileries, Versailles, 1948.
Paris, Orsay, 1988. *La photographie au musée d'Orsay,* Paris, Orsay Museum, 1988.
Paris, Orsay, 1990. *De Manet à Matisse: Nouvelle acquisitions du musée d'Orsay.* Paris, Orsay Museum, 1990.
Paris, Palais National des Arts, 1937. *Chefs d'oeuvre de l'art français,* Paris, Palais National des Arts, 1937.
Paris, Palais de Tokyo, 1980. *La grisaille,* Paris, Palais de Tokyo, 1980.
Paris, Petit Palais, 1936. *Gros, ses amis, ses élèves,* Paris, Petit Palais, 1936.
Paris, Rodin, 1993. *Le salon de photographie,* Paris, Musée Rodin, 1993.
Paris, Salons du Cercle, 1885. *Catalogue des dessins, aquarelles et estampes de Gustave Doré exposés dans les salons du Cercle de la librairie avec une notice bibliographique par M. G. Duplessis,* Paris, Salons du Cercle, 1885.
Recklinghausen, Amsterdam, 1961. *Polarität, das Apollinische und das Dionysische,* Recklinghausen, Städtische Kunsthalle, Amsterdam, Stedelijkmuseum, 1961.
Rome, 1959–60. *Il disegno francese da Fouquet a Toulouse-Lautrec,* Rome, Palazzo Venezia, 1959–60.
Rome, 1981–1982. *David et Rome,* Rome, Academy of France, 1981–82.
Rotterdam, Haarlem, 1958. *Hendrick Goltzius als Tekenaar,* Rotterdam, Museum Boymans, Haarlem, Teylers Museum, 1958.
San Francisco, 1947. *Nineteenth Century French Drawings,* San Francisco, California Palace of the Legion of Honor, 1947.
Strasbourg and Paris, 1983. *Gustave Doré, 1832–1883,* Strasbourg, Musée d'art moderne et cabinet des Estampes; Paris, Pavillon des Arts and Musée Carnavalet, 1983.
Vienna, 1976–77. *Von Ingres bis Cézanne, Aquarelle und Zeichnungen aus dem Louvre,* Vienna, Graphische Sammlung Albertina, 1976–77.
Washington, 1952–53. *French Drawings. Masterpieces from Five Centuries,* Washington, National Gallery of Art; Cleveland, Cleveland Museum of Art; Saint Louis, City Art Museum; Cambridge, Massachusetts, Harvard University, Fogg Art Museum; New York, Metropolitan Museum of Art, 1952–53.
Washington, 1988. *Michelangelo Draftsman,* Washington, National Gallery, 1988.

Photographic Credits
(Numbers refer to the illustrations)

Réunion des musées nationaux (M. Bellot)

With the exception of:
Agen, Museum of Fine Arts: 68
Amsterdam, Rijksmuseum-Stichting: 50
Angers, Museum of Fine Arts: 69
Cambridge (Mass.), Harvard University Art Museums: 14
Copenhagen, Statens Museum for Kunst: 96
Geneva, Museum of Art and History: 24
Madrid, Museo Thyssen-Bornemisza: 58
Paris, Bibliothèque Nationale: 2, 61, 17, 18, 25, 74, 86, 96
Paris, Documentation of the National Museum of Modern Art: 59, 60
(Giacomelli)
Saint-Lô, Museum of Fine Arts: 71
Patrice Astier: 93
J. Hyde: 4, 5

Acknowledgments

The presentation of the exhibit was conceived by Christophe Clément and realized under his direction by the Service des Travaux Muséographiques at the Louvre Museum.

Restoration of the drawings was provided by André Le Prat.

The Department of Graphic Arts wishes to express its profound gratitude to those in charge of the following collections for their generous loans:

Orsay Museum (Paris)
Bibliothèque Nationale (Paris)
Bibliothèque Littéraire Jacques Doucet (Paris)
Museum of Fine Arts of Agen

In particular, the organizers of the exhibit wish to thank Véronique Barjot-Faux, Varena Forcione, and Gabriele Gerling for their inestimable cooperation during all phases of the exhibit's realization.

For the valuable contributions of Agnès de la Beaumelle, Joëlle Cinq Fraix, Pierre Coural, François Chapon, Jean Galard, Françoise Heilbrun, Pierrette Jean-Richard, Nathalie Lorand, Bertrand Marchal, Philippe-Alain Michaud, Philippe Néagu, Véronique Goarin, and Catherine Scheck, we offer our warmest thanks.

Warm thanks as well to all of those who favored this exhibit with their distinguished assistance:

Christine André, Malika Berri, Giovanna Citi, Gilles Gratté, Gérard Haller, Jean-François Méjanès, Annie Madec, Gérard Lévy, Catherine Monbeig Goguel, Dominique Païni, Gérard Parus, Madeleine Pinault Sørensen, Maxime Préaud, Bernadette Py, Ilaria Quadrani, Brigitte Scart, Hélène Sueur, Brigitte Vincent, Léna Widerkehr, and the Services de Documentation of the Department of Graphic Arts and the Department of Paintings at the Louvre Museum, the Orsay Museum, the National Museum of Modern Art, the Musée de l'Homme, the Service Culturel, the Auditorium du Louvre, and the Service Photographique de la Réunion des Musées Nationaux.